AQA Biology for AS

Mike Bailey
Bill Indge
Martin Rowland

HODDER EDUCATION
PART OF HACHETTE LIVRE UK

The Publishers would like to thank the following for permission to reproduce copyright material:

p.iv both Bill Indge; **p.1** © Henri Bureau/Sygma/Corbis; **p.3** Robert Brook/Science Photo Library; **p.6** Bill Indge; **p.7** Bill Indge; **p.11** Bill Indge; **p.17** Figure 20 data from Christian B Anfinsen; **p.22** Bill Indge; **p.30** Bill Indge; **p.31** Wellcome Library, London; **p.33** both Bill Indge; **p.34** Moredun Animal Health Ltd/Science Photo Library; **p.35** Dr Gopal Murti/Science Photo Library; **p.36** Science Photo Library; **p.39** *t* CNRI/Science Photo Library, *b* Susumu Nishinaga/Science Photo Library; **p.40** A.R.Cavaliere, Department of Biology, Gettysburg College, Gettysburg, PA; **p.56** *l* James Steveson/Science Photo Library, *r* James Steveson/Science Photo Library; **p.60** *c* James Steveson/Science Photo Library, *b* CNRI/Science Photo Library; **p.62** Wellcome Images; **p.66** Jean-Yves Ruszniewski/TempSport/Corbis; **p.72** Bubbles Photolibrary/Alamy; **p.73** © Simon Rawles/Alamy; **p.74** *t* CNRI/Science Photo Library, *c* and *b* both Wellcome Images; **p.75** ISM/Science Photo Library; **p.76** Figure 19 based on data from Royal College of Physicians, 1983; **p.77** based on data from Royal College of Physicians, 1962; **p.78** Figure 21 data from 'Mortality in relation to smoking: 50 years of observations on male British doctors', Richard Doll et al, British Medical Journal, Jun 2004; **p.81** Table 2 data from 'Mortality in relation to smoking: 50 years of observations on male British doctors', Richard Doll et al, British Medical Journal, Jun 2004; **p. 82** JAMES King-Holmes/Science Photo Library; **p.84** John Radcliffe Hospital/Science Photo Library; **p.94** Science Photo Library; **p.97** Gavin Kingcome/Science Photo Library; **p.98** Table 1 and 2 data from National Heart Lung and Blood Institute www.nhlbi.nih.gov; **p.100** Peter Menzel/Science Photo Library; **p.102** Steve Gschmeissner/Science Photo Library; **p.103** Dr Klaus Boller/Science Photo Library; **p.112** Ian Hooton/Science Photo Library; **p.114** Figure 13 data from Dr Andrew Wakefield and Professor John O'Leary; **p.115** A. Barrington Brown/Science Photo Library; **p.116** Science Photo Library; **p.122** Adrian T Sumner/Science Photo Library; **p.123** L. Willatt, East Anglian Regional Genetics Service/Science Photo Library; **p.127** © Reuters/Corbis; **p.128** Bob Gibbons/Science Photo; p.131 Andrew Syred/Science Photo Library; **p.132** M.I. Walker/Science Photo Library; **p.135** ©NHPA/Stephen Krasemann; **p.136** Steve Gschmeissner/Science Photo Library; **p.137** Sinclair Stammers/Science Photo Library; **p.138** BIOPHOTO Associates/Science Photo Library; **p.139** Biophoto Associates/Science Photo Library; **p.140** Photo Insolite Realite/Science Photo Library; **p.142** Andy Walker, Midland Fertility Services/Science Photo Library; **p.143** Pascal Goetgheluck/Science Photo Library; **p.145** Microfield Scientific Ltd/Science Photo Library; **p.147** t © Papilio/Alamy, *b* © Doug Wilson/Corbis; **p.148** Eye Of Science/Science Photo Library; **p.149** both Susumu Nishinaga/Science Photo Library; **p.150** Ken M. Highfill/Science Photo Library; **p.151** Dr Jeremy Burgess/Science Photo Library; **p.157** CNRI/Science Photo Library; **p.160** *t* © Images of Africa Photobank/Alamy, *b* Andy Crump, TDR, WHO/Science Photo Library; **p.161** D. Phillips/Science Photo Library; **p.166** Claude Nuridsany & Marie Perennou/Science Photo Library; **p.167** *l* Steve Gschmeissner/Science Photo, *r* Dr Keith Wheeler/Science Photo Library; **p.170** all Bill Indge; **p.172** Bill Indge; **p.173** both Bill Indge; **p.175** t ©NHPA/Mike Lane, *b* © 2008 Antinolo Jorge Sierra/photolibrary.com; **p.176** *l* Bill Indge, *c* Bill Indge, *r* ©NHPA/Andy Rouse; **p.177** Bill Indge; **p.186** © 2008 by Terry Lynch; **p.188** Alfred Pasieka/Science Photo Library; **p.190** Figure 2 data from 'Geographic Diversity in Tuberculosis Trends and Directly Observed Therapy, New York City, 1991 to 1994', Amy L. Davidow, Michael Marmor, And Philip Alcabes, American Journal of Respiratory and Critical Care Medicine; **p.191** © NI Syndication Limited, The Sun, 22 February 2007; **p.197** *l* © superclic/Alamy, *r* © Mark Boulton/Alamy; **p.202** Bill Indge; **p.205** Bill Indge; **p.209** Bill Indge; **p.209** Bill Indge
t = top, *b* = bottom, *l* = left; *c* = centre, *r* = right

Every effort has been made to trace all copyright holders, but if any have been inadvertently overlooked the Publishers will be pleased to make the necessary arrangements at the first opportunity.

Although every effort has been made to ensure that website addresses are correct at time of going to press, Hodder Education cannot be held responsible for the content of any website mentioned in this book. It is sometimes possible to find a relocated web page by typing in the address of the home page for a website in the URL window of your browser.

Hachette Livre UK's policy is to use papers that are natural, renewable and recyclable products and made from wood grown in sustainable forests. The logging and manufacturing processes are expected to conform to the environmental regulations of the country of origin.

Orders: please contact Bookpoint Ltd, 130 Milton Park, Abingdon, Oxon OX14 4SB. Telephone: (44) 01235 827720. Fax: (44) 01235 400454. Lines are open 9.00–5.00, Monday to Saturday, with a 24-hour message answering service. Visit our website at www.hoddereducation.co.uk

First published in 2008 by
Hodder Education,
part of Hachette Livre UK
338 Euston Road
London NW2 3BH

Impression number 5 4 3 2 1
Year 2012 2011 2010 2009 2008

Cover photo: green lacewing (*Chrysopa sp.*), Dr. John Brackenbury/Science Photo Library
Illustrations by Barking Dog Art
Typeset in Palatino 10pt by Fakenham Photosetting Ltd, Fakenham, Norfolk NR21 8NN
Printed in Italy

A catalogue record for this title is available from the British Library
ISBN: 978 034 0 94599 5

Contents

Unit 1 Biology and disease

Unit 2 The variety of living organisms

Introduction

Pick up a newspaper, listen to the news on the television and biology will never be far from the headlines. When this introduction was being written, there was an outbreak of bird flu on turkey farms in East Anglia and questions were being asked that concerned biologists. What was the best way to stop the outbreak spreading? Where did it come from and, perhaps, the question that concerns us most, could it spread to humans? In South east Asia, rainforest is being cleared and oil palms planted. Much of the oil that this crop produces will go towards meeting the growing demand for biofuels for our vehicles. What are the ecological effects of replacing forest with palm oil plantations?

Figure 1 In Borneo and other parts of southeast Asia, rainforest is being cleared to meet the growing demand for palm oil. The ecological effects of this should concern us all.

Some of you will go on to become professional biologists and may investigate problems such as these. Many of you, though, will follow careers in other fields. It is just as important for you to be able to understand the issues involved and to be able to weigh up scientific evidence in coming to a decision.

This book is an introduction to the study of biology at A-level. It explains the biology you will need to understand and will help you to gain the skills you require for the AQA specification. It also looks at the way in which scientists work; how they investigate scientific problems and use the evidence they collect to draw their conclusions. All the way through the book we will be questioning the reliability of results and the validity of conclusions. Scientific advances have also greatly improved the quality of life for many people. We will look at some of these advances and the impact they have had.

The first six chapters of the book explore the topics covered in Unit 1. They look at the human digestive system, the heart and the gas exchange system and will show you how an understanding of the way in which they work allows us to appreciate how disease affects our bodies. They also introduce topics such as biological molecules, enzymes, cell structure and the ways in which substances get into and out of cells. These are topics that you will encounter many times during your biology course.

The main theme of Unit 2 of the AQA specification is biodiversity and this is covered by the remaining chapters in the book. They look at variation and its causes, consider the range of living organisms, some of the ways in which these organisms are similar to each other and differ from each other, and the use scientists make of these features in classifying organisms. The final chapters concentrate on the enormous impact that humans have on biodiversity.

About this book

Before you begin working from this book, it would be a good idea to look at the way it has been written. Each chapter has been presented in a similar way and shares a number of features.

The chapter opening

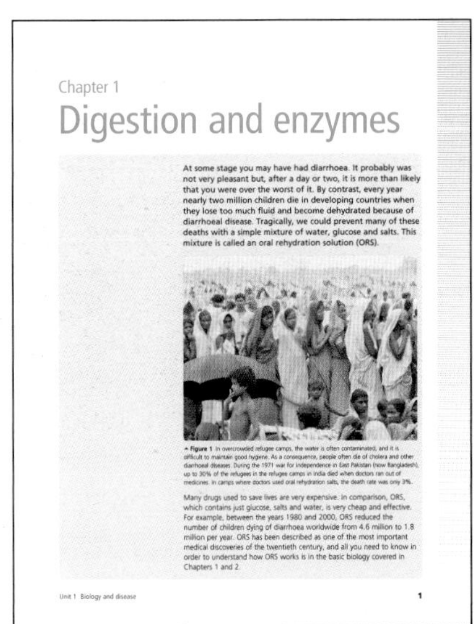

Chapter 1

Digestion and enzymes

At some stage you may have had diarrhoea. It probably was not very pleasant but, after a day or two, it is more than likely that you were over the worst of it. By contrast, every year nearly two million children die in developing countries when they lose too much fluid and become dehydrated because of diarrhoeal disease. Tragically, we could prevent many of these deaths with a simple mixture of water, glucose and salts. This mixture is called an oral rehydration solution (ORS).

▲ **Figure 1** In overcrowded refugee camps, the water is often contaminated, and it is difficult to maintain good hygiene. As a consequence, people often die of cholera and other diarrhoeal diseases. During the 1971 war for independence in East Pakistan (now Bangladesh), up to 30% of the refugees in the refugee camps in India died when doctors ran out of medicines. In camps where doctors used oral rehydration salts, the death rate was only 3%.

Many drugs used to save lives are very expensive. In comparison, ORS, which contains just glucose, salts and water, is very cheap and effective. For example, between the years 1980 and 2000, ORS reduced the number of children dying of diarrhoea worldwide from 4.6 million to 1.8 million per year. ORS has been described as one of the most important medical discoveries of the twentieth century, and all you need to know in order to understand how ORS works is in the basic biology covered in Chapters 1 and 2.

Unit 1 Biology and disease 1

Scientists use their knowledge and understanding to ask questions and suggest hypotheses. They carry out experiments which provide evidence that may or may not support their hypothesis. They may then be able to offer scientific explanations based on their experimental evidence and supported by the scientific community. In this way scientific advances are made and these may benefit humans. This is How Science Works and we have chosen something associated with this to start each chapter. It will help to show you the important part that the science of biology plays in the real world.

The text

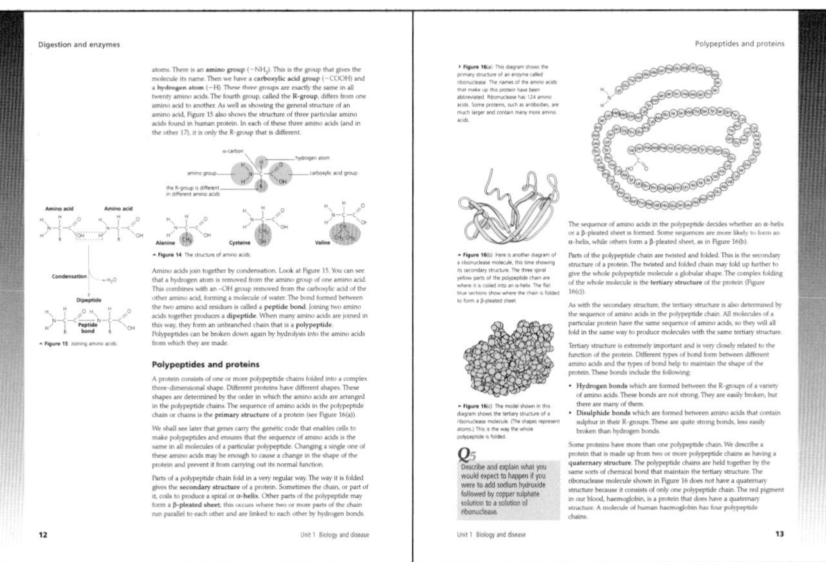

Digestion and enzymes

atoms. There is an **amino group** ($-NH_2$). This is the group that gives the molecule its name. Then we have a **carboxylic acid group** ($-COOH$) and a **hydrogen atom** ($-H$). These three groups are exactly the same in all twenty amino acids. The fourth group, called the **R-group**, differs from one amino acid to another. As well as showing the general structure of an amino acid, Figure 15 also shows the structure of three particular amino acids found in human protein. In each of these three amino acids (and in the other 17), it is only the R-group that is different.

▲ **Figure 14** The structure of amino acids.

▲ **Figure 15** Joining amino acids.

Amino acids join together by condensation. Look at Figure 15. You can see that a hydrogen atom is removed from the amino group of one amino acid. This combines with an –OH group removed from the carboxylic acid of the other amino acid, forming a molecule of water. The bond formed between the two amino acid residues is called a **peptide bond**. Joining two amino acids together produces a **dipeptide**. When many amino acids are joined in this way, they form an unbranched chain that is a **polypeptide**. Polypeptides can be broken down again by hydrolysis into the amino acids from which they are made.

Polypeptides and proteins

A protein consists of one or more polypeptide chains folded into a complex three-dimensional shape. Different proteins have different shapes. These shapes are determined by the order in which the amino acids are arranged in the polypeptide chains. The sequence of amino acids in the polypeptide chain or chains is the **primary structure** of a protein (see Figure 16(a)).

We shall see later that genes carry the genetic code that enables cells to make polypeptides and ensures that the sequence of amino acids is the same in all molecules of a particular polypeptide. Changing a single one of these amino acids may be enough to cause a change in the shape of the protein and prevent it from carrying out its normal function.

Parts of a polypeptide chain fold in a very regular way. The way it is folded gives the **secondary structure** of a protein. Sometimes the chain, or part of it, coils to produce a spiral or **α-helix**. Other parts of the polypeptide may form a **β-pleated sheet**; this occurs where two or more parts of the chain run parallel to each other and are linked to each other by hydrogen bonds.

12 Unit 1 Biology and disease

Polypeptides and proteins

▸ **Figure 16**(a) This diagram shows the primary structure of an enzyme called ribonuclease. The names of the amino acids that make up this protein have been abbreviated. Ribonuclease has 124 amino acids. Some proteins, such as antibodies, are much larger and contain many more amino acids.

▲ **Figure 16**(b) Here is another diagram of a ribonuclease molecule, this time showing its secondary structure. The three spiral yellow parts of the polypeptide chain are where it is coiled into an α-helix. The flat blue sections show where the chain is folded to form a β-pleated sheet.

▲ **Figure 16**(c) The model shown in this diagram shows the tertiary structure of a ribonuclease molecule. (The shapes represent atoms.) This is the way the whole polypeptide is folded.

Q5 Describe and explain what you would expect to happen if you were to add sodium hydroxide followed by copper sulphate solution to a solution of ribonuclease.

The sequence of amino acids in the polypeptide decides whether an α-helix or a β-pleated sheet is formed. Some sequences are more likely to form an α-helix, while others form a β-pleated sheet, as in Figure 16(b).

Parts of the polypeptide chain are twisted and folded. This is the secondary structure of a protein. The twisted and folded chain may fold up further to give the whole polypeptide molecule a globular shape. The complex folding of the whole molecule is the **tertiary structure** of the protein (Figure 16(c)).

As with the secondary structure, the tertiary structure is also determined by the sequence of amino acids in the polypeptide chain. All molecules of a particular protein have the same sequence of amino acids, so they will all fold in the same way to produce molecules with the same tertiary structure.

Tertiary structure is extremely important and is very closely related to the function of the protein. Different types of bond form between different amino acids and the types of bond help to maintain the shape of the protein. These bonds include the following:

- **Hydrogen bonds** which are formed between the R-groups of a variety of amino acids. These bonds are not strong. They are easily broken, but there are many of them.
- **Disulphide bonds** which are formed between amino acids that contain sulphur in their R-groups. These are quite strong bonds, less easily broken than hydrogen bonds.

Some proteins have more than one polypeptide chain. We describe a protein that is made up from two or more polypeptide chains as having a **quaternary structure**. The polypeptide chains are held together by the same sorts of chemical bond that maintain the tertiary structure. The ribonuclease molecule shown in Figure 16 does not have a quaternary structure because it consists of only one polypeptide chain. The red pigment in our blood, haemoglobin, is a protein that does have a quaternary structure. A molecule of human haemoglobin has four polypeptide chains.

Unit 1 Biology and disease 13

One of the most important words in the study of AS biology is 'understanding'. If you understand the basic ideas, you will be able to learn the necessary details later. If you don't understand the underlying biology, you will find it very difficult to remember the facts. In writing this book, we have kept this in mind and have tried to explain the basic ideas as clearly as possible. Most of you will have come to AS Biology from a background of GCSE Science so we have avoided introducing unnecessary technical terms. Where these terms are essential we have emboldened them and tried to make their meaning as clear as possible the first time we use them.

Q2

Suggest why it is not correct to say that food is absorbed through the small intestine wall into the blood.

Progress questions

The progress questions are all in blue boxes and are identified with the letter 'Q'. They should help you to understand what you have been reading and are meant to be answered as you go along. Some of them are very straightforward and can be attempted from information in the paragraph or so which come immediately before. Others require you to apply something that was explained earlier to a new situation. We haven't included any answers in the book but you will find them in the CD-ROM that accompanies this book.

Application and analysis

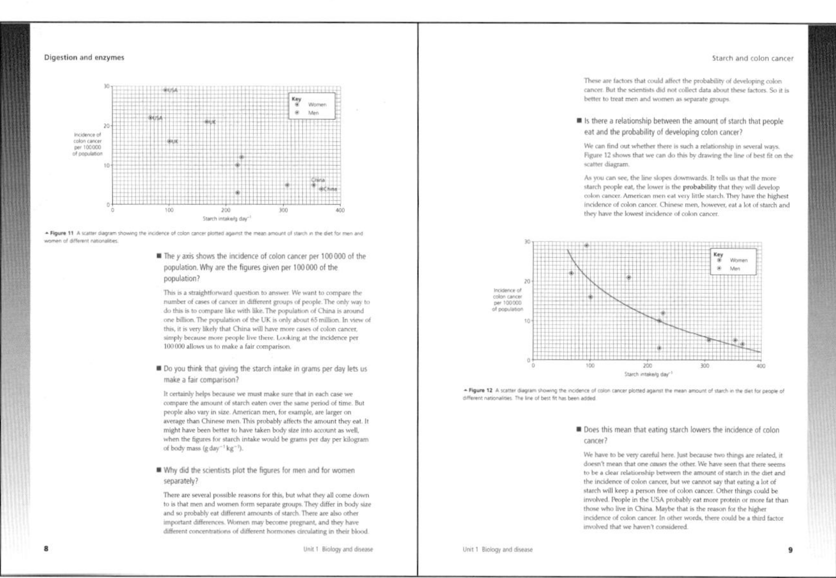

Digestion and enzymes

▲ **Figure 11** A scatter diagram showing the incidence of colon cancer plotted against the mean amount of starch in the diet for men and women of different nationalities.

■ The y axis shows the incidence of colon cancer per 100 000 of the population. Why are the figures given per 100 000 of the population?

This is a straightforward question to answer. We want to compare the number of cases of cancer in different groups of people. The only way to do this is to compare like with like. The population of China is around one billion. The population of the UK is only about 65 million. In view of this, it is very likely that China will have more cases of colon cancer, simply because more people live there. Looking at the incidence per 100 000 allows us to make a fair comparison.

■ Do you think that giving the starch intake in grams per day lets us make a fair comparison?

It certainly helps because we must make sure that in each case we compare the amount of starch eaten over the same period of time. But people also vary in size. American men, for example, are larger on average than Chinese men. This probably affects the amount they eat. It might have been better to have taken body size into account as well, when the figures for starch intake would be grams per day per kilogram of body mass ($g\ day^{-1}\ kg^{-1}$).

■ Why did the scientists plot the figures for men and for women separately?

There are several possible reasons for this, but what they all come down to is that men and women form separate groups. They differ in body size and so probably eat different amounts of starch. There are also other important differences. Women may become pregnant, and they have different concentrations of different hormones circulating in their blood.

8 Unit 1 Biology and disease

Starch and colon cancer

These are factors that could affect the probability of developing colon cancer. But the scientists did not collect data about these factors. So it is better to treat men and women as separate groups.

■ Is there a relationship between the amount of starch that people eat and the probability of developing colon cancer?

We can find out whether there is such a relationship in several ways. Figure 12 shows that we can do this by drawing the line of best fit on the scatter diagram.

As you can see, the line slopes downwards. It tells us that the more starch people eat, the lower is the **probability** that they will develop colon cancer. American men eat very little starch. They have the highest incidence of colon cancer. Chinese men, however, eat a lot of starch and they have the lowest incidence of colon cancer.

▲ **Figure 12** A scatter diagram showing the incidence of colon cancer plotted against the mean amount of starch in the diet for people of different nationalities. The line of best fit has been added.

■ Does this mean that eating starch lowers the incidence of colon cancer?

We have to be very careful here. Just because two things are related, it doesn't mean that one *causes* the other. We have seen that there seems to be a clear relationship between the amount of starch in the diet and the incidence of colon cancer, but we cannot say that eating a lot of starch will keep a person free of colon cancer. Other things could be involved. People in the USA probably eat more protein or more fat than those who live in China. Maybe that is the reason for the higher incidence of colon cancer. In other words, there could be a third factor involved that we haven't considered.

Unit 1 Biology and disease 9

These are opportunities for you to develop the skills of application and interpretation. The questions in these sections are in blue and have square bullet points in front of them. They are based on photographs and diagrams, graphs and tables and take you through the exercise step at a time. To get the most out of them, you should try to answer the questions before you look at the answers that are given underneath.

Principles boxes

As a result of working through the application and interpretation exercises you will find that you will have encountered some general principles. You will be able to apply these general principles to other similar problems. We have summarized these general principles in boxes.

Digestion and enzymes

■ Is it possible that eating starch does lower the incidence of colon cancer? How might it do this?

This is where scientists use their biological knowledge to suggest possible explanations for the results they collect. Food such as a banana contains different sorts of starch. Some of the starch in banana is digested only slowly in the human intestines. It is called resistant starch. When resistant starch enters the last part of our digestive system, the colon, it is broken down by the bacteria that live there. They produce substances such as butyric acid when they digest starch.

Resistant starch may help to prevent cancers developing in one of two ways. First, butyric acid is known to kill cancer cells. Second, resistant starch helps to increase the rate of movement of faeces through the colon. This means that any substances in the faeces that could cause cancer spend less time in contact with the cells that line the colon. Before we can say definitely what happens, a lot more work is necessary. On the evidence that we have here, all we can conclude is that it is possible that eating starch lowers the incidence of colon cancer.

General principles

Scatter diagrams

The graph in Figure 11 is a scatter diagram. You should know how to draw a scatter diagram.

- You draw a scatter diagram when you want to know if there is a relationship between two things. In Figure 11, we want to know if there is a relationship between the incidence of colon cancer and the mean amount of starch in the diet.
- The independent variable (the mean amount of starch in the diet) is plotted on the x axis, and the dependent variable (the incidence of colon cancer) is plotted on the y axis. You should use a similar scale on each axis so that the results are spread out equally in both directions.
- Ensure that you fully label the axes. Someone else should be able to look at the scatter diagram and know exactly what it shows without any further explanation.
- Plot each point as a dot with circle round it (⊙) or a cross (×).
- Draw a line of best fit like that shown in Figure 12.
- You should add a title explaining what the scatter diagram shows.

Interpreting scatter diagrams

- If your line of best fit slopes upwards, we can say that there is a positive correlation between the two variables. In other words, as one variable increases, so does the other.
- If your line of best fit slopes downwards, like that shown in Figure 12, we say that there is a negative correlation. In this case, as one variable increases, the other decreases.
- Sometimes the line of best fit is horizontal, sometimes it is vertical and sometimes it is completely impossible to draw a line of best fit. In these cases, all we can say is that there is no correlation between the variables concerned.
- We should always remember that just because two things are correlated, it doesn't mean that one causes the other.

10 Unit 1 Biology and disease

Interpretation exercises

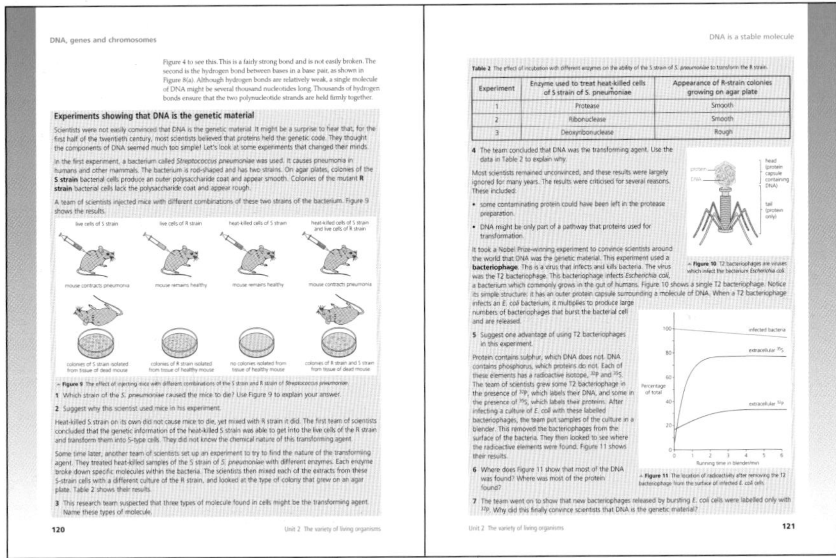

DNA, genes and chromosomes

Figure 4 to see this. This is a fairly strong bond and is not easily broken. The second is the hydrogen bond between bases in a base pair, as shown in Figure 8(a). Although hydrogen bonds are relatively weak, a single molecule of DNA might be several thousand nucleotides long. Thousands of hydrogen bonds ensure that the two polynucleotide strands are held firmly together.

Experiments showing that DNA is the genetic material

Scientists were not easily convinced that DNA is the genetic material. It might be a surprise to hear that, for the first half of the twentieth century, most scientists believed that proteins held the genetic code. They thought the components of DNA seemed much too simple! Let's look at some experiments that changed their minds.

In the first experiment, a bacterium called *Streptococcus pneumoniae* was used. It causes pneumonia in humans and other mammals. The bacterium is rod-shaped and has two strains. On agar plates, colonies of the **S strain** bacterial cells produce an outer polysaccharide coat and appear smooth. Colonies of the mutant **R strain** bacterial cells lack the polysaccharide coat and appear rough.

A team of scientists injected mice with different combinations of these two strains of the bacterium. Figure 9 shows the results.

Figure 9 The effect of injecting mice with different combinations of the S strain and R strain of *Streptococcus pneumoniae*.

1 Which strain of the *S. pneumoniae* caused the mice to die? Use Figure 9 to explain your answer.

2 Suggest why this scientist used mice in his experiment.

Heat-killed S strain on its own did not cause mice to die, yet mixed with R strain it did. The first team of scientists concluded that the genetic information of the heat-killed S strain was able to get into the live cells of the R strain and transform them into S-type cells. They did not know the chemical nature of this transforming agent.

Some time later, another team of scientists set up an experiment to try to find the nature of the transforming agent. They treated heat-killed samples of the S strain of *S. pneumoniae* with different enzymes. Each enzyme broke down specific molecules within the bacteria. The scientists then mixed each of the extracts from these S-strain cells with a different culture of the R strain, and looked at the type of colony that grew on an agar plate. Table 2 shows their results.

3 This research team suspected that three types of molecule found in cells might be the transforming agent. Name these types of molecule.

120 Unit 2 The variety of living organisms

DNA is a stable molecule

Table 2 The effect of incubation with different enzymes on the ability of the S strain of *S. pneumoniae* to transform the R strain.

Experiment	Enzyme used to treat heat-killed cells of S strain of S. pneumoniae	Appearance of R-strain colonies growing on agar plate
1	Protease	Smooth
2	Ribonuclease	Smooth
3	Deoxyribonuclease	Rough

4 The team concluded that DNA was the transforming agent. Use the data in Table 2 to explain why.

Most scientists remained unconvinced, and these results were largely ignored for many years. The results were criticised for several reasons. These included:

- some contaminating protein could have been left in the protease preparation.
- DNA might be only part of a pathway that proteins used for transformation.

It took a Nobel Prize-winning experiment to convince scientists around the world that DNA was the genetic material. This experiment used a **bacteriophage**. This is a virus that infects and kills bacteria. The virus was the T2 bacteriophage. This bacteriophage infects *Escherichia coli*, a bacterium which commonly grows in the gut of humans. Figure 10 shows a single T2 bacteriophage. Notice its simple structure: it has an outer protein capsule surrounding a molecule of DNA. When a T2 bacteriophage infects an *E. coli* bacterium, it multiplies to produce large numbers of bacteriophages that burst the bacterial cell and are released.

Figure 10 T2 bacteriophages are viruses which infect the bacterium *Escherichia coli*.

5 Suggest one advantage of using T2 bacteriophages in this experiment.

Protein contains sulphur, which DNA does not. DNA contains phosphorus, which proteins do not. Each of these elements has a radioactive isotope, ^{32}P and ^{35}S. The team of scientists grew some T2 bacteriophage in the presence of ^{32}P, which labels their DNA, and some in the presence of ^{35}S, which labels their proteins. After infecting a culture of *E. coli* with these labelled bacteriophages, the team put samples of the culture in a blender. This removed the bacteriophages from the surface of the bacteria. They then looked to see where the radioactive elements were found. Figure 11 shows their results.

Figure 11 The location of radioactivity after removing the T2 bacteriophage from the surface of infected *E. coli* cells.

6 Where does Figure 11 show that most of the DNA was found? Where was most of the protein found?

7 The team went on to show that new bacteriophages released by bursting *E. coli* cells were labelled only with ^{32}P. Why did this finally convince scientists that DNA is the genetic material?

Unit 2 The variety of living organisms 121

These exercises have a yellow background. They will provide you with an opportunity to work through more complex exercises on your own.

About your CD-ROM

There is a CD-ROM inside the back cover of this book, which contains an interactive copy of the book. Wherever the CD-ROM icon appears in the book, this links directly to a Tutorial (requires a web connection). Tutorials work through selected problems and concepts using a voiceover and animated diagrams.

All diagrams and photographs can be launched and enlarged directly from the pages. There are also Learning outcomes available at the beginning of every topic, and answers to all questions. All resources can be saved to your local hard drive.

Chapter 1

Digestion and enzymes

At some stage you may have had diarrhoea. It probably was not very pleasant but, after a day or two, it is more than likely that you were over the worst of it. By contrast, every year nearly two million children die in developing countries when they lose too much fluid and become dehydrated because of diarrhoeal disease. Tragically, we could prevent many of these deaths with a simple mixture of water, glucose and salts. This mixture is called an oral rehydration solution (ORS).

▲ **Figure 1** In overcrowded refugee camps, the water is often contaminated, and it is difficult to maintain good hygiene. As a consequence, people often die of cholera and other diarrhoeal diseases. During the 1971 war for independence in East Pakistan (now Bangladesh), up to 30% of the refugees in the refugee camps in India died when doctors ran out of medicines. In camps where doctors used oral rehydration solutions, the death rate was only 3%.

Many drugs used to save lives are very expensive. In comparison, ORS, which contains just glucose, salts and water, is very cheap and effective. For example, between the years 1980 and 2000, ORS reduced the number of children dying of diarrhoea worldwide from 4.6 million to 1.8 million per year. ORS has been described as one of the most important medical discoveries of the twentieth century, and all you need to know in order to understand how ORS works is in the basic biology covered in Chapters 1 and 2.

We can take the ORS story further. While children are suffering from diarrhoea, they are not absorbing the nutrients they need. As a result, they become weaker and weaker and less able to fight off the effects of the next attack of diarrhoea. Scientists have been thinking about this problem. Could they develop an even better ORS, one that not only prevents dehydration but also provides the valuable nutrients that a developing child needs?

The scientists investigated an ORS based on the starch in one type of rice flour. They found that it rehydrated diarrhoea sufferers and also helped to overcome malnutrition. However, at high concentrations, a rice-flour ORS is so thick that children cannot swallow it or take it from a feeding bottle. Scientists needed to find a suitable thickness for the rice-flour ORS. They took freshly made solutions of one type of rice flour at five different concentrations and made a measurement of the thickness of each solution. They measured with an instrument called a viscometer. Table 1 shows their results.

Table 1 The viscosity of different concentrations of rice-flour solution.

Concentration of rice flour/g 100 cm^{-3}	Viscosity of solution/cp
5	2 959
8	34 706
9	35 716
10	50 539
15	170 258

The viscosity of a solution is a measure of how thick it is. Viscosity is measured in centipoise (cp). The higher the viscosity of the solution, the thicker it is and the more difficult it is to drink. The table shows us that, as the concentration of the rice-flour solution increases, the thickness of the solution also increases.

Could we use the data in the table to produce a really effective ORS?

We know that solutions with a viscosity:

- below 1000 cp flow like water
- between 10 000 and 30 000 cp are thick and soup-like
- above 35 000 cp do not even flow out of a cup or feeding bottle.

At first sight, the data in the table look useful. A viscosity of 35 000 cp corresponds to a rice-flour concentration of about 8 g 100 cm^{-3}. Therefore, we might assume that the concentration of rice flour in a useful ORS should be something less than 8 g 100 cm^{-3}. But before we interpret the data in this way, we should ask ourselves:

Are the data in the table reliable?

We cannot say that the data are reliable because:

- the scientists used only one sort of rice flour, and others might give different results
- they obtained only one set of measurements
- values of 50 539 cp and 170 258 cp may look very impressive, but we should ask whether the viscometer was really this accurate.

Think of a hospital planning to make large amounts of a really effective rice-flour ORS. They first need a set of data that is reliable. So they would need a lot more data than the scientists had collected.

In this chapter we look at the biology behind diseases. We also look at the ways in which scientists work as they seek to understand the causes of disease and ways to combat it. We shall return to the story of a rice-flour ORS on page 28 at the end of this chapter.

Disease

Human diseases can be conditions that are not usually dangerous, such as the common cold, or they can be serious, life-threatening conditions such as AIDS, cholera and tuberculosis, cancer and heart disease. We can group all human diseases into two broad categories. Some are caused by microorganisms such as bacteria and viruses. These harmful microorganisms are called **pathogens**. They can be passed from one person to another, so the diseases they cause are called **infectious diseases**.

Q1

Several members of a family may develop a particular disease. Use your knowledge of infectious and non-infectious diseases to suggest two different reasons for this.

Non-infectious diseases, on the other hand, are not caused by microorganisms. They may result from the genes that we inherit from our parents, or they may be linked with our lifestyle and associated with factors such as diet, smoking and lack of exercise.

Our environment contains huge numbers of different microorganisms, and a small proportion of them are pathogens. They cause disease (see Figure 2).

▲ **Figure 2** Human sewage makes excellent fertiliser, and throughout the world it is spread on fields where crops are grown. Is this safe? Sewage contains many types of bacteria including a dangerous strain of *Escherichia coli* that can cause kidney damage. Research workers have found that the numbers of these dangerous bacteria decrease very rapidly when put on fields in sewage sludge. Using human sewage sludge as a fertiliser may therefore be much safer than was once thought.

Microorganisms that are also pathogens are present in and on the food we eat and in the water we drink. They are carried on the tiny droplets of moisture in the air that we breathe out or expel when we sneeze, and they are found in the soil and on objects that we touch. They find their way into our bodies through a number of body surfaces. We call these **interfaces** with the environment. They are shown in Figure 3.

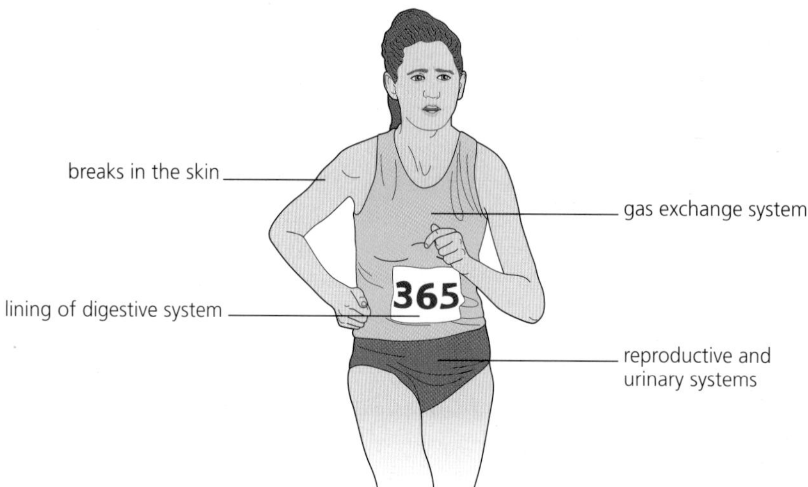

▲ **Figure 3** In order to cause disease, pathogens have to get into our bodies. They do this through interfaces with the environment.

The lining of the digestive system is one of these interfaces. Some pathogens attach themselves to the cells that form this lining. They include the bacteria *Salmonella* and *Campylobacter* that are responsible for many outbreaks of food poisoning, and others that cause more serious diseases such as cholera.

What does the digestive system do?

The **digestive system** consists of the gut which forms a tube extending from the mouth at one end, through the body, to the anus at the other end. Food is **ingested** – it is taken in. In the mouth, it is chewed, mixed with saliva, and swallowed. The food is now inside the gut but it is not yet inside the body itself. Before it can pass through the wall of the gut and into the blood, it must be **digested**. The food is mixed with digestive juices secreted by various glands as it is squeezed and pushed along by the muscular walls of the gut.

The digestive juices, made by gland cells of the digestive system, contain **enzymes**. The enzymes act on the large insoluble molecules of protein, starch and fats that are the main components of our food. The enzymes break them down into smaller soluble molecules:

- Protein is digested to amino acids.
- Starch is digested to glucose.
- Fats are digested to a mixture of fatty acids and glycerol.

These small molecules are **absorbed** through the **small intestine** wall into the blood and transported to the body's cells.

Q2

Suggest why it is not correct to say that food is absorbed through the small intestine wall into the blood.

Some substances in food, such as cellulose, cannot be digested by the human gut. They pass out through the anus, together with cells scraped from the gut lining, enzymes and bacteria, and are **egested** as faeces. Figure 4 summarises these processes.

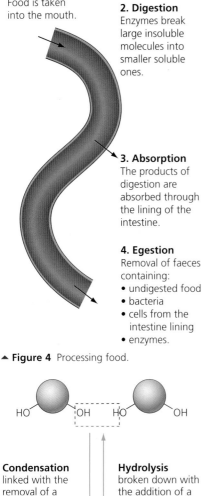

1. Ingestion
Food is taken into the mouth.

2. Digestion
Enzymes break large insoluble molecules into smaller soluble ones.

3. Absorption
The products of digestion are absorbed through the lining of the intestine.

4. Egestion
Removal of faeces containing:
- undigested food
- bacteria
- cells from the intestine lining
- enzymes.

▲ **Figure 4** Processing food.

Carbohydrates and their digestion

Large and small molecules

The food we buy in a supermarket may be processed but, whether it is a pizza or peanut butter, it has been derived from living organisms. It contains substances that once made up those organisms, although maybe not in the same proportions. Three groups of these substances are very important in our diet. They are carbohydrates, proteins and lipids, and they all contain carbon. We describe the molecules of substances in these groups as **organic** molecules. All other carbon-containing substances that were once in living organisms are also organic molecules.

Carbon atoms are unusual because they can form four chemical bonds. They can bond with other carbon atoms and with the atoms of other elements. The carbon atoms can join in long straight or branched chains. Many of the organic molecules found in living organisms are very large in size and are known as **macromolecules**. Macromolecules are built up from much smaller molecules. These small building blocks are called **monomers** and they may be identical or similar to each other. Several monomers join together to form a **polymer**.

Look at Figure 5. It shows how two monomers join together by a chemical reaction called **condensation** in which a molecule of water is formed. This water molecule is made up of the hydrogen atom (−H) that is removed from one of the two monomers, and a hydroxyl (−OH) group from the other. Because parts of the molecules have been removed (to form water), we refer to the larger parts that remain as **residues**. Joining a lot of monomer residues in this way produces a polymer.

Polymers may be broken down to the monomers that formed them by **hydrolysis**. This reaction is the opposite of condensation, because it adds −H and −OH from a molecule of water (see Figure 5).

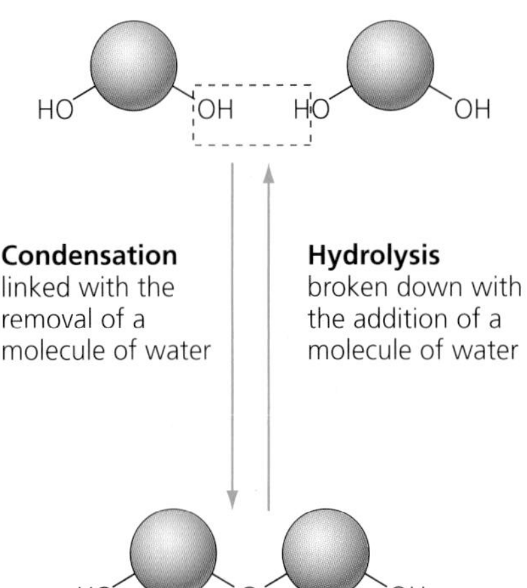

▲ **Figure 5** Monomers join together by condensation to form a polymer. This diagram shows two monomers joining together. When a large number of monomers are joined like this, we get a polymer. A polymer can be broken down to its monomers by hydrolysis.

Carbohydrates and food

A **carbohydrate** molecule contains carbon, hydrogen and oxygen. It has twice as many hydrogen atoms as oxygen atoms – the same proportion as in water. Carbohydrates are divided into three main types:

- **Monosaccharides** are single sugars. Different monosaccharides contain different numbers of carbon atoms. Most of those that are important in our food, such as glucose, fructose and galactose, contain six carbon atoms.
- **Disaccharides** are carbohydrates that contain two monosaccharide residues. Sucrose, maltose and lactose are disaccharides.
- **Polysaccharides** are very large molecules and contain many monosaccharide residues. Starch is a polysaccharide.

Glucose and other sugars

Glucose is a monosaccharide, so it is a single sugar. Its **molecular formula** is $C_6H_{12}O_6$. This formula simply tells us how many atoms of each element there are in each glucose molecule.

Now look at the structural formula shown in Figure 7. This shows a molecule of a particular form of glucose called α-glucose. Count each type of atom in diagram (a). There are 6 carbon atoms, 12 hydrogen atoms and 6 oxygen atoms, equal to the numbers of different atoms shown by the molecular formula, $C_6H_{12}O_6$. This diagram also shows you how the atoms are arranged.

Galactose and fructose are also monosaccharides and have exactly the same molecular formula as α-glucose. However, the atoms that make up these molecules are arranged in different ways. This means that, although all three substances are sugars, they have slightly different structures. This gives them slightly different properties.

Monosaccharides such as α-glucose are the monomers that join together to make many other carbohydrates. Two α-glucose molecules join by condensation to form a molecule of the disaccharide maltose. The bond forms between carbon 1 of one α-glucose molecule and carbon 4 of the other, and is called a **glycosidic bond** (see Figure 8).

Other disaccharides form in a similar way. Lactose, for example, is the sugar found in milk. It is formed in a condensation between a molecule of α-glucose and a molecule of another monosaccharide, galactose. Sucrose is formed from α-glucose and fructose.

When sugars such as α-glucose are boiled with Benedict's solution, an orange precipitate is formed because Cu(II) ions in Benedict's solution are reduced to orange Cu(I) ions. This reaction occurs because of the way

Q3

The molecular formula of galactose is $C_6H_{12}O_6$. What is the molecular formula of a molecule of lactose?

▲ **Figure 6** Most of the carbohydrate that we eat comes from plants. This crop is sugar cane, a plant that stores sucrose in its stem. The carbohydrate stored by other food plants such as potatoes and cereals is starch.

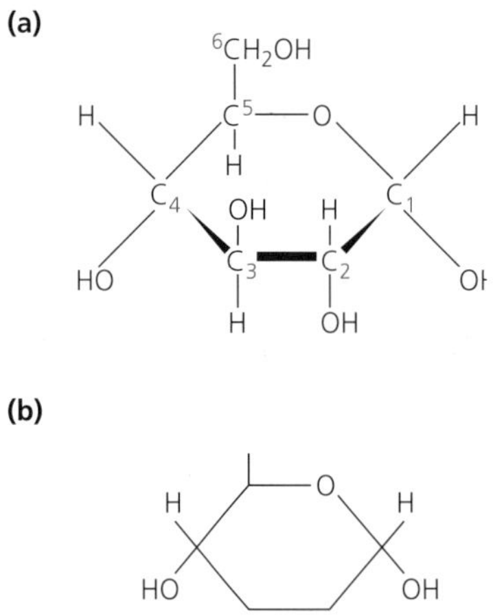

▲ **Figure 7** (a) This shows how the atoms in a molecule of α-glucose are arranged. The small numbers in red allow us to refer to particular carbon atoms, for example, when describing where particular chemical groups are attached and where bonds are formed. (b) This is a simplified version of its structure.

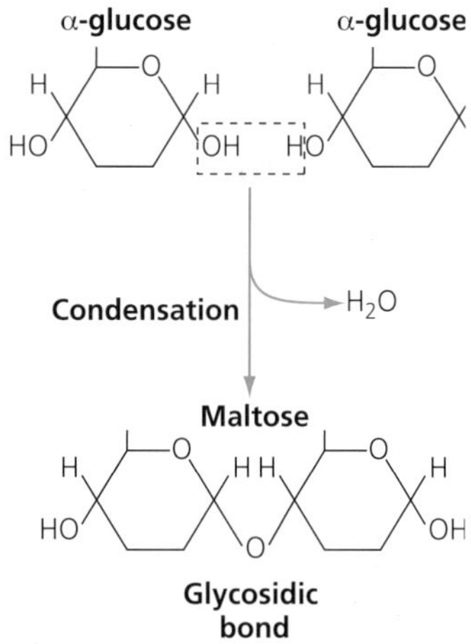

▲ **Figure 8** Two α-glucose molecules join together by condensation to give a molecule of the disaccharide maltose.

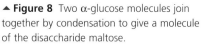

chemical groups are arranged in such sugars. These sugars are therefore called **reducing sugars**. Fructose, maltose and galactose are also reducing sugars.

Sucrose does not give an orange precipitate with Benedict's solution: it is a **non-reducing sugar**. However, when boiled with dilute acid, sucrose is hydrolysed to monosaccharides. The sucrose molecules are split into α-glucose and fructose, both reducing sugars. Then it will give a positive test with Benedict's solution. (See page 44 for details of food tests.)

Q4

Starch molecules from different plants may differ from each other. Give two ways in which they may be different.

Starch

Starch, a substance found in plants, is one of the most important sources of energy in the human diet. It makes up about 30% of what we eat. Starch is a mixture of two substances, amylose and amylopectin. Both these substances are polymers made from a large number of α-glucose molecules joined together by condensation.

Amylose
consists of a long chain of α-glucose residues

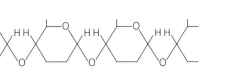

The chain is coiled into a spiral. Hydrogen bonds hold this spiral in shape.

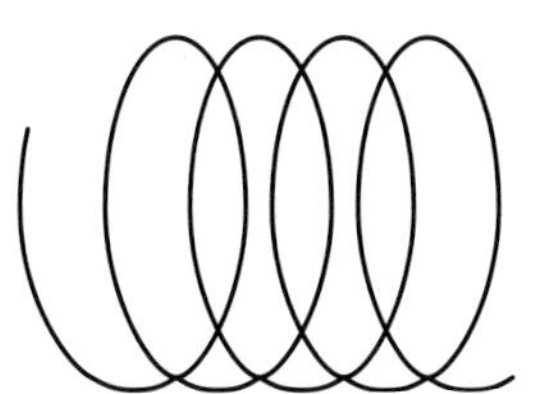

Amylopectin
consists of branched chains of α-glucose residues

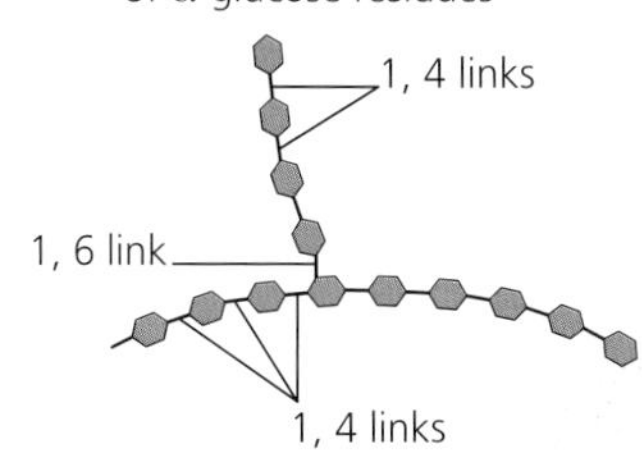

▲ **Figure 9** Starch consists of amylose and amylopectin. Starch from different plants contains different amounts of these two substances.

Figure 9 shows the structure of starch. You can see that **amylose** is a long chain of α-glucose molecules. They are linked by glycosidic bonds. This chain is coiled into a spiral and its coils are held in place by chemical bonds called hydrogen bonds. **Amylopectin** is also a polymer of α-glucose but its molecules are branched.

In the biochemical test for starch, you add a drop of iodine solution. Starch turns blue-black.

▲ **Figure 10** Most people like their bananas yellow. Yellow bananas taste sweet. Green bananas, however, may be better for you as they contain more starch. As a banana ripens and turns yellow, most of this starch is turned to sugars.

Starch and colon cancer

Scientists investigated the relationship between the food we eat and the probability of developing cancer of the colon. The colon is the last part of the digestive system. One of the factors that the scientists looked at was the amount of starch in people's diet. The scatter diagram in Figure 11 shows some of their results.

In considering any set of data, one of the first things we do is to look carefully at the data set and make sure that we understand exactly what it shows. We will start here by looking at the axes.

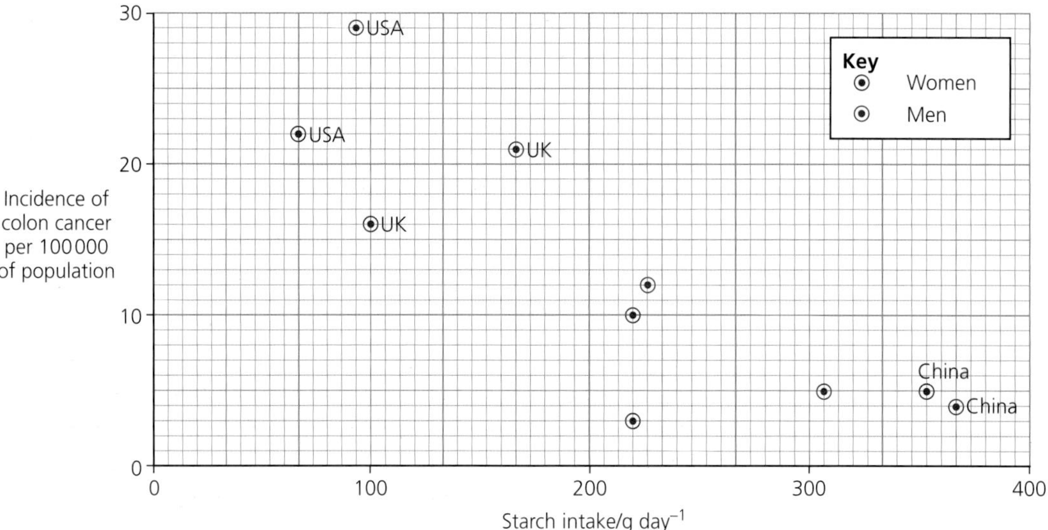

▲ **Figure 11** A scatter diagram showing the incidence of colon cancer plotted against the mean amount of starch in the diet for men and women of different nationalities.

The *y* axis shows the incidence of colon cancer per 100 000 of the population. Why are the figures given per 100 000 of the population?

This is a straightforward question to answer. We want to compare the number of cases of cancer in different groups of people. The only way to do this is to compare like with like. The population of China is around one billion. The population of the UK is only about 65 million. In view of this, it is very likely that China will have more cases of colon cancer, simply because more people live there. Looking at the incidence per 100 000 allows us to make a fair comparison.

Do you think that giving the starch intake in grams per day lets us make a fair comparison?

It certainly helps because we must make sure that in each case we compare the amount of starch eaten over the same period of time. But people also vary in size. American men, for example, are larger on average than Chinese men. This probably affects the amount they eat. It might have been better to have taken body size into account as well, when the figures for starch intake would be grams per day per kilogram of body mass (g day^{-1} kg^{-1}).

Why did the scientists plot the figures for men and for women separately?

There are several possible reasons for this, but what they all come down to is that men and women form separate groups. They differ in body size and so probably eat different amounts of starch. There are also other important differences. Women may become pregnant, and they have different concentrations of different hormones circulating in their blood.

These are factors that could affect the probability of developing colon cancer. But the scientists did not collect data about these factors. So it is better to treat men and women as separate groups.

Is there a relationship between the amount of starch that people eat and the probability of developing colon cancer?

We can find out whether there is such a relationship in several ways. Figure 12 shows that we can do this by drawing the line of best fit on the scatter diagram.

As you can see, the line slopes downwards. It tells us that the more starch people eat, the lower is the **probability** that they will develop colon cancer. American men eat very little starch. They have the highest incidence of colon cancer. Chinese men, however, eat a lot of starch and they have the lowest incidence of colon cancer.

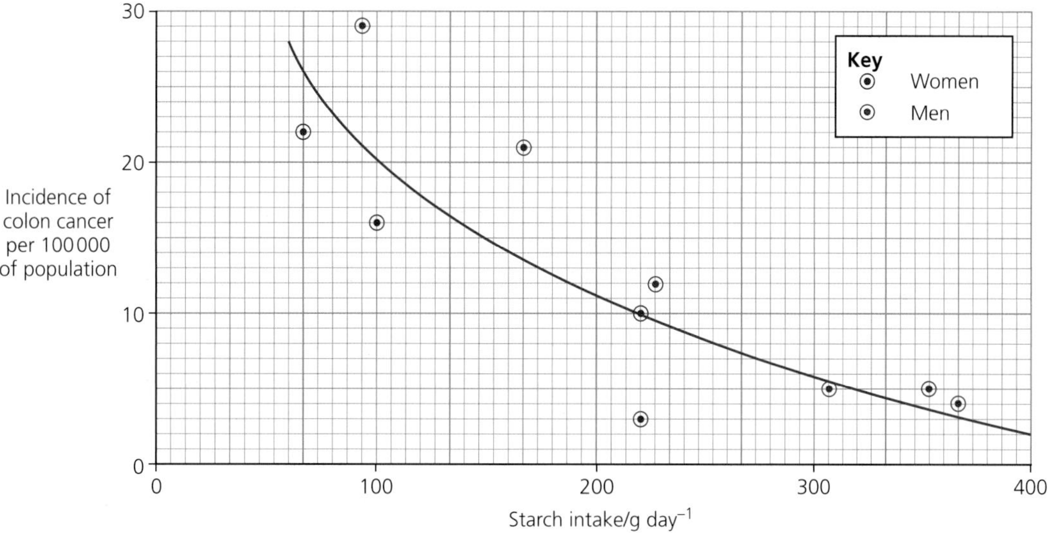

▲ **Figure 12** A scatter diagram showing the incidence of colon cancer plotted against the mean amount of starch in the diet for people of different nationalities. The line of best fit has been added.

Does this mean that eating starch lowers the incidence of colon cancer?

We have to be very careful here. Just because two things are related, it doesn't mean that one *causes* the other. We have seen that there seems to be a clear relationship between the amount of starch in the diet and the incidence of colon cancer, but we cannot say that eating a lot of starch will keep a person free of colon cancer. Other things could be involved. People in the USA probably eat more protein or more fat than those who live in China. Maybe that is the reason for the higher incidence of colon cancer. In other words, there could be a third factor involved that we haven't considered.

■ Is it possible that eating starch does lower the incidence of colon cancer? How might it do this?

This is where scientists use their biological knowledge to suggest possible explanations for the results they collect. Food such as a banana contains different sorts of starch. Some of the starch in banana is digested only slowly in the human intestines. It is called resistant starch. When resistant starch enters the last part of our digestive system, the colon, it is broken down by the bacteria that live there. They produce substances such as butyric acid when they digest starch.

Resistant starch may help to prevent cancers developing in one of two ways. First, butyric acid is known to kill cancer cells. Second, resistant starch helps to increase the rate of movement of faeces through the colon. This means that any substances in the faeces that could cause cancer spend less time in contact with the cells that line the colon. Before we can say definitely what happens, a lot more work is necessary. On the evidence that we have here, all we can conclude is that it is possible that eating starch lowers the incidence of colon cancer.

General principles

Scatter diagrams

The graph in Figure 11 is a scatter diagram. You should know how to draw a scatter diagram.

- You draw a scatter diagram when you want to know if there is a relationship between two things. In Figure 11, we want to know if there is a relationship between the incidence of colon cancer and the mean amount of starch in the diet.
- The independent variable (the mean amount of starch in the diet) is plotted on the *x* axis, and the dependent variable (the incidence of colon cancer) is plotted on the *y* axis. You should use a similar scale on each axis so that the results are spread out equally in both directions.
- Ensure that you fully label the axes. Someone else should be able to look at the scatter diagram and know exactly what it shows without any further explanation.
- Plot each point as a dot with circle round it (⊙) or a cross (×).
- Draw a line of best fit like that shown in Figure 12.
- You should add a title explaining what the scatter diagram shows.

Interpreting scatter diagrams

- If your line of best fit slopes upwards, we can say that there is a positive correlation between the two variables. In other words, as one variable increases, so does the other.
- If your line of best fit slopes downwards, like that shown in Figure 12, we say that there is a negative correlation. In this case, as one variable increases, the other decreases.
- Sometimes the line of best fit is horizontal, sometimes it is vertical and sometimes it is completely impossible to draw a line of best fit. In these cases, all we can say is that there is no correlation between the variables concerned.
- We should always remember that just because two things are correlated, it doesn't mean that one *causes* the other.

▲ **Figure 13** We eat different carbohydrates in our diet. Bread, pasta and potatoes all contain starch; fruit contains sucrose, glucose and fructose. Milk contains lactose.

Digesting carbohydrates

Respiration is the biochemical process by which we release energy from energy stores such as glucose. The glucose we use in respiration comes from the carbohydrates that we eat, so it is extremely important that our diet contains carbohydrate (Figure 13).

Any glucose that we eat can be absorbed as soon as it reaches the small intestine because glucose molecules are small and are able to pass through the cells that line the intestine and enter the blood. Starch, though, has large insoluble molecules that cannot be absorbed. They must be digested and broken down, first to maltose and then to glucose. This involves the enzymes amylase and maltase. Amylase hydrolyses starch to maltose and maltase hydrolyses maltose to glucose:

$$\text{starch} \xrightarrow{\text{amylase}} \text{maltose} \xrightarrow{\text{maltase}} \text{glucose}$$

The glucose can then be absorbed into the blood.

Enzymes such as amylase and maltase are proteins that act as catalysts.

Proteins and protein structure

Earlier in this chapter, we saw that starch is a polymer made up of a single type of monomer, α-glucose. Whether these α-glucose monomers are linked to form straight chains or branched chains, they still form starch. Different types of starch are very similar.

Proteins are different. The basic building blocks of proteins are amino acids. There are twenty different amino acids found in proteins and they can be joined in any order. In any living organism, there are a huge number of different proteins and they have many different functions.

If we take a single tissue, such as blood, we can get some idea of just how varied and important are the roles of proteins. Human blood is red because it contains haemoglobin. This is an iron-containing protein that plays an extremely important part in transporting oxygen from the lungs to respiring cells. When you cut yourself, blood soon clots. This is because another protein, fibrin, forms a mesh of threads over the surface of the wound, trapping red blood cells and forming a scab. Blood also contains enzymes, which are proteins. The antibodies produced by white blood cells are also proteins, and are important in protecting the body against disease.

The **biuret reaction** enables us to test for a protein. Sodium hydroxide solution is added to a test sample, and then a few drops of dilute copper sulphate solution. If there is a protein present, the solution will turn mauve.

Amino acids, the building blocks of proteins

Proteins are made up of twenty different amino acids, and they all have the same general structure. Look at Figure 14. Notice that there is a central carbon atom called the **α-carbon** and that it is attached to four groups of atoms. There is an **amino group** ($-NH_2$). This is the group that gives the molecule its name. Then we have a **carboxylic acid group** ($-COOH$) and a **hydrogen atom** ($-H$). These three groups are exactly the same in all twenty amino acids. The fourth group, called the **R-group**, differs from one amino acid to another. As well as showing the general structure of an amino acid, Figure 15 also shows the structure of three particular amino acids found in human protein. In each of these three amino acids (and in the other 17), it is only the R-group that is different.

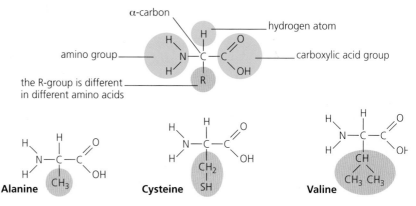

▲ **Figure 14** The structure of amino acids.

Amino acids join together by condensation. Look at Figure 15. You can see that a hydrogen atom is removed from the amino group of one amino acid. This combines with an –OH group removed from the carboxylic acid of the other amino acid, forming a molecule of water. The bond formed between the two amino acid residues is called a **peptide bond**. Joining two amino acids together produces a **dipeptide**. When many amino acids are joined in this way, they form an unbranched chain that is a **polypeptide**. Polypeptides can be broken down again by hydrolysis into the amino acids from which they are made.

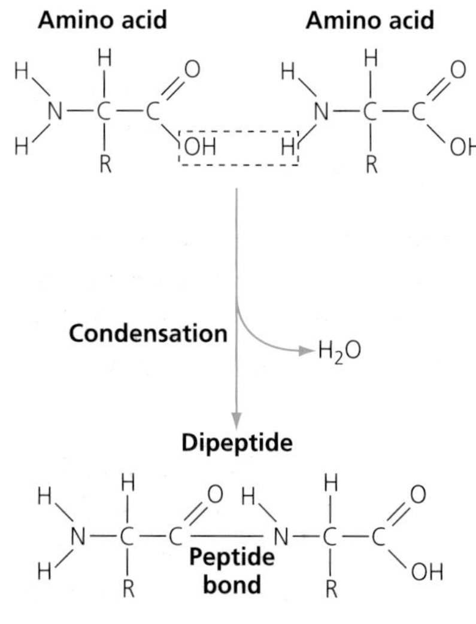

▲ **Figure 15** Joining amino acids.

Polypeptides and proteins

A protein consists of one or more polypeptide chains folded into a complex three-dimensional shape. Different proteins have different shapes. These shapes are determined by the order in which the amino acids are arranged in the polypeptide chains. The sequence of amino acids in the polypeptide chain or chains is the **primary structure** of a protein (see Figure 16(a)).

We shall see later that genes carry the genetic code that enables cells to make polypeptides and ensures that the sequence of amino acids is the same in all molecules of a particular polypeptide. Changing a single one of these amino acids may be enough to cause a change in the shape of the protein and prevent it from carrying out its normal function.

Parts of a polypeptide chain fold in a very regular way. The way it is folded gives the **secondary structure** of a protein. Sometimes the chain, or part of it, coils to produce a spiral or **α-helix**. Other parts of the polypeptide may form a **β-pleated sheet**; this occurs where two or more parts of the chain run parallel to each other and are linked to each other by hydrogen bonds.

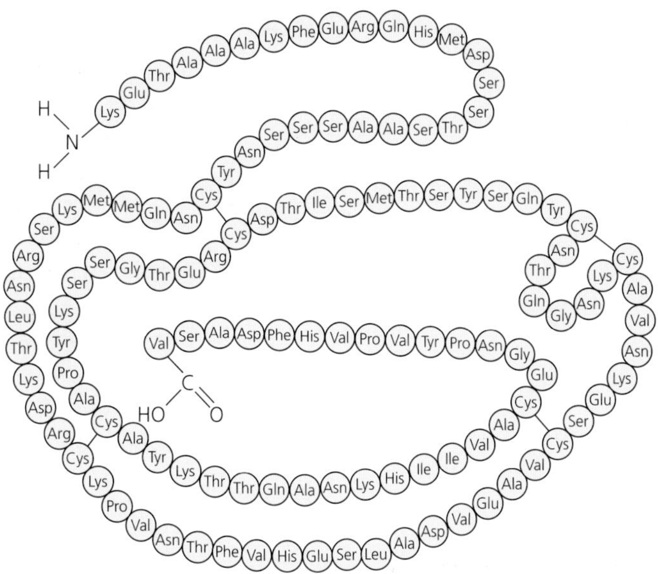

▸ **Figure 16**(a) This diagram shows the primary structure of an enzyme called ribonuclease. The names of the amino acids that make up this protein have been abbreviated. Ribonuclease has 124 amino acids. Some proteins, such as antibodies, are much larger and contain many more amino acids.

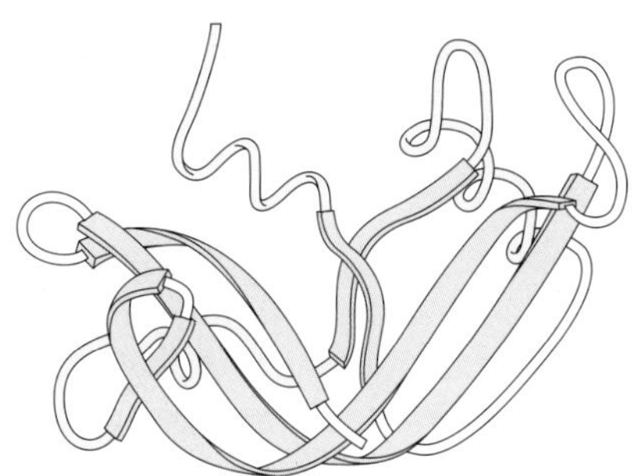

▲ **Figure 16**(b) Here is another diagram of a ribonuclease molecule, this time showing its secondary structure. The three spiral yellow parts of the polypeptide chain are where it is coiled into an α-helix. The flat blue sections show where the chain is folded to form a β-pleated sheet.

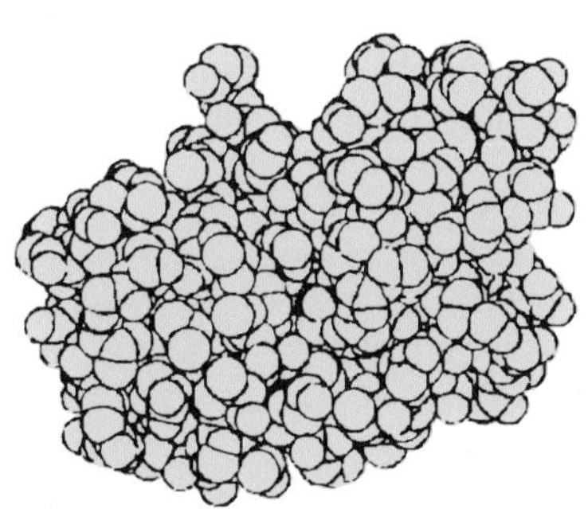

▲ **Figure 16**(c) The model shown in this diagram shows the tertiary structure of a ribonuclease molecule. (The shapes represent atoms.) This is the way the whole polypeptide is folded.

The sequence of amino acids in the polypeptide decides whether an α-helix or a β-pleated sheet is formed. Some sequences are more likely to form an α-helix, while others form a β-pleated sheet, as in Figure 16(b).

Parts of the polypeptide chain are twisted and folded. This is the secondary structure of a protein. The twisted and folded chain may fold up further to give the whole polypeptide molecule a globular shape. The complex folding of the whole molecule is the **tertiary structure** of the protein (Figure 16(c)).

As with the secondary structure, the tertiary structure is also determined by the sequence of amino acids in the polypeptide chain. All molecules of a particular protein have the same sequence of amino acids, so they will all fold in the same way to produce molecules with the same tertiary structure.

Tertiary structure is extremely important and is very closely related to the function of the protein. Different types of bond form between different amino acids and the types of bond help to maintain the shape of the protein. These bonds include the following:

- **Hydrogen bonds** which are formed between the R-groups of a variety of amino acids. These bonds are not strong. They are easily broken, but there are many of them.
- **Disulphide bonds** which are formed between amino acids that contain sulphur in their R-groups. These are quite strong bonds, less easily broken than hydrogen bonds.

Some proteins have more than one polypeptide chain. We describe a protein that is made up from two or more polypeptide chains as having a **quaternary structure**. The polypeptide chains are held together by the same sorts of chemical bond that maintain the tertiary structure. The ribonuclease molecule shown in Figure 16 does not have a quaternary structure because it consists of only one polypeptide chain. The red pigment in our blood, haemoglobin, is a protein that does have a quaternary structure. A molecule of human haemoglobin has four polypeptide chains.

Describe and explain what you would expect to happen if you were to add sodium hydroxide followed by copper sulphate solution to a solution of ribonuclease.

How do enzymes work?

Have you ever found an old newspaper, one that is perhaps months or even years old? If you have, you probably noticed that it had turned a yellowish-brown colour. What has happened? The paper has reacted with oxygen in the air, but it is a very, very slow reaction.

We can easily speed up this reaction. All we need to do is to touch the corner of the paper with a lighted match. The paper bursts into flame, reacting with oxygen in the air much faster. This reaction involves combustion. The newspaper is fuel and contains chemical potential energy. In order to release this energy in the chemical reaction with oxygen, we must supply some energy at the start. This is where the match comes in. It provides the **activation energy** necessary to start the reaction.

We sometimes compare what happens here with what would happen if you had a large rock at the top of a steep hill. There is a lot of potential energy in this situation but, under normal conditions, the rock will just sit there. But, give it a push and it will roll all the way down to the bottom of the hill. In other words, supply activation energy at the start, and the rock will give up a lot of its potential energy. Look at Figure 17. This is a graph showing, in a different way, the idea of the energy changes that take place as a chemical reaction progresses.

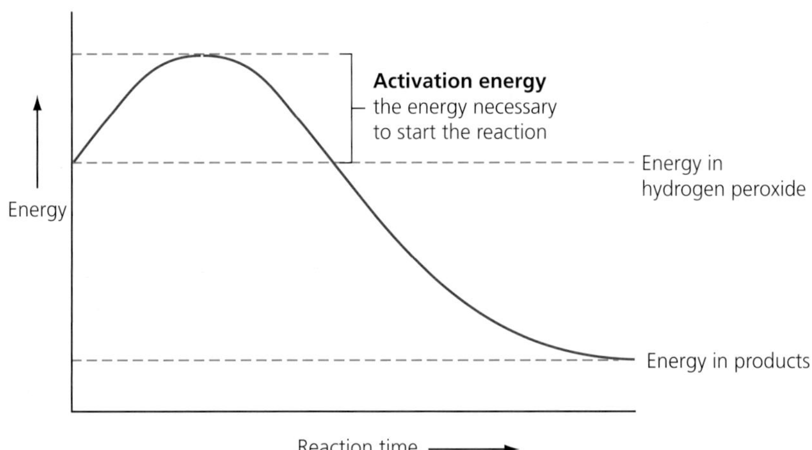

▲ **Figure 17** Activation energy is necessary before a chemical reaction will take place.

Hydrogen peroxide is a substance produced by reactions in many living cells. It is harmful, so it has to be removed. It breaks down very slowly to give the **products** water and oxygen:

$$2H_2O_2 \rightarrow 2H_2O + O_2$$

The products of this reaction, water and oxygen, are not only harmless, they are extremely useful to the organism.

We can pour some hydrogen peroxide into a test tube and it will slowly break down. We can make the reaction go faster by heating the hydrogen peroxide. Clearly, we cannot heat our cells to increase the rate at which the hydrogen peroxide they produce is broken down. This is where enzymes come in.

Cells produce an enzyme called **catalase**. Its **substrate**, the substance on which an enzyme acts, is hydrogen peroxide. Catalase lowers the activation energy needed to start the breakdown reaction of hydrogen peroxide. As a consequence, the hydrogen peroxide breaks down rapidly at the relatively low temperatures found inside living cells. Figure 18 shows this as a graph. Note that there is the same chemical potential energy at the start and there is the same amount in the products. The enzyme has simply lowered the activation energy necessary to start the reaction.

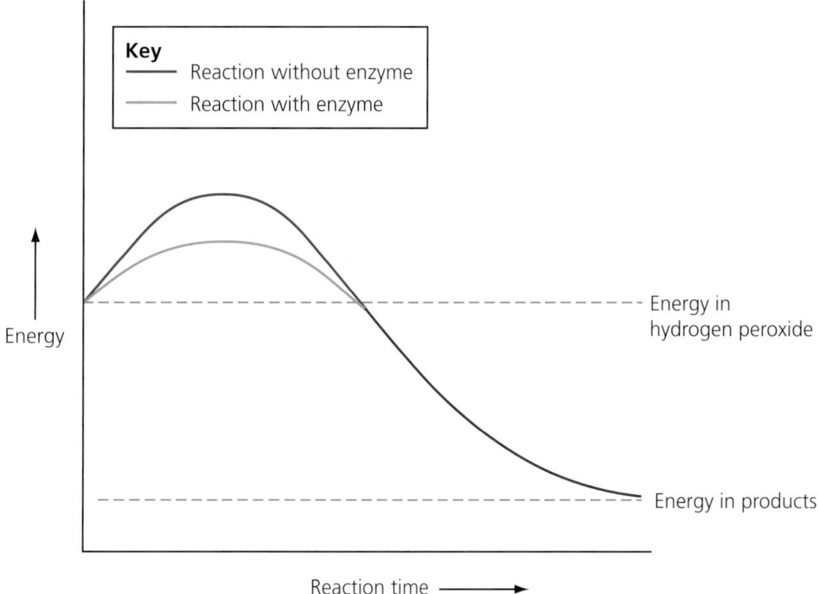

▲ **Figure 18** Adding an enzyme lowers the activation energy necessary to start a chemical reaction.

Enzyme shape and enzyme function: ribonuclease

A skill that a biologist must have is to be able to interpret unfamiliar data. Here we will look at some research carried out by Christian Anfinsen in the 1960s. It was very important research because it demonstrated the relationship between the structure of an enzyme and its function.

Anfinsen investigated the enzyme ribonuclease. This enzyme breaks down RNA (ribonucleic acid). There are different forms of ribonuclease. Look at the diagram in Figure 19 which shows the tertiary structure of one form of this enzyme.

The numbers on the diagram show positions along the polypeptide chain. For example, number 26 is the twenty-sixth amino acid along the chain. The large black dots represent the amino acid cysteine. This amino acid contains sulphur. Chemical bonds called disulphide bonds (see page 13) form between sulphur-containing amino acids. They are quite strong bonds and help to hold the tertiary structure of a protein together. In the diagram, the amino acid at positions 26 and 84 is cysteine. The dotted line between them is a disulphide bond.

When we look at unfamiliar data, it is very important to take the time to think about it carefully and make sure that we understand it. We should be able to answer some basic questions about Figure 19.

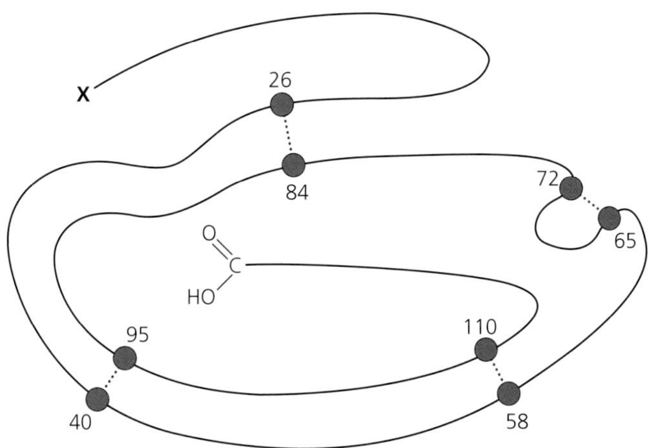

▲ **Figure 19** A molecule of one form of the enzyme ribonuclease.

■ What chemical group is shown by the letter **X** on the diagram?

This is an amino ($-NH_2$) group. Look back at Figure 15. You can see that the dipeptide has a $-COOH$ group at one end and an $-NH_2$ group at the other. The same is true of a polypeptide. There is always a $-COOH$ group at one end and an $-NH_2$ group at the other. Since the $-COOH$ group is shown on the diagram, position **X** must be where there is an $-NH_2$ group.

■ Figure 19 shows one form of the enzyme ribonuclease. How do you think other forms of ribonuclease will be different?

Different forms of ribonuclease will have different amino acids in different positions. In other words, each form will have a different primary structure. However, we would not expect them to differ much, because they are all forms of the same enzyme, ribonuclease.

■ All molecules of this form of ribonuclease have the same tertiary structure. Use information from the diagram to explain why.

This should be quite simple, if you have understood the diagram. All molecules of this form of ribonuclease will have the same sequence of amino acids. The cysteine molecules will therefore always be in the same positions and the disulphide bonds will form in the same place.

Hopefully, you have understood what the diagram of Figure 19 tells you. We will now look at the steps in Anfinsen's investigation.

- Anfinsen started by measuring the activity of untreated ribonuclease.
- He then treated the ribonuclease with mercaptoethanol. This substance broke the disulphide bonds in the ribonuclease molecules. He measured the activity of the treated ribonuclease.
- Finally, he removed the mercaptoethanol. As a result, the disulphide bonds re-formed.

His results are shown in Figure 20.

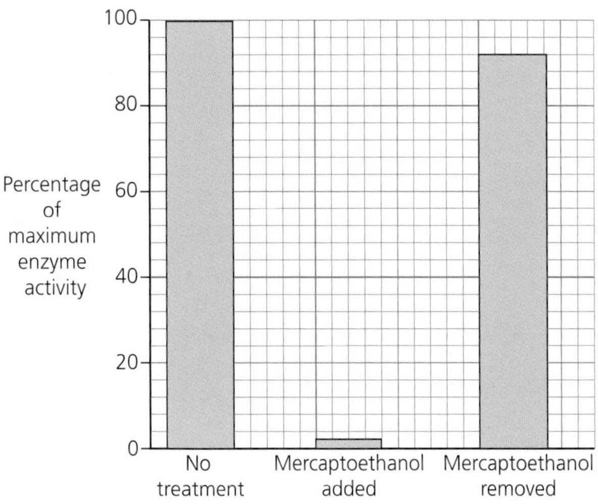

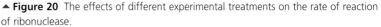

▲ **Figure 20** The effects of different experimental treatments on the rate of reaction of ribonuclease.

Again, the data shown in this graph are probably unfamiliar. We need to take the time to make sure that we understand the graph. We will start by looking at the axes. The *x* axis, the horizontal one, shows the three different treatments. The *y* axis, the vertical one, shows the enzyme activity. This is given as the percentage of maximum enzyme activity, so a value of 100 represents the fastest that the enzyme could possibly react.

To make sure that we really understand the information in the graph, we should ask, for example:

■ What does the second column show?

When the ribonuclease is treated with mercaptoethanol, the enzyme is not very reactive. It shows only about 2% of its maximum activity.

■ The graph shows us that mercaptoethanol had a considerable effect on the activity of ribonuclease. Why did it have this effect?

The tertiary structure of ribonuclease is held together by disulphide bonds. These have been broken, so the polypeptide chain loses its shape. We say that it is **denatured**. This means that the site into which the substrate molecules fit also loses its shape. As a result, the substrate will no longer bind to the enzyme. Not surprisingly, the activity of the enzyme falls.

■ What happened when the mercaptoethanol was removed from the ribonuclease? Can you explain this?

The bonds are re-formed and the tertiary structure of the enzyme is restored. The enzyme functions again.

General principles

Drawing a bar chart

The graph in Figure 20 is a bar chart. You should know how to draw a bar chart.

- You draw a bar chart when one of the things you plot does not have a numerical value. In the case of Figure 20, what is plotted is the treatment given to the enzyme, and this does not have a numerical value. The data are separate for each of the treatments.
- You should draw bars of equal width on the chart. These bars do not touch each other.
- The independent variable is the method of treatment. It is plotted on the *x* axis. The dependent variable is the activity of the enzyme and it is plotted on the *y* axis.
- Ensure that you fully label the axes. Someone else should be able to look at the bar chart and know exactly what it shows without any further explanation.
- You should add a title explaining what the bar chart shows.

Understanding graphs

You will come across a lot of graphs in biology. There are graphs in textbooks, in scientific journals, on the internet and in examination questions. You certainly need to be able to understand graphs.

- Read the information that comes before and the title of the graph, if it has one.
- Make sure you understand what the axes represent.
- Finally, make sure that you understand what the graph as a whole is telling you. With a barchart, look at one of the bars and see if you can explain what it means.

Explaining patterns

- Take your time. Make sure that you understand the data and have identified obvious patterns before you start explaining.
- Explain means give a reason. It does not mean describe. If you are required to explain something, make sure that you really do give a reason. In examinations, it is a good idea to start answers to 'explain' questions with the word 'Because'.
- You should be explaining a particular set of data, so you must relate your knowledge to the figures concerned.

Enzymes, substrates and products

If we mix an enzyme solution with biuret reagent, the solution goes violet in colour. This is the test for proteins, and we can use it to show that all enzymes are proteins. Now look at Figure 21. It shows some of the biochemical reactions that take place in a typical cell.

Each of the 520 dots is a particular substance and the lines connecting these dots are biochemical reactions. What is really important to understand is that each of these reactions is controlled by a different enzyme, so a single cell contains hundreds of different enzymes. These enzymes differ quite a lot in size. Some are rather small molecules, some are relatively enormous, but all of them are proteins.

In addition, each enzyme has a unique shape resulting from its tertiary structure. Somewhere on the surface of the enzyme, a group of amino acids forms a pocket. This pocket is the **active site** of the enzyme. When an enzyme catalyses a particular chemical reaction, a **substrate** molecule collides with the active site and binds with it to form an unstable intermediate substance called an **enzyme–substrate complex**. This complex then breaks down to the **product** molecules. The enzyme

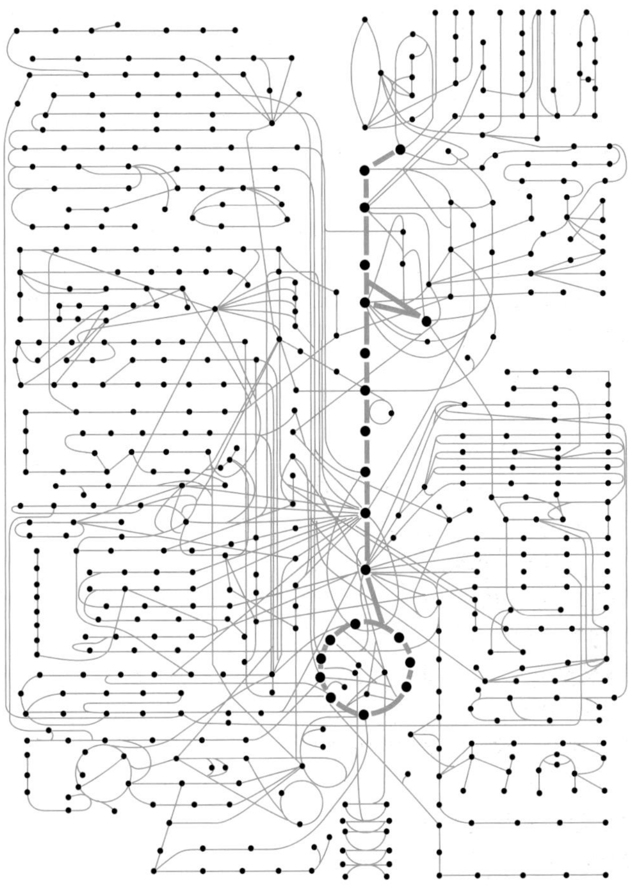

▲ **Figure 21** Believe it or not, this is a simplified diagram for the biochemical reactions that take place in a single cell. The dots represent different substances and the reactions are shown as lines linking the dots. Each one of the reactions is controlled by a different enzyme.

molecule is not used up in the reaction. It is now free to bind with another substrate molecule. Figure 22 summarises this.

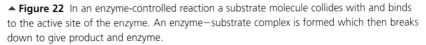

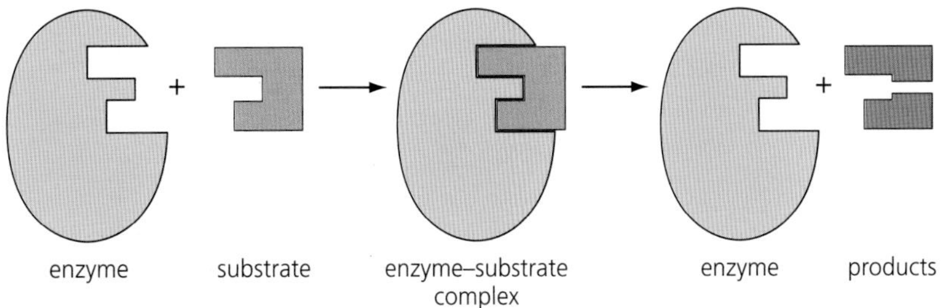

▲ **Figure 22** In an enzyme-controlled reaction a substrate molecule collides with and binds to the active site of the enzyme. An enzyme–substrate complex is formed which then breaks down to give product and enzyme.

An enzyme–substrate complex rapidly forms and breaks down. Forming a complex lowers the activation energy necessary to trigger the reaction. Scientists suggest different ways in which the activation energy might be lowered. The enzyme–substrate complex might bring together substrate molecules in positions that allow the reaction to take place more easily. It might put the substrate molecule under stress so that bonds break more readily. At present, we simply do not know exactly how enzymes lower activation energy.

Enzymes and models

Scientists use models to help them explain their observations. We have known for a long time that enzymes are specific, meaning that each enzyme catalyses just one type of reaction with one type of substrate. Amylase, for example, is an enzyme that hydrolyses starch. It breaks down starch to maltose. If we mix amylase and protein, however, nothing will happen, even though the breakdown of proteins to amino acids also involves hydrolysis. Amylase only hydrolyses its specific substrate, starch. It won't hydrolyse any other substance.

In 1894, the German chemist Emil Fischer produced a model that has proved very useful in explaining the specificity of enzymes. His model is known as the **lock and key model**. He suggested that the active site of an enzyme is similar to a lock and the substrate is like a key. In the same way that only one key will fit a particular lock, so only one substrate will fit into the active site of a particular enzyme (see Figure 23).

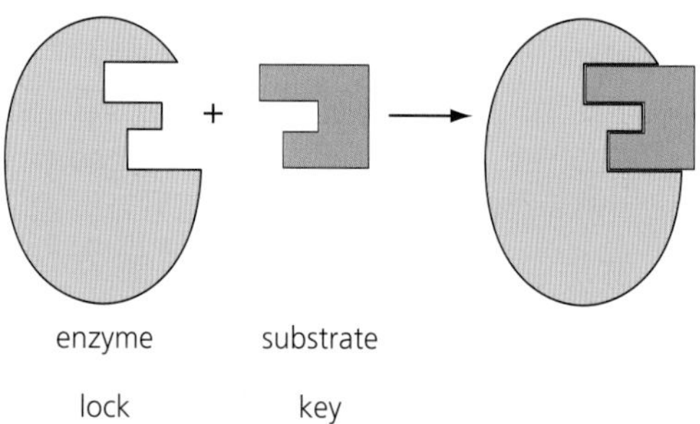

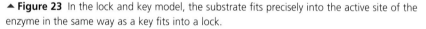

▲ **Figure 23** In the lock and key model, the substrate fits precisely into the active site of the enzyme in the same way as a key fits into a lock.

Biologists accepted this model for a long time. They used it to explain many of the properties of enzymes. For example, when you heat an enzyme you denature it. Heat alters its shape, including the shape of the active site, so that the substrate no longer fits. This is exactly what the lock and key model would predict. Distort the shape of a lock and the key cannot go in.

We can also use this model to explain why a substance with molecules shaped like the substrate can stop the activity of an enzyme. The similar shape of the molecule that is not the substrate also fits the active site, but a reaction does not happen. It blocks the site, so a substrate molecule cannot bind and react there. It is like putting a slightly different key into a lock and leaving it in. It goes in, but won't turn the lock, and blocks the way for the correct key. Molecules like this compete with substrate molecules, inhibiting the reaction, which is why this effect is called **competitive inhibition**. You can read more about inhibitors on page 23.

However, there are problems with the lock and key model. We know a lot more about proteins than Fischer did. For example, new techniques reveal that proteins are not the rigid structures that the idea of a lock suggests. We have found out that various parts of an enzyme molecule move. Some of

these movements are small. Others are quite large and may happen when the substrate binds to the enzyme. A new model was suggested. This is the **induced fit** model that is shown in Figure 24.

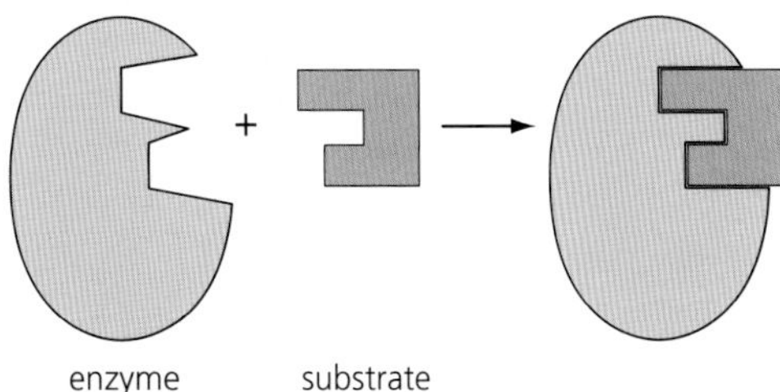

▲ **Figure 24** In the induced fit model, the substrate does not fit precisely until it binds with the active site of the enzyme. The active site then changes shape and moulds round the substrate, allowing a precise fit.

In this model, before the substrate binds to the enzyme, the substrate and the active site are not precisely complementary in shape. When the substrate binds, the active site changes shape and moulds closely round the substrate. It is a bit like a sock and a foot. Before you put your sock on, it is not foot-shaped at all. Put it on and it moulds round your foot.

It is one thing to come up with a new model, but in order to make real scientific progress we need to find evidence to support it. Is there any evidence for the induced fit model? We will look at one piece of evidence.

Hexokinase is an enzyme that catalyses the reaction shown below:

glucose + ATP → glucose 6-phosphate + ADP

Hexokinase transfers a phosphate group from a substance called ATP to a glucose molecule. This produces glucose 6-phosphate and ADP. Scientists used a technique called X-ray diffraction which enabled them to form 3D pictures of molecules. They investigated what happened to the shape of hexokinase when it binds to glucose.

Look at Figure 25. It shows you that the active site has changed in shape and has moulded round the glucose molecule.

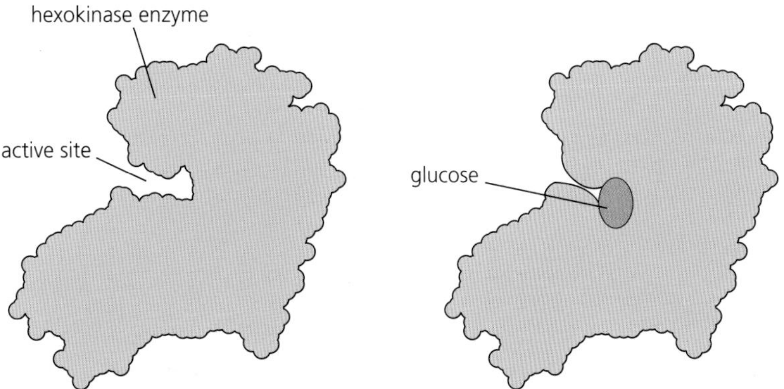

▲ **Figure 25** The diagram shows the shape of a hexokinase molecule before and after it has bound with its glucose substrate. Look at how the active site of the enzyme has changed shape.

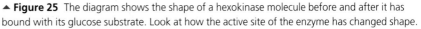

Q6

Enzymes are specific. This means that a particular enzyme will only catalyse a particular reaction. What causes enzymes to be specific?

The properties of enzymes – active sites and enzyme action

Enzyme-controlled reactions depend on substrate molecules fitting into the active site of the enzyme. An environmental factor that alters the shape of the active site will therefore alter the rate of a reaction. These factors include high temperatures, variations in pH and the presence of inhibitors.

High temperatures

Each enzyme has an optimum temperature. At this temperature, its rate of reaction is around its maximum. If we increase the temperature above its optimum, we increase the kinetic energy of the enzyme molecules. As a result, they vibrate more vigorously, and this breaks the chemical bonds that maintain the tertiary structure of the enzyme molecules. Once these bonds have broken, the enzyme changes its shape. It has been **denatured**. Its active site also changes shape, and as a result, substrate molecules will no longer fit and form an enzyme–substrate complex (Figure 26).

▲ **Figure 26** Saliva contains amylase. This enzyme most actively digests starch at body temperature. Jacket potatoes are served hot, so very little of the starch in a jacket potato will be digested in your mouth.

Temperature and enzymes

Acetylcholinesterase is an enzyme that exists in several different forms. It is found in the nervous system of many animals including fish. Table 2 shows the temperature at which the rate of reaction of this enzyme is at its maximum in different species of fish.

1 Describe the relationship between the temperature of the fish's habitat and the temperature at which the rate of reaction of acetylcholinesterase is at a maximum.

2 Trout have two forms of acetylcholinesterase. One has a maximum rate of reaction at 2 °C; the other has a maximum rate of reaction at 18 °C. Suggest the advantage of this to trout.

Table 2 The temperature at which the rate of reaction of acetylcholinesterase is at its maximum in different species of fish.

Species	Habitat	Temperature at which the rate of reaction is at a maximum/°C
Icefish	under the ice in the Antarctic	−2
Trout	freshwater lakes and streams in Britain	2 and 18
Grey mullet	Mediterranean	25

3 Acetylcholinesterase is found in icefish and grey mullet, but it has slightly different properties in each species of fish.

(a) The acetylcholinesterase in both fish breaks down a substance called acetylcholine. Explain why it is able to do this.

(b) Use your knowledge of protein structure to explain why the acetylcholinesterase found in these two fish has slightly different properties.

pH

The **pH** of a solution is a measure of its hydrogen ion concentration. The higher the concentration of hydrogen ions (H^+), the lower the pH, and the more acid the solution. Look at the graph in Figure 27. It shows that the rate of a reaction rises to a peak at pH 6.5. It then falls sharply. The peak value of 6.5 is the **optimum** pH for this enzyme.

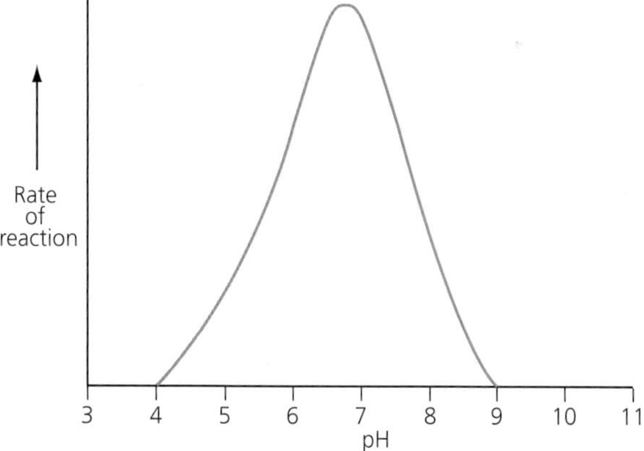

▲ **Figure 27** Enzymes work efficiently over a very narrow pH range. This graph shows the effect of pH on a typical enzyme from a human cell.

Changing the pH above or below the optimum of an enzyme affects the rate at which the enzyme works. The change in pH alters the concentration of hydrogen ions (H^+) or hydroxyl ions (OH^-) in the surrounding solution. If the change is small, the main effect is to alter charges on the amino acids that make up the active site of the enzyme. As a result, substrate molecules no longer bind. A large change in pH breaks the bonds that maintain the tertiary structure of the enzyme. The result is that the enzyme is denatured.

Inhibitors

Inhibitors are substances that slow down the rate of enzyme-controlled reactions. As we have seen on page 20, competitive inhibitors have

Q7

Uric acid is a substance that is made in the body. Gout is a painful condition caused when too much uric acid is produced and crystals form in the joints. Gout can be controlled by a drug called allopurinol. Allopurinol is a competitive inhibitor. Suggest how allopurinol controls gout.

molecules that are very similar in shape to the substrate of the enzyme, as shown in Figure 28. They are described as competitive inhibitors because they compete with the substrate for the active site. They fit into the active site and block it. This prevents substrate molecules from entering and stops an enzyme–substrate complex being formed.

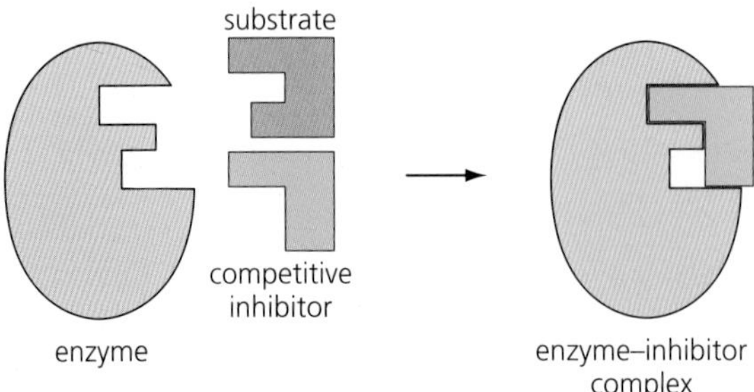

▲ **Figure 28** A competitive inhibitor competes with substrate molecules for the active site of the enzyme.

Figure 29 shows how **non-competitive** inhibitors work. Notice that a non-competitive inhibitor doesn't fit into the active site of the enzyme and block it in the way that a competitive inhibitor does. Instead, it binds somewhere else on the enzyme. This causes the active site to change shape and, as a result, substrate molecules no longer fit and so no enzyme–substrate complex is formed.

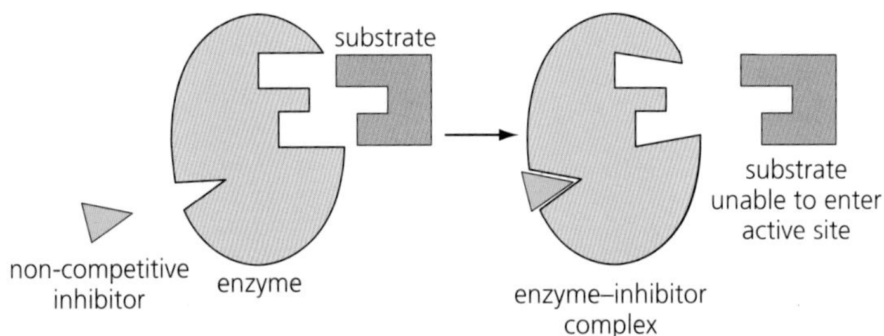

▲ **Figure 29** Non-competitive inhibitors bind to the enzyme somewhere other than the active site. This causes the active site to change shape.

The properties of enzymes – collisions come first

An enzyme and its substrate must come together before an enzyme-controlled reaction can take place. They must collide with each other with enough energy to break existing chemical bonds and form new ones. The greater the number of successful collisions in a given period of time, the faster will be the rate of reaction. Increasing the temperature and increasing the concentration of the substrate can increase the probability that a successful collision will take place and that an enzyme–substrate complex will form.

Temperature

We have already seen that high temperatures denature enzymes and stop them from working (page 22). At temperatures below the optimum, an increase has a different effect (see Figure 30). An increase in temperature increases the kinetic energy of the enzyme and substrate molecules. As a result, they move faster. This increases the probability that enzyme and substrate molecules will collide with each other. In most enzyme-controlled reactions, a rise of 10 °C more or less doubles the rate of reaction, provided that temperature stays below the optimum.

▲ **Figure 30** The tuatara is a New Zealand reptile. Being a reptile, its body temperature is very similar to the temperature of its environment. The tuatara is active and its enzymes can digest food at temperatures as low as 6 °C. With an increase in temperature, its enzymes work faster and it digests its food faster.

An increase in temperature therefore increases the rate of reaction until the temperature reaches an optimum value. Above this, an increase causes the enzyme to be denatured, and the rate of reaction decreases. This is summarised in Figure 31.

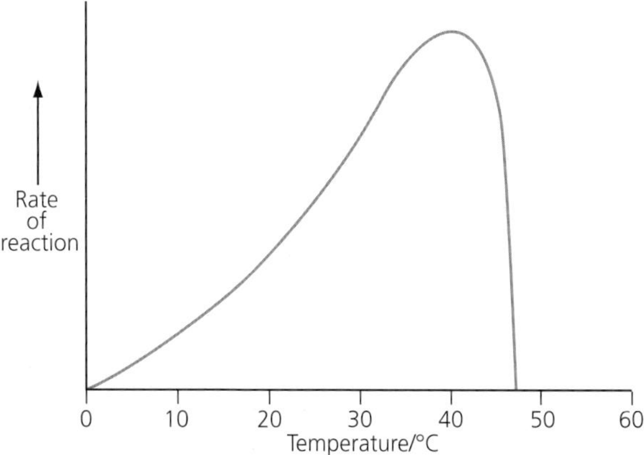

▲ **Figure 31** The effect of temperature on the rate of reaction of an enzyme-controlled reaction.

Limiting factors and substrate concentration

The shape of the curve in Figure 32 is one that you will often come across. It is an example that has nothing to do with biology. Supporters are going to a football match. To get into the ground, they have to pass through turnstiles. The graph shows the rate at which the supporters get into the ground plotted against the number of people outside who are trying to get in.

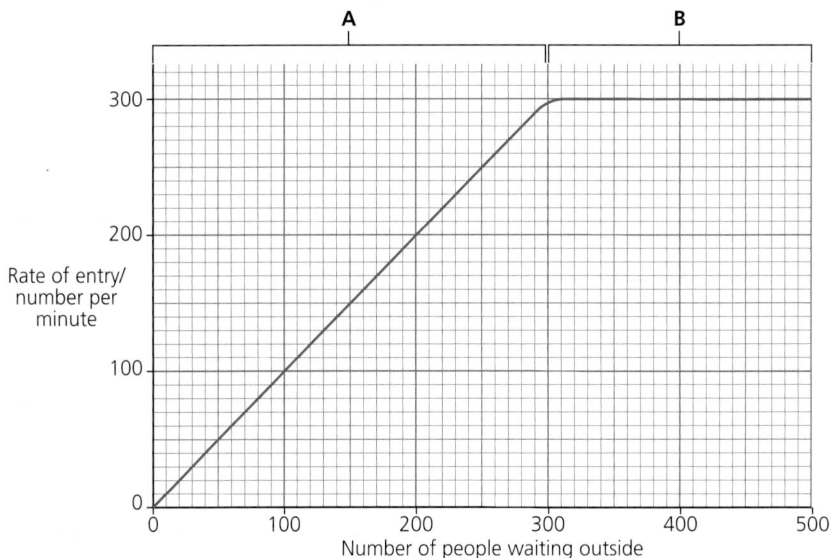

▲ **Figure 32** The rate of entry to a football ground plotted against the number of people outside.

We have divided this curve into two parts. Look at part **A** first. It shows that the rate of entry into the ground is directly proportional to the number of people outside. Three hours before the game starts, very few people are trying to get in. They can go straight to a turnstile and walk through. As more and more people arrive, the rate of entry into the ground increases.

There comes a point, however, when there are so many people outside that all the turnstiles are working as fast as possible and queues start to build up. The rate of entry to the ground cannot get any faster. We are now on the part of the curve labelled **B**. We say that over part **A** of the curve, the number of people outside is the **limiting factor** as it limits the rate of entry to the ground. The curve levels out in part **B**. It does not matter how much faster supporters arrive at the ground, the rate of entry stays the same. Something else is acting as the limiting factor. It is probably the number of turnstiles.

We will now look at a biological example that is based on the same principles. Figure 33 shows what happens to the rate of reaction when the concentration of the substrate is increased. In this reaction, both the temperature and the pH are at their optimum values.

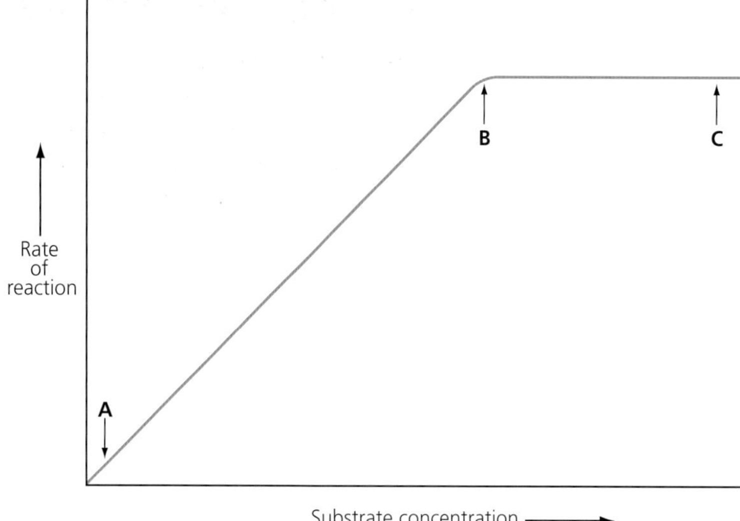

▲ **Figure 33** The effect of substrate concentration on the rate of an enzyme-controlled reaction.

- Look at the part of the curve between point **A** and **B** on the graph. What limits the rate of reaction over this part of the curve?

The answer is substrate concentration.

- What is the evidence from the graph for this answer?

As we increase the concentration of the substrate, the rate of reaction also increases.

- What causes the rate of reaction to increase over this part of the curve?

The more substrate molecules there are, the greater is the probability that one of these molecules will collide successfully with the active site of an enzyme and a reaction will take place.

- Now look at the part of the curve between **B** and **C**. How does increasing the substrate concentration after point B affect the rate of reaction?

The rate of reaction stays the same.

- What caused the rate of reaction to stay the same over this part of the curve?

At any one time, all the enzyme active sites are occupied. The enzyme cannot work any faster. The only way that the rate of reaction can be increased is to increase the number of enzyme molecules.

General principles

Watch for curves of the shape shown in Figures 32 and 33. They are very common in biology and their explanation relies on the same principles every time. We will call what we plot on the *x* axis X, and what we plot on the *y* axis Y.

- The first part of the curve rises. Y is limited by X because an increase in X produces an increase in Y.
- The *y*-axis value on the second part of the curve stays constant. On this part of the curve, an increase in X has no effect on Y. Something other than X is limiting Y.

Making a better oral rehydration solution

We started this chapter by looking at the work of a group of scientists who wanted to make an oral rehydration solution (ORS) from rice flour. The problem they faced was that useful rice-flour solutions are too thick to drink. They decided to use the enzyme amylase to digest the starch. This reduces its viscosity so that a patient can drink it from a cup or a feeding bottle. They investigated the effect of different concentrations of amylase on reducing the viscosity of rice-flour solution. This is an investigation that you could do in your school or college laboratory. How would you go about it?

In all investigations you change something. This is the **independent variable**. In the ORS investigation, the independent variable is the concentration of amylase. As a result of these changes, you have to measure something else. This is the **dependent variable**. In this investigation, the dependent variable is the viscosity of the rice-flour solution.

The first step in any investigation is to identify these two variables. The next is to plan how to change the independent variable.

Changing the independent variable

An experimental result that occurs only once could be due to **chance**. It could also be because the scientist who carried out the investigation did it in a particular way. Experiments are only **reliable** if they can be repeated by someone else. This means that you should give enough detail in describing your method for another scientist to follow the technique exactly as you intended, without the need for any help other than your set of instructions. In this case it is not enough, for example, to say, 'Put the mixture in a water bath.' Another scientist would want to know what temperature you used. 'Put the mixture in a water bath at a constant temperature of 35 °C' is much better.

In most experiments, variables other than the one you are planning to change might also affect the results. We call these **confounding variables**. You should design your experiment so that these confounding variables are kept constant. There are several confounding variables here. The incubation time of the enzyme and rice-flour solutions, temperature, pH and substrate concentration could all affect the rate of this reaction. If we keep these factors constant, then there is a reasonable chance that any difference in viscosity will be due to the concentration of amylase.

Once you have decided how you are going to change the independent variable and have identified the various confounding variables whose values you must keep constant, you need to ask another question:

Is there anything, other than the independent variable, in the way I have set up this experiment that could have produced these results?

If there is, you need a **control**. A control experiment is one that you set up to eliminate certain possibilities. In this investigation it is possible that the rice-flour solution would have become runnier anyway if you just left it. We ought to have a control experiment where everything is the same as in the experimental container but without amylase. By setting up this control you eliminate the possibility that something other than amylase reduced the viscosity of the solution.

Measuring the dependent variable

Once you have decided how you will change the independent variable, you should decide how to determine the effect of this on the dependent variable. You need quantitative data and this means taking measurements. These measurements must be made with the appropriate degree of precision and must be reliable.

In this investigation, you could measure viscosity. You could use a viscometer but it is not very likely that you would have one in your laboratory. There are other, simpler methods however. You could pour the solution into a burette and see how long it took for the liquid to drain out through the tap, or you could take the time for a marble or other object to fall through a column of the solution.

You also need to bear in mind that if you carry out the experiment once only, you do not know if the results are reliable. Carrying it out twice doesn't help you much either. If the results are different, which is the reliable one? You need to carry it out several times. Only in this way can you separate reliable data from anomalies.

General principles

Designing an investigation

Here is a summary of the important things that you should always consider in designing an investigation.

At the start

- Write out a title for your investigation. It should take the form:
  The effect of [independent variable] on [dependent variable]
- Use this title to identify what you are going to change (the independent variable) and what you will measure as a result (the dependent variable).

The independent variable

- Make sure that you have described your method of changing the independent variable in enough detail so that another person in your class could carry out the investigation exactly as you intended.

- Consider the range of values of the independent variable which you will need for a comprehensive set of results.
- List the other variables that might influence the results. Describe how these confounding variables may be kept constant.
- Ask yourself whether anything else in the way that the experiment has been set up, other than the independent variable, could have produced the results you might expect. If there is, you need a control.

The dependent variable

- Describe how you will measure the dependent variable and obtain quantitative results.
- Describe the limits of the scale of the apparatus you use. The smallest scale division determines the precision of the measurement.
- Specify the number of times you will repeat each reading. The more repeats you have, the more reliable your results are likely to be. Unfortunately, the more repeats you carry out, the longer the investigation will take. You will obviously need to compromise.

Chapter 2

Cholera

Cholera is not a disease we usually think people will catch in Britain today, but it was once a real threat. In 1826, an outbreak started in India and advanced westwards through Afghanistan and Iran into Europe. It arrived in Sunderland in north-east England in 1831, and then spread rapidly through the rest of Britain. In Scotland there were 3166 deaths, 2400 in Manchester and Liverpool, 2000 in the Midlands and nearly 5300 in London.

Cholera is a dreadful disease. It starts with severe muscle and stomach cramps. Vomiting and fever soon follow, and then the victim develops diarrhoea. This leads to a huge loss of body fluid. An adult can lose as much as 20 dm^3 of liquid a day in diarrhoea. Without treatment, a person with cholera usually dies. This is because they lose so much liquid that their circulatory system fails.

Cholera returned to Britain repeatedly over the thirty years following 1831. At the time, doctors did not know what caused cholera or how to prevent it.

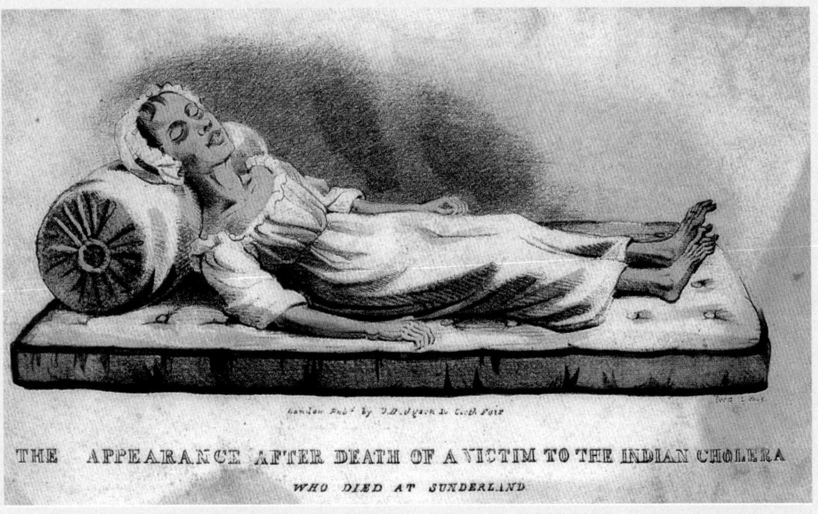

THE APPEARANCE AFTER DEATH OF A VICTIM TO THE INDIAN CHOLERA
WHO DIED AT SUNDERLAND

▲ **Figure 1** This picture is of a young victim of cholera who died at the time when John Snow was working in London. She has the appearance of someone who has lost a lot of water from her body.

Cholera

In 1854, there was an outbreak of cholera in London. A doctor named John Snow decided to investigate it. He already suspected that cholera was spread by contaminated water. He searched the records of the area affected by cholera and found that the water was supplied by two companies. The Southwark and Vauxhall Water Company drew its water from a part of the River Thames known to be contaminated with sewage, while the Lambeth Water Company took its water from an uncontaminated supply upriver from the contaminated area. When Snow learned about this, he saw an opportunity to test a hypothesis he had made. His hypothesis was that cholera was spread by contaminated water. In his own words:

> 'No fewer than three hundred thousand people of both sexes, of every age and occupation, and of every rank and station, from gentle folks down to the very poor, were divided into two groups without their choice, and, in most cases, without their knowledge; one group being supplied with water containing the sewage of London, and amongst it, whatever might have come from the cholera patients – the other group having water quite free from such impurity.'

If you have read this passage carefully, you will realise that Snow designed an excellent experiment. He took a very large sample of people, three hundred thousand, so we can assume that his results were reliable. He also had an experimental group and a control group. The only difference between the two groups was that one drank water that was contaminated by sewage, and the other did not.

Snow then investigated each house in which someone had died of cholera and found which water company supplied it. Table 1 shows his results.

Table 1 Populations and deaths from cholera in houses supplied by two London water companies.

House water supply	Population in 1851	Cholera deaths in 14 weeks ending 14 October 1854	Deaths per 100 000 living people
Southwark and Vauxhall Water Company	266 516	4 093	153
Lambeth Water Company	173 748	461	26

Snow was excited by these results and thought that the evidence in support of his hypothesis was very convincing. His colleagues, however, refused to accept his results. They claimed that because Snow did not find any 'poison' in the water, he couldn't possibly be right.

A little later, cholera broke out in Soho, an area of London very close to Snow's home. He immediately collected a sample of water from the pump in Soho's Broad Street. He thought that the water from this pump might have been contaminated, so he examined it. But it looked fairly clear. He compared it with water from a number of pumps nearby and could see no difference.

▲ **Figure 2**(a) The site of the Broad Street pump. This pump supplied the contaminated water that caused the 1854 Soho cholera outbreak.

The Red Granite kerbstone
marks the site of the historic
BROAD STREET PUMP
associated with Dr. John Snow's
discovery in 1854
that Cholera is conveyed by water

▲ **Figure 2**(b) The plaque is on the wall of the John Snow pub named after the man whose scientific experiments led to discovering that cholera is transmitted by water.

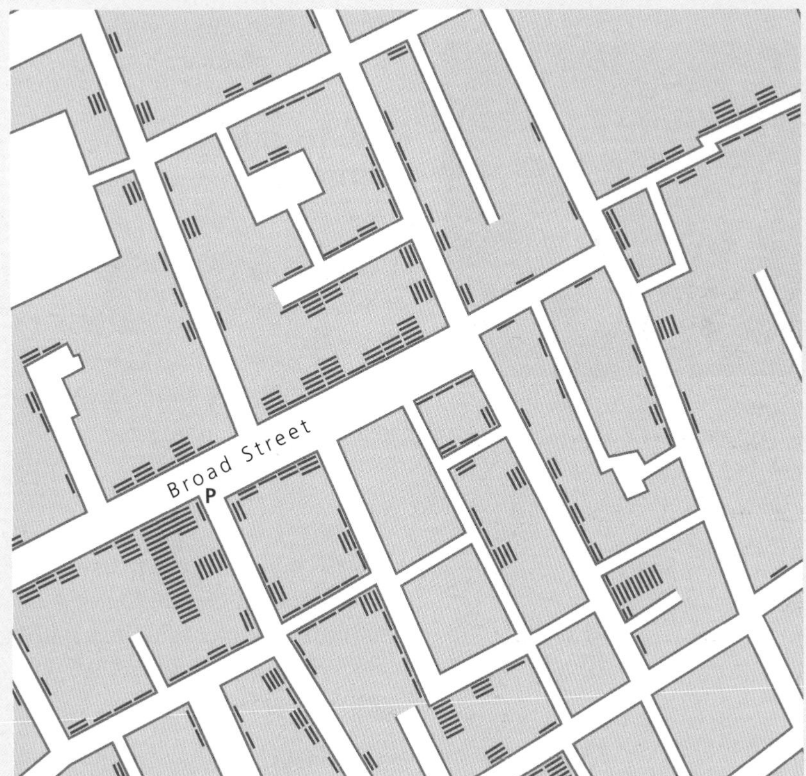

▶ **Figure 2**(c) The map is a copy of Snow's original map showing the position of the Broad Street pump and where the cholera victims lived.

Snow then decided to collect evidence to show where the cholera victims lived and where they got their water. He found that 73 of the 83 victims lived closer to the Broad Street pump than to any other pump. He was also told that 8 of the remaining 10 victims had drunk water from the Broad Street pump. Snow took his evidence to the Board of Guardians controlling that area of Soho. They were not convinced, but agreed to remove the handle of the Broad Street pump. Soon after this, the epidemic was over.

John Snow was not only a doctor. He was also an outstanding scientist. He used his knowledge and his observations to produce a **hypothesis**. He then **tested** this hypothesis with a well-designed experiment. The evidence from his investigations confirmed his hypothesis that cholera was spread by contaminated water.

Snow's problems came in trying to persuade the decision makers of his time that if they accepted his findings they could greatly improve the health of many people. They believed that cholera was caused by an evil 'miasma' or vapour present in the air, so they were reluctant to cut off the water supplies that Snow said caused cholera.

We will concentrate on the story of cholera in the rest of this chapter. When we understand the basic biological principles, we can then understand what causes the disease, its symptoms and the way it can be treated.

Cholera bacteria

John Snow died without knowing that cholera was a disease caused by bacteria. In fact, it wasn't until thirty years after the Soho outbreak that the German microbiologist Robert Koch finally isolated cholera bacteria. Look at Figure 3. It shows a single cholera bacterium magnified 10 000 times. We will use this information to work out its actual size.

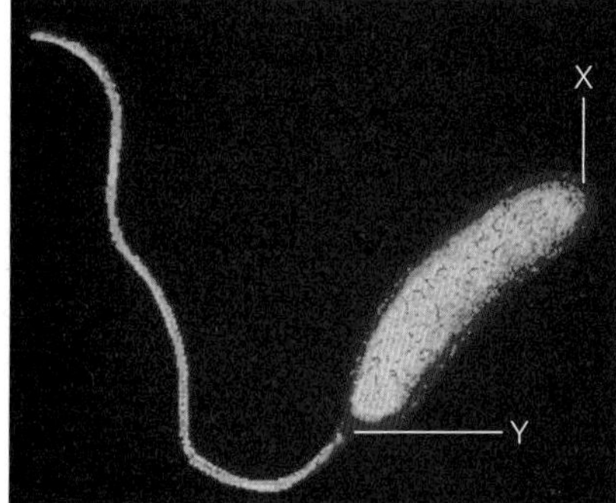

▲ **Figure 3** This photograph shows a cholera bacterium. It has been magnified 10 000 times.

How to calculate the actual length of a cholera bacterium

The magnification of an object in a photograph is its length in the photograph divided by its real length. We can write this as a simple formula:

$$\text{magnification} = \frac{\text{length in photograph}}{\text{real length}}$$

If we rearrange this formula, we can calculate the real length of the cholera bacterium in the photograph:

$$\text{real length} = \frac{\text{length in photograph}}{\text{magnification}}$$

We have been given the magnification, but we need to know the length of the bacterium in the photograph. That is straightforward. All we have to do is use a ruler to measure the length of the bacterium in the photograph. We won't include the flagellum. We will just measure the cell between points **X** and **Y** in the photograph.

It is 30 mm in length, so we substitute these figures in the rearranged formula:

$$\text{real length} = \frac{30}{10\,000}\ \text{mm}$$

$$= 0.003\ \text{mm}$$

The calculation is really very simple, but the units we have used are not very practicable. It is like measuring the cost of a postage stamp in pounds rather than pence. It would be better in this case to give the answer in micrometres (μm). There are a thousand micrometres in a millimetre, so the length of the bacterium is 0.003 × 1000 or 3 μm.

General principles

Calculating the real length where the magnification is given

The magnification is usually given as a magnification factor such as ×10 000.

- Measure, in millimetres, the length of the structure in the image. This is the image length.
- To find the real length of the structure, divide the image length you have measured in millimetres by the magnification you have been given using the formula:

$$\text{real length} = \frac{\text{image length}}{\text{magnification}}$$

- This will give you a real length in millimetres. To convert it to micrometres, multiply by 1000.

Calculating magnification

- To calculate the magnification of a structure, use the formula:

$$\text{magnification} = \frac{\text{image length}}{\text{real length}}$$

You shouldn't need to remember this because you should realise that magnification is how big something looks (its image length) compared with how big it really is (its real length).

Prokaryotes and their structure

Cholera bacteria are very small, much smaller than the human cells they infect. Small size is a feature of the cells of all bacteria, and they differ from human cells in a number of other ways. One is that a bacterial cell does not have a nucleus. It does contain DNA, but this DNA is only present as a loop in the cytoplasm of the cell. It doesn't form chromosomes in a nucleus.

We describe bacterial cells as **prokaryotes** and bacteria as **prokaryotic organisms**. The word prokaryote means 'before the nucleus'. Another feature of prokaryotic organisms such as cholera bacteria is that some of the DNA they contain, the genetic material, is found in tiny circular strands called **plasmids**.

A cholera bacterium is surrounded by a **cell surface membrane**. (This membrane is also called the plasma membrane.) Outside this membrane is

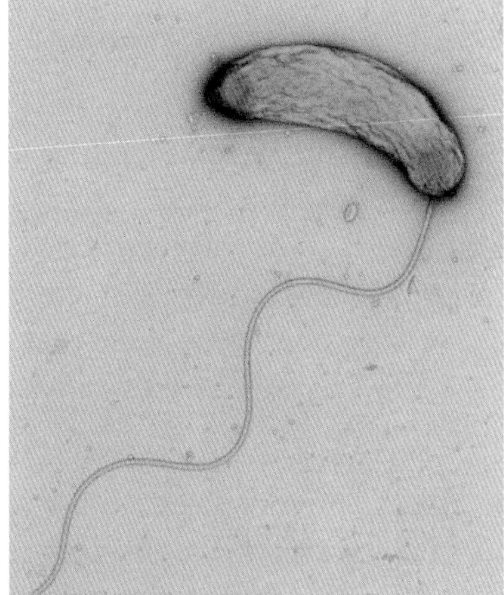

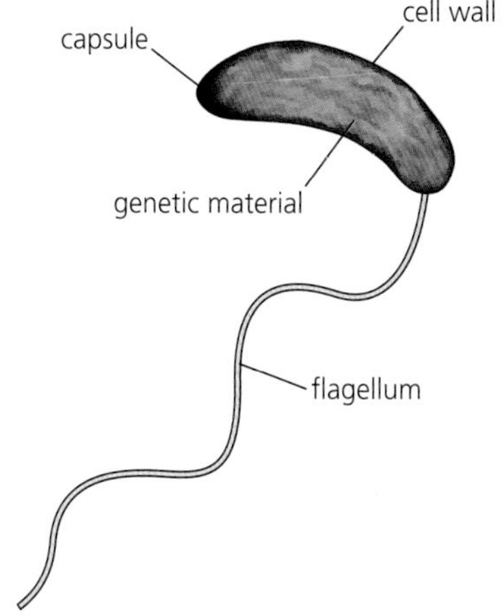

Figure 4 This photograph shows the main features of a cholera bacterium. The drawing has been made from the photograph to enable you to identify the various features.

a **cell wall**, but unlike plant cell walls, it is not made from cellulose. It is made from other substances. Outside the cell wall is another layer. This is the protective **capsule**. A cholera bacterium has a long whip-like **flagellum** which helps the cell to move. Flagella are found only in some bacteria. Not all species have them.

Look now at Figure 4. This shows another photograph of a cholera bacterium, together with a drawing showing its main features.

Looking at eukaryotic cells

Q1

Calculate the actual length of the epithelial cell labelled **A** in Figure 5.

The cells that line the small intestine are called **epithelial** cells. Figure 5 shows epithelial cells from the human small intestine. This photograph was taken through an optical microscope.

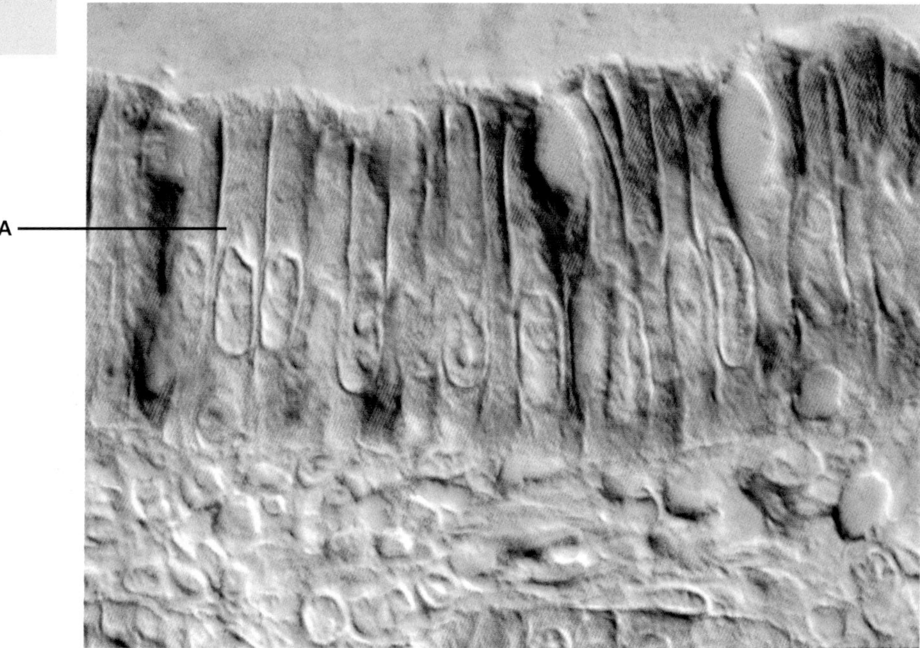

Figure 5 Epithelial cells from the human small intestine. This photograph has been magnified 3300 times.

Look at it carefully and you will see that each cell contains a large **nucleus**. We call animal and plant cells **eukaryotic** cells because they possess a nucleus. The word eukaryote means 'true nucleus'.

You will also see that the boundary of the cell, where it lines the lumen of the intestine, shows up as a rather fuzzy thick line. If we magnify this a bit more, it does not help a lot. All we get is a slightly thicker fuzzy line. Magnification on its own is not enough. What we need is greater resolution. **Magnification** is making things larger. **Resolution** involves distinguishing between objects that are close together. To resolve objects that are close together, we need a microscope that will produce a sharper image.

Light waves limit the resolution of an optical microscope. Using light, it is impossible to resolve two objects that are closer than half the wavelength of the light by which they are viewed. The wavelength of visible light is between 500 and 650 nanometres, so it would be in optical microscope that would distinguish between of this value. That is good enough for a lot of purpo for looking at cells from animals and plants. But it w very small structures inside a cell. For that we need a

The transmission electron microscope

If the wavelength of light limits the resolution of an optical microscope, then one solution is to use a beam of electrons instead. Electrons have very much smaller wavelengths than light, so a beam of electrons should be able to resolve two objects that are very close together. That is the way an electron microscope works, as you can see in Figure 6.

We cut a very thin section through the tissue that we are going to examine. This section, the specimen, is preserved and stained, and then it is put inside a sealed chamber in the microscope. The air is sucked out of the chamber and this produces a vacuum. Finally, a series of magnetic lenses focuses a beam of electrons through the specimen and produces an image on a screen.

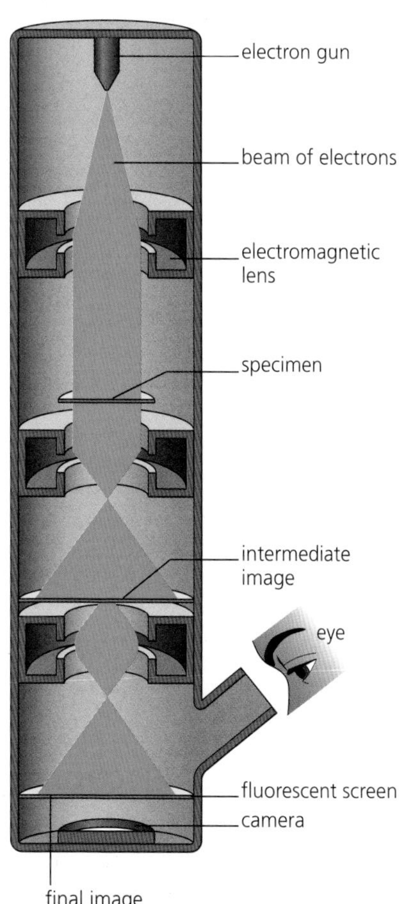

▲ **Figure 6** The diagram shows the main features of a transmission electron microscope.

The big advantage of using a transmission electron microscope is its resolving power. It lets us see the structure of a cell in much more detail than we could ever hope to see with an optical microscope. Look at Figure 7. It gives you a clear idea of just what can be seen with a human eye, a good quality optical microscope and a transmission electron microscope.

2

Can you see the cell surface membrane surrounding an animal cell with an optical microscope? Use the information in Figure 7 to explain your answer.

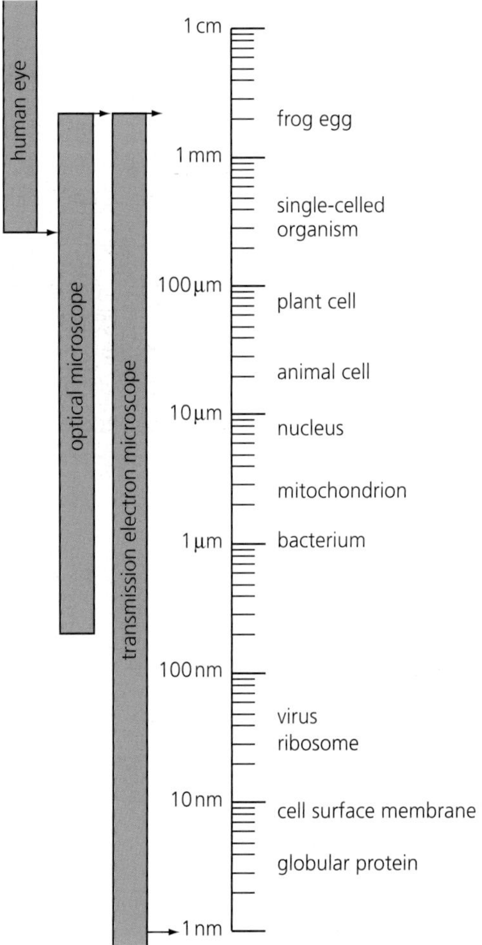

▲ **Figure 7** The scale on this diagram goes from 1 nanometre to 1 centimetre. These values have been plotted on a log scale because this is the best way of representing such a large range of measurements. The diagram shows that a human eye is able to see large single-celled organisms. With an optical microscope, we can see things as small as bacteria. With modern transmission electron microscopes, we can see large molecules.

A high resolving power means that a transmission electron microscope has a useful magnification of up to 100 000 times.

Electron microscopes have their limitations

You might think that a transmission electron microscope with a magnification of 100 000 times is the perfect instrument to investigate cell structure. However, such a microscope has limitations. Because there is a vacuum inside, all the water must be removed from the specimen. This means that you cannot use a transmission electron microscope to look at living cells. They must be dead.

Sections through different planes

There are also problems in interpreting what you see. Some of these arise because a very thin slice has to be cut through the specimen. Look at Figure 8(a). It shows a red blood cell. The shape of a red blood cell is often described as a biconcave disc because it is thinner in the centre and thicker at the edge.

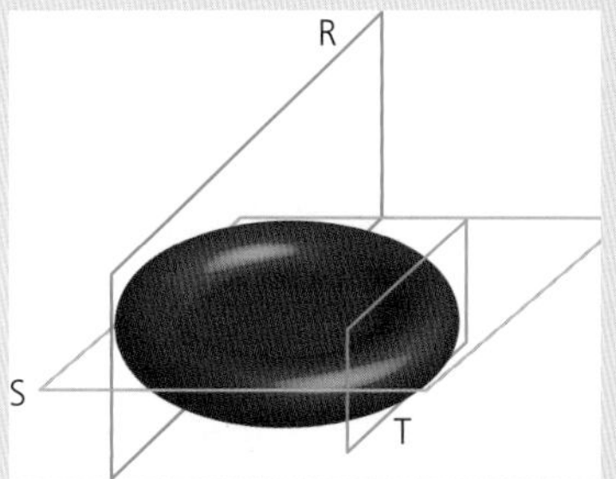

▲ **Figure 8(a)** A drawing of a red blood cell. Sections have been cut through it in different planes.

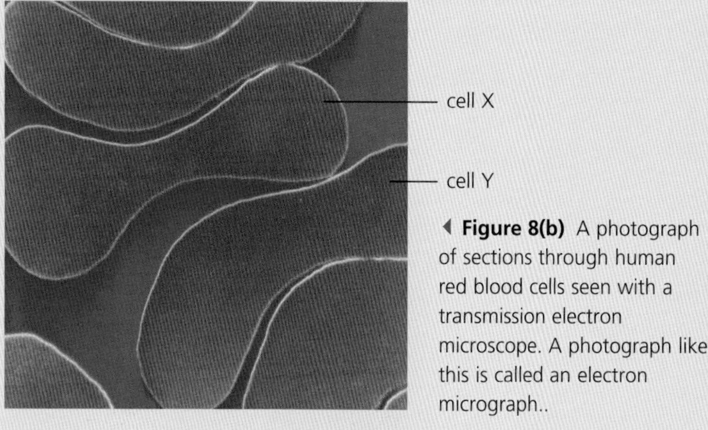

◀ **Figure 8(b)** A photograph of sections through human red blood cells seen with a transmission electron microscope. A photograph like this is called an electron micrograph..

1 Make simple drawings to show what the cut surface of the cell in Figure 8(a) would look like if it were cut through each of the planes shown in the figure.

2 Look at Figure 8(b). It shows very thin sections of red blood cells. Through which of the three planes shown in diagram (a), is the cell labelled **X** cut?

3 The cell labelled **Y** has a bent shape. This bent shape resulted when the cell was sliced. Suggest what caused this bent shape.

When the beam of electrons in a transmission electron microscope strikes a specimen, some of the electrons pass straight through and some are scattered by dense parts of the specimen. The parts of the specimen that scatter the electrons appear dark coloured on an electron micrograph.

4 Red blood cells show as a uniform dark colour on an electron micrograph. Explain why.

5 A human red blood cell measures 7 µm in diameter. Calculate the magnification of the electron micrograph in Figure 8(b).

A **scanning electron microscope** works in a slightly different way to a transmission electron microscope. In a scanning microscope, the electron beam bounces off the surface of the object. Figure 9 shows a scanning electron micrograph of red blood cells.

6 What additional information can you get about red blood cells from Figure 9?

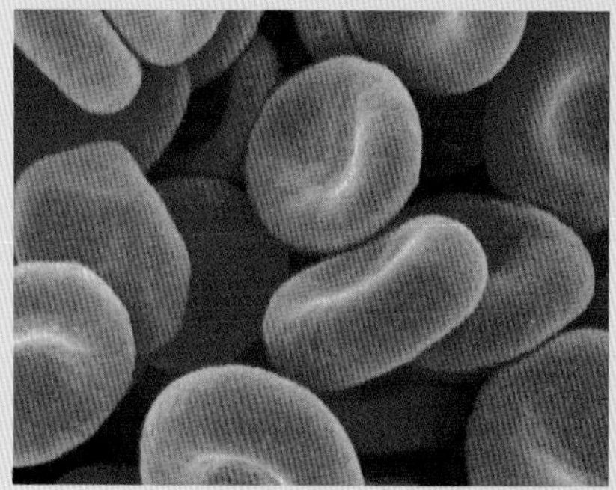

▲ **Figure 9** A scanning electron micrograph of red blood cells.

The ultrastructure of epithelial cells

Figure 5 on page 36 shows some epithelial cells from the human small intestine as they appear when looked at with an optical microscope. Now look at Figure 10. This shows part of one of the same cells, but it has been taken with a transmission electron microscope, so you can see much more detail.

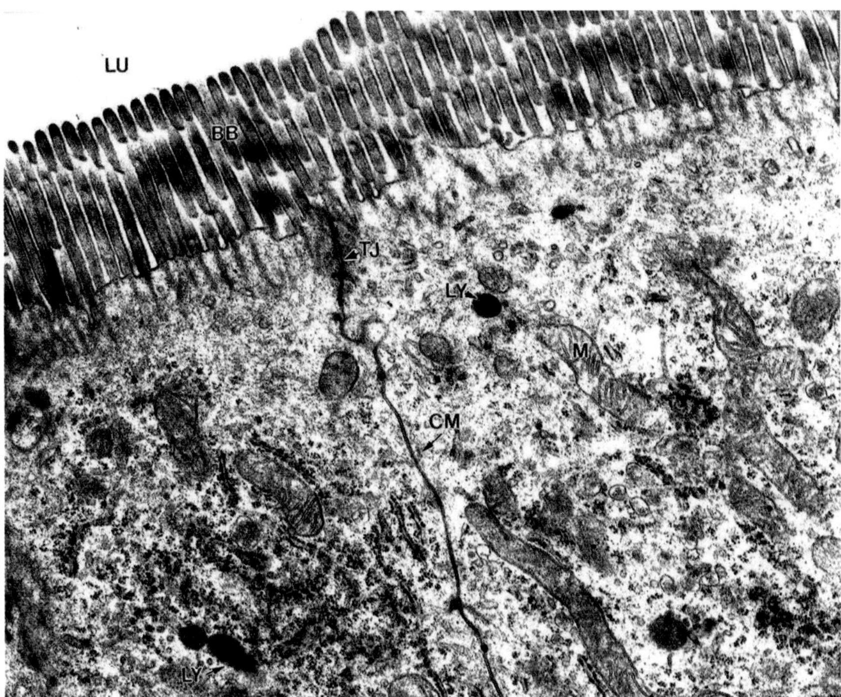

▲ **Figure 10** An electron micrograph of an epithelial cell from the small intestine.

Look again at the boundary of the cell, where it lines the lumen of the intestine. It shows that the fuzzy thick line that you saw in Figure 5 is made up of tiny finger-like folds in the membrane called **microvilli**. The nucleus can be seen clearly as well. The rest of the cell is made up of cytoplasm in which there are many tiny structures called **organelles**. These organelles have particular functions in the cell. Table 2 on page 41 summarises the functions of the organelles found in an epithelial cell from the small intestine.

Because of the high resolution of a transmission electron microscope, the organelles in the cell can be seen clearly. You could not see most of these organelles with an optical microscope.

Separating cell organelles

Understanding the structure of an organelle is not the same as understanding its function. To find out about function, biologists need a pure sample containing lots of the organelle that they want to investigate. We separate cell organelles from each other using the process of **cell fractionation**. In this process, a suitable sample of tissue is broken up and then centrifuged at different speeds. Figure 11 is a flow chart which summarises the main steps in this process.

The tissue is broken up in a **homogeniser**. This is a machine rather like a kitchen blender. The tissue is suspended in a buffer solution which keeps the pH constant. This solution is kept cold and has the same water potential as the tissue.

↓

The homogenised mixture is filtered. This removes large pieces of tissue that have not been broken up.

↓

The filtrate is now put in a **centrifuge** and spun at low speed. Large organelles such as nuclei fall to the bottom of the centrifuge tube where they form a **pellet**. They can be resuspended in a fresh solution if they are wanted.

↓

The liquid or **supernatant** is now spun in the centrifuge again. This time, smaller organelles such as mitochondria separate out into a pellet.

↓

▲ **Figure 11** The organelles in a sample of tissue can be separated from each other by the process of cell fractionation in a centrifuge. This flow chart shows the main steps in the process.

Table 2 The main organelles found in an epithelial cell from the small intestine.

Organelle	Main features	Function
Cell surface membrane	The membrane found round the outside of a cell. It is made up of lipids and proteins.	Controls the passage of substances into and out of the cell.
Microvilli cell surface membrane	Tiny finger-like projections of the cell surface membrane.	Increase the surface area of the cell surface membrane.
Nucleus	The largest organelle in the cell. It is surrounded by a nuclear envelope consisting of two membrane layers. There are many holes in the envelope called nuclear pores.	Contains the DNA which holds the genetic information necessary for controlling the cell.
Mitochondrion	A sausage-shaped organelle. It is surrounded by two membrane layers. The inner one is folded and forms structures called cristae.	Produces ATP from respiration. The molecule ATP is the source of energy for the cell's activities.
Lysosome	An organelle containing digestive enzymes. These enzymes are separated from the rest of the cell by the membrane that surrounds the lysosome.	Digests unwanted material in the cell
Ribosome	A very small organelle, not surrounded by a membrane.	Assembles protein molecules from amino acids.
Rough endoplasmic reticulum ribosome	Endoplasmic reticulum is made of membranes that form a series of tubes in the cytoplasm of the cell. The membranes of rough endoplasmic reticulum are covered with ribosomes.	Collects and transports proteins around the cell.
Smooth endoplasmic reticulum	Similar to rough endoplasmic reticulum, but the membranes do not have ribosomes.	Synthesises lipids.
Golgi apparatus	A stack of flattened sacs, each surrounded by a membrane. Vesicles are continually pinched off from the ends of these sacs.	Packages and processes molecules such as the proteins that are made in the cell. Forms lysosomes.

Now that you know something about the structure of an epithelial cell from the small intestine, you can begin to understand how cholera bacteria cause such terrible diarrhoea. As John Snow found out, the bacteria usually enter the body in contaminated drinking water. They multiply inside the small intestine where they produce poisonous substances called toxins. The cholera toxin is what eventually causes diarrhoea. In order to understand the link between the cholera toxin and diarrhoea, you need to know a little more about the cell surface membrane and how it regulates the passage of substances into and out of cells.

The cell surface membrane

Triglycerides

You saw in Table 2 that the **cell surface membrane** is made up of lipids and proteins. The commonest lipids found in living organisms are **triglycerides**. We call most of the triglycerides found in animals fats because they are solid at a temperature of about 20 °C. A triglyceride is made up of a molecule of glycerol and three fatty acid molecules. The basic structures of these molecules are shown in Figure 2.12.

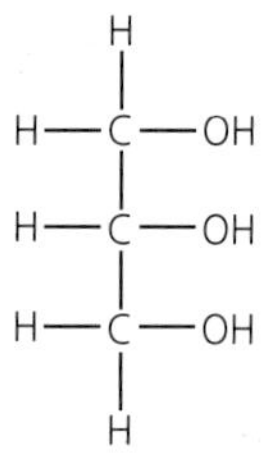

```
        H
        |
    H—C—OH
        |
    H—C—OH
        |
    H—C—OH
        |
        H
```

(a) Glycerol is a type of alcohol. It has three –OH groups, each of which can condense with a fatty acid.

R.COOH

(b) This is the simplest formula for a fatty acid molecule. The letter R represents a hydrocarbon chain consisting of carbon and hydrogen atoms.

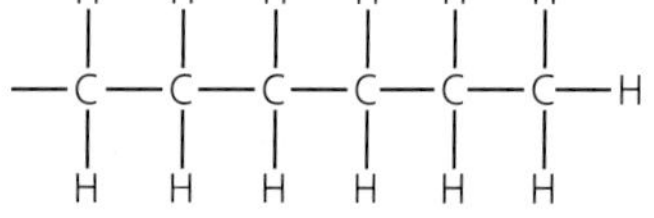

```
  H  H  H  H  H  H
  |  |  |  |  |  |
—C—C—C—C—C—C—H
  |  |  |  |  |  |
  H  H  H  H  H  H
```

(c) In saturated fatty acids, each of the carbon atoms in this chain, with the exception of the last, has two hydrogen atoms joined to it.

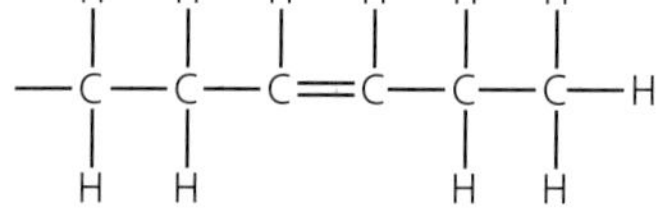

```
  H  H  H  H  H  H
  |  |  |  |  |  |
—C—C—C=C—C—C—H
  |  |        |  |
  H  H        H  H
```

(d) In unsaturated fatty acids, there are one or more double bonds between the carbon atoms in the chain. Because of this, some carbon atoms will be joined only to a single hydrogen atom.

▲ **Figure 12** The basic structure of a molecule of (a) glycerol and (b) fatty acid; (c) shows the structure of a saturated fatty acid and (d) shows the structure of an unsaturated fatty acid.

Glycerol is a type of alcohol. Look at Figure 12(a). You will see that there are three –OH groups in glycerol. These groups allow the molecule to join with three fatty acids to produce a triglyceride. Figure 12(b) is the simplest possible way of showing the structure of a fatty acid molecule. The letter **R** represents a chain of hydrogen and carbon atoms. In the fatty acids found in animal cells there are often 14 to 16 carbon atoms in this chain. These fatty acids may be described as **saturated** or **unsaturated**. The difference between them is shown in Figures 12(c) and 12(d).

When a triglyceride is formed, a molecule of water is removed as each of the three fatty acids is joined to the glycerol. You may remember, from when you looked at the structure of proteins and polysaccharides, that this type of chemical reaction is called **condensation**. The formation of a triglyceride from glycerol and fatty acids is shown in Figure 13.

- Draw a diagram to show a glycerol molecule.
- Draw three fatty acid molecules 'the wrong way round' next to it.

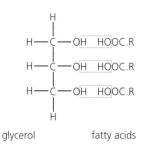

```
        H
        |
    H—C—OH   HOOC.R
        |
    H—C—OH   HOOC.R
        |
    H—C—OH   HOOC.R
        |
        H
  glycerol        fatty acids
```

- Remove three molecules of water, taking the H from the glycerol and the –OH from the fatty acids.

```
        H
        |
    H—C—OOC.R
        |
    H—C—OOC.R + 3H2O
        |
    H—C—OOC.R
        |
        H
```

- Close everything up to show the completed triglyceride.

▲ **Figure 13** This diagram is a simple way of showing how a molecule of glycerol joins with three fatty acid molecules to form a triglyceride.

You can use the emulsion test to test for lipids such as triglycerides. Crush a little of the test material and mix it thoroughly with ethanol. Pour the resulting solution into water in a test tube. A white emulsion shows that a lipid is present.

The tests for substances in foods are summarised in Table 3.

Table 3 Tests for food substances.

Substance	Test	Brief details of test	Positive result
Protein	Biuret test	• Add sodium hydroxide to the test sample • Add a few drops of dilute copper sulphate solution	Solution turns mauve
Carbohydrates Reducing sugars	Benedict's test	• Heat test sample with Benedict's reagent	Orange-red precipitate is formed
Non-reducing sugars		• Check that there is no reducing sugar present by heating part of the sample with Benedict's solution. • Hydrolyse rest of sample by heating with dilute hydrochloric acid. • Neutralise by adding sodium hydrogencarbonate • Test sample with Benedict's solution	Orange-red precipitate is formed
Starch	Iodine test	• Add iodine solution	Turns blue-black
Lipid	Emulsion test	• Dissolve the test sample by shaking with ethanol • Pour the resulting solution into water in a test tube	A white emulsion is formed

Phospholipids

A phospholipid has a very similar structure to a triglyceride, but as you can see from Figure 14, it contains a phosphate group instead of one of the fatty acids. It is quite a good idea to think of a phospholipid as having a 'head' consisting of glycerol and phosphate and a 'tail' containing the long chains of hydrogen

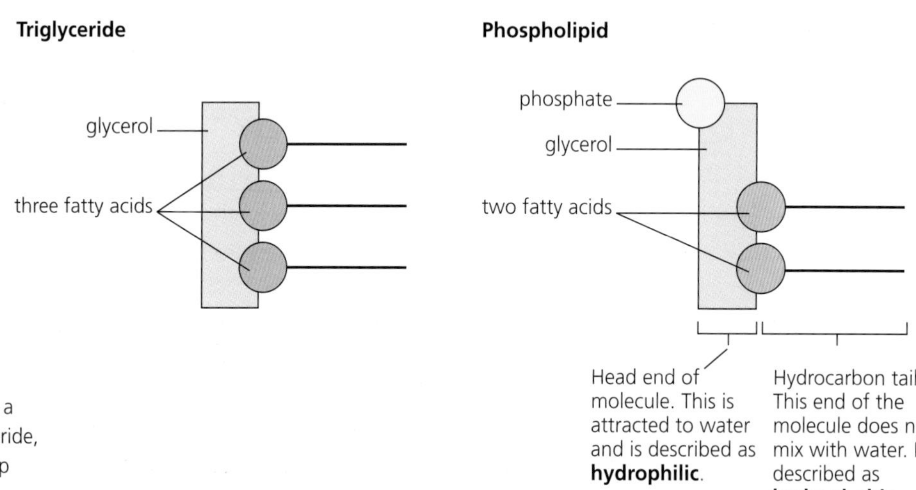
Triglyceride
glycerol
three fatty acids
Phospholipid
phosphate
glycerol
two fatty acids
Head end of molecule. This is attracted to water and is described as **hydrophilic**.
Hydrocarbon tail. This end of the molecule does not mix with water. It is described as **hydrophobic**.

▸ **Figure 14** A phospholipid has a structure very similar to a triglyceride, but it contains a phosphate group instead of one of the fatty acids.

and carbon atoms of the two fatty acids. The presence of the phosphate group means that the head is attracted to water. It is described therefore as being **hydrophilic** or 'water loving'. The hydrocarbon tails do not mix with water, so this end of the molecule is described as **hydrophobic** or 'water hating'.

When phospholipids are mixed with water, they arrange themselves in a double layer with their hydrophobic tails pointing inwards and their hydrophilic heads pointing outwards. This double layer is called a **phospholipid bilayer** and forms the basis of membranes in and around cells.

Fatty acids in milk

Milk contains triglycerides. Scientists investigated how the fatty acids in human milk depend on the food that the mother eats. The scientists collected samples of milk from two groups of women. The women in one group were vegans and only ate food obtained from plants. Those in the other group, the control group, ate food obtained from both animals and plants. Table 4 shows the concentrations of different fatty acids in the milk samples.

Table 4 The concentrations of different fatty acids in vegan and control group milk samples.

Fatty acid	Number of double bonds in hydrocarbon chain	Number of carbon atoms in hydrocarbon chain	Concentration of fatty acid in milk sample/mg g^{-1}	
			Vegan group	Control group
Lauric	0	12	39	33
Myristic	0	14	68	80
Palmitic	0	16	166	276
Stearic	0	18	52	108
Palmitoleic	1	16	12	36
Oleic	1	18	313	353
Linoleic	2	18	317	69
Linolenic	3	18	15	8

1 The first four fatty acids in the table are saturated fatty acids. Explain why they are described as saturated.

2 Construct a table to show all of the following.
- The total concentration of saturated fatty acids in milk from the vegan group.
- The total concentration of unsaturated fatty acids in milk from the vegan group.
- The total concentration of saturated fatty acids in milk from the control group.
- The total concentration of unsaturated fatty acids in milk from the control group.

3 Use an example from the table to explain what is meant by a polyunsaturated fatty acid.

4 Describe the difference between the total concentration of polyunsaturated fatty acids in milk produced by the vegan group and by the control group. Suggest an explanation for this difference.

The fluid mosaic model

A cell surface membrane is only about 7 µm thick, so we cannot see all the details of its structure, even with an electron microscope. Because of this, biologists have produced a model to explain its properties. This is called the **fluid mosaic model**. The model was given this name because it describes how the molecules of the different substances that make up the membrane are arranged in a mosaic. These molecules don't just stay in one place. They move around, so we also describe the membrane as being fluid.

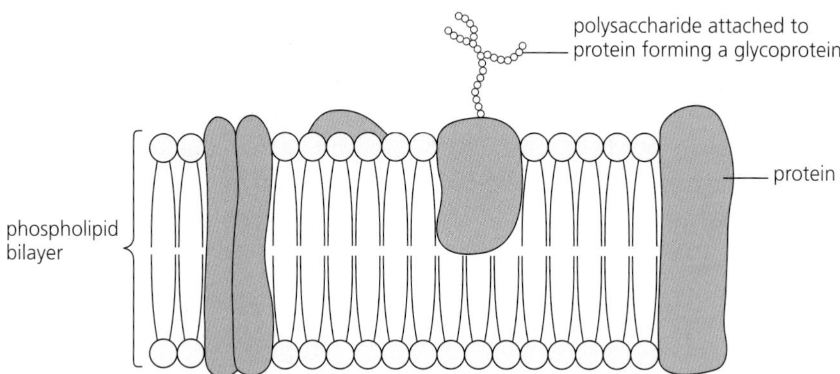

▲ **Figure 15** A simple diagram showing the structure of a cell surface membrane. The main components are the phospholipids, which form a bilayer, and proteins.

Look at Figure 15. This is a very simple diagram showing a section through a cell surface membrane. It illustrates how the phospholipids and proteins are arranged. The membrane is based on a phospholipid bilayer. Very small molecules, and molecules that dissolve in lipids, can pass easily through this bilayer. Water-soluble substances, however, must pass through pores in the protein molecules that span the membrane. The phospholipid layer therefore forms a very important barrier. Since molecules of some substances are unable to pass through it directly, passage into or out of the cell is controlled by the protein molecules in the membrane.

Some of the proteins move freely in the phospholipid bilayer of the cell surface membrane. Others are attached to both the cell surface membrane and structures in the cytoplasm of the cell.

Membrane proteins have a variety of different functions:

- They may act as enzymes. Enzymes that digest carbohydrates are found in the cell surface membranes of the epithelial cells that line the small intestine.
- They act as carrier proteins and play an important part in transporting substances into and out of the cell.
- They act as receptors for hormones. A hormone will only act on a cell that has the right protein receptors in its cell surface membrane.

Carbohydrates are attached to lipids and proteins on the outside of the cell surface membrane, forming glycolipids and glycoproteins. They are important in allowing cells to recognise one another.

Diffusion, osmosis and active transport

Diffusion

Diffusion is the passage of the ions or atoms or molecules that make up a substance, from where they are at a high concentration to where they are at a lower concentration. In other words, particles of the substance diffuse down a **concentration gradient**. Think about what happens if you put a drop of ink into a beaker of water. The ink molecules will gradually spread through the water. They will have diffused from where they were in a high concentration in the original drop to where they are in a lower concentration in the surrounding water.

These particles are moving at random. You can see this quite easily if you look at a tiny drop of toothpaste mixed with water under the microscope. The toothpaste particles move around, twisting and turning. They are moving because the molecules of water in which they are suspended are moving at random and are bumping into them. The kinetic energy that the molecules possess results in this movement.

In a solid, the particles are fixed and cannot move relative to one another; in a liquid, the molecules are free to move, but are close together, so bump into each other and change direction; and in a gas, the molecules travel much further before colliding with each other.

Diffusion is also one of the ways in which substances pass into and out of cells. During respiration for example, cells produce carbon dioxide. So there is a higher concentration of carbon dioxide inside a cell than outside. Carbon dioxide will diffuse from where it is in a high concentration inside a cell through the cell surface membrane to where it is in a low concentration outside the cell. We call surfaces through which diffusion takes place **exchange surfaces**.

The **rate of diffusion** is the amount diffused through the surface divided by the time taken. This depends on a number of factors. These include the following:

- **Temperature**. The higher the temperature, the more kinetic energy molecules possess. Molecules therefore move faster at higher temperatures, so the higher the temperature, the faster the rate of diffusion.
- **Surface area**. The greater the surface area of the exchange surface, the faster the rate of diffusion
- **The difference in concentration on either side of the exchange surface**. The greater this difference, the faster the rate of diffusion. In the intestine, the blood is continually transporting the products of digestion away from the intestine wall. This ensures a large difference in concentration and a faster rate of diffusion.
- **A thin exchange surface**. Diffusion is only efficient over very short distances. Exchange surfaces such as the epithelium of the intestine are very thin.

Q3

Fish have gills. They use these gills to obtain oxygen from the water by diffusion. Suggest three properties of fish gills that are adaptations for efficient diffusion.

Facilitated diffusion

Molecules such as those of glucose cannot pass directly through the phospholipid bilayer of a cell surface membrane. They need to be taken across by carrier proteins in the membrane. These carrier proteins have a binding site on their surface which has a specific shape. A glucose carrier, for example, has a binding site into which only glucose molecules will fit. In addition, different sorts of cells have different carrier proteins. This explains why a particular cell will take up some substances but not others.

Diffusing molecules bind to a carrier protein. The protein changes shape and takes the molecules through the membrane.

Ion channels help the diffusion of ions. Some ion channels have gates that open and close.

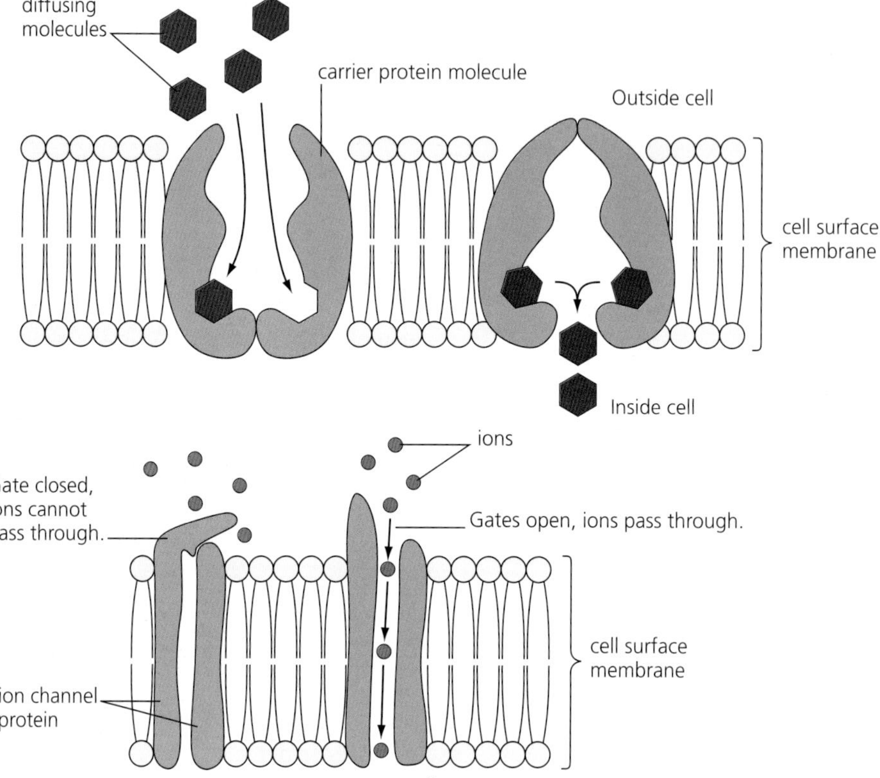

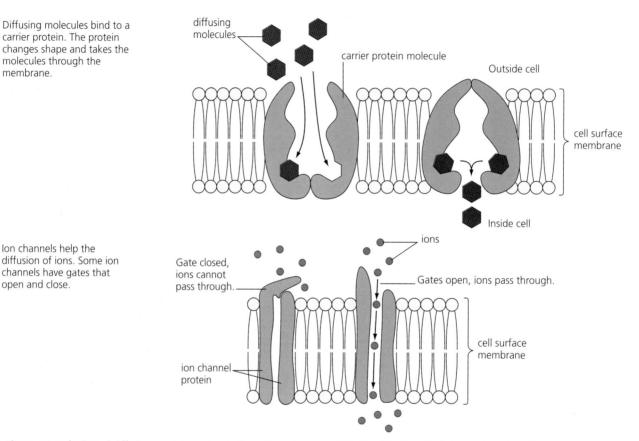

▲ **Figure 16** In facilitated diffusion, protein carriers in the cell membrane assist in the diffusion of substances into the cell.

Carrier proteins are able to change shape. Look at Figure 16. It shows you that in one form the binding site is exposed to the outside of the cell. In the other form, it is on the inside. Taking glucose as an example, you can see that it will fit into the binding site when it is exposed on the outside of the cell. The carrier protein then changes shape, bringing the glucose molecule through the membrane and into the cell. This process, in which a protein carrier transfers a molecule that would not otherwise pass through the membrane, is called **facilitated diffusion**. As with simple diffusion, facilitated diffusion relies on the kinetic energy of the molecules. It is also described as a passive process because it does not require energy from respiration.

Water potential and osmosis

Look at Figure 17. It shows water molecules surrounded by a membrane. These water molecules are in constant motion. As they move around randomly, some of them will hit the membrane. The collision of the molecules with the membrane creates a pressure on it. This pressure is

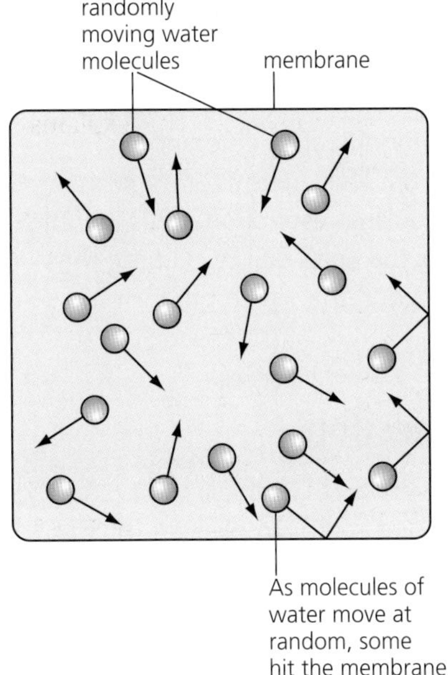

▲ **Figure 17** Water molecules move at random. Some will hit the surrounding membrane and create a pressure on it. This pressure is the water potential.

known as the **water potential** and it is measured in units of pressure, usually kilopascals (kPa) or megapascals (MPa).

Obviously, the more water molecules that are present and able to move about freely, the greater is the water potential. The greatest number of water molecules that it is possible to have in a given volume is in distilled water because this is pure water and nothing else is present. Distilled water therefore has the highest water potential. It is given a value of zero. All other solutions will have a value less than this. They will have a negative water potential.

Now look at Figure 18. This shows a cell surrounded by distilled water. The cell surface membrane separates the cytoplasm of the cell from the surrounding water. It is **partially permeable**. This means that it allows small molecules such as water to pass through but not larger molecules. The cytoplasm of the cell contains many soluble molecules and ions. They attract water molecules which form a 'shell' round them. These water molecules can no longer move around freely in the cytoplasm. Therefore, there is a much higher concentration of free water molecules in the water surrounding the cell than there is in the cell's cytoplasm.

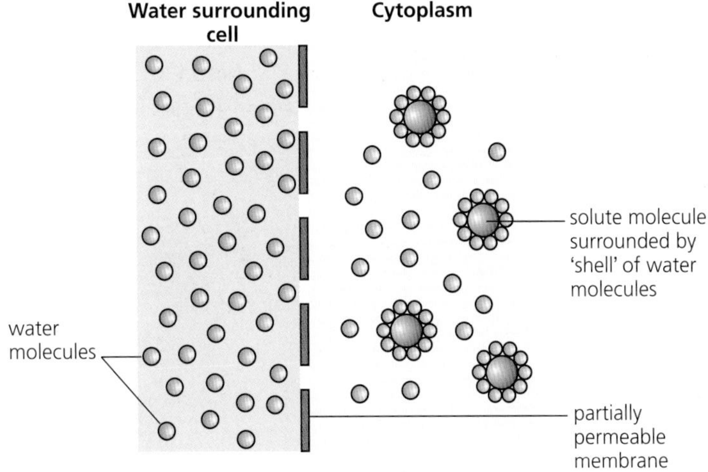

▲ **Figure 18** In this diagram, the concentration of water molecules that are able to move freely is higher outside the cell than inside the cell. As a result, water will move into the cell by osmosis.

The water potential is higher outside the cell than inside it, and water molecules therefore diffuse from the distilled water into the cell. Water molecules will also diffuse from any solution with a higher water potential to a solution with a lower water potential. This is **osmosis**. We can, therefore define osmosis in terms of water potential:

> *Osmosis is the net movement of water molecules from a solution with a higher water potential to a solution with a lower water potential through a partially permeable membrane.*

Active transport

Most cells are able to take up substances that are present in low concentrations in their environment. Plant cells, for example, take up mineral ions which are present in very small concentrations in the surrounding soil. **Active transport** is a process by which a cell takes up a substance *against* a concentration gradient.

As with facilitated diffusion, protein carrier molecules are involved, and they transport the substance across the membrane. The difference is, however, that active transport requires energy. This energy comes from molecules of the substance ATP produced during respiration. Cells in which a lot of active transport takes place, such as the epithelial cells lining the small intestine, have large numbers of mitochondria which produce the necessary ATP.

Absorbing the products of digestion

You read in Chapter 1 that digestion results in large insoluble molecules such as starch being broken down into smaller soluble molecules. By the time that digested food is half way along the small intestine, it is like soup. It has been mixed with digestive juices secreted from various glands and with sodium and chloride ions from the epithelial cells lining the first part of the small intestine.

Adding these ions lowers the water potential of the digested food, and this results in a water potential gradient. The water potential in the lumen of the first part of the small intestine is lower than that in the epithelial cells. Water therefore moves by osmosis from the cells into the lumen. You can see this in Figure 19.

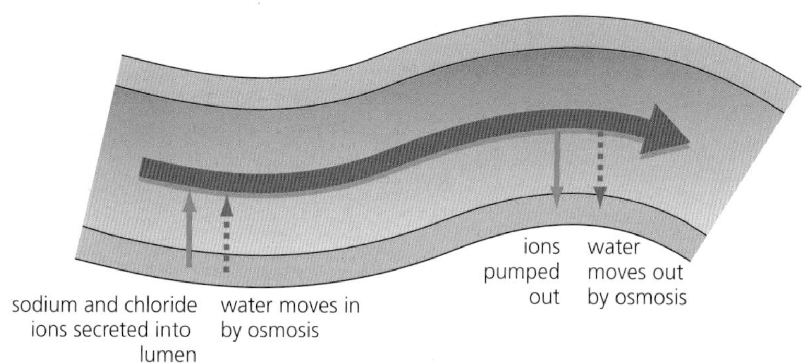

▲ **Figure 19** Sodium and chloride ions are secreted into the first part of the small intestine. This results in osmosis and water moving from epithelial cells into the lumen of the intestine. The processes of digestion and absorption are much more efficient in the resulting soupy mixture. Further along the small intestine, the ions and water are reabsorbed into the intestine lining.

Further along the small intestine, these ions are taken back from the lumen contents into the epithelial cells. This involves active transport through the cell surface membranes of the epithelial cells. As a result, the water potential in the cells is now lower than in the lumen of the intestine, so water moves out from the lumen into the epithelial cells by osmosis.

One of the most important products of carbohydrate digestion is glucose. The intestine absorbs glucose by a combination of facilitated diffusion and active transport. Look at Figure 20. You will see that there are carrier molecules called **co-transport proteins** in the cell surface membranes of the epithelial

Q4

The epithelial cells in the small intestine contain many mitochondria. Explain the link between the large number of mitochondria and the transport of sodium ions out of the cells into the blood.

cells. These are carrier molecules that only transport glucose in the presence of sodium ions. Each time a glucose molecule is transported into the cell, so is a sodium ion. This part of the process involves facilitated diffusion. Facilitated diffusion, however, will only work if substances can move down a concentration gradient. This gradient is maintained by actively transporting sodium ions out of the cell into the blood. The glucose molecules pass from the inside of the cells into the blood by facilitated diffusion.

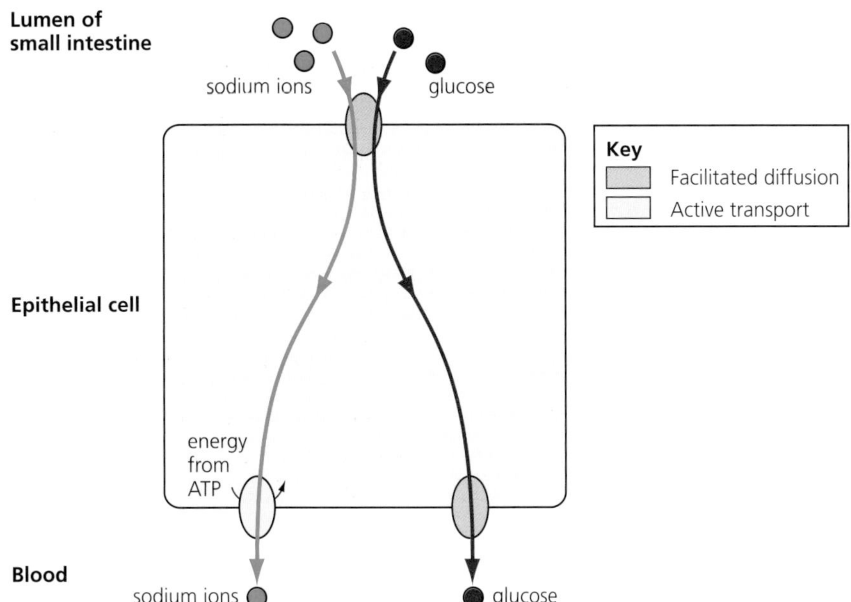

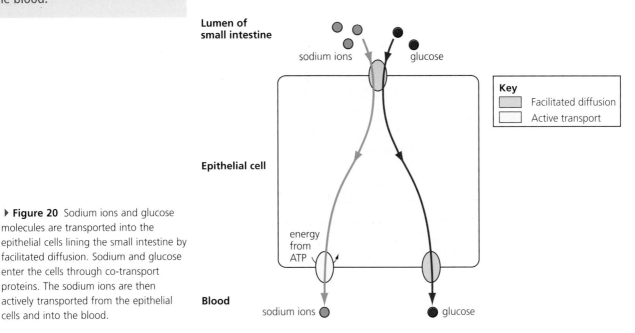

▸ **Figure 20** Sodium ions and glucose molecules are transported into the epithelial cells lining the small intestine by facilitated diffusion. Sodium and glucose enter the cells through co-transport proteins. The sodium ions are then actively transported from the epithelial cells and into the blood.

Identifying variables

Scientists investigated how different factors affected the rate of absorption of glucose from a piece of small intestine. The results of their investigation are shown in the graph in Figure 21.

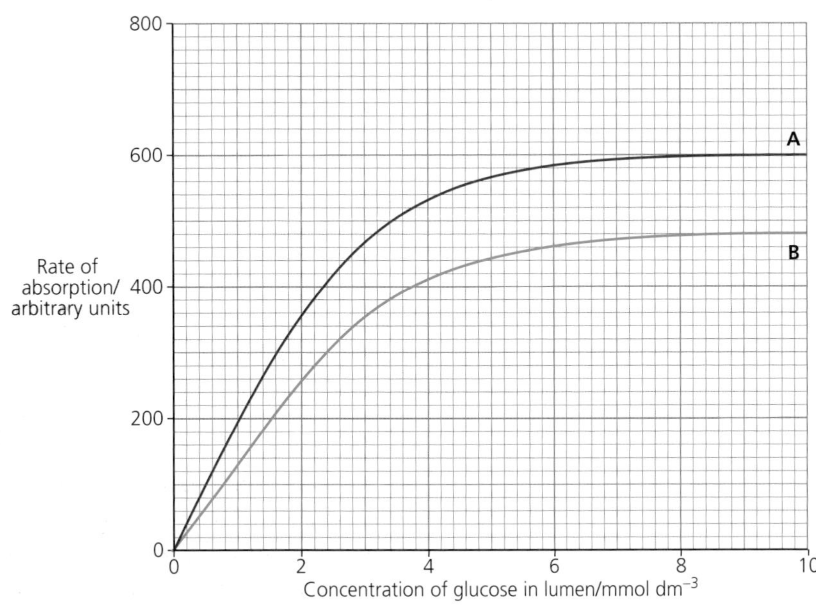

▸ **Figure 21** The graph shows the effect of glucose concentration on the rate of absorption of glucose from the small intestine. Curve **A** shows the results when the glucose solution in the intestine was stirred. Curve **B** shows the results when the glucose solution was not stirred.

■ **Look carefully at this graph. What are the independent variables in this investigation?**

There are two: the concentration of glucose in the lumen of the intestine, and whether or not the glucose solution was stirred. They are the independent variables because they were the factors that the scientists changed.

■ **What is the dependent variable?**

The dependent variable is the factor that is measured as a result of changing the independent variable. In this investigation, it is the rate of absorption of glucose from the small intestine.

In this investigation, the scientists measured the rate of glucose absorption.

■ **What is meant by the *rate* of absorption?**

The rate is the amount absorbed divided by the time taken. We often use rates in biology because they allow comparisons to be made.

When the scientists carried out the investigation, they kept the temperature constant.

■ **Why did the scientists keep the temperature constant?**

Temperature affects the rate of absorption. If the scientists allowed the temperature to vary as well as, say, the concentration of glucose in the lumen of the intestine, they would not know what caused any change in the rate of absorption.

■ **Now look at curve B on the graph. Describe how the concentration of the glucose solution in the lumen of the small intestine affects the rate of absorption.**

The rate of absorption increases as the concentration of glucose in the small intestine increases, and then gradually levels off. After a concentration of approximately 5 mmol dm^{-3}, it remains constant.

■ **The rate of absorption is more or less constant above a concentration of 5 mmol dm^{-3}. Explain why.**

This is another graph where limiting factors are involved (see page 26 where we looked at the effect of substrate concentration on the rate of an enzyme-controlled reaction).

There must be something other than the concentration of glucose in the lumen of the small intestine that is limiting the rate of absorption here. It is probably the number of glucose carrier molecules in the cell surface membrane of epithelial cells lining the intestine.

■ Describe and explain the effect of stirring on the rate of absorption.

The graph shows that stirring increases the rate of absorption, whatever the concentration of glucose in the lumen of the small intestine. Think about what happens when the glucose solution has not been stirred. As it is absorbed into the cells, the concentration in the intestine will fall, and the difference in lumen and cell concentrations will become less and less. Obviously, this fall in the concentration gradient will slow the rate of diffusion. Stirring maintains the concentration gradient. This results in a higher rate of absorption.

General principles

Drawing a line graph

Drawing a graph helps you to see the relationship between two variables much more clearly than a table. You will come across a lot of line graphs in Biology, like the one in Figure 21. You should know how to draw a line graph.

- The independent variable, in this case the concentration of glucose in the lumen of the small intestine, is plotted on the *x* axis, and the dependent variable (the rate of absorption) is plotted on the *y* axis.
- The axes should be fully labelled and you should include units. Someone should be able to look at the graph and know exactly what it shows without any further explanation.
- Choose a suitable scale.
  - Make sure all the points you need to plot will fit on the graph.
  - Avoid a scale which involves fractions of grid squares. This makes it difficult to plot points accurately.
- Plot the individual points as clearly and accurately as possible. Use either a dot with a circle round it (⊙) or a cross (×).
- Join the points. Draw either a smooth curve or straight lines joining the points. You should only draw a smooth curve if your data are sufficiently reliable for you to feel that you can confidently predict intermediate values. Otherwise, join the individual points with straight lines.
- You should add a title explaining what the graph shows.

Interpreting rates of change

- Where a graph shows two curves for two different conditions, you can compare the rates by comparing the slopes of the curves.

Cholera and diarrhoea

You saw at the start of this chapter that cholera bacteria produce a poisonous substance called a **toxin**. This toxin is called **choleragen**. Molecules of choleragen toxin bind to the cell surface membranes of the epithelial cells lining the small intestine and bring about a huge increase in the active transport of ions into the lumen of the small intestine. The result is a higher than normal concentration of ions and therefore an abnormally low water potential in the intestinal lumen. Consequently, very large amounts of water move by osmosis out of the tissues surrounding the intestine. This causes the massive diarrhoea that is a characteristic symptom of cholera.

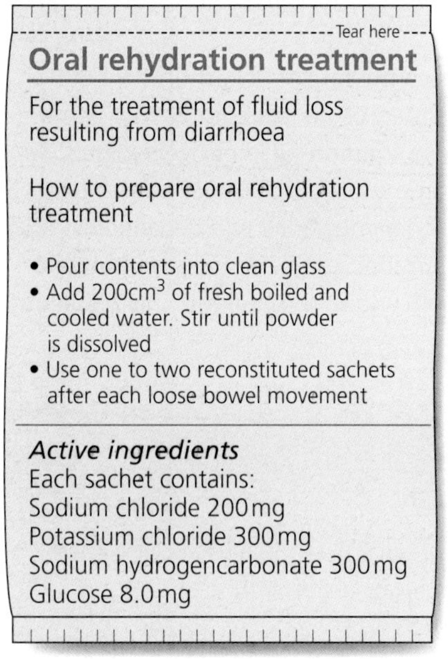

Oral rehydration treatment

For the treatment of fluid loss resulting from diarrhoea

How to prepare oral rehydration treatment

- Pour contents into clean glass
- Add 200cm^3 of fresh boiled and cooled water. Stir until powder is dissolved
- Use one to two reconstituted sachets after each loose bowel movement

Active ingredients
Each sachet contains:
Sodium chloride 200 mg
Potassium chloride 300 mg
Sodium hydrogencarbonate 300 mg
Glucose 8.0 mg

▲ **Figure 22** Oral rehydration solutions are cheap and very effective. The contents of this sachet may cost only a few pence, but if used correctly, it can save lives from cholera.

Q5

Oral rehydration solutions like the one made up from the sachet shown in Figure 20 contain a set concentration of glucose. Would doubling the concentration of glucose in the solution make a more effective oral rehydration solution? Explain your answer.

Oral rehydration solutions and the treatment of cholera

Although the toxin produced by cholera bacteria affects the transport of ions from the epithelial cells lining the small intestine, it has very little effect on the co-transport proteins that reabsorb ions in the lower part of the small intestine. So, if we can get these proteins to work a little better, we could ensure that adequate amounts of glucose and sodium ions are taken back from the lumen of the intestine into the cells. This should go some way towards limiting the diarrhoea.

This is the basis of the oral rehydration solutions (see Figure 22) that we looked at the start of Chapter 1. The sachet of glucose and mineral salts is mixed with a set volume of clean water. The patient drinks the resulting solution and this stimulates sodium and glucose to be taken up by the co-transport proteins. Water is now absorbed from the intestine by osmosis, and the diarrhoea is brought under control.

Milk, the perfect food?

Milk is produced by the mammary glands of female mammals from shortly after they give birth. It contains all the nutrients that a newborn mammal requires in the early stages of its life. The sugar found in milk is lactose. You may remember from Chapter 1 that lactose is a disaccharide and is formed by the condensation of a molecule of α-glucose and a molecule of galactose. Lactose cannot pass through the epithelium of the small intestine into the blood. It must be digested first. Newborn mammals produce the enzyme **lactase**. Lactase hydrolyses lactose, producing glucose and galactose. These two are monosaccharides which can therefore be absorbed into the blood.

When most mammals are weaned they no longer drink milk. The genes that are responsible for producing lactase are switched off and no more lactase is produced. It would be inefficient for the body to produce an enzyme that is no longer required. So most adult mammals, whether they are aardvarks or zebras, do not produce lactase. This is also true of humans who come from those parts of the world where milk has never been part of the diet of an adult. We describe people as **lactose intolerant** if they cannot digest lactose because they do not produce the enzyme lactase. There is nothing wrong with people who are lactose intolerant. In fact, the condition is perfectly normal, and more people are lactose intolerant than lactose tolerant. Most people in the UK, however, are able to drink milk and digest lactose as adults. In these people, the gene for lactase production has not been switched off.

In a person who is lactose intolerant, the undigested lactose passes along the gut to the colon. The gut bacteria ferment this lactose and produce a variety of smaller soluble substances and gases such as methane and carbon dioxide. The small soluble molecules lower the water potential of the colon contents, so water moves in by osmosis. The result is diarrhoea.

Interpreting lactose tolerance tests

Miguel has recently arrived in the UK from South America. He has noticed that since arriving in this country he often feels bloated. He also suffers a lot from wind (and that can be very embarrassing) and has explosive diarrhoea. What is wrong with him? He decides to go to the doctor. She examines him. Is Miguel lactose intolerant or has he simply got a bacterial infection? The symptoms are very similar.

She decides to send Miguel to the hospital for a lactose tolerance test. He is given a solution containing 50 g of lactose to drink. The amount of glucose in his blood is then measured at intervals over the next two hours. Look at the graphs in Figure 23. Graph **A** shows the results of a person who is able to drink milk without showing signs of lactose intolerance. Graph **B** shows Miguel's test results.

Look at Graph **A**.

1 What is the maximum increase in the concentration of glucose in the blood?

2 The glucose concentration increases in the first 30 minutes after the person drank the solution of lactose. What causes this increase?

3 The glucose concentration decreases after 30 minutes. What causes this decrease?

Now look at Graph **B**.

4 What is the maximum increase in the concentration of glucose in Miguel's blood?

5 The glucose concentration hardly increases at all in the first 30 minutes after Miguel drank the solution of lactose. Miguel is lactose intolerant. Explain why his blood glucose concentration hardly increases.

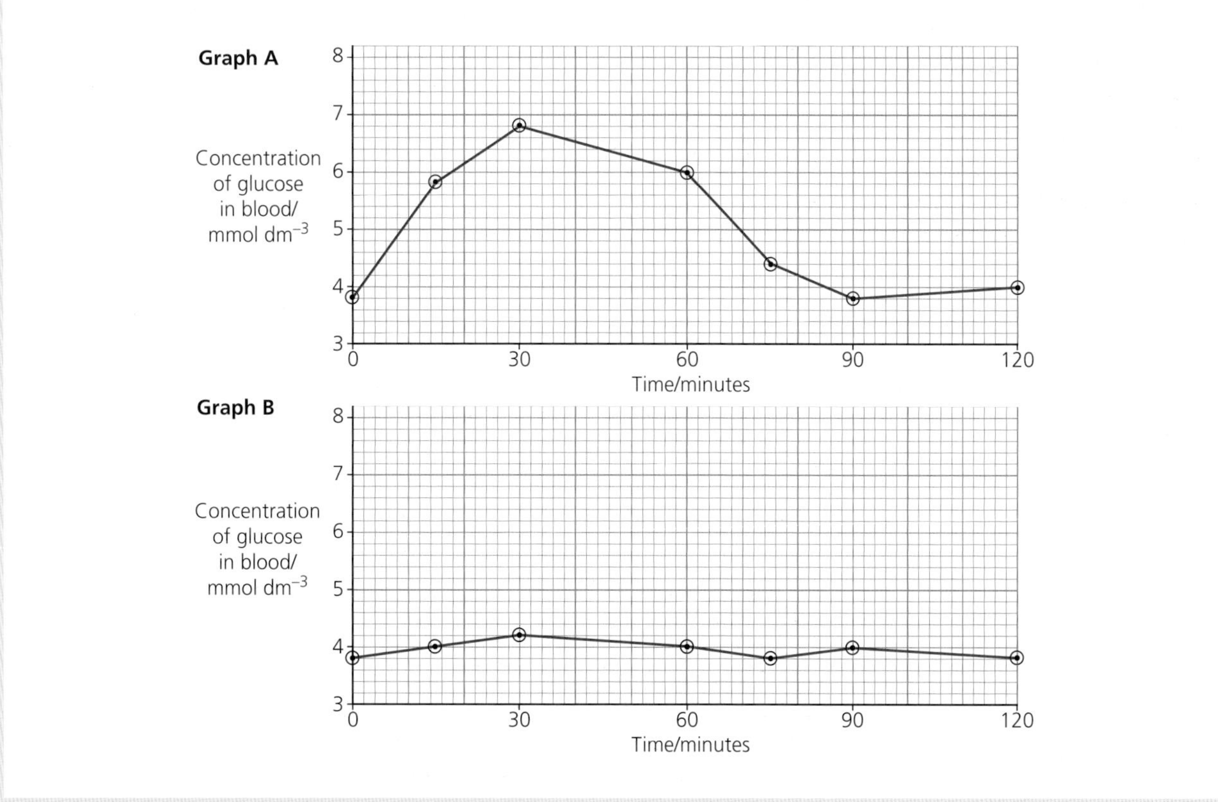

▲ **Figure 23** These graphs show the changes in blood glucose concentration after drinking a solution of lactose. Graph **A** shows the results for a healthy person who is able to drink milk without showing symptoms of lactose intolerance. Graph **B** shows Miguel's test results.

Chapter 3

The lungs and lung disease

Tobacco smoke contains a vast mixture of substances. These include the addictive ingredient nicotine and the highly toxic gas, carbon monoxide. Of over 4000 organic compounds in the tar, at least 60 are known to cause cancer. All of these substances reach the delicate cell lining in a smoker's lungs. Some get swept out again when the smoker exhales, some stay in the lungs and some pass into the blood and reach all parts of the body. After a few years, a smoker's lungs are lined with tar, as the photograph in Figure 1 shows.

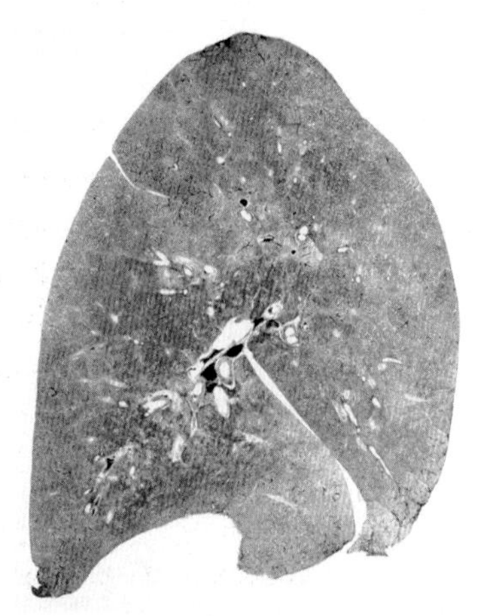

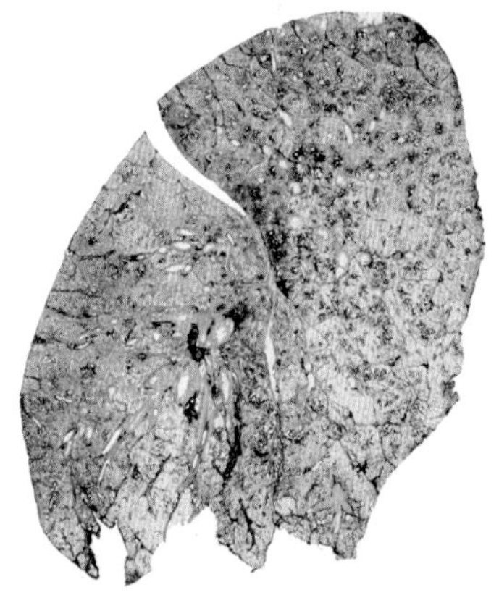

Figure 1 Left: section through a clean non-smoker's lung. Right: section through a tar-filled smoker's lung.

Common sense suggests that deposits of substances like these must be harmful, but it can be difficult to convince smokers of exactly how dangerous it is. All smokers seem to know someone who has smoked like a chimney for years and lived to be ninety. People vary greatly in the effects that tobacco smoke has on them – their reaction to a particular toxin can vary widely. Researchers have had to depend on data from large-scale surveys that provide statistics that establish the true effects of smoking.

One large survey was carried out in Norway. Over 2000 healthy middle-aged men were given a wide range of health and fitness tests. Some were non-smokers and others smokers. Seven years later, the same group was followed up. By then, about 30% of the non-smokers and 60% of the smokers had died or disappeared or had developed a serious health problem such as heart disease or cancer.

The data in Table 1 show the results of two of the fitness tests for those who were apparently still healthy after seven years. In one of the tests, the men rode an exercise bike for as long as possible. In another test, the men took a deep breath and then breathed out with as much force as they could – a forced expiration test.

Table 1 Data for two fitness tests carried out by non-smokers and smokers.

Fitness test (all results are mean values)	Non-smokers (n = 791)		Smokers (n = 347)	
	At start	After 7 years	At start	After 7 years
Time riding exercise bike before exhaustion/minutes	14.8	14.1	12.9	11.3
Total work done riding exercise bike/kJ	124	118	102	86
Maximum volume of air that could be expired in one second/cm^3	3638	3522	3341	3070

n = number of men who did the fitness tests

Look at the results for the exercise bike test. You can see that the non-smokers were able to ride for longer than the smokers before they gave up through exhaustion. They also rode more strongly and therefore did more work before giving up. Seven years later, both groups did less well, but the decline in performance of the smokers was greater. The smokers also failed to breathe out as quickly and with as much force as the non-smokers. At first sight, the differences may not seem very large, but bear in mind that they show results for large numbers of men.

Statisticians used calculations that tested whether or not the results were showing real differences between the two groups of men. Their calculations demonstrated that the differences were statistically significant: statistically, it was very unlikely that the differences were just due to chance. In fact, the calculations showed that the probability that the differences were just due to chance was less than one in a thousand. Since the number of men tested was large, the investigators could be confident that their results were also reliable. In addition, they had selected groups of men who, apart from their smoking habit, were as similar as possible: the age range of the men was restricted, they were all from a similar background and they lived in similar areas of Norway. Also, men with any obvious signs of heart or lung disease had been excluded.

From the results of these fitness tests it was possible to conclude that there was a link between smoking and lack of fitness. However, the study did not identify the cause of the link. Working out the cause is complicated because there are probably a number of factors involved, including the effects of smoking on the lungs and on the heart and blood vessels. The forced expiration test, however, suggests that one factor is the rate at which air is able to pass through the airways of the lungs. The results suggest that the airways of the smokers may have become narrower or partially blocked, and that the lung tissues may have become stiffer, so that the lungs were not able to expel air so rapidly or in such volume as in non-smokers.

In this chapter we look at the structure of the breathing system and how it functions. This will enable us to explain how some diseases can affect breathing, and to evaluate other evidence for the damaging effects of smoking on the lungs.

Why we need to breathe

Fortunately, we breathe without having to think about it: for most of the time we are hardly conscious of the regular chest movements that take air into and out of our lungs. It is only when we exert ourselves more than usual that we become aware of our breathing.

The primary function of breathing is to supply oxygen for **respiration**. Respiration is the biochemical process by which energy is released from glucose, or from other energy stores such as fats. The rate at which cells require energy varies. Active muscle cells need large supplies of energy for contraction. Cells that make digestive enzymes or that are growing rapidly use energy for the synthesis of complex molecules. The electrochemical activities of our brain cells need a constant supply of energy from respiration, and brain cells are damaged if deprived of oxygen for more than a few minutes.

Just as vital as obtaining oxygen is the removal of carbon dioxide, the waste product of respiration. Carbon dioxide produces an acid solution, so as carbon dioxide accumulates, the pH of the cells and blood is lowered. The pH of the blood plasma and intercellular fluid is normally maintained very close to pH 7.4. Any variation from this upsets the ionic balance, and can rapidly lead to unconsciousness and death. To avoid this, a build-up of carbon dioxide very quickly stimulates an increase in the rate of breathing.

The lungs are where oxygen passes from the atmosphere into the blood and where carbon dioxide passes out. We refer to this process as **gas exchange**. Note that the movement of oxygen is quite independent of the movement of carbon dioxide; oxygen and carbon dioxide do not swap with one another.

The movement of the gases is entirely by **diffusion**. As you saw in Chapter 2, diffusion occurs when there is a difference between concentrations of a substance in two places. The substance moves from a place of high concentration to a place of lower concentration. Breathing air with a particularly high concentration of carbon dioxide can be lethal, even when there is a good supply of oxygen. Carbon dioxide will not diffuse from the blood if the concentration in the lungs is even higher than its concentration in the blood. Carbon dioxide is odourless, so it can be hard to detect when its concentration is dangerously high. As an example, seeds slowly produce the gas by respiration; grain in a store raises carbon dioxide concentration, so farmers take care to ensure that grain stores are well ventilated before entering them.

Breathing movements maintain a supply of fresh air at the internal surface of the lungs. The sequence of breathing processes that replace air in the lungs is called **ventilation**. Without active ventilation, air could not find its way into our lungs anywhere near fast enough to supply our need for oxygen. Also, as our energy demands change, for example when we start to run, we are able to vary the rate at which we ventilate our lungs.

The structure of the lungs

Our lungs almost fill the **chest cavity** which occupies the upper part of the body enclosed by the ribs. The heart and its major blood vessels tuck in between the lungs and above the diaphragm that separates the chest cavity from the abdomen. The main parts of the human breathing system are shown in Figure 2.

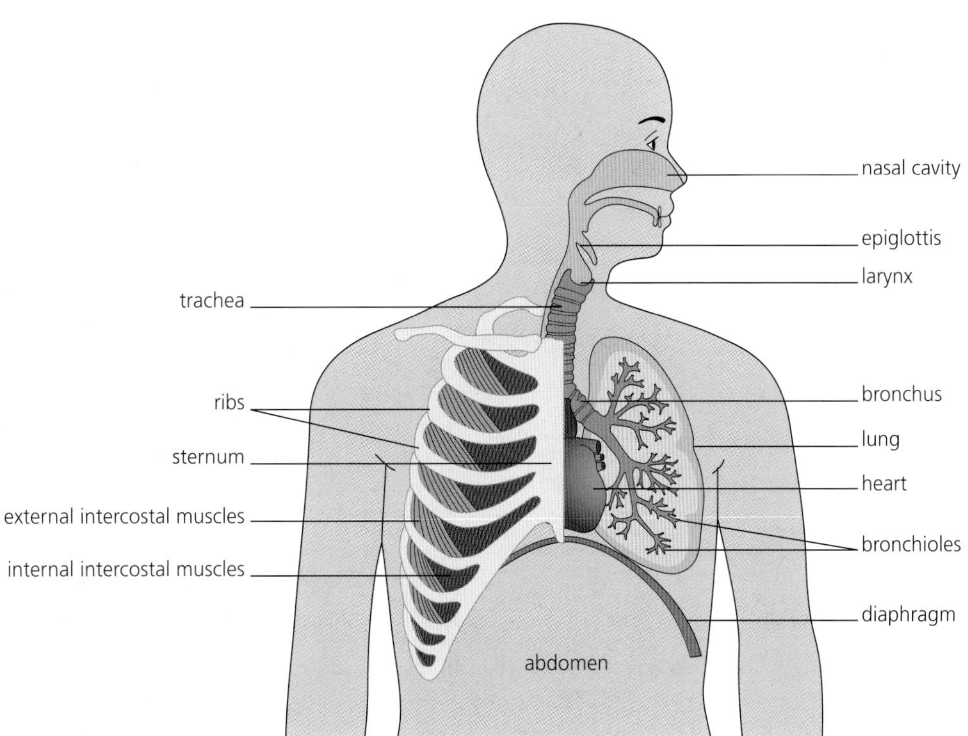

Figure 2 The human breathing system.

Interpreting a photomicrograph of the lung

Figure 3 shows lung tissue without magnification. It appears to be quite solid and not obviously full of air. However, you can see some of the bronchioles that transport air in the lungs.

The photomicrograph in Figure 4 shows a very thin slice of lung tissue as seen through a microscope. At this magnification, the lung looks rather like a sponge. The sponginess is due to tiny cavities called **alveoli**. When we breathe in, the alveoli fill with air and become roughly spherical. It is in these balloon-shaped cavities that gas exchange occurs.

To obtain a slice for a microscope slide, some lung tissue is first embedded in a waxy substance that makes the tissue rigid. Then very thin slices are cut with the blade of a machine like a small bacon slicer. The alveoli appear to have irregular shapes because they are not inflated as they would be in a living lung after inhalation. The outline of their walls is wavy, not smooth and rounded. As the cells are almost transparent, the section is stained and this shows the nuclei as dark dots.

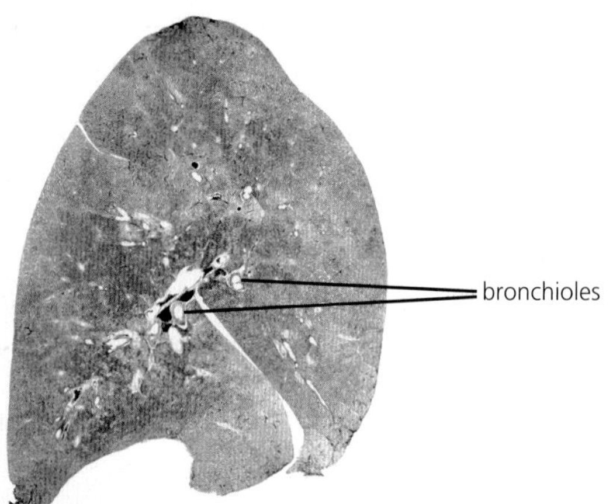

Figure 3 A section of part of a lung.

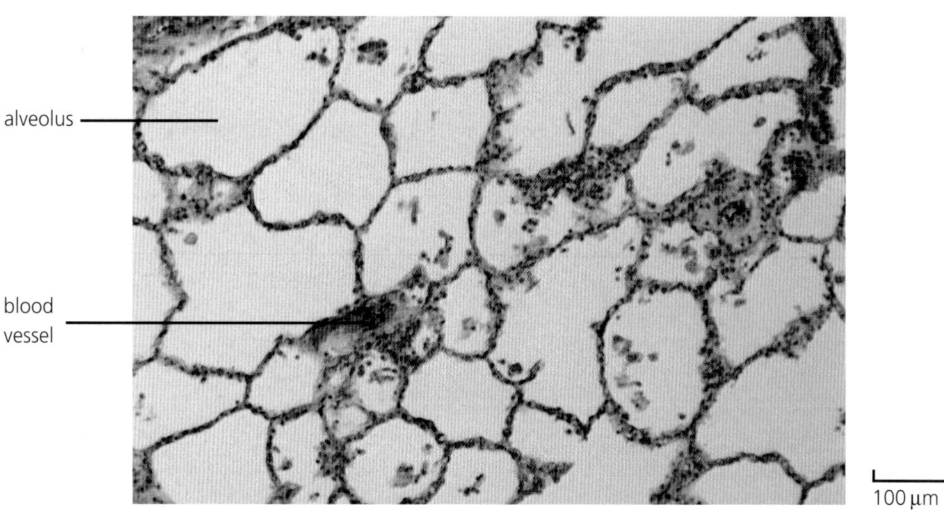

Figure 4 A photomicrograph of a small section of lung tissue. Since it is magnified, the spongy texture of the lung is clear.

■ Why do the alveoli look to be different sizes, rather than all the same as the diagram in Figure 6 shows?

You can answer this by thinking what happens if you cut straight across a bunch of round grapes. Some will be cut through the middle, but others will be cut to one side of the middle and these sections will look much smaller.

■ How do we calculate the actual size of an alveolus from the photomicrograph?

In Chapter 2 you were shown how to work out the actual size from a photomicrograph when you were given the magnification factor. In this photo, the size is shown as a scale line drawn on the photo. You can see that the line is labelled 100 μm. This means that the length of the line represents 100 μm on the photo. To find the actual size of an alveolus we need to compare its dimensions with the length of the scale line.

- Measure the maximum length and width in millimetres of the alveolus labelled **A** in Figure 4.
- Again in millimetres, measure the length of the scale line. Note that this length represents 100 μm.

To work out an actual length, multiply the image length by the distance that the scale line represents, and divide it by the length of the scale line. This is the formula:

$$\text{actual length} = \frac{\text{image length (mm)} \times \text{distance represented by the scale line (units given)}}{\text{measured length of scale line (mm)}}$$

On the photomicrograph, the maximum length of the alveolus is about 30 mm and the width is 15 mm.

The length of the scale line is 10 mm.

So, using the formula, the maximum width is $\frac{30 \times 100}{10} = 300\,\mu\text{m}$

■ Use the same formula to work out the minimum width.

You should find that the maximum dimensions of the alveolus in the photomicrograph are about 300 μm and 150 μm. If the alveolus was inflated, its diameter would probably be about 225 μm in diameter.

Analysing a photomicrograph

Remember when interpreting a micrograph of biological material that what you see through a microscope is only a very thin slice of tissue. Cutting a thin slice may alter the shape of the tissue. The slice may cut across structures in different planes (see also Chapter 2, page 39). For example, a blood vessel may be cut straight across or lengthways. The tissue may be stained to show structures that would otherwise be transparent. The colours are not natural.

A light microscope has a maximum magnification of about 1500 times. At this magnification, it is impossible to distinguish structures that are less than about 2 μm apart. For example, cell surface membranes (also called plasma membranes) are too small to be distinguished from adjacent material.

To form an image, an electron microscope uses a beam of electrons instead of light. This allows structures as small as about 1 nanometre (nm) to be distinguished. A nanometre is one-thousandth of a micrometre; 1 μm = 1000 nm. Specialised equipment is required to make a section thin enough to show structures clearly with an electron microscope. Also, in the electron microscope the specimen has to be placed in a vacuum, and this treatment can distort it.

General principles

- A micrograph often shows just a small section of a tissue, organ or organism. You should be able to visualise three-dimensional forms from thin slices in a slide or photograph.
- You should be able to calculate the actual size of a part in a section using accurate measurements you make and either the magnification factor or scale line.
- If your measurements are in millimetres, for example, ensure that you convert units accurately when you give the size of the part in micrometres or nanometres.

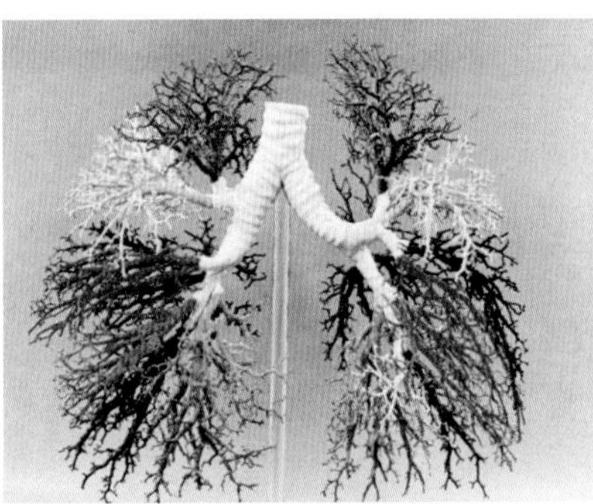

Figure 5 The branching network of bronchioles in a lung. The bronchioles have been filled with plastic resin and then the other tissue of the lung has been dissolved away.

How oxygen gets into the blood

For efficient diffusion, a **gas exchange** surface needs to have:

- a large surface area, compared with the volume of the organism
- a short distance for the gas to diffuse
- a large difference in the concentration of gas on opposite sides of the surface.

In human lungs, the large surface area is achieved by having a vast number of very small alveoli. Each lung contains about 350 million alveoli. As shown in Figure 6, the airways in the lung, called **bronchioles**, branch hundreds of times so that the diameter at their ends is tiny. At the end of each branch is a cluster of alveoli. These are rather like bunches of tiny hollowed out grapes connected to the network of bronchioles.

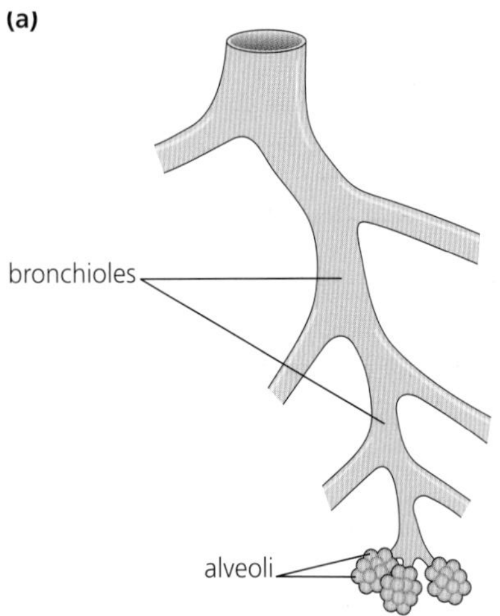

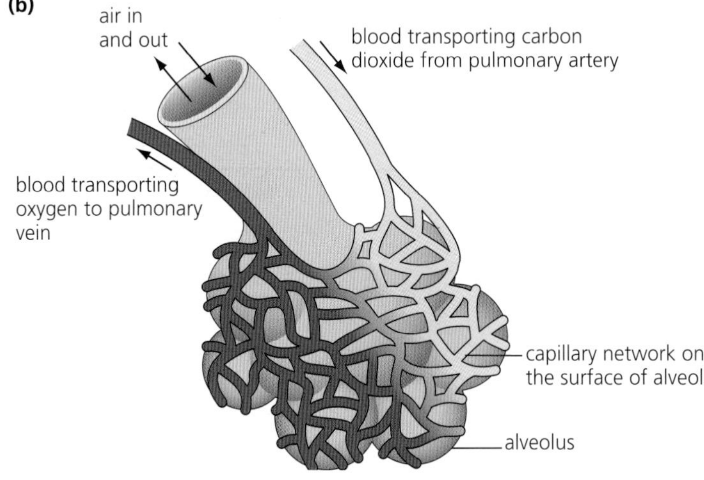

Figure 6 The diagrams show that the bronchioles have thin branches, each branch ending in a cluster of alveoli surrounded by capillaries.

The gas exchange surface

The alveoli are covered with a network of blood capillaries (see Figure 6(b)). The walls of the alveoli and of the capillaries form a very thin barrier between the air in the alveoli and the blood (see Figure 7). The alveolar wall cells are flattened, with only a thin layer of cytoplasm between their cell surface membranes. The capillary walls also consist of very thin cells. These cells are curved to form narrow tubes (see cross section in Figure 7). The capillaries are so narrow that the red blood cells, which carry oxygen and carbon dioxide, touch the walls as the blood flows through the capillaries.

Because of this cell arrangement, the distance between the air in the alveoli and the red blood cells is very short. This minimises the distance that oxygen has to diffuse from air to blood, and carbon dioxide from blood to air.

The inner surface of the alveolus wall is covered in a very thin film of water because the plasma membranes of its cells are permeable to water. The rate of diffusion of a gas in water is much lower than its rate of diffusion in air, and the film of water increases the distance that gases have to diffuse. Both these factors slightly lower the rate of diffusion of gases. However, a membrane that is not permeable to water is also not permeable to oxygen. Consequently a moist surface is an unavoidable feature of a gas exchange surface. In infections such as pneumonia, the layer of liquid on the surface of the alveoli gets much thicker. This seriously slows the rate of gas diffusion.

Between the alveoli and the capillaries is a very thin layer of tissue fluid that contains elastic fibres. These fibres help to maintain the structure of the alveoli and hence the lungs. The fibres are made by cells that fit in between the alveoli and form **connective tissue**, as seen in Figure 7.

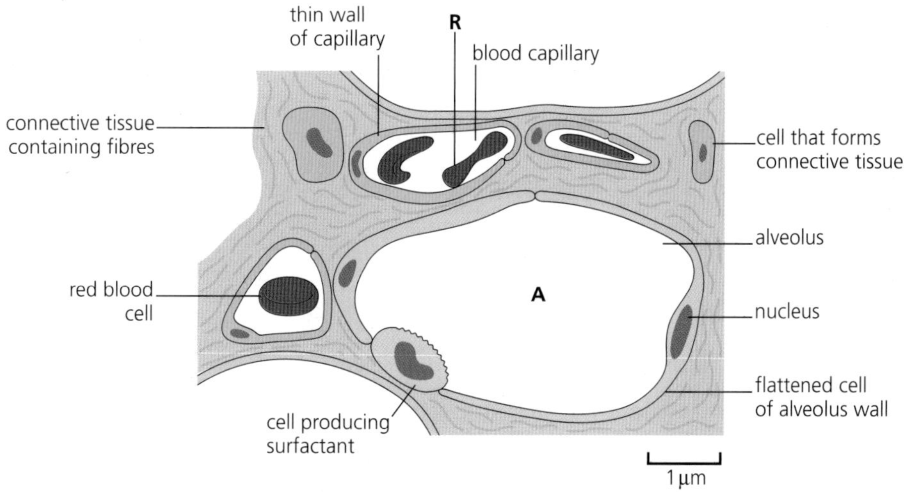

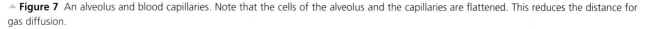

Figure 7 An alveolus and blood capillaries. Note that the cells of the alveolus and the capillaries are flattened. This reduces the distance for gas diffusion.

Q1

Use the scale line in Figure 7 to calculate the minimum distance that oxygen would have to diffuse to pass from the air in the alveolus (**A**) to the red blood cell (**R**).

A **concentration gradient** is essential for gas exchange. The gradient is maintained by ventilation in the lungs coupled with the continuous flow of blood. Breathing movements constantly change the air in the alveoli, providing fresh oxygen and removing carbon dioxide. Oxygen diffuses into the red blood cells. As the blood flow rapidly moves the red blood cells on, they are replaced by oxygen-poor cells.

This ensures that the concentration of oxygen in the alveoli is always much higher than the concentration in the blood.

The structure of the breathing system

If you could take out your lungs and carefully spread out all the alveoli, they would cover most of the floor area of a typical school laboratory. That's about 70 m^2. The total surface area of the skin of an adult is slightly less than 2 m^2. The lungs therefore have an area that is roughly 35 times the area of the surface of the body. This shows how large a surface area we need for gas exchange, and it makes up for the low surface area to volume ratio of human bodies. It would obviously be impractical to have such a huge area outside our bodies, billowing out like a massive sail, or as an array of flaps sticking out from the side like external gills. Having the gas exchange surface folded away in the chest has the advantage of protecting the thin surface membrane from damage. It also reduces the loss of water.

Since the lungs are tucked away inside the chest, it is essential that a good supply of oxygen reaches the gas exchange surface. Breathing movements serve this purpose: they constantly replace the air in the alveoli by the process of **ventilation**. Without active ventilation, air could not reach our lungs anything like fast enough to supply our oxygen needs. Our energy demands change, for example when we start to run. So we must also vary the rate at which we ventilate our alveoli.

The ventilation route

The ventilation route (see Figure 2 on page 59), is:

- nose and nasal passages, or mouth and mouth cavity
- trachea (windpipe)
- bronchi
- bronchioles
- alveoli.

It may seem curious that we can breathe through both the nose and the mouth. The advantage of breathing through the **nose** is that air has to pass through a maze of narrow cavities behind the nose called **sinuses**. The membrane lining the sinuses has a good blood supply. The blood warms the air to the lungs, so maintaining core body temperature. Also, warm air holds more water vapour than cold air, so moister air reaches the lungs through the nose than through the mouth. This reduces loss of water by evaporation from the surface of the lungs.

Cells in the sinus membrane secrete mucus that contains a sticky protein which traps dust and bacteria. Other membrane cells are covered with tiny hair-like structures called cilia. The cilia beat and move the mucus towards the throat where it is swallowed. This lowers the chance of infectious organisms reaching the delicate tissues of the lungs.

The sinuses of the nose are narrow and can easily become blocked, so breathing through the **mouth** gives the air an alternative route, for instance when we have a cold. The cold virus irritates the mucous membrane and it produces excessive amounts of mucus. We can take in air through the mouth much faster than through the nose. At times such as when we are running, it is more important to supply oxygen rapidly than it is to warm the air or reduce infection.

The **trachea** is a wide tube. Air passes from the throat, through the trachea, down the neck and into the chest. Food must not go down with the air, so when we swallow a flap of cartilage called the **epiglottis** closes over the entrance to the trachea. Normally, this is precisely coordinated by a reflex action. But occasionally some food may go down the wrong way. This stimulates us to cough, which usually expels the food from the trachea and stops us from choking.

While you read, you probably lean forward and bend your neck. You do not choke since the trachea does not kink and close up as a piece of soft rubber tubing would. This is because its structure is more like a shower hose.

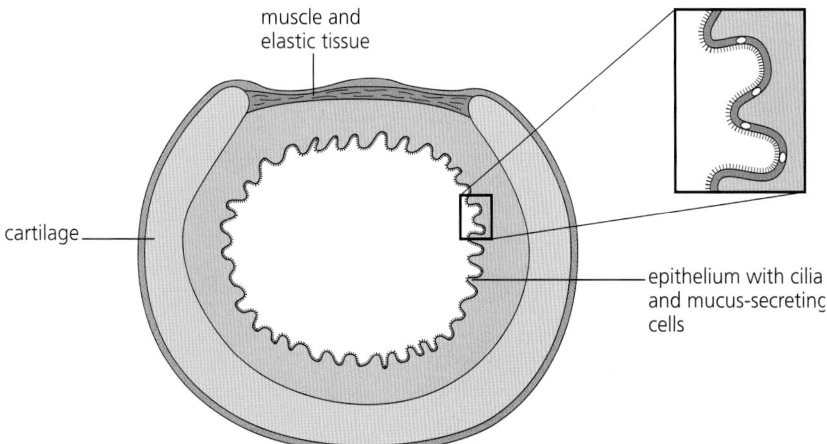

Figure 8 A section across the trachea. The stiff cartilage keeps the airway open. The muscle and elastic tissue allows flexibility. Cells of the epithelium that line the airway secrete mucus which traps bacteria and dust particles. Hair-like cilia beat upwards and sweep the mucus to the throat.

The tracheal wall contains about 20 rings of hard cartilage separated by narrow bands of soft muscular and elastic tissue. The soft tissue allows the trachea to be flexible and to stretch, while the cartilage rings hold it wide open, even when the neck is bent. They also prevent the trachea from collapsing as we breathe in hard (think of a soft straw being sucked flat). The cartilages are C-shaped, and are not quite complete rings. This allows the gullet, which passes down the neck just behind the trachea, to expand as food is swallowed.

The top section of the trachea is adapted to form the **larynx** (the voice box). To produce the sounds that make up our voice, two things happen. We use precise muscular actions to adjust the position of two folds of tissue (the vocal cords) inside the larynx, and at the same time we expel air from the lungs.

Q2

List the features of the breathing system that (a) keep the airways open, (b) reduce the evaporation of water, (c) protect the lungs from infection.

The trachea branches into two **bronchi**, one to each lung, and these have many branches (see Figure 2, page 59). The smaller branches are called **bronchioles**, themselves repeatedly branched. The smallest branches end in the clusters of alveoli (Figure 6, page 62). The bronchi and the larger bronchioles also have cartilage in their walls, but here the cartilage is in small sections connected by muscle and elastic fibres. The smaller bronchioles have only muscle and elastic fibres, so that these tubes can both expand and contract easily during ventilation.

Inspiration

Breathing movements make the chest expand and draw air into the lungs. This process is called **inspiration**. As the volume of the chest begins to increase, the air pressure inside the lungs starts to decrease. It becomes slightly lower than the atmospheric air pressure outside. This small difference in pressure causes air to rush into the lungs. The air movement is surprisingly rapid and forceful, yet similar small differences in pressure create the strong winds of our weather.

The volume of the chest can be increased in two ways. The chest is separated from the abdomen by a domed sheet rather like a bulging mini-trampoline. This sheet is the **diaphragm**. It is a tough membrane attached by muscles to the inner wall of the chest at the bottom of the ribcage. It completely seals off the chest and lungs from the organs of the abdomen. When the muscles of the diaphragm contract, the dome flattens. The centre of the diaphragm may be lowered by as much as 10 cm, so increasing the chest volume considerably. When we are resting, only a small movement of the diaphragm is needed for us to get enough air into the lungs during each inspiration.

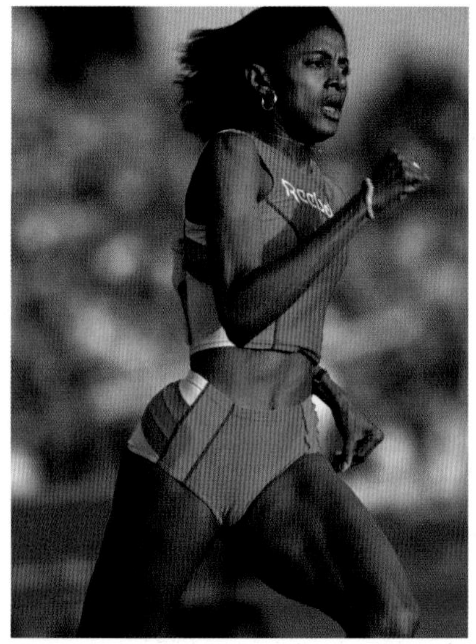

Figure 9 The sprinter is just finishing a 200 m sprint. She now needs to get oxygen into the blood very rapidly in order to restore the reserves used up by her muscles.

When we are more active, our oxygen requirements increase. Then, as well as the diaphragm becoming flatter, we can also move our ribs to produce a larger increase in volume. As Figure 2 (page 59) shows, the ribs are connected to each other by two layers of **intercostal muscles**. During a deep inspiration, the muscles in the outer layer called the external intercostal muscles contract. They pull the whole ribcage upwards and outwards: each rib swings up from the backbone and its front end moves up and out (see Figure 10).

Expiration

At rest, breathing out is mainly due to the lungs recoiling from being stretched. As the external intercostal muscles relax, the elastic fibres round the alveoli shrink and squeeze air out. But when we are exercising it is more important to push air out forcibly. The internal layer of **intercostal muscles** (Figure 2 page 59), which slopes in the opposite direction to the external

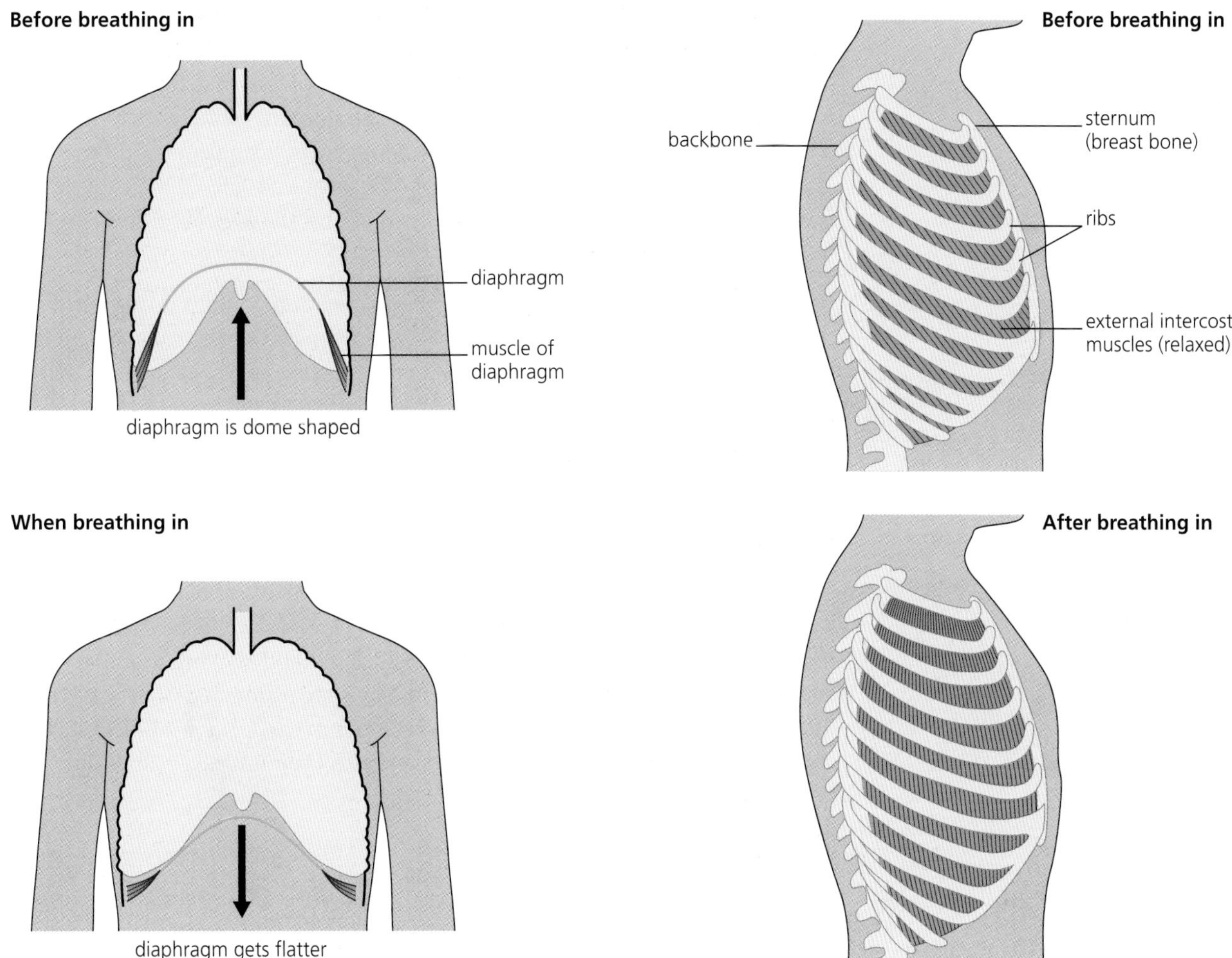

Figure 10 The position of the diaphragm (left) and the ribcage (right), before and after taking a deep breath.

layer, contracts and helps to pull the ribs back down. We may also contract the muscles in the wall of the abdomen. This forces the liver, intestines and stomach upwards against the diaphragm, pushing it back into its domed position.

Why the lungs and chest wall stick together

Together, the movements of the diaphragm and ribs can increase the internal volume of an adult man's chest by as much as 4 litres. The lungs are not actually attached to the chest wall, but both the lungs and the wall are covered by smooth membranes called the **pleural membranes**. Between them is a very thin layer of tissue fluid, so the two membranes stick together by surface tension, just as two wet glass plates will stick to each other. (Try pulling apart two wet microscope slides.) When the chest expands, the lung membrane sticks to the chest wall, forcing the alveoli to open up. As internal air pressure drops below atmospheric pressure, air flows into the alveoli.

As we have seen on page 63, the inner surfaces of the alveoli are also moist. If the alveolar walls were to stick together as the pleural membranes do, breathing would require a very great effort. To prevent this, cells in the alveolar walls secrete a substance called a **surfactant** which consists of phospholipid molecules (see page 44). These form a single layer on the surface film of water, with the hydrophobic fatty acid tails of the molecules sticking into the alveolar cavity. This layer allows the alveoli to open up with little effort.

When a baby is born, its lungs are unexpanded and contain no air. Normally a full-term baby makes strong movements of the chest muscles that draw air into the lungs and open up the moist passages that end in the alveoli. Surfactant helps to minimise the effort the baby needs to make. Loud cries are a good sign that the baby has been successful.

Premature babies, however, have too little or no surfactant. The walls of their alveoli remain stuck together because the baby's breathing movements are not strong enough to overcome surface tension and pull the walls apart. The lungs do not start secreting surfactant until a fetus is about 23 weeks old. It takes about another 10 weeks for enough surfactant to build up and prevent the alveoli from collapsing and sticking together again. Premature babies need help with their breathing and often have to be given artificial ventilation. It is also routine in the UK for medical staff to assist them by passing artificial surfactant into their lungs.

Q3

Use your knowledge of phospholipid structure to explain how the surfactant stops the walls of the alveoli sticking together.

Deep breathing

We do not breathe at a constant rate. When we run, our breathing gets deeper and faster. Look at Figure 11. It shows the changes in the volume of air in a man's lungs when he changes his activities.

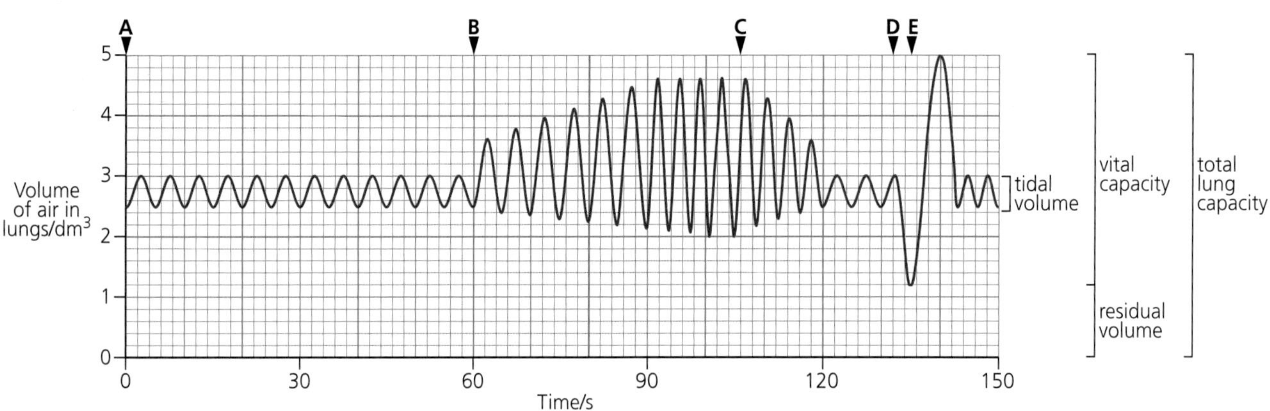

Figure 11 Graph to show the changes in rate and depth of breathing of a man who changes his activities.

- During the period between **A** and **B**, the man is at rest. His breathing is shallow and steady.
- At **B** he starts to exercise and he takes deeper breaths.
- He stops exercising at **C** and his breathing starts to return to its resting state.
- At **D** he breathes out as fully as he can by contracting his abdomen muscles so that the abdominal organs push up against the diaphragm (see page 67). He also uses his internal intercostal muscles to pull down his ribcage as far as possible. This empties his lungs much more than when breathing at rest. That still leaves quite a lot of air in the lungs that cannot be expired. This amount of air is the **residual volume** of his lungs.
- Then at **E**, he breathes in as deeply as he can (his maximum chest expansion).

The volume of air inspired per breath when at rest is the **tidal volume**. Breathing is at a steady rate and the volume taken in is the same each time. Therefore, to work out the volume of air inspired per minute, the **minute ventilation rate**, simply multiply the tidal volume by the number of breaths per minute, as represented by the equation:

$$\text{Minute ventilation rate} = \text{tidal volume} \times \text{number of breaths per minute}$$

Use the graph in Figure 11 to answer the following questions.

(a) What is the tidal volume for the man when he is at rest?
(b) How many breaths per minute does the resting man take?
(c) Calculate the minute ventilation rate of the resting man.
(d) What was the maximum volume of a single breath while exercising?
(e) Calculate the percentage increase for the maximum volume inspired during exercise compared with the resting tidal volume.
(f) The vital capacity is the maximum volume of air that can be inspired after expiring as fully as possible. What is the vital capacity for this man?
(g) What is the total lung capacity, including the residual volume, that cannot be expired?

Interpreting pressure changes during breathing

Look carefully at the two graphs in Figure 12 and make sure that you understand what they show.

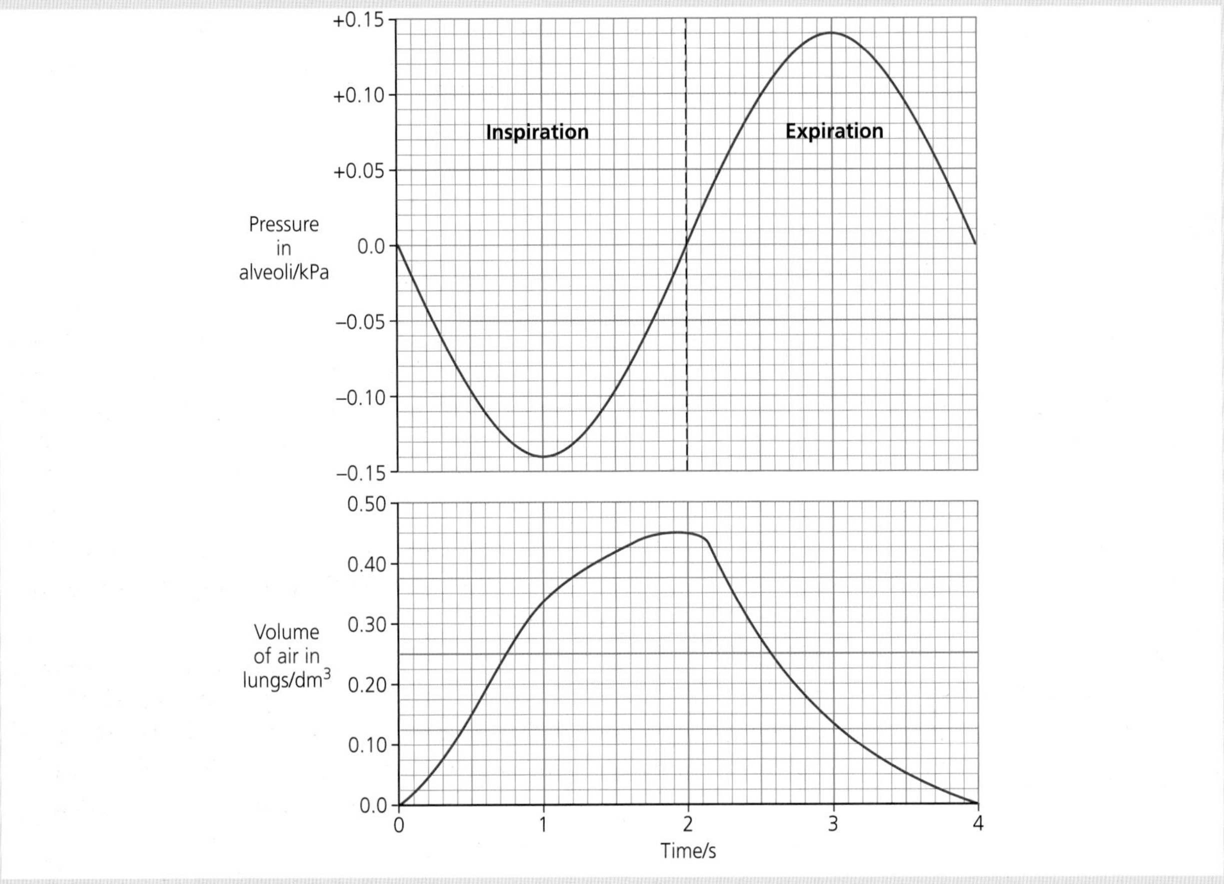

Figure 12 Graphs showing changes in alveolar air pressure and lung volume during inspiration and expiration in an adult man.

- The upper graph shows the changes in pressure in the alveoli during one breath, that is, during both inspiration and expiration. Pressure is measured in kilopascals (kPa). Zero on the *y* axis is when the pressure in the alveoli is the same as the atmospheric pressure outside the body. Atmospheric pressure is normally about 100 kPa, but it varies according to weather conditions.
- The lower graph shows the changes in the volume of the lungs during the same breath. As lung volume increases, pressure falls and air enters the lungs. The volume is measured in cubic decimetres (dm^3). Remember that 1 dm^3 is 1 litre, which equals 1000 cm^3.

1 (a) What is the maximum increase in the volume of the lungs?

(b) Do you think these data were measured when the man was at rest or during exercise? Explain the evidence for your answer.

2 Describe the pattern of change in volume of the lungs during inspiration.

3 Describe the pattern of change in pressure in the alveoli during inspiration.

4 Explain what causes the decrease in pressure in the alveoli at the beginning of inspiration.

5 Explain why the pressure in the alveoli returned to zero at the end of inspiration.

6 Describe the pattern of change in volume in the alveoli during expiration.

7 Describe the pattern of change in pressure in the alveoli during expiration.

8 Explain the changes in pressure and volume during expiration.

9 A chest wound (such as a stab or bullet wound) that allows air into the space between the chest wall and the lungs can prevent normal inspiration, even though breathing movements occur. Suggest an explanation for this.

General principles

Interpreting data from line graphs

- When results of an investigation are in the form of a graph, the horizontal axis, the *x* axis, normally shows the **independent variable**. This is the variable for which the values are selected by the investigator. For example, in Figure 12, time is the independent variable because the investigator has chosen the time intervals at which the pressure and volume were measured.
- The vertical axis, the *y* axis, shows the **dependent variable**, that is, the variable for which the investigator measures values. In Figure 12, these are the pressure and volume.

Taking measurements

- Look at the **scale** on each axis in a graph and its units. Check what each small division of the graph's grid represents. It might be equal to one unit, but it might be two or more units, or one- or two-tenths of a unit, for example. Be careful because examiners do not always use easy scales in exam questions. Candidates often misinterpret awkward scales.
- If there are no small subdivisions on the axis scales, rule a horizontal and a vertical line to find the value of a particular point on a curve. (Remember that the line joining points on a graph is called a '**curve**', even if it appears to be a straight line.)
- Do not forget to include the units in your answer.

Describing patterns and trends

- Describe whether the graph shows the dependent variable increasing, decreasing or staying constant. Describe each significant change in the **gradient** of the curve, and, if relevant, state the value at which the change occurs. Remember to include the units!
- Do not describe every small change if the curve keeps going up and down. Look for the overall patterns of increase or decrease.
- Look at the scales and judge whether a change on the graph is likely to be significant, or whether it might simply be the result of variability in the **accuracy** of measurement. Very small increases or decreases may show that a factor is in fact staying constant.
- One common reason for variability in accuracy in biological investigations is that living things vary a lot. Small differences may simply be the result of minor differences between organisms.
- Before you select intermediate values from a graph, think how the measurements were made and how the graph was plotted. For a smooth curve showing a continuously varying dependent variable, such as rate of an enzyme reaction over time, it is reasonable to assume that values you read from the graph between the plotted points are **valid** measures. But a variable might only be measured at lengthy intervals. If a bird population was counted only once a year in summer, it would not be valid to take a value half way between two plotted points as the winter population size.

Figure 13 People with asthma use an inhaler to keep the airways open and ease breathing.

What is asthma?

Jenny makes the mistake of stroking her friend's cat. She knows that she is allergic to the dust from animal fur and that it quickly causes the lining of her airways to become inflamed and swollen. As a result, she has one of her asthma attacks. As she struggles for breath, it feels as though as her chest is being gripped in a vice. She makes a strange wheezing noise as she breathes.

Fortunately she has her inhaler; she presses the top and a drug is propelled into her lungs that relaxes and opens up her airways. Soon she is able to breathe normally again. Although she finds the attacks a nuisance, Jenny is able to lead an active life, and there is a good chance that she will grow out of them as she gets older.

Asthma affects about 5 million people in the UK and this number appears to be increasing for reasons that are not yet fully understood. Attacks can be triggered by a wide variety of **allergens** (substances that cause allergies) including substances in fur and feathers, pollen, tobacco smoke and the dust mites that scavenge the tiny flakes of skin that we shed all the time, and that build up as dust in our homes. Anxiety and exercise may bring on an attack, but sometimes there is no obvious trigger. Children whose parents or other close relatives suffer from allergies such as hay fever or eczema seem to be more prone to asthma, so it is likely that there is some genetic link.

During an asthma attack:

- The muscle tissue in the walls of the bronchi and bronchioles contracts. This reduces the diameter of the airways.
- The cells in the linings of the walls that secrete mucus go into overdrive, and mucus further obstructs the thinner tubes.
- Other cells, called **mast cells**, react as though the lungs are infected. They produce histamine which makes the linings inflamed and swollen. The blood vessels dilate and become more leaky. This allows white blood cells to escape into the surrounding tissue, where they make the attack response that would occur if bacteria and other invaders were present.

All of these responses restrict the flow of air and make breathing more difficult. Normally, these responses help to stop harmful substances such as smoke getting too deep into the lungs, but in asthmatics the response

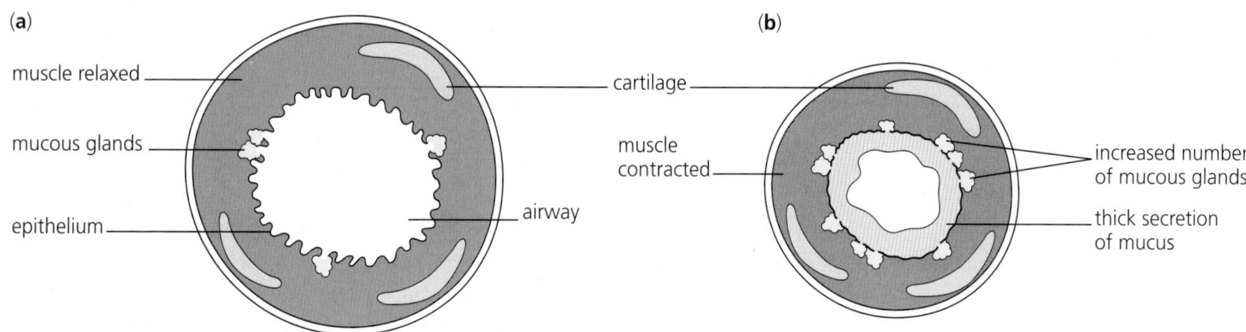

Figure 14 Cross section of the bronchus (a) in a person who does not have asthma and (b) during an attack in an asthma sufferer.

seems to be too sensitive. The dangerous effect is that the volume of air reaching the alveoli and therefore of oxygen getting into the blood is much reduced. In severe cases the victim may start to turn bluish (a condition called **cyanosis**) as the supply of oxygen in the blood to the skin declines. If the oxygen supply to the brain is severely reduced, the person can die. Urgent medical attention is needed if an attack cannot be controlled by an inhaler.

Asthma sufferers can take steps to reduce the chance of exposure to the allergens that trigger an attack. A measure that is often effective is not to keep furry or feathered pets at home. Dust mites thrive in homes with wall-to-wall carpets, so having wooden floors instead can be beneficial. Using bed sheets which mites cannot get through and which are regularly vacuum-cleaned may reduce the problem.

It is very difficult to avoid all allergens completely, so most sufferers need to use the drugs in an inhaler at times. These drugs relax the muscles in the bronchial walls, so that the airways open up again. Other drugs reduce the inflammation. Adults with chronic asthma may suffer from permanent damage to the bronchi and bronchiole walls. They may need to take a daily dose of steroid drugs to prevent asthma attacks. However, many people with asthma lead fully active lives. For example, in the 1984 Olympic Games, the American swimmer Nancy Hogshead won three gold medals and a silver, despite having asthma.

Q5

Suggest what causes the wheezing noise when a person suffers from an asthma attack.

Fibrosis – a poor reward for a miner

Albert has difficulty climbing stairs. Every third step, he has to pause to catch his breath. For over 30 years he worked as a coal miner. Despite precautions, the atmosphere in the mine was often full of particles of coal and rock dust. As particles accumulated deep in his lungs, the lung tissues gradually became stiff, and he developed a condition called pulmonary ***fibrosis*** *which severely limits his capacity to lead an active life.*

Figure 15 The dust inhaled by miners permanently damages the lining of the lungs. This damage restricts oxygen intake and consequently the ability of a person to be active.

Mining and quarrying have always been dangerous occupations because they produce so much fine dust. Mucus generally traps most tiny particles that reach the bronchi and bronchioles, and cilia sweep out the mucus (see Figure 8 on page 65). But dust-laden air is drawn into the alveoli where there are no cilia to sweep particles back out.

However, there are large cells in the alveoli called **macrophages** that can engulf bacteria and foreign particles such as dust. They can move into the connective tissue round alveoli (see Figure 7 on page 63) from the inner surface of alveoli by squeezing between the cells of the alveolar walls. They wrap round the particles and then enter the lymph system (see page 160). In this way they remove bacteria and particles from the lungs.

But when there are very large amounts of dust, many of the macrophages stay in the connective tissue between the alveoli. Over the years, they stimulate the formation of fibrous tissue that develops into hard lumps in the connective tissue. It is these fibrous nodules that make Albert's lungs stiff. They are no longer able to expand normally when he breathes in, and they do not collapse fully to expel air when he breathes out. Consequently his breathing is very shallow.

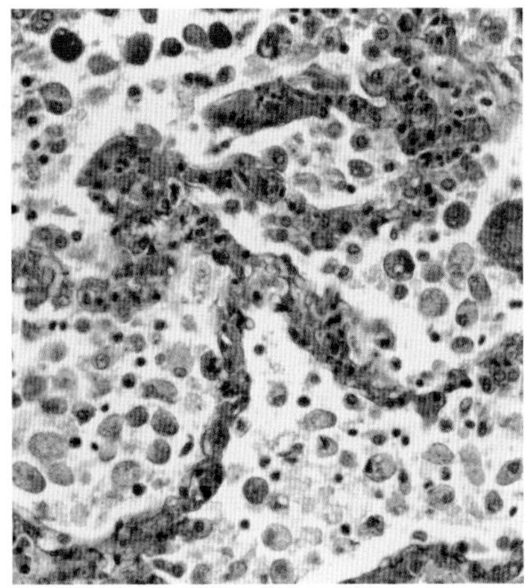

Figure 16 A section of a lung from someone suffering from pulmonary fibrosis. The alveolar walls (darker bands) are thickened by fibrous tissue that stiffens them, so they are limited in their ability to expand and take air in, and to recoil and expel air. The alveoli can gradually fill up with the bacteria and dust particles seen in this photograph.

Q6

Explain how fibrous tissue in the lungs makes activity such as climbing stairs difficult.

Q7

Explain how damage to the alveoli makes it difficult for a person with emphysema to obtain enough oxygen.

Q8

Explain how enzymes break down the walls of the alveoli.

Emphysema – a smoker's reward

People who have been heavy smokers since their teenage years may, by their forties, have developed **emphysema.** This is a condition in which their airways have been so damaged by the irritating effect of cigarette smoke that they must regularly breathe oxygen-rich air from a machine in order to carry on with daily activities. Even so, they can be severely restricted in what they are able to do.

Lung cancer is a well-known result of smoking. However, almost as many deaths result from the physical damage that tobacco smoke causes to lung tissue. One effect of smoke is to stimulate white blood cells to release protein-digesting enzymes that slowly break down the walls of many of the alveoli, leaving large spaces in the lungs. One of these enzymes targets the elastic tissue in the lungs. Loss of elasticity reduces the ability of the lungs to recoil after breathing in – the person can no longer breathe out effectively.

Compare the photographs of lung tissue in Figure 17. You can see that there are many clear spaces where the walls of the alveoli have broken down. This is the effect of emphysema.

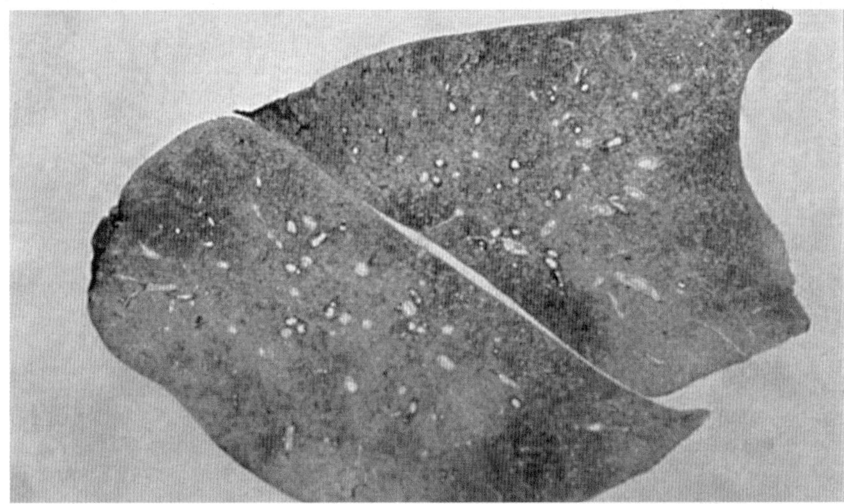

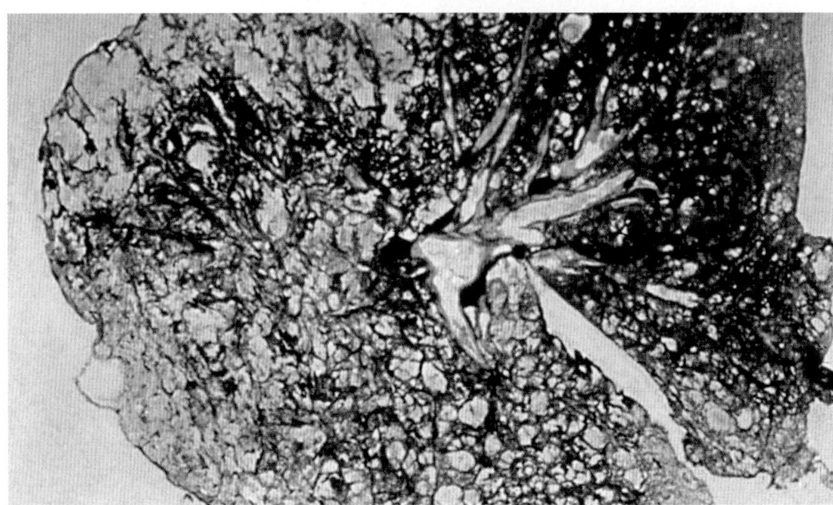

Figure 17 Top: healthy lung tissue. Bottom: lung tissue showing emphysema.

Tuberculosis

Each year about 9 million people worldwide are infected with the bacterium that causes **tuberculosis**, better known simply as TB. In 2006, over one and a half million died of the disease, even though there are drugs that can provide effective treatment. The numbers have been increasing in recent years because the disease is associated with overcrowded living conditions and with HIV infection, which are both on the increase.

In many parts of Africa and Asia in particular, large numbers of people have moved from rural areas into slums in urban areas where living space is very restricted and facilities such as the provision of clean water and sewage disposal are limited. Frequently there is very little health care, and those who do contract TB cannot afford the drugs to cure it. The damaging effect of HIV on the immune system greatly increases the susceptibility of victims to TB infection. For many of those who develop AIDS, TB is the main cause of death.

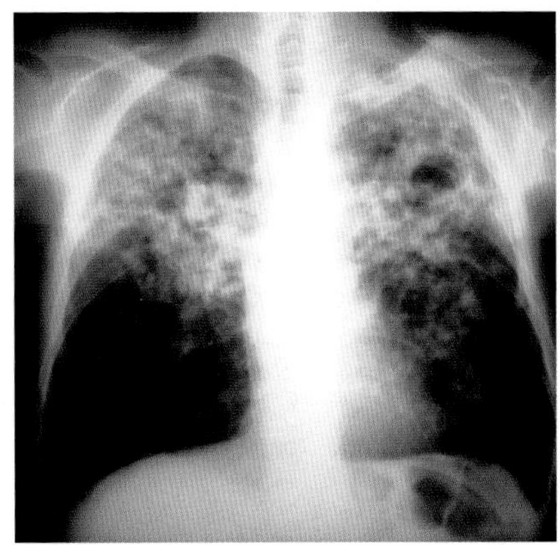

Figure 18 X-ray of a lung showing tubercles caused by infection by the tuberculosis bacterium.

The commonest way in which TB is spread is by sneezing and coughing. The bacteria are sprayed out in tiny droplets that others can breathe in. The bacteria multiply in the lung tissues, producing small lumps, rather like little boils. It is these lumps, called tubercles, that give the disease its name. In most healthy adults the immune system responds to the infection and the bacteria are killed. It is possible for victims to suffer only from a short fever, similar to a mild dose of flu, and be unaware that they have been infected. The damaged tissue leaves scars, which give the lungs a grainy appearance on an X-ray.

However, tuberculosis bacteria are unusually difficult to kill, and in many people they remain in a dormant state inside cells. Months, or even years, later they may start to grow and multiply again, especially when the person is under stress or has a weakened immune system. As they spread through the lungs they create cavities, rather like emphysema, and parts of the lungs may collapse. Fluid collects in the lungs and breathing becomes difficult. Common symptoms are coughing, often with blood in the sputum, chest pain, fever and loss of appetite. If untreated, a victim becomes weak, loses weight and gradually wastes away. The illness used to be called 'consumption' because the muscles and other body tissues appear to be consumed – eaten away.

Before antibiotic drugs to treat TB became available, sufferers were often isolated in hospitals in country areas where the clean air was assumed to help cure the disease. Because of a vaccination programme, tuberculosis is relatively uncommon in Britain. Each year there are only about 8000 cases and fewer than 400 deaths. However, health officials are concerned that in recent years TB is becoming more common again.

It had been hoped that with a combination of vaccination and drug treatments the disease would soon be more or less eradicated. The BCG vaccine that was used regularly to immunise children is no longer found to be effective. The vaccine contains live TB bacteria from a weak strain that is harmless and does not actually cause tuberculosis. Because this strain has many of the same proteins as the bacteria that do cause TB, it should stimulate the immune system to make antibodies and provide long-term

Q9

Explain how the fluid in the lungs would affect a person suffering from tuberculosis.

Q10

Suggest why people with TB often cough up blood.

immunity against the disease (see page 103). It now appears that in many people the immune system destroys the bacteria in the vaccine *before* the immune memory is formed. Therefore an increasingly large proportion of the population is now liable to be infected by TB bacteria.

Of even greater concern is the discovery of strains of TB bacteria that are resistant to most, or even all, of the antibiotic drugs currently used to cure the disease. You will find out more about resistance to the antibiotics used to treat TB in Chapter 11.

Smoking kills

It is estimated that each year in the UK, about 115 000 people die early due to their smoking habit. Of these, about 28 000 die from lung cancer, and over 30 000 die from other chronic lung diseases such as emphysema and bronchitis. Smoking accounts for between 80% and 90% of deaths from lung diseases. On average, of those who continue to smoke regularly from their teenage years, about a quarter die prematurely in middle age, 20 years before the normal life expectancy.

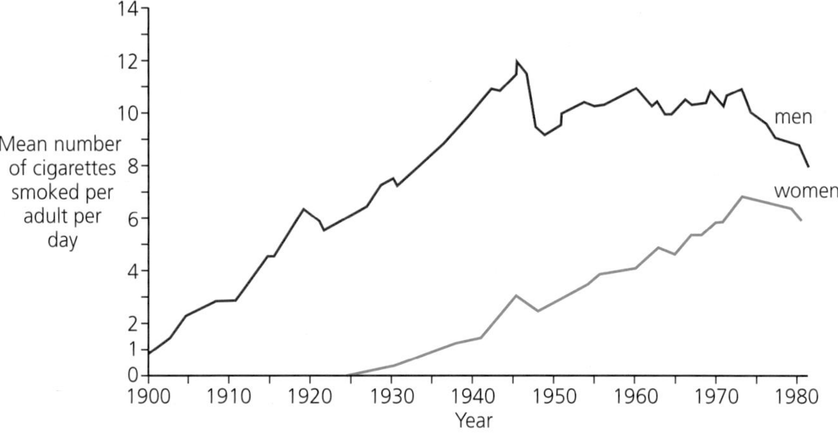

Figure 19 Graph of cigarette consumption by men and women in the UK from 1900–1980.

So, what is the evidence for the link between smoking and disease? Tobacco was introduced into Britain over 400 years ago. It was another 300 years before smoking cigarettes began to be both popular and affordable. By the 1930s, doctors were beginning to suggest that smoking might be damaging to health as they were seeing greatly increased numbers of patients suffering from lung cancer. Their concerns did not affect the smoking behaviour of the general public. The graph in Figure 19 shows how the consumption of cigarettes in the UK grew during the twentieth century.

The graph in Figure 20 shows the changes in the number of deaths from lung cancer up to 1960 compared with cancers of other organs.

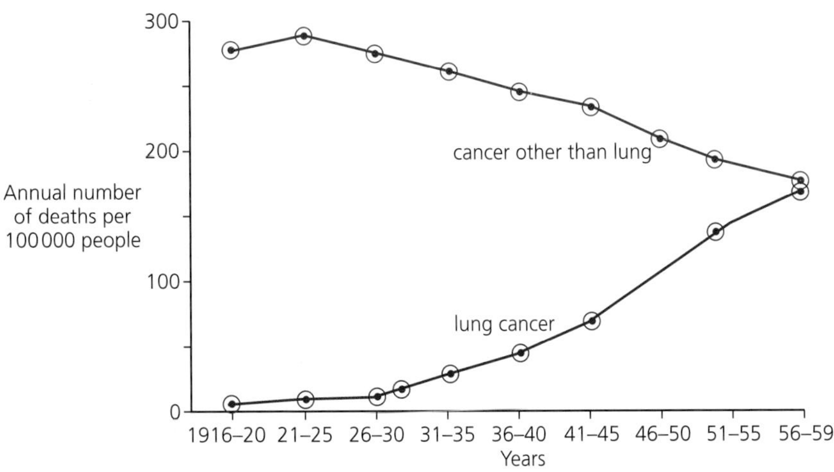

Figure 20 Death rates from cigarette lung cancer and other cancers between 1916 and 1959.

Q11

Look at the curve in Figure 19 for the number of cigarettes smoked by women. Explain how you would expect the data for deaths from lung cancer in women to give evidence supporting the hypothesis that smoking is a cause of lung cancer.

Q12

As well as deaths from lung cancer, Figure 20 shows the number of deaths from other cancers. How do these data support the hypothesis that smoking causes lung cancer?

Look at Figure 19. Notice that the number of cigarettes smoked by men rises steadily from 1900. How does this compare with the number of deaths from lung cancer, shown in Figure 20? This also rises, but the rise only becomes steep after about 1930. Then, both the number of cigarettes smoked and the number of lung cancer deaths go up steeply, so there is a **positive correlation** (see page 80) between them.

How could the delay in the rise in lung cancer deaths be explained? Bear in mind that cancer develops only slowly, so it may be 20 years or more before smokers start to show signs of the disease and die.

It is important to note that this positive correlation could not prove that smoking causes lung cancer. Many other factors were also increasing over the same period (such as the number of cars), and it was possible that one of these factors could explain the increase in lung cancer. The correlation did, however, provide one piece of evidence that supported the hypothesis and justified further research.

Much more evidence was needed to prove that smoking really does cause lung cancer. In 1950, two epidemiologists, Richard Doll and Austin Hill, published the results of a study of patients in four hospitals in the UK. Two groups of patients were selected – those who were suffering from lung cancer and those who had been admitted to hospital for other conditions. The patients were questioned about their smoking habits. They were, for example, asked whether they were regular smokers or had given up smoking, and about their daily consumption of cigarettes. Doll and Hill showed that a higher proportion of the lung cancer patients than the control group were regular smokers. Although other studies were showing similar results, they were still not considered to be absolute proof of a link between smoking and lung cancer. Critics suggested that some unknown factor might make people both more likely to take up smoking and to be susceptible to lung cancer without smoking causing the cancer. The research was also criticised on the grounds that the answers to questions about past smoking habits might be unreliable, either due to inaccurate memory or deliberate fibbing.

In 1951, Doll and Hill set about obtaining data that would be more convincing. Instead of checking the past history of people who already had lung cancer, they decided to select a group of healthy people and monitor who developed the disease. They chose British doctors as their subjects. Perhaps surprisingly, many doctors were smokers at the time. Doll and Hill reckoned that doctors would be more honest and reliable in recording their smoking habits. It was also easy to keep track of doctors because they have to be registered with the Medical Council. In all, the smoking habits and death rate of over 34 000 doctors were recorded for the next 50 years.

Analysing the evidence of the study by Doll and Hill

Q13

Use the graph in Figure 21 to determine the percentage of smokers and non-smokers surviving at ages 60, 70 and 80.

Q14

For each of these ages, calculate the difference in the percentage surviving.

Q15

By approximately how many years was the average lifespan reduced in smokers?

The graph in Figure 21 shows one set of results from this investigation. It shows the percentage of smoking and non-smoking doctors who survived to various ages over the 50 years of the study which ended in 2001. The smoking group was all those doctors who continued to smoke throughout the investigation, whereas the non-smoking group were those who had never smoked.

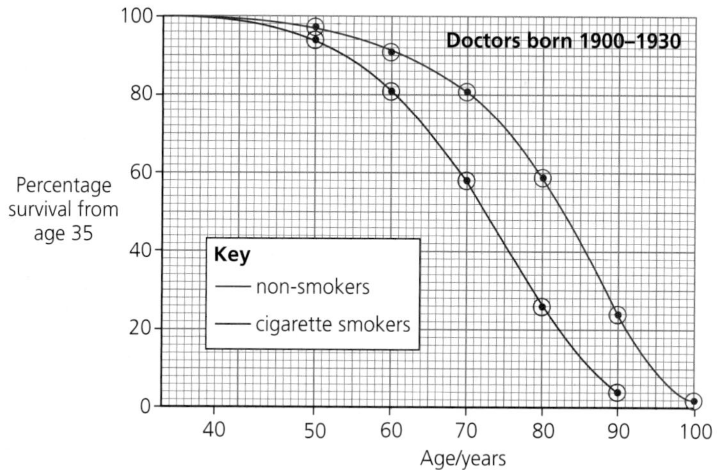

Figure 21 Graph showing the percentage of smoking and non-smoking doctors surviving at each decade of age until age 100.

Interpreting data relating to the effects of smoking and pollution

Collecting the evidence

Researchers investigating the effects of smoking or other pollution cannot carry out controlled experiments on people. It is just not ethically acceptable, for example, to select randomly two groups of people and make one group smoke 20 cigarettes a day for 10 years, while banning the control group from smoking altogether. Evidence must be based on people who were exposed to smoking, or another pollutant, and then comparing them with others who were not exposed.

In **retrospective studies** (collecting data from the past), researchers select groups of people who have already developed a disease such as lung cancer. They then question the people about their past experiences and look for common factors. They may also compare their experiences with the experiences of a control group who do not have the disease being studied. These studies can be unreliable because people may have forgotten details such as how long they have smoked, or they may deliberately deceive or exaggerate.

In **prospective studies** (collecting data as it accumulates), researchers select groups and then follow what happens to them over a period of years. This makes it easier for the researchers to keep track of changes, such as changes in smoking habits, as long as frequent checks are made. The researchers can also keep records of a wider range of possible variables. However, this adds to the time it takes to get useful results.

General principles

Interpreting the results of studies on health risks

You will understand that there are often great difficulties in collecting data on health risks:

- There are often many factors involved.
- Controlled experiments in which one variable only is studied cannot be carried out on people for ethical reasons.
- It is hard to find enough people with similar lifestyles to act as matched control groups.
- It is often several years before the effects of health risks become apparent, and following up groups of people for long periods is difficult and expensive.
- Data obtained by asking people about their past is often unreliable.

When looking at the results of a health risk study, you need to consider the following:

- Find out the number of people who were investigated. You can have more confidence in the evidence if a large number of people were involved than if the number was small.
- Identify the different levels of exposure to the health risk that were investigated, for example, the number of cigarettes smoked per day.
- Assess whether the control group is well matched with the group exposed to the factor being tested. They should, for example, come from similar backgrounds, be of similar ages and so on.
- Assess whether the differences between the results for the two groups are sufficiently large to indicate that the factor which is thought to be a health risk is indeed a risk.
- Find out whether tests have been done to check that the differences are statistically significant.

If the incidence of the disease or the mortality rate is given, calculate the **relative risk**; for example, calculate the *difference in the percentages* of the two groups that develop the disease.

The following terms are often used in investigations of the causes of diseases.

- **Incidence**. The incidence of a disease is the number of cases that occur in a particular group of people in a given time, such as the number of smokers that develop lung cancer in a year. To make it easy to compare how common a disease is in different groups, the incidence is calculated as the number of cases in a standard size of group, for example, number of cases of lung cancer per 1000 smokers per year. When looking for possible effects of pollution on asthma, researchers might compare the incidence of asthma in children living in urban areas with those in rural areas.
- **Mortality rate**. The mortality rate is the number of deaths per number of the population per year from a particular disease or other cause, such as road accidents. A rate of 2.5 lung cancer deaths per 1000 smokers would mean that, out of 10 000 smokers, on average 25 died each year.

- **Correlation**. A correlation is an association between two variables. If measurements of both variables increase, there is a positive correlation. For example, there is a well-established correlation between the number of cigarettes smoked per day and the incidence of lung cancer. It is important to note that a positive correlation is *not* proof that one factor is the cause of another. You might find a correlation between baldness and wearing a hat, but that would not mean that wearing a hat causes baldness.
- **Statistically significant**. Investigations of the effects of smoking, pollution, drugs or diet on people never give absolutely certain results. You do not find, for example, that everyone who smokes 30 cigarettes a day for 5 years gets lung cancer. People are highly variable and do not always behave consistently. Researchers carry out statistical tests on their results to find out whether it is likely that that they have discovered a genuine effect. These tests check how likely it is that a difference, for example, between smokers and non-smokers, is just due to chance. This will depend on the number of people tested and the size of the differences in results for the two groups. The results are usually considered to be statistically significant if they show a 95% probability that the difference is real. Even so, this is not absolute proof. There is still a 1 in 20 probability that these particular results were due to chance.
- **Risk factor**. A risk factor is something, such as smoking, that correlates with an increased chance of suffering from a particular disease or condition. The relative risk can be calculated by finding the ratio between the incidence of the disease in those exposed to the factor and the incidence in those not exposed. For example, if the incidence of a lung disease in smokers is 30 cases per 1000 per year and in non-smokers it is 10 cases, the relative risk is 3.0, which means that smokers are 3 times more likely to develop the disease.

Causes of death amongst male doctors

Table 2 Mortality rate of male doctors per 1000 per year.

Cause of death	Mortality rate of male doctors per 1000 per year				
	Never smoked	Given up smoking	Still smoking/cigarettes per day		
			1–14	15–24	25 or more
Lung cancer	0.17	0.68	1.31	2.33	4.17
Cancer of mouth, throat, gullet	0.09	0.26	0.36	0.47	1.06
Other cancers	3.34	3.72	4.21	4.67	5.38
Other chronic lung disease, e.g. emphysema	0.11	0.64	1.04	1.41	2.61
Heart disease	6.19	7.61	9.10	10.07	11.11

Table 2 shows more of the results of the Doll and Hill study of doctors. The mortality rate is the average number of deaths per year per 1000 doctors from each cause. A mortality rate of 2.0 means that, on average, two doctors in every thousand died each year. Out of 30 000 doctors, this would mean a total of 60 deaths. However, in this study the rates were calculated separately for each 5-year age group, for example for doctors aged 55 to 59. The rates have then been adjusted because the number of deaths at the younger age groups is much lower than in the older groups. The figures therefore indicate the effect of each cause on both the overall death rate per 1000 doctors and the age of death.

Study the data in the table.

1 What do the data show about the effect of smoking on mortality from lung cancer?

2 What do the data show about the effect of smoking on the other causes of death shown in the table?

3 For each cause of death, calculate by how much the risk is increased by smoking 25 cigarettes a day compared with not smoking at all.

4 Describe the effects of giving up smoking.

5 Describe and explain the results for heart disease.

Chapter 4

The heart and heart disease

The man in the photograph suffered a serious heart attack. Feeling tired after a morning digging his garden, he started to feel faint. He had a severe pain in his chest, and he became breathless and felt sick. Fortunately, an ambulance reached him within minutes, and paramedics were able to get his heart beating again. He was one of the lucky ones who survived and was soon on the way to recovery.

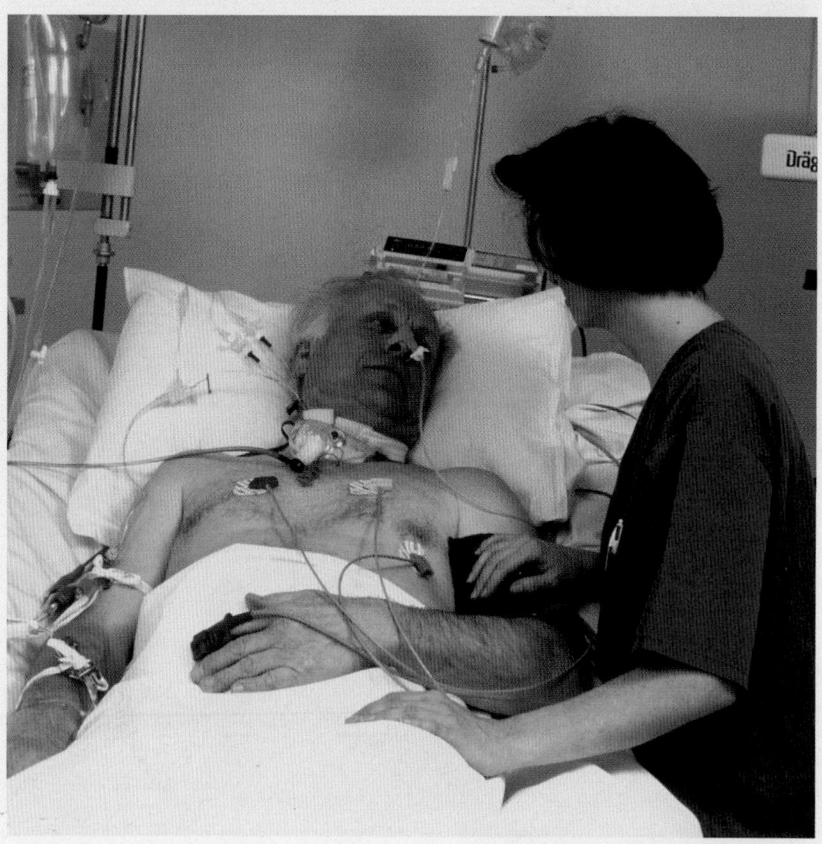

▲ **Figure 1** A person who has had a heart attack is first treated in intensive care.

Diseases of the heart and blood vessels are by far the commonest causes of death in the UK. More than one in three people die from what doctors call cardiovascular disease. That's over 200 000 deaths each year in the UK. Over 60% of these people die of disease of the heart itself, properly known as coronary heart disease (CHD). The coronary arteries are the vessels that supply blood to the heart muscle. When a person has a heart attack, a clot in a coronary artery stops blood from reaching part of the heart muscle, which then stops contracting.

Since everyone will die of something eventually, perhaps it's not surprising that failure of one of the major organs very commonly causes death. However, it is estimated that about a third of the deaths from heart disease occur prematurely, before the average lifespan of the rest of the population. There are also large numbers who recover from a heart attack, but whose activities are seriously restricted, at least for a time.

It was first suggested in the 1960s that aspirin might help to prevent heart attacks when it was discovered that aspirin helps to stop blood clots. This is because aspirin interferes with the action of blood platelets. The platelets are cell fragments that play an important role in blood clotting. Aspirin stops the platelets from sticking together and so reduces the chance that clots will block the vessels taking blood to the heart muscle.

At the time, most doctors were very scornful of the idea that such a cheap and common drug as aspirin could prevent heart attacks. Nevertheless, the Medical Research Council tested the idea, and in 1969 it set up a trial in Cardiff. The researchers decided to test the effect of giving a daily dose of aspirin to men who had recently recovered from a heart attack. One group of the men took a daily pill containing 300 mg of aspirin. The others, the control group, took a dummy pill containing no aspirin. The patients in each group were selected randomly, so neither the doctors nor the patients knew who was being treated with aspirin. Over 1200 men were studied, but only the coded records of the researchers enabled them to trace which of the men had taken the aspirin. After treatment for a year, 12% fewer of the men taking the aspirin had died of another heart attack compared with the control group. However, the difference between deaths in the two groups was not enough for the results to be statistically significant. This one study had not given convincing evidence for doctors to start using aspirin as a regular part of the treatment for heart attack victims.

However, the research continued. Evidence was gathered from larger numbers, for longer times after the heart attack, from women as well as men, for different age groups and with different doses of aspirin. The results from these studies were collected and analysed. All showed that treatment with aspirin gave some benefit. In fact, the combined results of about 20 years of studies involved large enough numbers to show that aspirin gave a significant advantage after a first heart attack. During these studies, compared with the control groups, on average 34% fewer of the patients taking a daily dose of aspirin died.

Trialling aspirin as a treatment to prevent heart attacks

It is now common for people who have had a heart attack to take aspirin. The evidence shows that this simple treatment prevents, or at least delays, many thousands of deaths a year. At the same time, this example illustrates some of the difficulties of developing new treatments in medicine. People vary enormously and respond differently to drugs and other treatments. Trial results rarely show absolutely clear-cut benefits, and some people may have unexpected side effects.

1 The men gave permission to take part in the first trial, but they could not choose to receive the treatment that might help to save their lives.

(a) Do you think they should have been allowed to choose?

(b) How might the results of the trial have been affected if they had been able to choose?

2 How should dummy pills be made in order to make sure the results are reliable?

3 Why do you think the doctors were not told which patients were getting the aspirin?

Aspirin can have side effects. For example, if a person also develops a stomach ulcer, it may bleed excessively because the aspirin reduces clotting. Yet the improvements in the survival rate after a heart attack show that the benefits from aspirin treatment are much greater than the risks from this side effect. However, because the benefits of aspirin were publicised, some people started taking aspirin to prevent a heart attack, even though they had never either suffered from one or shown signs of having one.

4 Suggest what advice could be given to the public and to doctors about this use of aspirin.

The function of the heart

The heart is the most obviously active organ in the human body. It is constantly busy, even during sleep. When the heart stops beating we die. Traditionally the heart was thought to be the seat of our emotions – bravery, love, passion, excitement. This is not surprising since we can feel the changes in our heartbeat when we are frightened or get excited.

In reality, the function of the heart is relatively simple – to pump the blood round the body, forcing it to all parts of the body. Strictly, the human heart is two pumps since it has two halves. One half pumps blood to the lungs where it is oxygenated. The oxygenated blood returns to the other half of the heart and is then pumped to all the other organs.

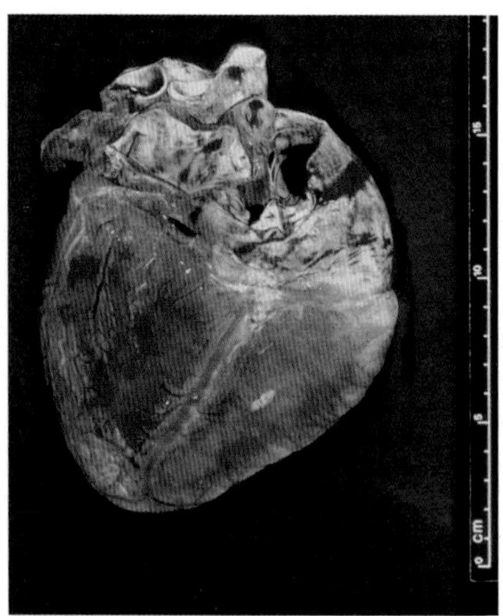

▲ **Figure 2** The outside of the heart.

The blood transports both oxygen and the glucose required for respiration. When the heart stops beating, the whole of the body is deprived of oxygen and fuel. Cells do not have reserves of oxygen. The brain cells are particularly sensitive to a shortage of oxygen. Within about five minutes, brain cells will start to die. Rapid first aid to restart the heart is essential if brain damage is to be avoided.

The rate and strength of the heartbeat must be able to change according to the body's requirements. When we are at rest, the heart can potter along at a steady 60 to 70 beats per minute. But during exercise, when the muscles require a much greater supply of oxygen, the rate of heartbeat may more than double. In this chapter we will look at the structure and functions of the different parts of the heart, as well as the control system that varies the rate of heartbeat. We will also explain the causes of heart attacks.

The heart as a pump

Look at the diagram of the heart in Figure 3. Remember that it is the view from the front of a person, so you see the right side of the heart on the left of the diagram.

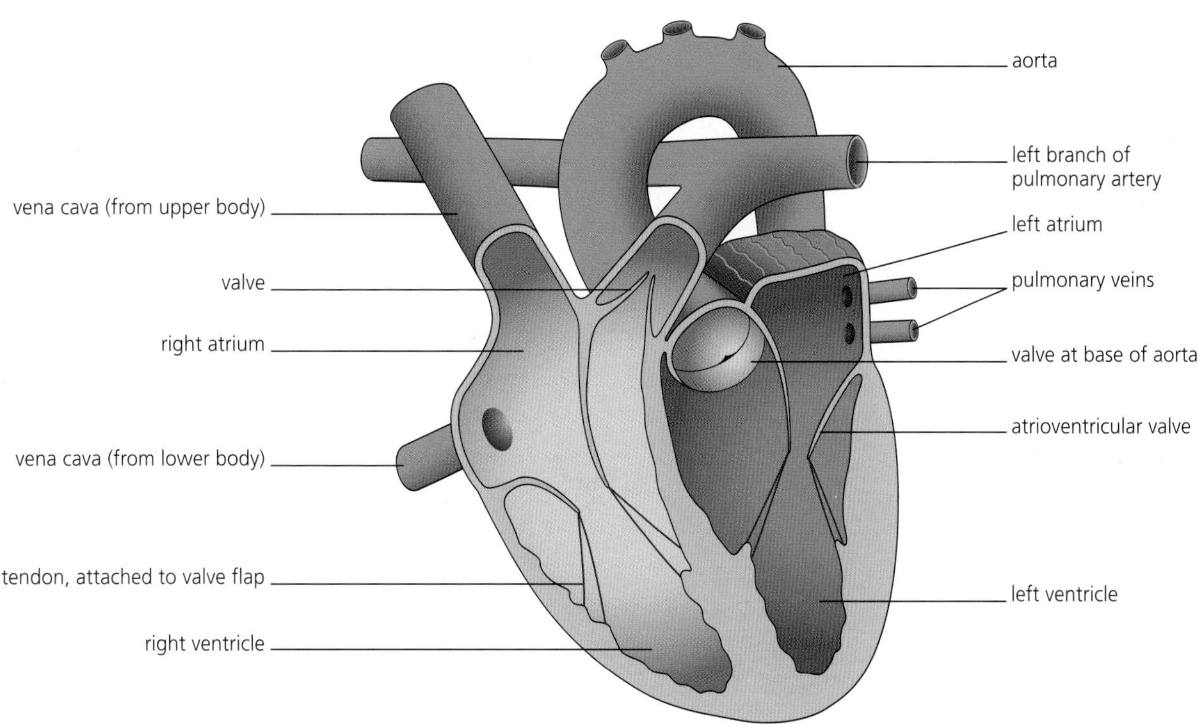

▲ **Figure 3** A vertical section through the human heart.

Q1

You can see that the muscular walls of the ventricles are much thicker than the walls of the atria. Why do you think the ventricles have thick walls?

Q2

The walls of the left ventricle are thicker than the walls of the right ventricle. Suggest an advantage of this.

Q3

The walls of the atria are quite thin. Suggest why the atria only have thin walls.

Notice that the heart has two halves, separated by a wall down the middle. Each half has two sections called chambers. The lower chambers are the **ventricles**. The right ventricle pumps blood to the lungs, and the left ventricle pumps it to the rest of the body. The two upper chambers are the **atria** (singular: atrium). The blood that returns from the lungs and the other parts of the body enters the atria. It is the job of the atria to pump this blood into the ventricles.

Between the atrium and the ventricle on each side is a **valve**, called an atrioventricular valve. The valve that separates each atrium from its ventricle has flaps made of thin but tough tissue. The atrium muscles relax and the atrium fills with blood from the vena cava. Its muscles then contract. This pushes the flaps down, and blood flows into the emptied ventricle which has relaxed muscles. Then, when the ventricle muscles contract, the flaps are pushed together. This stops blood from flowing back from the ventricle into the atrium.

In Figure 3, you can see that thin tendons join the edges of the valve flaps to the wall of each ventricle. These tendons are like tough pieces of string and do not stretch. The function of the tendons is to ensure that blood does not flow back into the atrium through the valve.

Q4

Suggest how the tendons prevent backflow when the ventricle contracts.

When the ventricles contract, blood is forced from the ventricles into large blood vessels that pass out of the top of the heart. From the left ventricle, blood enters the **aorta**. Outside the heart, the aorta has branches to the head, arms, intestines, legs, and so on. From the right ventricle, the **pulmonary artery** has a branch to each lung. Notice that there is a valve at the lower end of both the aorta and the pulmonary artery. These valves stop blood from flowing back into the ventricles when the ventricle muscles relax and the ventricles start to open up again.

Blood returns to the heart through large veins. The **pulmonary veins** return blood from the lungs to the left atrium. Veins called **vena cavae** bring blood from the upper and lower parts of the body into the right atrium.

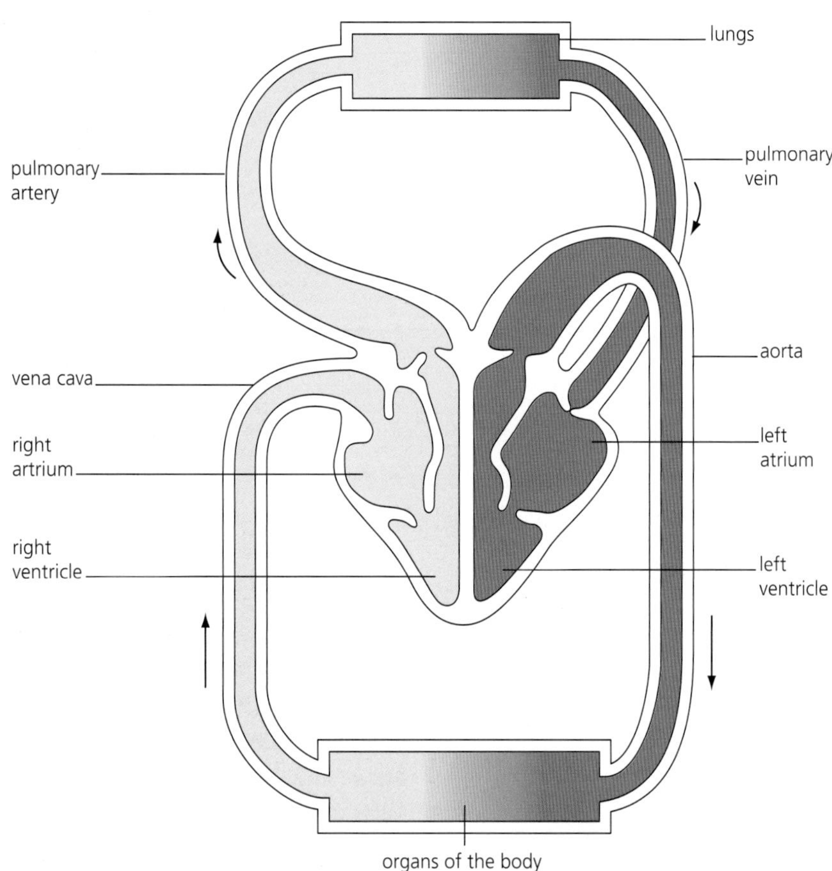

▲ **Figure 4** The human double circulation.

Blood is pumped from the left ventricle to organs of the body where it becomes deoxygenated. The blood returns to the right atrium. It then passes into the right ventricle which pumps it to the lungs where it is re-oxygenated. It returns to the left atrium and then reaches the left ventricle again.

The cardiac cycle

Since you are reading this, you must be alive and your heart must be beating. To confirm this, gently press a fingertip on your neck just to one side of your windpipe. Here, each time the heart beats, you should feel the pulse caused by the surge of blood through one of the arteries that goes to your head. If you are relaxed, you will feel a pulse roughly every second. The time between each pulse represents the length of the cardiac cycle.

The **cardiac cycle** is the sequence of stages that happens during one heartbeat. The term for a stage in the cardiac cycle when the heart muscles are contracting is **systole**. The relaxation stage is called **diastole**. Therefore, the three stages shown in Figure 5 are atrial systole, ventricular systole and diastole.

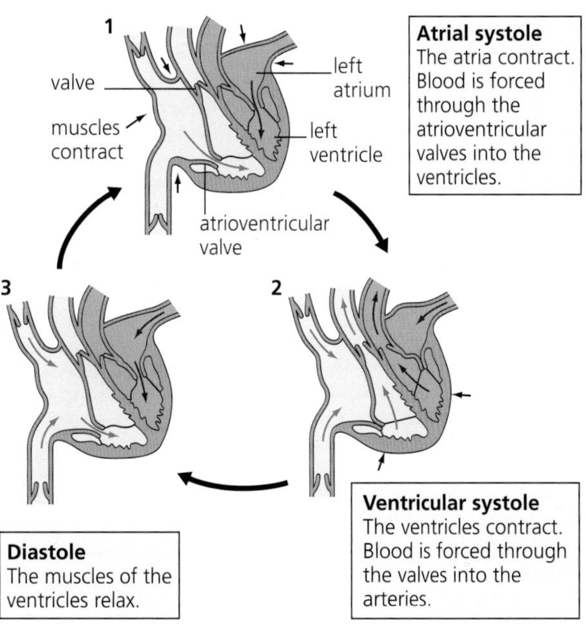
1
valve
muscles contract
left atrium
left ventricle
atrioventricular valve
Atrial systole
The atria contract. Blood is forced through the atrioventricular valves into the ventricles.
2
Ventricular systole
The ventricles contract. Blood is forced through the valves into the arteries.
3
Diastole
The muscles of the ventricles relax.

▸ **Figure 5** The three stages in the cardiac cycle. The atria contract (atrial systole), the ventricles contract (ventricular systole), and finally the ventricles relax (diastole).

Contraction of the muscles in the walls of the ventricles creates the pressure that circulates the blood. The left and right ventricles contract at the same time. As the ventricles contract they build up a high pressure which forces open the valves at the base of the aorta and the pulmonary artery and drives blood out through these vessels.

After passing round the lungs and the rest of the body, the blood flows back into the atria of the heart at a much lower pressure. When the blood flows back in, the muscular walls of the heart are relaxed, so even at low pressure the returning blood expands the relatively thin walls of the atria. As the atria fill, some blood does pass through the valves into the ventricles. However, as the atria fill up, the muscles in their walls contract. This forces the valves open and pushes the blood quickly into the ventricles.

Each time the heart beats, the left ventricle squirts out the same volume of blood as the right ventricle. This may seem surprising, since the lungs are much nearer and smaller than the rest of the body, but otherwise the continuous circulation would not be maintained. If the right ventricle pumped out less blood each time, there would be less returning to the left atrium and therefore less for the left ventricle to pump to the body. The left ventricle would soon run out of blood to send to the body.

Analysing the pressure changes in the heart during the cardiac cycle

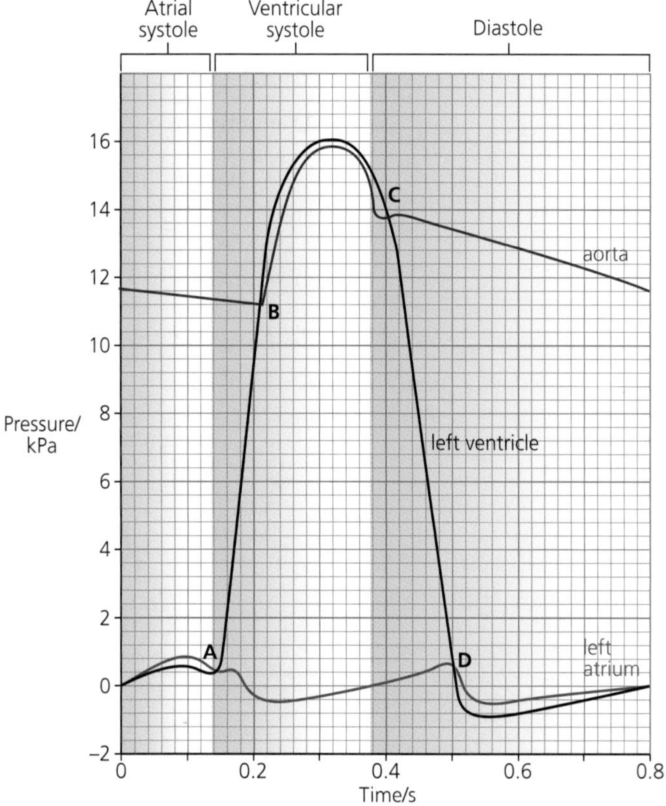

▸ **Figure 6** A graph showing changes in pressure during one cardiac cycle for the left atrium and left ventricle and the aorta.

The graph in Figure 6 shows the changes in pressure that occur in the left side of the heart and in the aorta during one cardiac cycle. Let us look first at the curve showing pressure in the left ventricle. Key points on the curve are labelled with the letters **A** to **D**.

- Notice that at the start of atrial systole the pressure in the left ventricle is more or less 0 kPa. At this time the muscles in the walls of the ventricle are relaxed and therefore not putting any pressure on the blood. During atrial systole, the pressure rises slightly as the left atrium contracts and pushes blood into the ventricle.
- At point **A**, the start of ventricular systole, the ventricle walls contract strongly and the pressure shoots up. The atrioventricular valve is forced shut, preventing blood from being pushed back into the atrium.
- At **B**, the pressure in the ventricle becomes the same as the pressure in the aorta. As soon as the pressure exceeds the pressure in the aorta, the valve at the base of the aorta is forced open and blood is pushed into the aorta.
- By **C**, the ventricle has been emptied of blood. The muscles in the ventricle wall relax, and pressure in the ventricle falls back to zero.
- At **D**, for a short time there is a slight negative pressure as the ventricle expands and its internal volume increases.

Remember that one cardiac cycle follows another in a continuous process. There is never a gap between cycles, so blood immediately starts to flow into the expanding ventricles from the atria because the pressure in the atria is now greater than the pressure in the empty, expanding ventricles. This in turn causes blood to flow into the atria from the veins. The pressure in the ventricles rises again as they fill.

Analysing pressure changes in the left atrium and the aorta

Now see if you can analyse the curves for the left atrial and aortic pressures shown in Figure 6.

Try to answer the questions in blue before you study the answers.

- Describe and explain what happens to the pressure in the atrium between the start of the cycle and **A**.

  The pressure rises as the muscles in the atrium wall contract and force blood through the valve into ventricle. The pressure falls again as the atrium empties.

- The atrioventricular valve closes at **A.** When does it open again? Explain your answer.

  The valve opens at D. Notice that the curves for pressure in the ventricle and atrium cross at this point, so the pressure on either side of the valve is briefly the same. The pressure in the ventricle then falls slightly below the atrial pressure, so blood again flows through the valve into the ventricle.

- Soon after **A**, the pressure falls as the atrium expands after atrial systole. Explain why the pressure then rises again until **D**.

  The pressure of blood in the pulmonary vein, even though it is quite low, is pushing blood into the atrium and raising the pressure in the atrium as it fills up.

- Explain why the maximum pressure in the atrium is much lower than the maximum pressure in the ventricle.

  There is much less muscle in the walls of the atria. They exert much less force when they contract compared with the thick walls of the ventricle.

The pressure in the aorta stays high throughout the cycle. Its walls are elastic and are stretched during ventricular systole. The stretched walls exert pressure on the blood in the aorta, just as an elastic bandage on your leg continues to squeeze the leg.

- Between which points on the curve is blood entering the aorta from the left ventricle?

  Blood enters the aorta between B and C. The valve opens at B and closes again when the pressure in the ventricle falls below the pressure in the aorta.

■ Figure 6 shows the pressures on the left side of the heart. How would you expect a similar graph showing pressures on the right side to differ? Explain your answer. It may help you to refer to the drawing of the heart in Figure 3.

The maximum pressure in the right ventricle would be lower because the walls are less muscular and exert less force. In fact, the maximum pressure in the right ventricle is normally less than a quarter of the maximum in the left ventricle. The pressure in the pulmonary artery would also be much lower. However, since the two sides pump together, the timing and pattern of events would be much the same.

Cardiac output and control of heartbeat

Figure 7 shows the internal volume of the left ventricle during one cardiac cycle. This graph is on exactly the same time scale as the graph of pressure changes in Figure 6. The same positions have been labelled **A** to **D**, so you can match up with the changes in pressure in the left ventricle.

You can see that between **B** and **C** the volume of the ventricle decreases rapidly. This matches the period when pressure increases as the ventricle contracts. During this stage, blood is being pumped out into the aorta. As the muscles of the ventricle relax after **C**, its volume increases, the pressure falls and blood flows in from the atrium. At this stage, the muscles of the atrium are still relaxed. Atrial systole, when atrial muscles contract, merely tops up the blood in the ventricle between zero and point **A** on the curve in this graph.

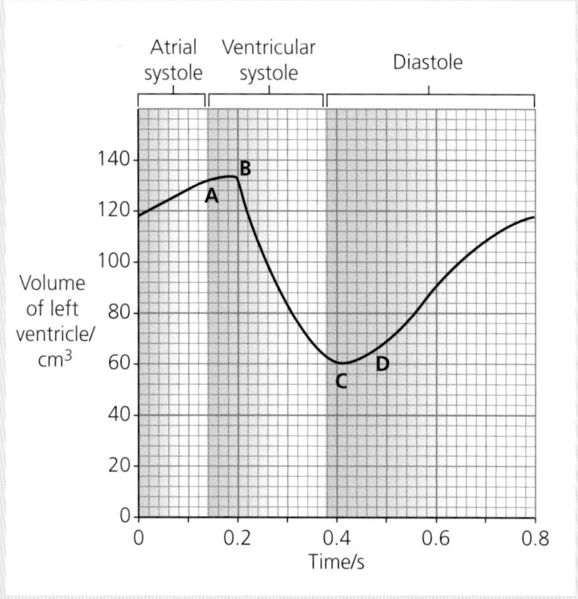

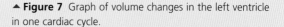

▲ **Figure 7** Graph of volume changes in the left ventricle in one cardiac cycle.

1 Notice in Figure 7 that the volume of the left ventricle stays almost constant between A and B. How can this be explained?

The volume of blood pumped out of the left ventricle during one cardiac cycle is called the **stroke volume**.

2 Use the scale on the *y* axis in Figure 7 to calculate the stroke volume shown by this graph.

We call the volume of blood that the left ventricle pumps out to the body per minute the **cardiac output**. To work out the cardiac output, you first need to calculate the **heart rate**, which is the number of cardiac cycles per minute. To find the number of cycles per minute you have to divide 60 by the time in seconds taken for one cycle.

3 How long is the cardiac cycle shown in Figure 7?

You can then use the following equation to find the cardiac output:

$$\text{cardiac output} = \text{stroke volume} \times \text{heart rate}$$

4 Calculate the cardiac output shown in Figure 7.

For a man lying down and doing nothing, the average cardiac output is about 5 dm^3 (5000 cm^3). During exercise the cardiac output can increase to be about four times as great. This caters for the much higher oxygen and glucose requirements of active muscles. The increase can be produced by changing either the heart rate or the stroke volume, or both.

In an investigation, groups of trained athletes and untrained students were required to ride an exercise bike as fast as they could for a few minutes. Their maximum stroke volume and heart rate were measured. The mean maximum stroke volume for the athletes was 160 cm^3 and for the students 100 cm^3. The mean maximum heart rate was 190 beats per minute for the athletes and 200 beats per minute for the students.

5 (a) Calculate the mean maximum cardiac output for each group.

(b) Explain which factor accounts for the difference.

(c) Suggest how training may have affected the stroke volume.

Coordinating the heartbeat

The muscle of the heart is amazing. For a start, it doesn't get tired. Even in someone who is bone idle it can go on steadily contracting and relaxing 70 times a minute, 24 hours a day for 80 years or more. (That works out at about 3 billion contractions in a lifetime, assuming a life with very little exercise or excitement.)

Secondly, it can carry on contracting and relaxing rhythmically without any nerve impulses from the brain. This ability to work on its own is called **myogenic** (meaning 'arising from muscle'). A heart can be removed from the body and, as long as it is given an oxygen and nutrient supply, it will carry on beating.

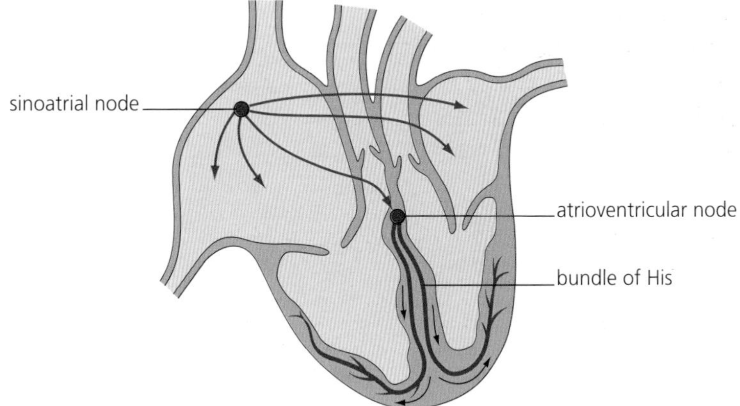

▲ **Figure 8** The diagram shows the route of the electrical activity that makes the heart beat in a smooth sequence.

It is essential that the sequence of muscle contraction and relaxation that we have seen in the cardiac cycle takes place in the right order. The sequence is coordinated by a group of cells called the **sinoatrial node (SAN)** near the top of the right atrium. These cells produce regular waves of electrical activity, similar to nerve impulses. The rate at which the SAN produces these waves determines the rate of heartbeat because they start off atrial systole. For this reason the SAN is often called the heart's pacemaker. A wave of electrical excitation spreads over the walls of both atria, as shown in Figure 8. This makes the muscles in the atrial walls contract. Notice that contraction spreads outwards from the top of the atria, squeezing blood towards the ventricles.

The electrical activity cannot pass from the walls of the atria to the muscles of the ventricles, because it is stopped by a ring of insulating fibrous tissue. At the lower end of the wall that separates the atria is another group of specialised cells, the **atrioventricular node** (AVN). These cells can conduct electrical activity, although after a slight delay. From the AVN, specialised fibres called the **bundle of His** conduct electrical impulses rapidly down the wall between the ventricles to the bottom of the heart. From here, other fibres extend back up the walls of the ventricles. These fibres stimulate the muscles of the ventricles to contract rapidly from the base of the heart upwards. This produces ventricular systole.

Analysing the control of the cardiac cycle

The features of the heart described above make sure that blood is pumped efficiently and in the right direction. Explain how each of the following is important. Think about the advantages of each before you refer to the answers.

- The spread of electrical activity across the atria from the SAN.

  The muscles of the atria contract from the top downwards. This pushes blood down through the atrioventricular valves into the ventricles.

- The insulating fibrous tissue between the atria and the ventricles.

  This stops the wave of atrial muscle contraction continuing through to the ventricle muscles. If contractions started at the *top* of the ventricles, blood would just be forced towards the bottom of the heart.

- The short delay in the transmission of electrical activity through the AVN.

  The delay allows the atria to complete contraction and empty blood into the ventricles before the ventricles start to contract.

- Passing impulses down the bundle of His to the lower end of the heart.

  This makes the muscles contract from the bottom of the ventricles so that the blood is forced upwards and out through the aorta and pulmonary artery at the upper end of the ventricles.

- The rapid spread of the impulses through the fibres to the muscles of the ventricles.

  The contraction of the muscles spreads quickly up the ventricles. Pressure builds up rapidly and the blood is forced out at speed, as you can see in the curve for the ventricle in Figure 6.

Changing heart rate

The SAN can maintain a steady heartbeat by itself and without any control from nerve impulses, but it cannot change the rate at which the heart beats. Nerves from the brain to the SAN help to regulate the heart rate. Impulses travelling in these nerves alter the rate at which the SAN sends out the waves of electrical activity. The heart rate is varied according to the requirements of the body. In fact, there are two separate nerves, one that speeds up the rate and one that slows it down. These nerves originate from the part of the brain that automatically controls activities essential to life, such as breathing and blood circulation. We have no conscious control over the beating of our heart. The greatest increase in rate occurs during exercise, but the rate also goes up when we are excited or frightened. Obviously the rate has to be slowed down again when the exercise or excitement finishes. The stroke volume can also be changed. During exercise the muscle fibres contract further, and more blood is forced out during each contraction of the ventricles.

Sometimes the SAN becomes diseased and starts to operate unevenly. Since the way it works depends on a simple series of electrical impulses, it can be replaced by an artificial pacemaker.

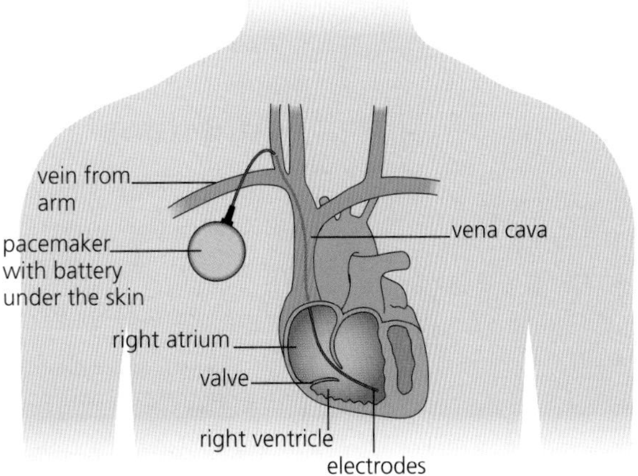

▲ **Figure 9** An artificial pacemaker, showing its wires in position in the heart.

In a minor operation under local anaesthetic, the battery-operated pacemaker is inserted under the skin below the collarbone. Two thin wires are passed along the major vein into the right ventricle of the heart. The electrodes at the end of the wires emit electrical impulses from the pacemaker that stimulate the atrium and ventricle muscles to contract at a regular rate, usually about 70 beats per minute.

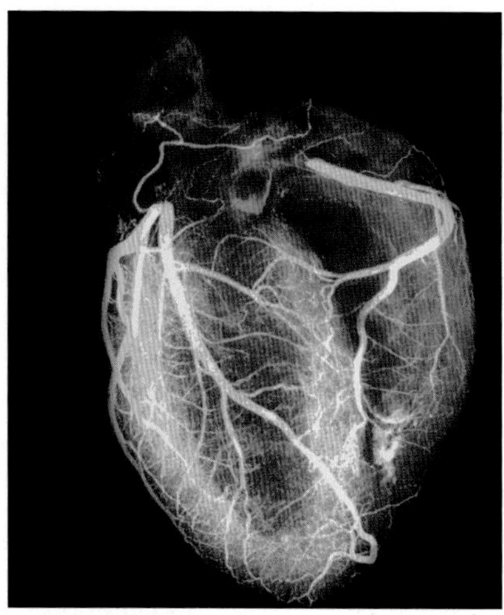

▲ **Figure 10** An angiogram of the heart, showing the coronary blood supply to the heart muscle.

Coronary heart disease (CHD)

Coronary heart disease refers to any condition that interferes with the coronary arteries that supply blood to the heart muscle. Being very active, the muscle requires a continuous supply of oxygen and glucose. This supply does not enter the muscle from the blood in the chambers of the heart. It reaches the muscle from arteries that branch from the aorta and spread over the surface of the heart, as you can see in Figure 10. Small vessels penetrate the heart muscle so that all parts are close enough to the blood supply for the oxygen and glucose to diffuse to the muscle cells.

Problems arise when blood vessels taking blood to the heart muscle become very narrow or blocked so that the supply of oxygen and glucose is reduced or cut off. How serious this is depends on where the blockage occurs and how much of the muscle is affected.

Arteries may become partly blocked when fatty deposits form in their walls. These fatty deposits are called **atheroma**. The resulting narrowing of the arteries is referred to as atherosclerosis or, in common language, 'hardening of the arteries'. Blood clots often form in a narrowed artery. If the blood supply to a major part of the heart muscle is completely blocked, the muscle starts to die due to lack of a blood supply. A heart attack follows. The medical term for heart muscle death is **myocardial infarction** (an infarction is the death of tissue; myocardial means that it occurs in the heart muscle).

Atheroma

Fatty deposits start to build up in an artery when the layer of cells lining the inside of the artery (called the endothelium) becomes damaged and inflamed. This often happens at a junction where a smaller artery branches off, possibly because uneven blood flow has damaged the junction.

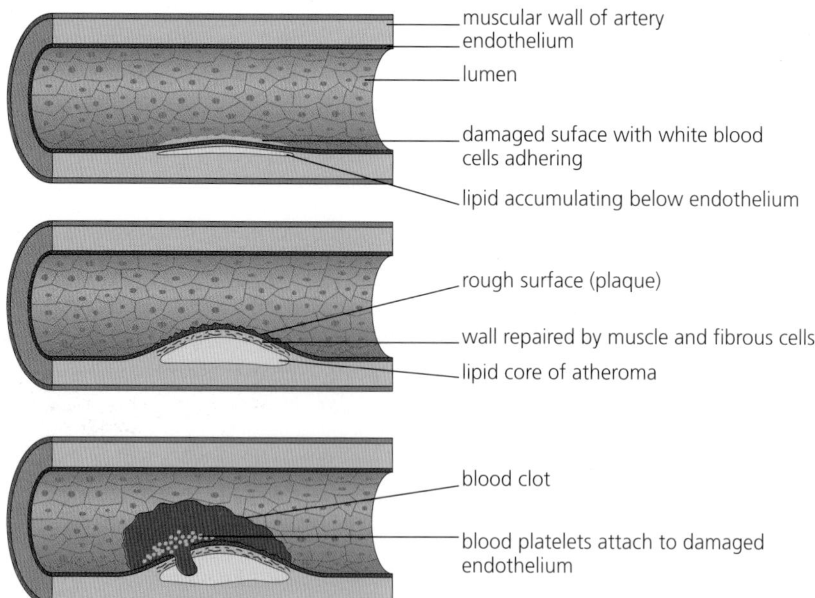

▲ **Figure 11** The sequence of diagrams shows the formation of atheroma and plaque in an artery.

The endothelium may also be damaged by high blood pressure, viral infection or chemical pollutants in the blood. As with damage to cells in other parts of the body, certain types of white blood cell are attracted to the site. These white cells pass from the blood and squeeze between the cells of the endothelium into the surrounding muscular wall. They absorb fatty materials from the blood, in particular low-density lipoproteins (LDL). Lipoproteins are complex substances containing both fatty (lipid) and protein components. The fatty part is derived from **cholesterol**, which is often portrayed as a 'baddie' in articles on diet.

New muscle and fibrous cells repair the damaged wall, but these leave a lumpy area with a rough surface called a **plaque**. This may remain for a long time without causing much trouble, but eventually its cells age and die. The surface of the lump becomes rougher. If the endothelium breaks down, blood platelets stick to the damaged site and a blood clot forms, a condition that is called **thrombosis**. As the blood clot grows, it is more likely to completely block the lumen of the artery (the central space through which the blood flows) and cause a heart attack.

One complication is that bits of the clot may break away and then get stuck in some of the smaller arterioles, where they cut off the blood supply to small sections of heart muscle. This may damage the heart without causing a full-scale heart attack. Another possibility is that the artery is weakened by the damage to its wall so that it starts to bulge due to the blood pressure. This swelling is called an **aneurysm**. In a minority of cases the aneurysm can actually burst, which is likely to be disastrous and fatal. Both thromboses and aneurysms can occur in arteries in other parts of the body, especially in the brain where they are the cause of strokes.

Myocardial infarction

It is possible to survive for many years with atheroma without being seriously incapacitated, or even aware of its existence. One symptom may be pain in the centre of the chest brought on by vigorous exercise. This is called **angina**, and the pain normally dies away when the exercise stops. The pain is caused because the atheroma prevents certain areas of heart

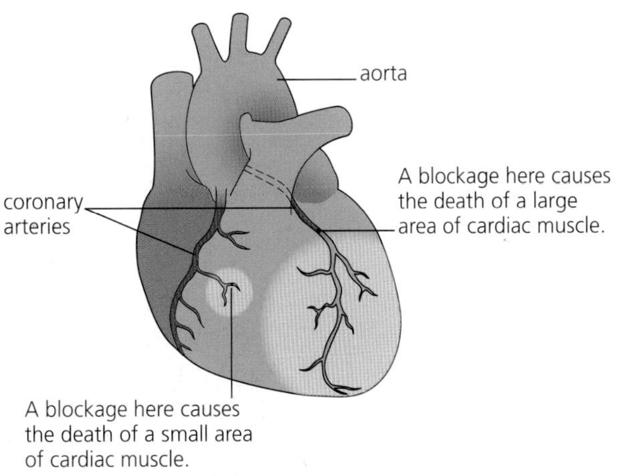

▲ **Figure 12** Where cardiac muscle dies when coronary arteries are blocked.

muscle from getting the increased blood supply needed during exercise. People with angina need to be monitored to prevent the condition from worsening and causing a myocardial infarction. Regular treatment with aspirin can reduce the chance of blood clots forming, as described in the introduction to this chapter.

Most myocardial infarctions are caused when a clot blocks a coronary artery at the site of an atheroma. The symptoms are severe pain in the chest, often described as feeling as though the chest is being crushed by a heavy object. The victim may also feel sick and breathless and have a rapid but weak pulse.

Anyone who has these symptoms needs urgent medical attention. The seriousness of the condition depends on where the blockage occurs and how much of the heart muscle is deprived of oxygen. Affected muscle will soon stop working, and this often disrupts the heartbeat. The impulses that normally make muscle fibres in the ventricles contract together become uncoordinated. The result is fibrillation, when the fibres contract independently. The left ventricle no longer produces enough force to pump the blood out into the aorta and no pulse can be felt in the victim's neck.

Emergency defibrillation is urgently needed before too much damage occurs. A defibrillator gives the chest brief electric shocks until the heartbeat stabilises. This equipment is kept in ambulances. Shops and workplaces often have a defibrillator and staff trained to use it.

About a third of victims die within an hour unless defibrillation is administered, ideally within a few minutes of the attack. Until a defibrillator is available, and as a first aid measure to keep some circulation going, the heart can be squeezed by rapidly compressing the chest. Artificial respiration is also often needed, since breathing stops when the muscles involved lose their oxygen supply. It is a good idea to be familiar with these first aid techniques to use in an emergency.

Risk factors

Many factors increase the risk of suffering from coronary heart disease. Some of these factors are unavoidable, such as increasing age. But others are the result of particular lifestyles, and a person can choose to alter the risk from them. The main risk factors include:

- **Age and sex**. Deaths from CHD can occur in young adults, but the numbers involved are small. Not surprisingly, the risk increases with age as damage to arteries develops slowly and as the effects of other factors take effect. Men are much more likely than women to get CHD in middle age, but after this the risk becomes fairly similar.
- **Genetic factors**. CHD tends to run in families, especially where heart attacks occur in middle age or earlier. This may be partly due to members of families having similar lifestyles, but there is evidence for some genetic causes. For example, the risk of two identical twins both dying from CHD is about four times as great as the risk for non-identical twins.
- **Smoking**. As we saw in Chapter 3, in addition to its effects on the lungs, smoking can significantly increase the risk of dying from CHD. Table 2

on page 81 shows that the risk for doctors who smoked heavily was nearly double that of non-smokers. Working out the precise effect is difficult. For heavy smokers it is likely that smoking will damage both the lungs and the heart. It may be chance as to which is the first to cause death. It is not certain how smoking affects the heart. One possible explanation is that nicotine makes arteries constrict, and this causes an increase in blood pressure, another risk factor.

- **High blood pressure.** It is normal for blood pressure to increase during exercise, when the heart beats more forcefully. However, in some people the pressure is high even when they are at rest. The risk factors linked to high blood pressure include genetics, high salt intake, lack of exercise and alcoholism. One effect of high blood pressure is that the arteries develop thicker walls. As the wall of an artery thickens, the lumen gets narrower. As anyone who has attached rubber tubing to a tap and then squeezed will know, the water jet comes out with much greater force. The narrowing of the arteries therefore has the knock-on effect of raising blood pressure even more. This can damage their inner surface, making it more likely that atheroma will develop. It can also result in damage to the heart itself. The ventricles can enlarge, and in the worst cases the beating of the heart can become so irregular that heart failure results.
- **High concentration of low-density lipoproteins in the blood.** As we have already seen, low-density lipoproteins (LDL) are involved in the formation of atheroma. Lipoproteins are a complex association of triglycerides, cholesterol and proteins. Although cholesterol has a bad reputation because of its link to heart disease, it is essential for the synthesis of cell membranes. Cholesterol is transported in the blood by LDL from the liver where the lipoproteins are made from fats and cholesterol in the diet. However, research shows that when the diet contains an excess of fats, especially saturated fats, the quantity of LDL in the blood rises and there is a greatly increased risk of developing coronary heart disease.

  The blood also contains high-density lipoprotein (HDL), which has a higher proportion of protein in their structure. These are the 'goodies' because they absorb excess cholesterol and return it to the liver where it is removed from the blood. People with a high ratio of HDL to LDL have a lower risk of developing heart disease. Blood tests can determine the ratio of HDL to LDL, and the results can be used to advise on protective changes to lifestyle. Drugs called statins may also be used to lower the concentration of LDL.

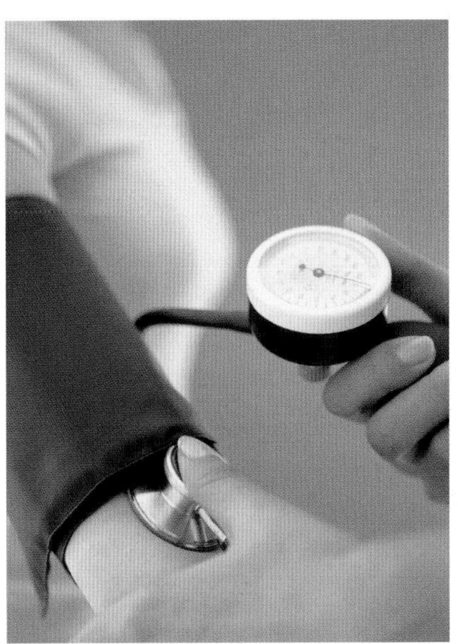

▲ **Figure 13** A sphygmomanometer is the equipment that a doctor uses to measure a person's blood pressure.

Q5

Explain what causes the difference between maximum and minimum blood pressure in the artery.

Q6

A doctor reports a person as having a blood pressure of 130/85. What would the pressures be in kPa?

Measuring blood pressure

Although scientists use kilopascals as the units of pressure, doctors still measure blood pressure in old units. These were the units in which a mercury barometer measured atmospheric pressure. Mean atmospheric pressure is 760 millimetres of mercury (mmHg), which is the height of a column of mercury that atmospheric pressure will support. Atmospheric pressure is 100 kPa, so 760 mmHg = 100 kPa.

Blood pressure is measured by finding the maximum and minimum pressures in the artery in the arm. In an adult, a healthy reading is taken to be less than 140 and 90 for these two measurements.

Risk factors work together

There are some other factors that show a statistical increase in the risk of heart disease, such as obesity, lack of exercise and diabetes. In some cases, the explanation for the increased risk is clearly linked to other factors. For example, obesity is likely to be linked to eating fatty foods, which in turn is likely to lead to high concentrations of cholesterol and LDL in the blood. For many people, their statistical risk of having a heart attack is the result of a combination of different risk factors.

Calculating risk of CHD

Table 1 Estimates of the risk of coronary heart disease over the next 10-year period for different age groups of men.

Factor	Range	Points for each age group			
		Age groups/years			
		40 to 49	50 to 59	60 to 69	70 to 79
Age		3	7	10	12
Blood cholesterol/ mg 100 cm^{-3}	<160	0	0	0	0
	160–199	3	2	1	0
	200–239	5	3	1	0
	240–279	6	4	2	1
	280+	8	5	3	1
Smoking	Smoker	5	3	1	1
	Non-smoker	0	0	0	0
Systolic blood pressure/mmHg	<120	0	0	0	0
	120–129	0	0	0	0
	130–139	1	1	1	1
	140–159	1	1	1	1
	160+	2	2	2	2
Blood HDL content/ mg 100 cm^{-3}	<40	2	2	2	2
	40–49	1	1	1	1
	50–59	0	0	0	0
	60+	−1	−1	−1	−1

Table 2 Point scores for men and the percentage probability that they will develop CHD in the next 10 years.

Point Score	1	2	3	4	5	6	7	8	9	10	11	12	13	14	15	16	17+
Percentage increased risk of CHD over next 10 years	1	1	1	1	2	2	3	4	5	6	8	10	12	16	20	25	30

For each risk factor, statisticians can assess the chance of developing coronary heart disease. Table 1 gives points for some risk factors for men in different age groups. The points are based on statistical evidence for the increased risk for healthy men over a 10-year period. For example, the point score of a man aged between 40 and 49 is increased by 5 points if he is a smoker. His total point score in Table 1 shows the probability that he will develop CHD during the next ten years of his life, assuming that he is healthy at the time of assessment.

To calculate the point score, you add together the scores for all of the five categories in Table 1. For example, a 42 year-old non-smoking man, with a cholesterol concentration of 180 mg per 100 cm^3 of blood, blood pressure of 140 mmHg and an HDL concentration of 55 mg per 100 cm^3, has these scores:

Age 3
Cholesterol 3
Smoking 0
Blood pressure 1
HDL 0.

The total score is 7.

From Table 2, you can see that this man has a 3% increased risk of suffering from CHD during the following 10 years. This is called his '10-year risk'.

1 Suggests explanations for each of the following:

(a) The point score rises steeply for older age groups.

(b) The point score for blood cholesterol is greatest for the youngest age group.

(c) Blood HDL content above 60 mg per 100 cm^3 has a negative score.

2 Work out the 10-year risk for each of the following men and suggest what advice about their lifestyle should be given in each case.

(a) A smoker, aged 48, blood cholesterol 265 mg per 100 cm^3; blood pressure 146 mmHg and HDL 44 mg per 100 cm^3.

(b) A non-smoker, aged 68, blood cholesterol 188 mg per 100 cm^3; blood pressure 140 mmHg and HDL 62 mg per 100 cm^3.

Chapter 5

The body's defence against disease

Look at the baby in Figure 1. He lives in the plastic cage or bubble that you can see around him. The bubble is completely airtight. The air that he breathes has to be filtered before it is pumped into the bubble. The food and water that he consumes must pass through an air lock before he can touch them. Anyone who wishes to touch him must work through the plastic gloves you can see in the photograph. This boy can never leave the plastic bubble. He will not be able to go to school. He will not be able to play out with friends. He will not be able to touch his mother, his father or his siblings. Can you imagine a life like this?

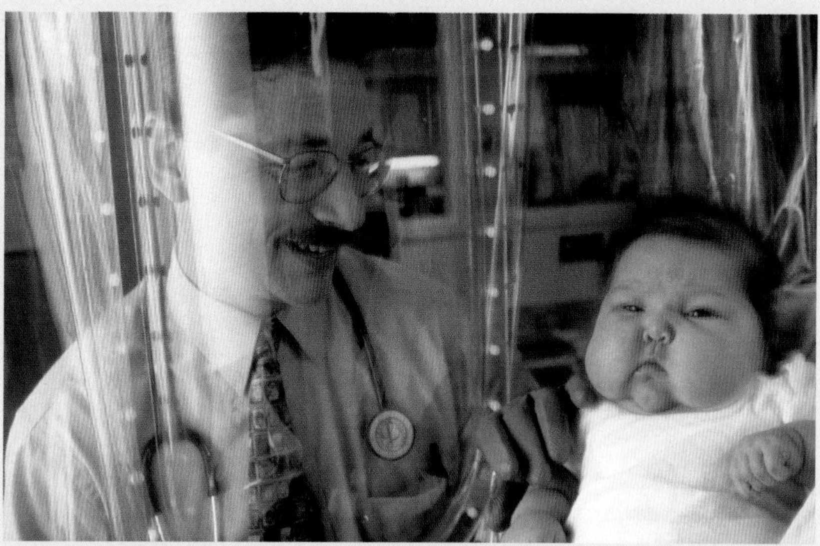

Figure 1 This boy suffers from SCID. The plastic bubble in which he lives protects him from infection.

This boy was born with an inherited condition, called **s**evere **c**ombined **i**mmuno**d**eficiency (SCID). He is unable to produce enough white blood cells. White blood cells are part of the immune system, the system that helps to protect us against disease. If he were to suffer any infection, he could not fight it off. As a result, even the mildest infection could kill him.

A baby born with SCID survives infection provided it is breast-fed. Its mother's milk contains antibodies that she has produced. The baby is able to absorb these without digesting them, so that they work in the baby's own blood system. However, once the baby is weaned, it loses its supply of these ready-made antibodies. At this stage, it is likely to die unless transferred to a bubble like the one shown in the photograph.

There is some hope for SCID sufferers. Bone marrow contains **stem cells**. Stem cells are cells that can divide to make any type of human cell. A transplant of bone marrow from a healthy person has helped some SCID sufferers to make the white cells they lack.

More recently, scientists have genetically modified stem cells from a SCID sufferer's own bone marrow to compensate for the single gene that he lacks. The scientists first removed stem cells from the patient's own bone marrow. Then, they used a harmless virus as a vector (carrier) to put copies of the healthy gene into the stem cells. After this, they put these genetically modified cells back into the patent's own bone marrow, where they multiplied and enabled him to produce the white blood cells he needs.

In this chapter we will look at how the immune system of a healthy person works.

Our bodies are ideal incubators for pathogens

Your body contains an abundant supply of nutrients, including water. You also maintain your body at a constant temperature and pH. These conditions provide an ideal environment for your own growth, and also for the growth of many types of microorganism. These microorganisms include bacteria, viruses and fungi. They are present in the air that you inhale and in the food and water that you swallow. Whilst many of these microorganisms are harmless, a few cause disease, that is, they are **pathogenic**.

Thankfully, your body has a number of defences against pathogens. The first is to prevent the entry of pathogens. If this fails, the second defence is for the region invaded by the pathogen to swell and become red, in what is called a non-specific inflammatory response. If this fails, the third defence occurs. Here, the body targets that particular pathogen, in a specific immune response. Let us look at each of these in turn.

Physical and chemical barriers to infection

Preventing pathogens from getting into your body is the first line of defence. Your skin provides a good barrier. It has many layers of cells, and this makes it difficult to penetrate. The membranes lining your digestive, reproductive, and respiratory systems act as barriers to the entry of most pathogens, too. These external and internal surfaces also provide chemical barriers to infection. The waxy oils that make your skin supple contain fatty acids that are toxic to many microorganisms. Tears, saliva and urine contain enzymes that destroy the proteins in pathogens by hydrolysis (see page 5).

Q1

Suggest how the bacteria living in your intestines help to prevent infection by pathogens.

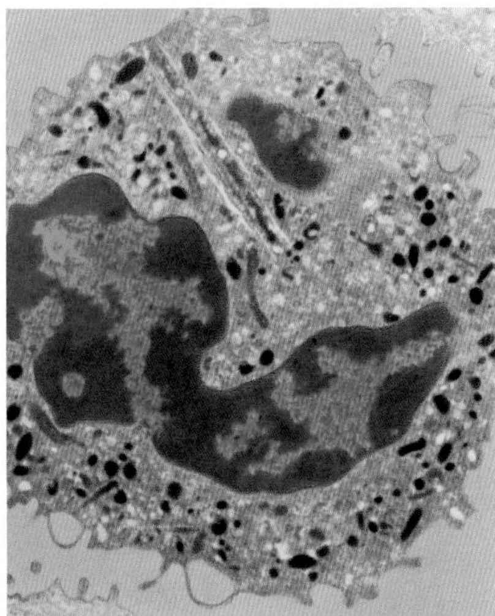

Figure 2 This blood cell is a phagocyte. Phagocytes are cells that can ingest and then digest microscopic pathogens. Notice that their cytoplasm is full of lysosomes (coloured red). These contain enzymes that are important in destroying ingested pathogens.

Non-specific inflammatory response – phagocytes and lysosomes

If a pathogen gets into your body, an **inflammatory response** is your second line of defence. This type of response is non-specific, meaning that it is the same for all pathogens. Blood contains two types of blood cell, red cells and white cells. Unlike red cells, there are many different types of white cell. Some of these are **phagocytes.** This means that they can surround and digest microscopic pathogens. Look at the two different types of phagocyte in Figure 2. You can see that their cytoplasm is full of lysosomes. You learned about lysosomes in Chapter 2 (page 41). They contain enzymes that can digest proteins, lipids and carbohydrates and are important in destroying pathogens.

A phagocyte surrounds a microscopic pathogen, engulfing it (see Figure 3). This is the process of **ingestion**. You came across the term 'ingestion' in Chapter 1, page 4. You can see that we use it to mean 'take in', whether it is humans or white cells that take in material. When a phagocyte ingests a pathogen, the pathogen is wrapped in membrane which forms a tiny sac around it. This sac is called a **vacuole**.

Lysosomes move to this vacuole and their membranes fuse with the membrane around the vacuole. This fusion releases the lysosomal enzymes onto the ingested pathogen. The enzymes digest the pathogen and the phagocyte absorbs the harmless products of digestion. In this way, phagocytes kill pathogens that have entered the body.

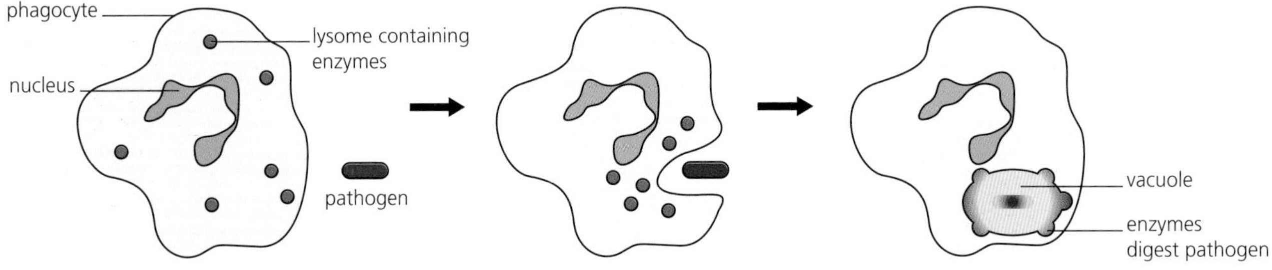

Figure 3 How a phagocyte ingests a pathogen.

Q2

The pathogens are harmful, but the products of their digestion are not. Explain why.

Phagocytes are present in the blood, but they can also leave the blood and attack microscopic pathogens in other tissues. They leave the blood by squeezing through tiny gaps between the cells that form capillary walls (see page 158). Substances called **histamines** help this process. Histamines are released when tissues are damaged.

You might have noticed that the area around a cut on your finger becomes red and slightly swollen. These symptoms are caused by histamines, which stimulate the small arteries leading to infected tissues to become dilated. If the cut becomes infected, it may produce yellowish pus. Pus contains phagocytes that have attacked the pathogens which caused the infection.

Q3

An infected cut on your finger becomes hotter than the skin on the rest of your finger. Explain why.

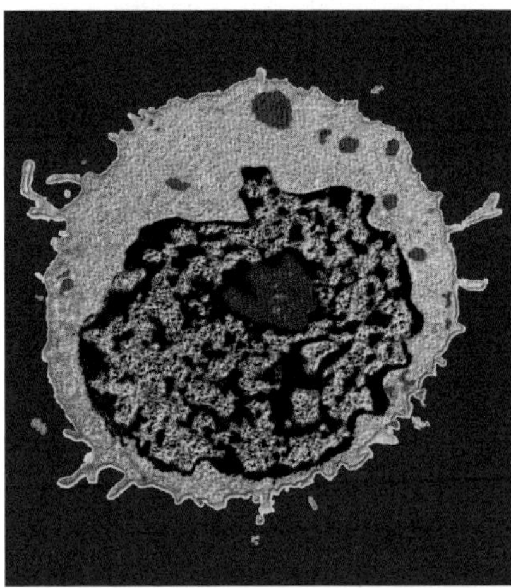

Figure 4 Lymphocytes are a type of white blood cell. They are involved in cellular and humoral immunity.

B cells and T cells

Phagocytes do not respond in a specific way to a microscopic pathogen; they ingest and destroy any foreign cells. In contrast, **lymphocytes** are specific. Lymphocytes are another type of white blood cell. Each lymphocyte attacks only one type of foreign cell. Figure 4 shows the appearance of a lymphocyte. You can see that these cells do not have the lysosomes in their cytoplasm that we have seen in phagocytes.

Lymphocytes go through a maturing process before they are capable of fighting infection. The maturing process begins before birth, and results in two types of lymphocyte.

- B lymphocytes, known as **B cells**, mature in bone marrow. They cause a **humoral response** to infection. This means that they secrete antibodies into the blood.
- T lymphocytes, known as **T cells**, mature in the thymus. They cause a **cellular response** to infection. This means that they do not secrete antibodies into the blood.

Before going further, we need to be clear about three terms used in immunology.

Antigen

An **antigen** is a molecule that triggers an immune response. Small molecules, like amino acids, sugars and triglycerides do not trigger an immune response. Antigens are large, complex molecules, such as proteins, polysaccharides and **glycoproteins**. Figure 5 shows that antigens are located on the outer surface of cells.

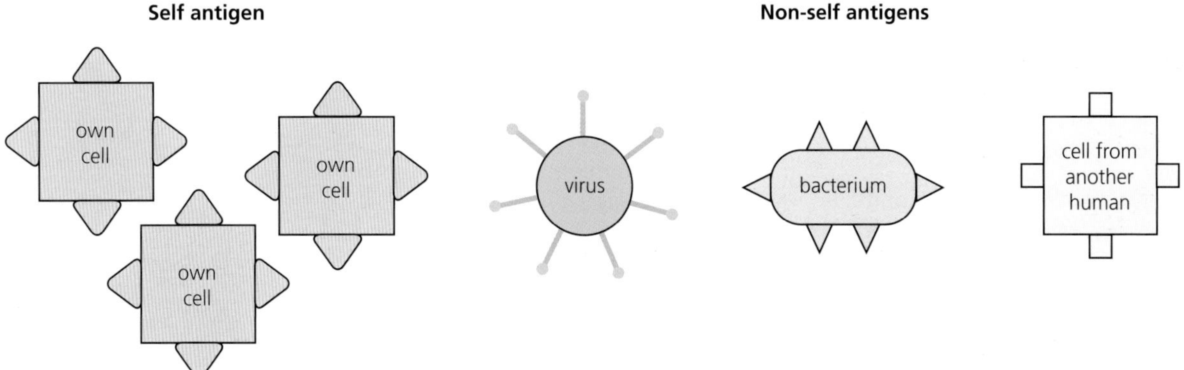

Figure 5 Every mammal has self antigens on the surface membranes of its cells. The antigens on the surface of cells from another organism, non-self antigens, trigger an immune response. (Drawings are not to scale.)

Each cell in your body has **self antigens** on its surface membrane. These self antigens help the body's cells to recognise each other, and act as receptors of substances such as hormones. Mammals do not normally produce antibodies against their own self antigens. However, in the body of another mammal, these antigens trigger an immune response.

Antibody

An **antibody** is a protein that a B cell secretes in response to a non-self antigen. Every antibody is a Y-shaped molecule, made of four polypeptide

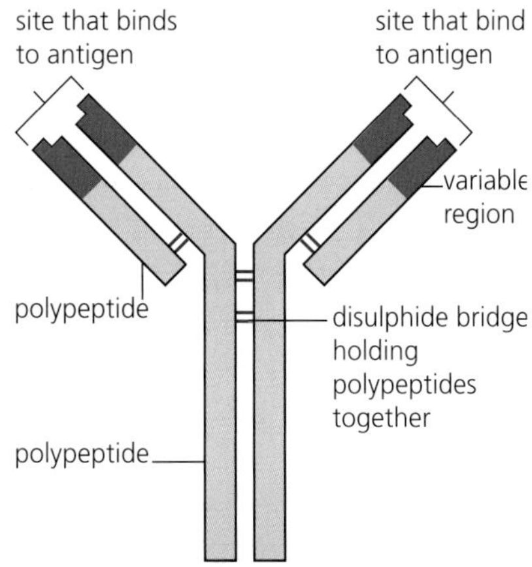

Figure 6 Every antibody is a protein molecule made of two long and two short polypeptide chains. The variable region shown in the diagram is the part of the molecule that combines with an antigen to make an antigen–antibody complex.

chains. Figure 6 shows you that two of the polypeptides are large and two are small. It also shows the two key parts of the antibody molecule – the sites that bind with a specific antigen. Every mammal is able to make millions of different antibodies, each with a different pair of binding sites for one type of antigen only.

Antigen–antibody complex

An antigen and an antibody have complementary molecular shapes, meaning that they fit into each other. When an antibody collides with a cell carrying a non-self antigen that has a complementary shape, it binds to the antigen. When this happens, the two molecules form an **antigen–antibody complex**. This is the first stage in the destruction of a cell carrying a non-self antigen.

B cells and the humoral immune response

A single B cell has only one type of **receptor** molecule on its surface membrane. However, you randomly make millions of different B cells, each with a different receptor on its surface membrane. By chance, one of these B cells might have receptors with a shape exactly complementary to the shape of an antigen on a cell that has entered your blood. In that case, the receptors bind with this antigen. Figure 7 summarises what then happens.

This B cell divides rapidly to produce a large number of daughter cells. Since the divisions are by mitosis, these daughter cells are genetically identical, that is, they are **clones**. The majority of these cells form **plasma cells**, which release antibodies. A small number remain as **memory cells**. If cells carrying the same antigen enter the blood again, the memory cells will 'recognise' them and produce new plasma cells faster than before.

Q4

Give two ways in which antibodies are similar to enzymes.

Q5

A collision between a B cell and an antigen is less likely than the collision between a memory cell and the same antigen. Explain why.

Q6

Give two differences in the way that a T cell and a B cell react to their respective antigens.

T cells and the cellular immune response

Like B cells, a single T cell has one type of receptor on its surface membrane. Blood contains a vast number of T cells, each with a different receptor on its surface membrane. However, T cells are different from B cells in two important ways:

- T cells never release antibodies into the blood.
- T cells respond to an antigen only if this antigen is present on the surface of an infected cell. This infected cell is called an **antigen-presenting cell**. It is one of your body's own cells that is infected by a pathogen.

Look at Figure 8. It shows how a T cell responds to infection. Each infected cell has antigens from the pathogen on its own surface membrane, that is, it is an antigen-presenting cell. A T cell with receptors that are complementary to the antigen attaches to the antigen. This T cell is now 'sensitised' and begins to divide rapidly to form a clone. An important function of the T cells in this clone is to stimulate B cells to divide.

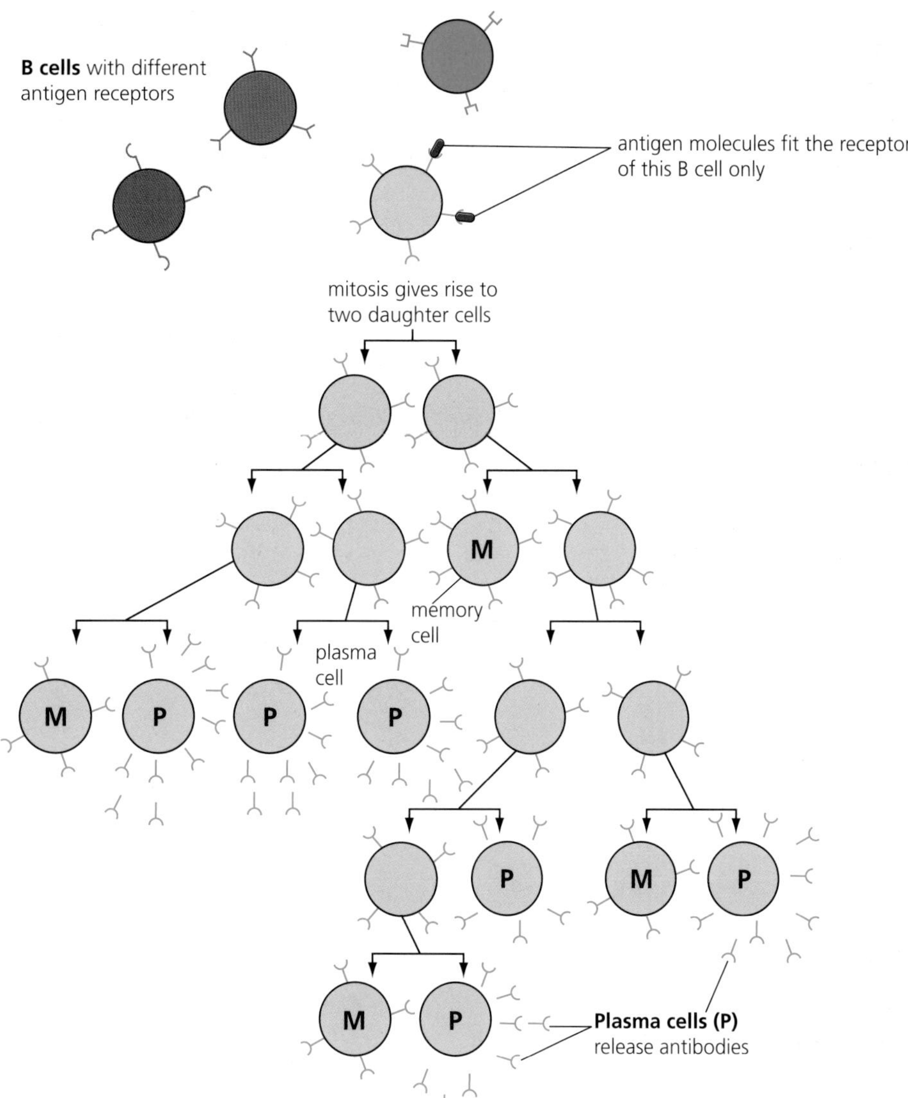

Figure 7 The diagram shows what happens when, by chance, an antigen meets a B cell. If this B cell has a complementary receptor, it will bind to the antigen. This stimulates the B cell to divide rapidly, forming a large clone of daughter cells. Most of these are **plasma cells** (labelled P), which release antibodies into the blood. A few are memory cells (labelled M), which remain dormant in the blood.

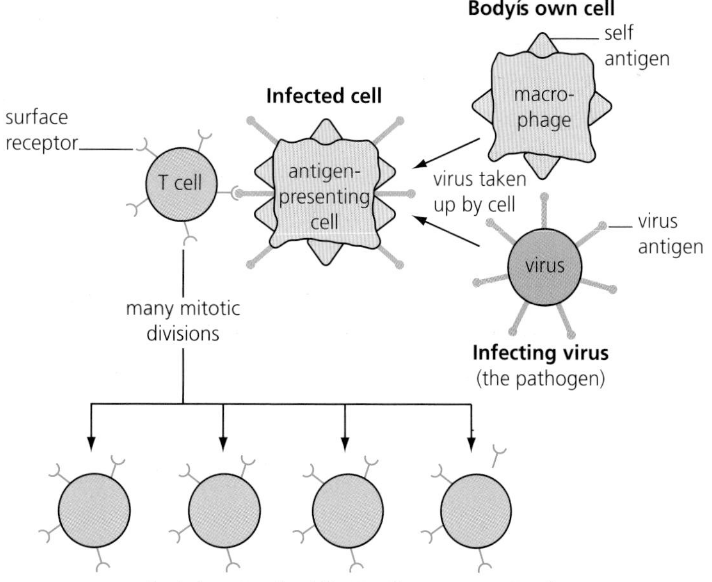

Figure 8 When the surface receptor of a T cell combines with a complementary antigen, the T cell becomes sensitised and starts dividing. However, T cells will combine with a complementary antigen only if it is on the surface of an antigen-presenting cell – one of the body's own infected cells. The sensitised T cell then divides rapidly to form a clone of cells.

HIV and T cells

The human immunodeficiency virus (HIV) infects one sort of T cell and destroys all these cells. People infected by this virus are HIV-positive. Without treatment, they will develop Acquired Immune Deficiency Syndrome (AIDS). Without their T cells, AIDS sufferers lose their ability to overcome infections. As a result, people with AIDS often die from diseases, such as tuberculosis, from which other humans could recover.

Worldwide, about 22.6 million people are either HIV-positive or suffer from AIDS. About 63% of these people live in sub-Saharan Africa. Some people are at greater risk of HIV infection than others because of their lifestyles. People in 'high-risk' groups include intravenous drug users who share needles and people who have unprotected sex with many partners. Unprotected sex means sexual intercourse without using a condom that would prevent the virus passing from partner to partner. However, scientists have found to their surprise that in many 'high-risk' groups there are a few people who seem to be resistant to HIV infection.

1 Drug users who share needles are at increased risk of becoming HIV-positive. Explain why.

Medical investigators studied a group of prostitutes at a special clinic in Nairobi, the capital of Kenya. The group included an unusually large number of HIV-resistant women. The investigators tested the blood of all the prostitutes for the presence of HIV.

2 Suggest why the investigators chose to work

(a) with prostitutes;

(b) in sub-Saharan Africa.

3 The investigators tested for the presence of HIV rather than for antibodies against HIV. Suggest why.

Although most of the prostitutes were HIV-positive, a few were not. To check their findings, the investigators tested the blood of the HIV-negative women in a different way. The investigators took white blood cells from the HIV-negative women and put them into Petri dishes with HIV-infected cells. The women's cells did not become infected.

4 The investigators did these tests in Petri dishes. Do their results prove that the women were immune to infection by HIV? Explain your answer.

The investigators concluded that the T cells of these women had already been exposed to the HIV and had managed to destroy it. As a result, this group of women had acquired resistance to HIV.

In a different study, scientists in New York found that some people in a different 'high-risk' group appeared to have a natural immunity to HIV. These people had inherited two defective copies of a gene called CKR-5. This gene encodes a protein which is found on the surface membrane of T cells and to which the HIV must attach in order to cause infection.

5 (a) What effect would you expect defective copies of the CKR-5 gene to have on the shape of the encoded protein in the membrane of T cells?

(b) Use your answer to suggest why people with two copies of the defective CKR-5 gene cannot be infected by HIV.

Why don't we catch the same infection twice?

If you suffered an illness such as chicken pox when you were a child, you might have wondered why you never caught the disease again. We can explain this using our knowledge of antibodies, plasma cells and memory cells.

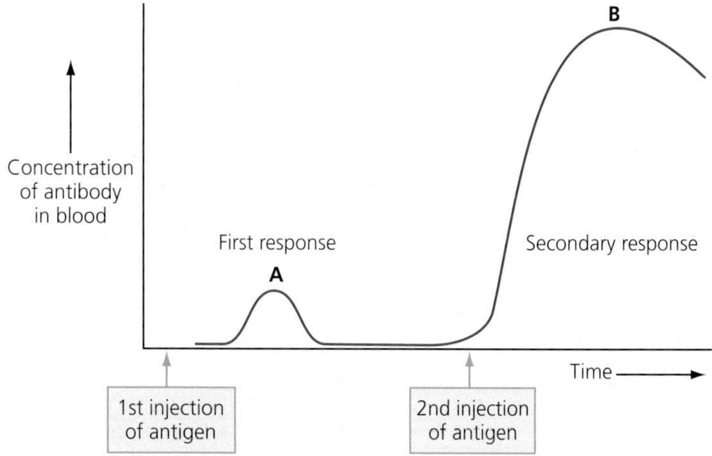

Figure 9 The effect of repeated injections of antigen on the concentration of antibodies in the blood.

Look at Figure 9. It shows the concentration of an antibody in the blood of a person who is injected twice with the same antigen. The part of the curve labelled **A** shows what happens after the first injection. After a short delay, there is a small rise in the concentration of antibody in the blood. This is the **primary response**. The antibody concentration quickly falls again. We can use the information from Figure 7 (page 105) to explain this. The short delay represents the time for a complementary, specific B cell to collide randomly with the antigen, bind with the antigen to form an antigen–antibody complex and then divide to form a clone of plasma cells that release their antibodies.

As the antibodies destroy the antigens, so fewer and fewer B cells are made, and the concentration of antibody falls again. The part of the curve labelled **B** shows what happens after the second injection. This **secondary response** is more rapid and results in a higher concentration of the antibody in the blood. Again, we can explain this using information from Figure 7. After the first response, many memory cells that are specific for the antigen remain in the blood. As a result:

- the memory cells are much more likely to collide with the antigen and bind with it. This means that the memory cells start to divide to produce plasma cells. This explains why the secondary response is more rapid than the first response.
- a larger number of plasma cells are produced, so the concentration of antibodies is higher during the secondary response.

The same events occur when we suffer infections. The first time we become infected by a particular pathogen, our response is slow and we produce few antibodies. During this primary response, we exhibit the symptoms of that infection. We talk about catching the disease. However, the next time we become infected by the same pathogen, our response is very rapid and we produce a large concentration of antibodies. We are able to destroy the pathogen before it causes disease.

Q7

Bottle-fed babies have more infections than breast-fed babies. Explain why.

Why do we get colds and flu every winter?

As we have seen, the surface receptors on lymphocytes have a shape complementary to only one antigen. This is why they are specific. Memory cells can only be effective against a pathogen that always has the same antigen. If the antigen on a pathogen were to change, the receptors on our memory cells would no longer bind with it.

Some pathogens show **antigen variability**. This means that they frequently change the antigens on their surface. The cold virus and the influenza virus show antigen variability. As a result of mutations, the cold virus and the influenza virus frequently change their antigens. This means that the 'new' cold or flu viruses have antigens that are no longer complementary to the surface receptors of the memory cells remaining from the cold or flu you caught last year. You never have a secondary response, so you catch a cold or flu all over again.

Testing the clonal selection hypothesis

Scientists propose explanations for the observations they make. We refer to these explanations as **hypotheses**. In order to test the validity of a hypothesis, scientists use it to make predictions and then devise experiments to test these predictions. If their results are always consistent with their predictions, they become confident in their hypothesis.

The **clonal selection hypothesis** proposes an explanation for the way that we produce antibodies against non-self antigens. We can summarise this hypothesis in the following way:

> Our immune systems randomly produce millions of different types of B and T cells. Each type has a unique protein receptor on its surface membrane. When, and only when, one of these cells binds with a complementary antigen, it is stimulated to produce large numbers of cells that are identical to itself and, consequently, to each other. We call a group of identical cells a **clone**. Thus, in response to the presence of a particular antigen, a B or T cell is selected and it forms a clone. Within the clone, each cell has the identical protein receptor on its surface.

In an experiment to test this hypothesis, scientists injected two rats, **R** and **S**, with antigens from two different strains of pneumococcal bacteria. They injected each rat twice, with the second injection made 28 days after the first.

- Why do you think the scientists injected each rat twice, with a gap of 28 days between injections?

Figure 9 will help you to answer this question. After the first injection, the rats would produce only a small quantity of antibodies against the pathogen (the primary response). After the second injection, the rats would produce much more of the antibody (the secondary response).

■ Which type of immune cell do you think the scientists were attempting to stimulate?

Hopefully, you spotted that the scientists were going to look for antibodies. This means that the scientists must have been trying to stimulate B cells, since T cells do not produce antibodies.

The scientists injected rat **R** with antigens from strain **X** of the bacterium (type **X** antigens) and injected rat **S** with antigens from strain **Y** of the pneumococcal bacterium (type **Y** antigens).

■ What do you think the scientists were predicting would happen as a result of these injections?

Using the clonal selection hypothesis, the scientists were predicting that the blood of both rats would already contain one or more B cells with a protein receptor that was complementary to each of the antigens from the two strains of bacterium. If the clonal selection hypothesis is correct, the cells in rat **R** with a protein receptor complementary to type **X** antigens should be stimulated to form a clone. However, this should not happen in rat **S**. Instead, the cells with a protein receptor complementary to type **Y** antigens should be stimulated to form a clone in rat **S**.

The scientists now needed a way to find out which cells had been stimulated to produce a clone. The method they chose was rather neat. They coated inert beads with the type **X** antigens and put the beads into two glass columns (labelled 1 and 3 in Figure 10). They then did the same with type **Y** antigens and put these beads into another two glass columns (labelled 2 and 4 in Figure 10). They reasoned that if they washed samples of lymphocytes through these columns, those lymphocytes that had the appropriate complementary protein receptors would bind to the antigens on the inert beads. As a result, they would stay in the glass column and not emerge at the bottom.

■ Why was it important that the beads they used were inert?

You might not have come across the term 'inert' before. Something that is inert will not react with anything. This was important because the scientists did not want any of the lymphocytes to react with the beads and stick to them. They wanted them to bind only with the antigens that coated the beads.

One week after the second injection, the scientists removed a sample of blood from each of the two rats and separated the lymphocytes from the rest of the blood. They put half of each sample into a column of inert beads coated with type **X** antigen and half into a column of inert beads coated with type **Y** antigen. They then washed the samples through the columns and collected any lymphocytes that passed through the column.

■ What type of fluid do you suppose they used to wash the lymphocytes through the columns?

Hopefully, you used your knowledge of water potential and osmosis to answer this question. Since the scientists wanted to recover some cells at the bottom of the column, they would have to use a solution with the same water potential as the lymphocytes. If they had used water, the lymphocytes would have taken up water by osmosis and burst.

Finally, the scientists tested the lymphocytes that had passed through each column to see whether they could make antibodies against either of the two antigens used in the experiment. Figure 10 summarises the method they used and their results.

Now let's look at their results and see if we can interpret them. Let's start with the results from column 1. First we need to make sure we have understood what they show by describing them.

■ How would you describe the results from column 1?

Remember that a description translates information from one form to another. At this stage we are not attempting to explain the result. In this case, an adequate description is that the lymphocytes washed through the column could not produce type **X** antibodies at all, but could produce a small quantity of antibodies against type **Y** antigens.

■ Can you explain the two parts of that description?

The clonal selection hypothesis proposes that, by chance, rat **R** would have some lymphocytes with protein receptors that were complementary to type **X** antigen, and other lymphocytes with protein receptors that were complementary to type **Y** antigen. So, the rat had the potential to make antibodies against both types of antigen. Since rat **R** was injected with type **X** antigen, we predict that it would produce a large clone of cells with receptor proteins complementary to that antigen. However, these would bind with the type **X** antigen on the beads in column 1. That is why none of the lymphocytes emerging from column 1 could produce antibodies against type **X** antigen (called anti-X antibody in Figure 10). The cells with a receptor protein complementary to type **Y** antigen would not bind with the type **X** antigen in column 1 and so emerged at the bottom of the column. The cells can produce anti-Y antibody but, since there are so few of them, they only produced a small quantity.

Now let's describe the results from column 2. Here, the emerging cells produced large quantities of anti-X antibody but no anti-Y antibody.

■ Explain why cells emerging from column 2 give large quantities of anti-X antibody but no anti-Y antibody.

We predicted that rat **R** would produce a large clone of cells with receptor proteins complementary to type **X** antigen. Since column 2 contained

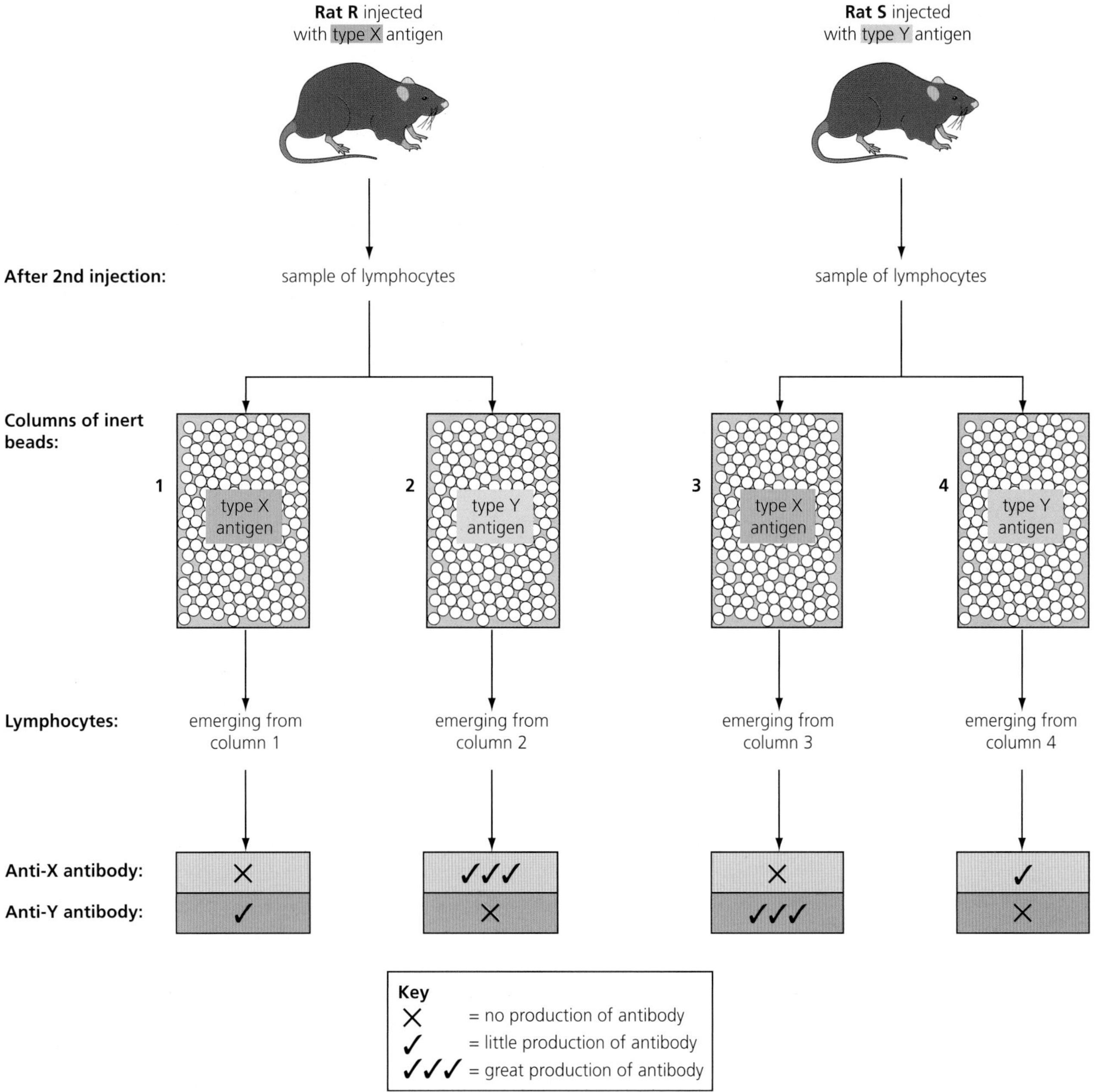

Figure 10 This diagram summarises the method and results of an investigation into antibodies from rats injected with antigens.

beads coated with type **Y** antigen, these cells would not bind to this antigen and would emerge at the bottom of the column. Since there were lots of cells, they produced a large quantity of anti-X antibodies. The few cells with protein receptors for type **Y** antigen bound with the antigen in column 2; none emerged at the bottom of the column.

You should be able to use similar arguments to explain the results from columns 3 and 4. We can then **evaluate** the experiment. This means we ask whether the experiment was a good test of the clonal selection hypothesis. If the results had not been consistent with this prediction, they would have cast serious doubt on the hypothesis. By using two rats injected with different antigens of the same bacterium, and by using columns with only type X antigen or only type Y antigen, the scientists had built a **control** into

Figure 11 This child is being vaccinated. The vaccine will cause him to make antibodies against a pathogen without ever suffering the disease it causes.

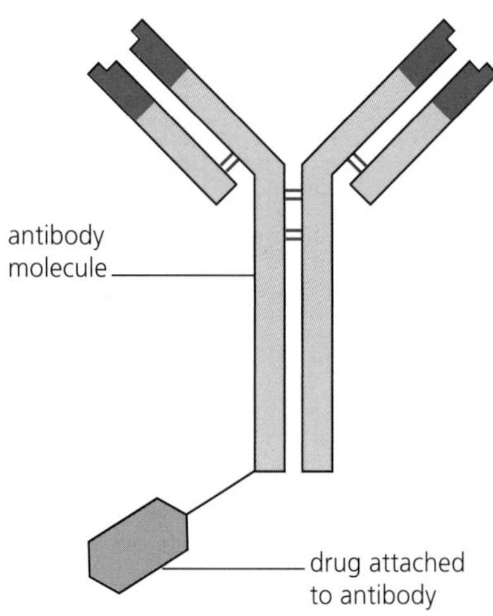

Figure 12 'Magic bullets' are monoclonal antibodies each with a molecule of a drug attached to them. These antibodies attach specifically to cells carrying the complementary antigen on their surface. In this way, the drug gets directly to the cells where it is needed.

Q8

When making monoclonal antibodies to direct a drug to a patient's cells, scientists would not use B cells from the patient's own body. Explain why.

their experiment. Without further details, we must assume that the scientists made sure that the conditions under which the rats were reared were kept constant. You could criticise the scientists for using only two rats, since this was a small sample size. In fact, they used large groups of rats. This account has been simplified to help us understand what as done. Therefore, we can conclude that the experiment was a valid test of the clonal selection hypothesis.

Vaccines

You are lucky not to have suffered potentially lethal diseases in order to become immune to them. Instead, you were given vaccinations, like the child in Figure 11. As a result, your body made antibodies. A **vaccine** is a preparation of antigen from a pathogen. The vaccine can be injected or, in some cases, it is swallowed. After the first treatment, you make antibodies against the antigens; you also make memory cells. After the second treatment, you show the secondary response seen in Figure 9, making large numbers of B cells and memory cells.

Obviously, it would be crazy to inject someone with a really dangerous pathogen. Vaccines are made harmless in a number of ways. These include:

- killing the pathogen in a way that leaves its antigens unaffected, e.g. vaccine against cholera
- weakening the pathogen in a way that leaves its antigens unaffected, e.g. Sabin oral vaccine against polio
- removing the antigens from the surface of the pathogen and using the purified antigens to make a vaccine, e.g. vaccine against hepatitis B.

Monoclonal antibodies

Scientists can make a new cell by fusing a tumour cell with a B cell. Because it is made from two different cells, this new cell is called a **hybridoma cell**. It has the properties of the two cells from which it was made. Like a tumour cell, it grows rapidly in laboratory cultures. Like a B cell, it produces one type of antibody, namely **monoclonal antibody**.

Because hybridoma cells can be cultured in laboratories, scientists can harvest large quantities of monoclonal antibody. Monoclonal antibodies have a number of uses. They can be injected into someone in the initial stages of a particular infection, providing him or her with a high concentration of antibodies to overcome the disease.

Figure 12 shows another use of monoclonal antibodies. A drug has been attached to the molecule of antibody. Since the antibody will attach only to cells with the specific antigen on their surface, the drug will be carried directly and solely to those cells on which it is designed to work.

To vaccinate or not? A parent's dilemma

Parents must make many decisions about the health and safety of their child. Vaccination is one of these decisions. You might think that the decision is obvious – if you have your child vaccinated, you protect it against a potentially lethal disease. However, all vaccinations carry a small risk. Suppose that you believe this risk is too high; would you have your child vaccinated?

Table 1 The proportion of children affected as a result of getting measles or after their first dose of a vaccine offering protection against measles.

Condition	Proportion of children affected as a result of:	
	getting measles	their first dose of MMR vaccine
Convulsions	1 in 200	1 in 1000
Brain disease (meningitis or encephalitis)	Between 1 in 200 and 1 in 5000	Less than I in a million
Death	Between 1 in 2500 and 1 in 5000, depending on age	0

Parents recently faced exactly this dilemma. In the 1980s, a new triple vaccine, MMR, was introduced. The MMR vaccine gives protection against three diseases:

- measles, which can lead to severe illness, convulsions, lifelong disability and death
- mumps, which can cause meningitis and permanent deafness
- rubella, which during pregnancy can affect the fetus by causing deafness, blindness, heart defects and other difficulties.

The triple vaccine is thought to be a better protection than three separate vaccines because it reduces the time over which babies are exposed to rubella, measles and mumps. The MMR vaccination is made in two doses. The first dose is given at 12 to 15 months. The second dose is given at school entry.

1 The first dose of MMR coincides with the time when many breast-fed babies are weaned. What is the advantage of this timing?

2 Rubella affects the fetus of pregnant women, yet it is important that boys are vaccinated against rubella. Explain why.

3 Look at Table 1. What can you conclude from this about the safety of the MMR vaccine?

In February 1988, Dr Wakefield, a British doctor, published a research report suggesting that MMR might cause autism, a behavioural disorder. Dr Wakefield proposed that, in some children, MMR vaccination causes inflammation of the intestine, which causes toxins to leak into the blood. These toxins then pass into the brain, producing the damage that causes autism.

4 Dr Wakefield carried out his initial research on 12 children. How reliable were his findings?

In April 2000, Dr Wakefield and Professor John O'Leary, director of pathology at a Dublin hospital, presented further research findings to the United States Congress. They reported that tests on 25 children with autism showed 24 had traces of the measles virus in their guts. Professor O'Leary said this was now 'compelling evidence' of a link between autism and MMR.

5 Does the evidence of Dr Wakefield and Professor O'Leary show that MMR causes autism? Explain your answer.

Many other scientists performed investigations to check these research findings. None could find any evidence to support Dr Wakefield's proposal that MMR caused autism. Despite this, public confidence in the MMR vaccine fell dramatically in the UK. Many parents prevented their children from receiving the MMR vaccine. Some parents of autistic children began to sue the pharmaceutical companies that had produced the MMR vaccine.

6 Dr Wakefield acted as a consultant for some of the parents who were suing the pharmaceutical companies. This led to criticism from his scientific peers. Explain why.

7 Figure 13 shows the results of research in California. Do these data support the theory that autism is linked to the use of MMR vaccine? Explain your answer.

There is now an overwhelming body of evidence to suggest there is no link between MMR vaccinations and autism. Despite this, the proportion of children in the UK receiving an MMR vaccination by their second birthday fell from 91% in 1997–1998 to 81% in 2004–2005. Would you have had your baby vaccinated with MMR? We must each use the available scientific evidence intelligently to inform our decisions.

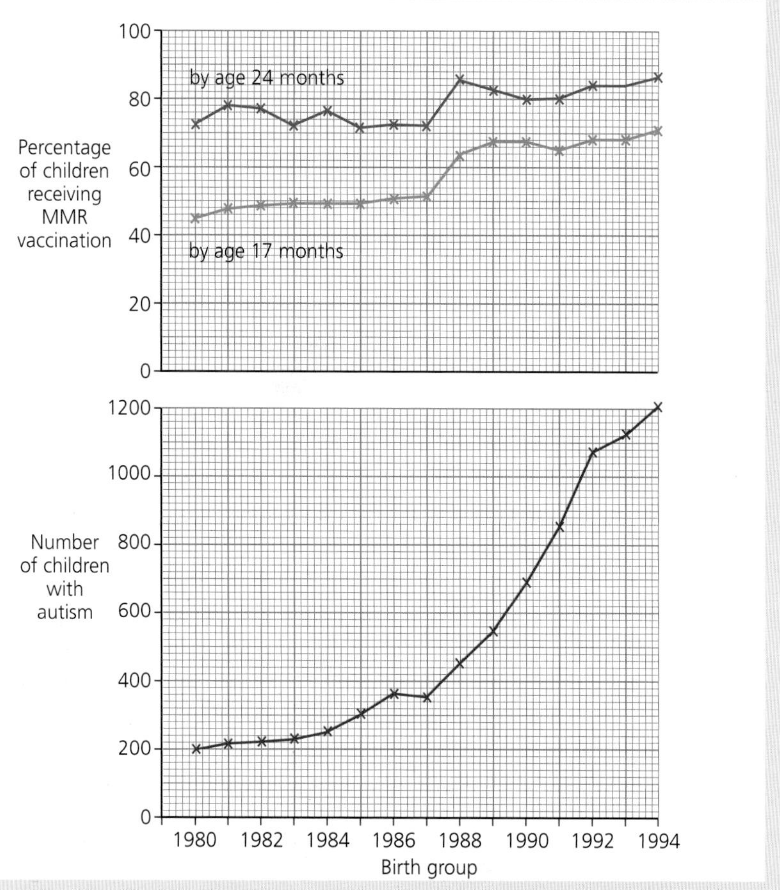

Figure 13 Is there a link between the use of MMR vaccine and autism? The upper graph shows the percentage of two-year-old children who received MMR vaccinations between 1980 and 1994. The lower graph shows the number of reported cases of autism among the children born in these years. The data are from a study in California, USA.

Chapter 6

DNA, genes and chromosomes

The two men in Figure 1 are James Watson and Francis Crick. They worked out the structure of DNA. The photo shows them standing by the model of DNA that they produced in 1953.

Throughout your GCSE Science course, you learned about the way that scientists work, and continue to do so during your AS Biology course. As James Watson tells us in his book *The Double Helix*, Watson and Crick worked on the structure of DNA without doing scientific experiments, as we shall see later.

Figure 1 James Watson and Francis Crick first proposed the structure of DNA that you will learn about in this chapter. Here, the two researchers are posing in front of the DNA model they built in 1953. Crick is pointing at the model.

In 1952, James Watson had completed his PhD in the USA and was carrying out research at the University of Cambridge in the UK. Here he met Francis Crick, who had yet to finish the research for his PhD in physics and was becoming quite bored with it. The two men were fascinated by DNA and spent many hours discussing its possible structure.

They knew from experiments performed in the previous 20 years that DNA is the hereditary material of organisms – a substance that carries information (the genetic code) for characteristics from one generation to the next. They knew that DNA, deoxyribonucleic acid, was one type of the cell substances called **nucleic acids**. They also knew that it contained chemical groups of atoms called deoxyribose and phosphate, and four types of a group called organic bases. These bases are adenine, thymine, cytosine and guanine. Watson and Crick also knew Chargaff's rule. This was that the number of adenine bases in a molecule of DNA is always the same as the number of thymine bases, and similarly for the pair of bases cytosine and guanine. This was something which Chargaff himself thought was a 'strange but possibly meaningless phenomenon'. But Watson and Crick's discovery was to give far-reaching meaning to these equal numbers of base pairs.

At the same time, other scientists around the world were racing to be the first to discover the nature of the genetic code. The American biochemist Linus Pauling had already won a Nobel Prize for work on chemical bonding, and Watson and Crick feared he would be the first to find the code. Two others, Maurice Wilkins and Rosalind Franklin, were working at Kings College in London. In their research, they bombarded crystals of DNA with X-rays and obtained photographic images that were patterns made by the diffracted X-rays. By studying these images and making careful measurements from them, these two scientists were able to learn about the internal structure of DNA. Figure 2 shows one of the X-ray images that Rosalind Franklin made. As soon as she saw this image she knew she had evidence that DNA has a helical structure, of two coils winding round together. At that moment, she was the only person in the world who both had that evidence and understood it.

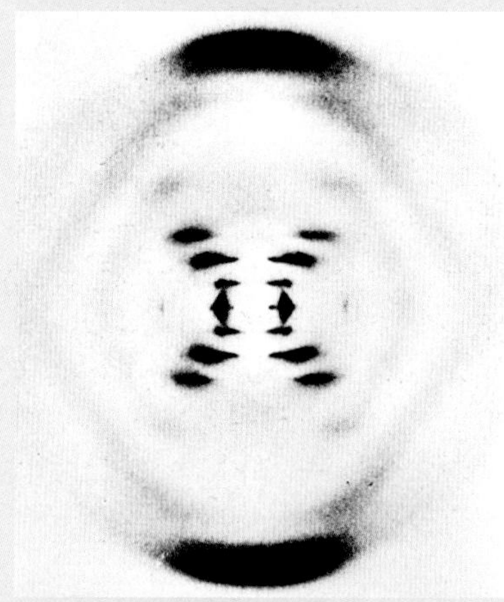

▲ **Figure 2** This photograph, that Rosalind Franklin produced from X-rays diffracted through a DNA molecule on to a photographic plate, told her that DNA is a double helix. Unfortunately for her, Watson and Crick saw her evidence and used it before she did.

As James Watson tells us in his book, during the time he and Crick collaborated over DNA, they did no scientific research of the usual kind, which involved experimenting and gathering data. Watson's sister was dating the son of Linus Pauling, whom they knew to be working on the genetic code. She was able to provide snippets of information about Pauling's research. Watson himself was able to obtain confidential information from the laboratories in which Wilkins and Franklin worked.

Using solely this information, molecular models and some very inspired guesswork, Watson and Crick came up with the structure of DNA. They published a 900-word report of their proposed structure in the journal *Nature* in April 1953 and won a Nobel Prize in 1962 for their discovery. Reflecting their reliance on the work of others, their Nobel Prize was shared with Maurice Wilkins, whose confidential research findings they had used. Unfortunately, by that time, Rosalind Franklin had died of cancer; otherwise she would also have shared the Nobel Prize. In his own autobiography, *The Third Man of the Double Helix*, Maurice Wilkins concludes that if only he and Rosalind Franklin had been able to work better together, they would have found the structure of DNA much earlier themselves. As in other walks of life, teamwork is important in scientific research.

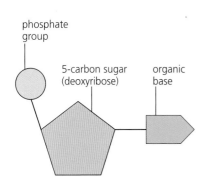

▲ **Figure 3** A single DNA nucleotide is made from a molecule of a 5-carbon sugar (a pentose) called deoxyribose, a phosphate group and an organic base. Nucleotides are the monomers from which nucleic acids are made.

Nucleotides

Like other molecules you have learned about, nucleic acids are polymers made up of repeated subunits. In this case, the subunit is called a **nucleotide**. Figure 3 shows the structure of a single nucleotide from DNA. It has three components:

- a **pentose** (5-carbon sugar). DNA gets part of its name from the sugar in each of its nucleotides. The sugar is called **deoxyribose** (which is the sugar ribose with one oxygen atom missing).
- a **phosphate group**. This has a negative charge, which makes DNA a highly charged molecule. This negative charge enables us to separate fragments of DNA by electrophoresis. You will learn more about this technique during your A2 course (see *A2 Biology*).
- an **organic base**. DNA contains only four of these bases. Two are **adenine** (A) and **guanine** (G), bases known as purines. The other two are **thymine** (T) and **cytosine** (C), bases known as pyrimidines.

Q1

What makes one DNA nucleotide different from another?

Polynucleotide strand

Figure 4 shows how two nucleotides join together by condensation (see page 5). You can see that the two deoxyribose groups (also called residues) become linked together through one of the phosphate groups. When many nucleotides become linked together like this, they form a **polynucleotide**. You can see the diagram of a single polynucleotide strand in Figure 5(a). Notice how the pentoses and phosphates form a sugar–phosphate backbone. As we will be more interested in the organic bases, we can simplify the polynucleotide strand to the structure shown in Figure 5(b).

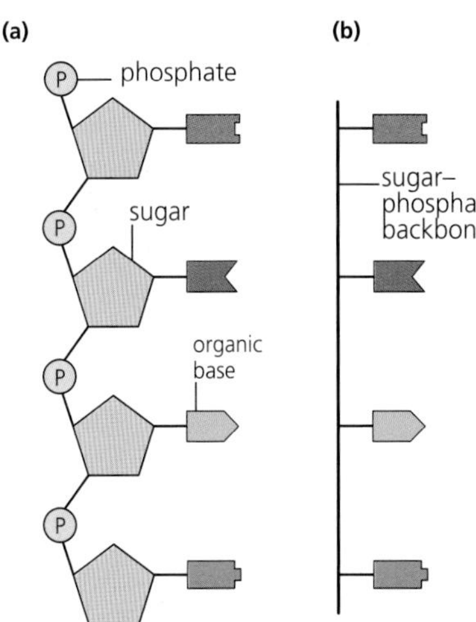

▲ **Figure 5** (a) Part of a single polynucleotide strand. (b) A simpler way to represent the same polynucleotide strand.

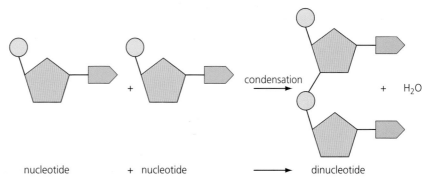

▲ **Figure 4** Two nucleotides react to form a dinucleotide.

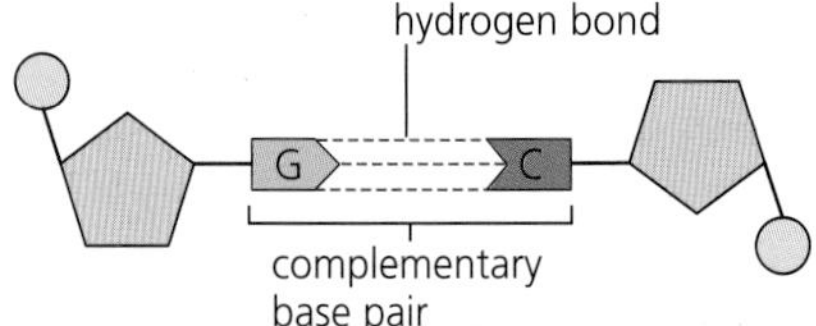

▲ **Figure 6** Hydrogen bonds form between the complementary bases of two nucleotides, producing a complementary base pair.

Base pairing

We saw in Figure 4 how two nucleotides condense to form a dinucleotide. Figure 6 shows a different way that two nucleotides can join together. The two nucleotides with complementary bases are joined by chemical bonds called **hydrogen bonds** between the bases. In this way the bases become a complementary base pair. Hydrogen bonds are weaker than the bonds holding the sugar–phosphate backbone together.

Base pairing occurs only between complementary bases. In DNA, adenine always pairs with thymine, with two hydrogen bonds (A=T) and cytosine always pairs with guanine, with three hydrogen bonds (C≡G).

Table 1 Complementary base pairs include one purine base and one pyrimidine base. A and T are complementary bases (A=T pair); C and G are complementary bases (C≡G pair).

Purine base	Pyrimidine base
Adenine (A)	Thymine (T)
Guanine (G)	Cytosine (C)

DNA has two polynucleotide strands

Some types of nucleic acid molecule are made of a single polynucleotide strand, like the one shown in Figure 5. You will learn more about these during your A2 course. DNA is not single-stranded; it is made from two polynucleotide strands. The two strands are held together by hydrogen bonds between the complementary base pairs shown in Table 1.

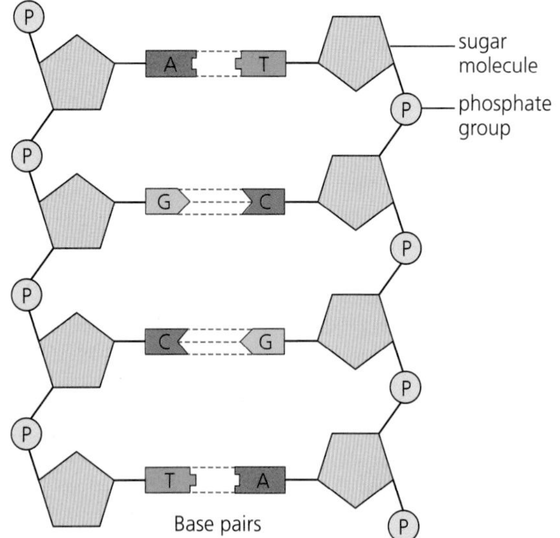

▲ **Figure 7** Part of a molecule of DNA showing that it has two anti-parallel strands.

Look at Figure 7, which shows part of a molecule of DNA. You should be able to identify individual nucleotides, the sugar–phosphate bonds holding together the nucleotides in one polynucleotide strand, and hydrogen bonds between complementary base pairs that are holding together the two polynucleotide strands. Look closely at the base sequence of each polynucleotide strand. Notice that one strand has a base sequence that is complementary to the base sequence on the other strand, and that the two strands run in opposite directions. For this reason, we call them **anti-parallel strands**.

Q2

A hydrogen bond is a relatively weak bond. Explain why the hydrogen bonds in DNA hold the molecule together strongly.

Figure 8(a) shows a simpler version of part of a DNA molecule. Here, the sugar–phosphate backbones are shown as single lines. Figure 8(b) shows the final complication of a DNA molecule. The two polynucleotide strands are twisted into a coil called a helix. This diagram shows why a DNA molecule is often referred to a **double helix**.

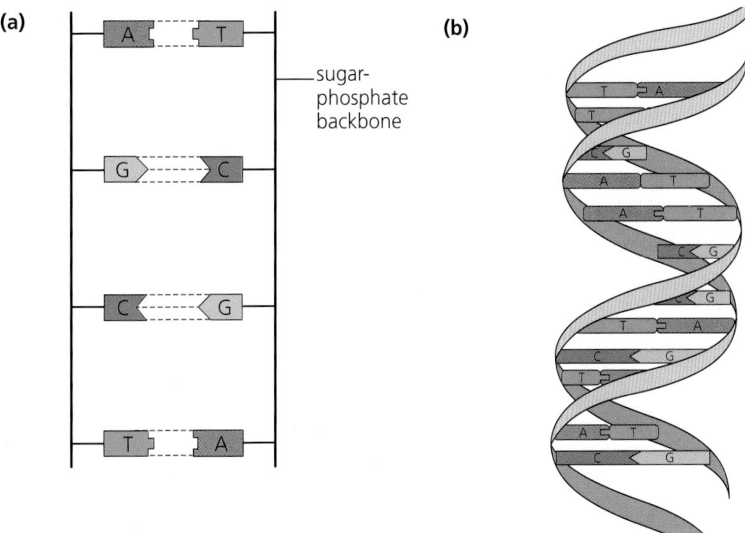

▲ **Figure 8** (a) A simpler version of Figure 7. (b) A molecule of DNA, showing the double helix of polynucleotide strands.

DNA and the genetic code

The **genetic code** is the order of bases in an organism's DNA. This sequence determines the amino acid sequence of each polypeptide (page 12) that a cell can produce. One or more very long polypeptides assemble to form proteins. Proteins include haemoglobin found in red blood cells, and enzymes that regulate all the chemical reactions of substances in cells. The genetic code controls the sequence of amino acids in polypeptides, and hence the nature of proteins formed from them. The code thereby controls how an organism develops and behaves.

You will learn more about the way in which the genetic code is used to make polypeptides in Unit 5 during your A2 course. For now, you need only know that it is the *order* of the bases, adenine, cytosine, guanine and thymine, which forms this genetic code. In fact, a sequence of three bases, called a **base triplet**, carries the genetic code for each amino acid.

DNA is a stable molecule

Since DNA carries the code that cells use to produce their polypeptides, it is important that a DNA molecule does not change. Two types of chemical bond hold DNA molecules together. The first is the bond that joins the phosphate group of one nucleotide to the sugar of the next. Look again at

Figure 4 to see this. This is a fairly strong bond and is not easily broken. The second is the hydrogen bond between bases in a base pair, as shown in Figure 8(a). Although hydrogen bonds are relatively weak, a single molecule of DNA might be several thousand nucleotides long. Thousands of hydrogen bonds ensure that the two polynucleotide strands are held firmly together.

Experiments showing that DNA is the genetic material

Scientists were not easily convinced that DNA is the genetic material. It might be a surprise to hear that, for the first half of the twentieth century, most scientists believed that proteins held the genetic code. They thought the components of DNA seemed much too simple! Let's look at some experiments that changed their minds.

In the first experiment, a bacterium called *Streptococcus pneumoniae* was used. It causes pneumonia in humans and other mammals. The bacterium is rod-shaped and has two strains. On agar plates, colonies of the **S strain** bacterial cells produce an outer polysaccharide coat and appear smooth. Colonies of the mutant **R strain** bacterial cells lack the polysaccharide coat and appear rough.

A team of scientists injected mice with different combinations of these two strains of the bacterium. Figure 9 shows the results.

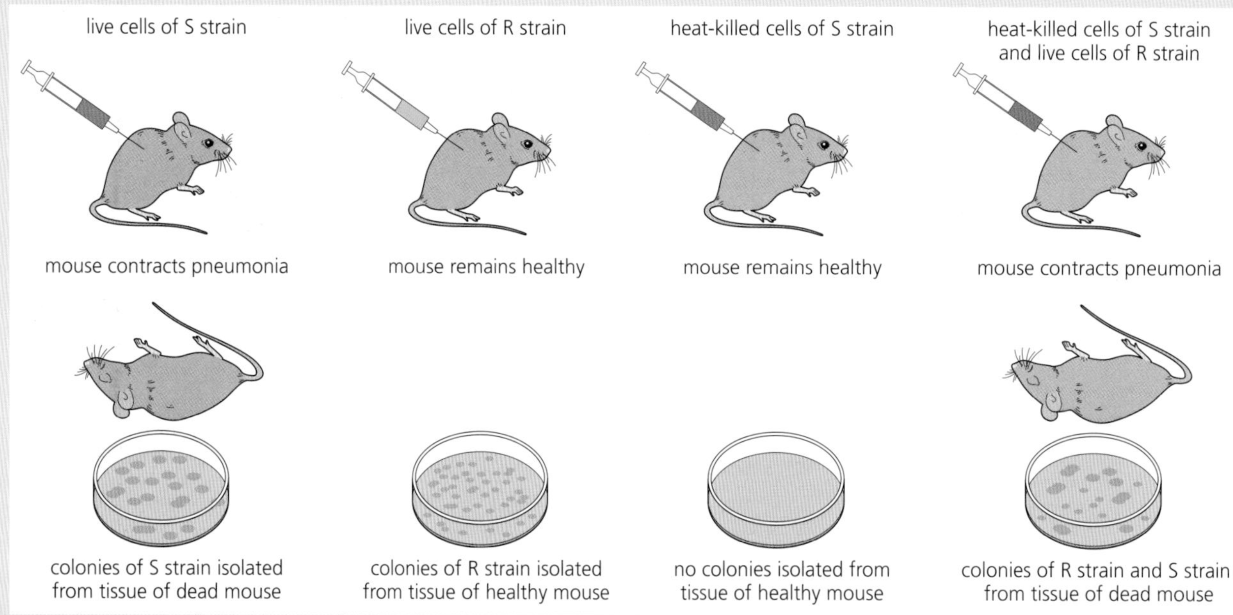

▲ **Figure 9** The effect of injecting mice with different combinations of the S strain and R strain of *Streptococcus pneumoniae*.

1 Which strain of the *S. pneumoniae* caused the mice to die? Use Figure 9 to explain your answer.

2 Suggest why this scientist used mice in his experiment.

Heat-killed S strain on its own did not cause mice to die, yet mixed with R strain it did. The first team of scientists concluded that the genetic information of the heat-killed S strain was able to get into the live cells of the R strain and transform them into S-type cells. They did not know the chemical nature of this transforming agent.

Some time later, another team of scientists set up an experiment to try to find the nature of the transforming agent. They treated heat-killed samples of the S strain of *S. pneumoniae* with different enzymes. Each enzyme broke down specific molecules within the bacteria. The scientists then mixed each of the extracts from these S-strain cells with a different culture of the R strain, and looked at the type of colony that grew on an agar plate. Table 2 shows their results.

3 This research team suspected that three types of molecule found in cells might be the transforming agent. Name these types of molecule.

Table 2 The effect of incubation with different enzymes on the ability of the S strain of *S. pneumoniae* to transform the R strain.

Experiment	Enzyme used to treat heat-killed cells of S strain of S. pneumoniae	Appearance of R-strain colonies growing on agar plate
1	Protease	Smooth
2	Ribonuclease	Smooth
3	Deoxyribonuclease	Rough

4 The team concluded that DNA was the transforming agent. Use the data in Table 2 to explain why.

Most scientists remained unconvinced, and these results were largely ignored for many years. The results were criticised for several reasons. These included:

- some contaminating protein could have been left in the protease preparation.
- DNA might be only part of a pathway that proteins used for transformation.

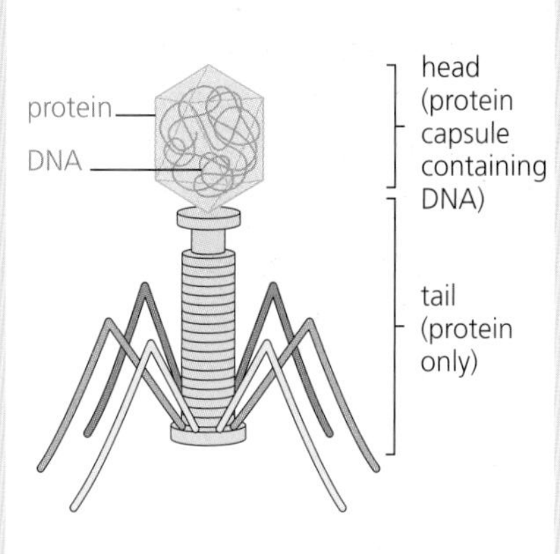

▲ **Figure 10** T2 bacteriophages are viruses which infect the bacterium *Escherichia coli*.

It took a Nobel Prize-winning experiment to convince scientists around the world that DNA was the genetic material. This experiment used a **bacteriophage**. This is a virus that infects and kills bacteria. The virus was the T2 bacteriophage. This bacteriophage infects *Escherichia coli*, a bacterium which commonly grows in the gut of humans. Figure 10 shows a single T2 bacteriophage. Notice its simple structure: it has an outer protein capsule surrounding a molecule of DNA. When a T2 bacteriophage infects an *E. coli* bacterium, it multiplies to produce large numbers of bacteriophages that burst the bacterial cell and are released.

5 Suggest one advantage of using T2 bacteriophages in this experiment.

Protein contains sulphur, which DNA does not. DNA contains phosphorus, which proteins do not. Each of these elements has a radioactive isotope, ^{32}P and ^{35}S. The team of scientists grew some T2 bacteriophage in the presence of ^{32}P, which labels their DNA, and some in the presence of ^{35}S, which labels their proteins. After infecting a culture of *E. coli* with these labelled bacteriophages, the team put samples of the culture in a blender. This removed the bacteriophages from the surface of the bacteria. They then looked to see where the radioactive elements were found. Figure 11 shows their results.

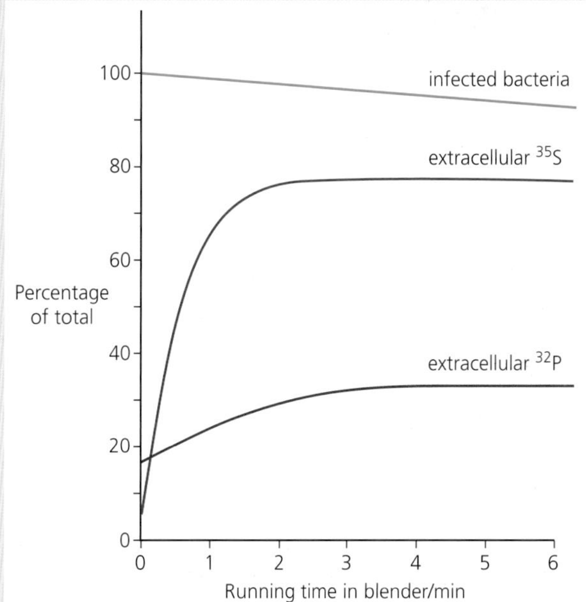

▲ **Figure 11** The location of radioactivity after removing the T2 bacteriophage from the surface of infected *E. coli* cells.

6 Where does Figure 11 show that most of the DNA was found? Where was most of the protein found?

7 The team went on to show that new bacteriophages released by bursting *E. coli* cells were labelled only with ^{32}P. Why did this finally convince scientists that DNA is the genetic material?

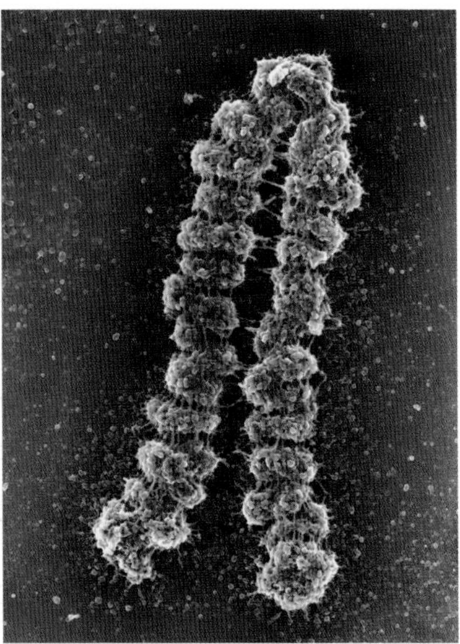

▲ **Figure 12** An electron micrograph of a chromosome. If you look closely, you can see some bits of the polynucleotide strand that is tightly coiled in the chromosome.

DNA, chromosomes and genes

The DNA of prokaryotic cells is different from the DNA in eukaryotic cells (see page 35). In prokaryotes, each molecule of DNA forms a closed loop, which is found in the cytoplasm of their cells. Although a single prokaryotic cell might contain many of these loops, they are all copies of the same DNA molecule.

In contrast, a single eukaryotic cell always has many, different molecules of DNA. In eukaryotic cells, each DNA molecule is surrounded by proteins called **histones**, and forms a rod-like structure (with two ends) called a **chromosome**. Figure 12 shows a chromosome from a eukaryotic cell. In it, the DNA helix is tightly coiled, so that the chromosome looks much thicker than a DNA molecule. Look closely at Figure 12. Can you see some of the polynucleotide strands within the thick chromosome?

Each chromosome carries the genetic code for a large number of polypeptides. The code for a single polypeptide is called a **gene**. Look at Figure 13. It shows a chromosome as a long string of genes. Each gene has a specific position on a chromosome, called its **locus**. For example, the human gene that codes for pancreatic amylase (see Chapter 1, page 11) is located at the locus p21 on the short arm of chromosome 1. The sequence of organic bases in each gene encodes the amino acid sequence of a single polypeptide molecule.

Q3

Give three ways in which the DNA of prokaryotic cells is different from DNA in eukaryotic cells.

It might surprise you to learn that much of the DNA in eukaryotic cells does not code for polypeptides. In fact, less than 2% of human DNA is thought to code for them. Figure 14 shows how some non-coding DNA is found within a gene, and some is found between genes. The non-coding regions of DNA within a gene are called **introns**; the coding regions are called **exons**.

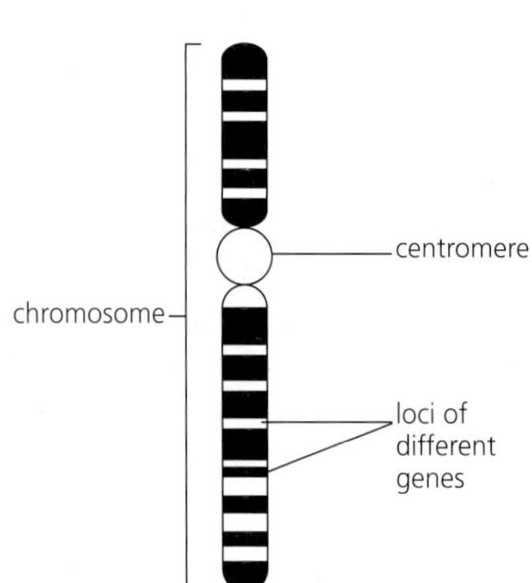

▲ **Figure 13** A chromosome contains many genes. Each gene occurs on one chromosome only and occupies a particular place called its locus.

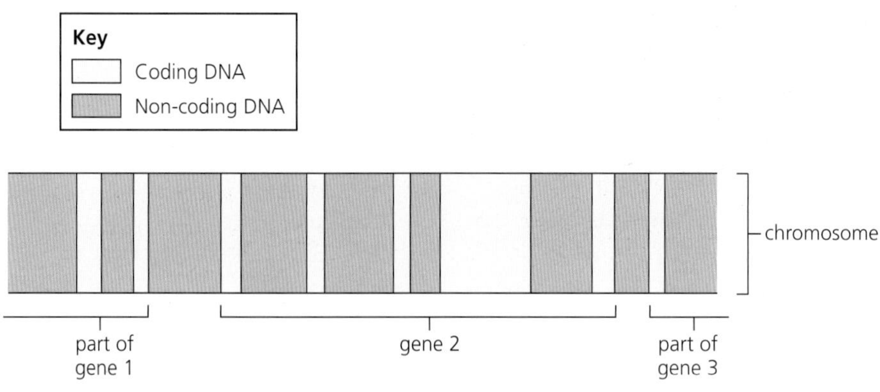

▲ **Figure 14** Non-coding DNA is found within a gene and between adjacent genes.

Differences between the DNA found in prokaryotic and eukaryotic cells have been described above. These differences are summarised in Table 3. Because of these differences, we should not refer to the genetic material of a prokaryotic cell as a chromosome. However, as a shorthand description, we sometimes refer to bacterial 'chromosomes'.

Table 3 A comparison of the DNA molecules found in prokaryotic and eukaryotic cells.

Feature of DNA	Prokaryotic cells	Eukaryotic cells
Relative length of molecule	Short, i.e. few genes	Long, i.e. many genes
Shape of molecule	Circular, forming a closed loop	Linear, forming a chromosome
Number of different molecules per cell	One	More than one
Association with proteins	Not associated with proteins	Associated with proteins, called histones
Non-coding DNA	Absent	Present within genes (introns) and as **multiple repeated sequences** between genes

Meiosis separates homologous chromosomes and produces haploid cells

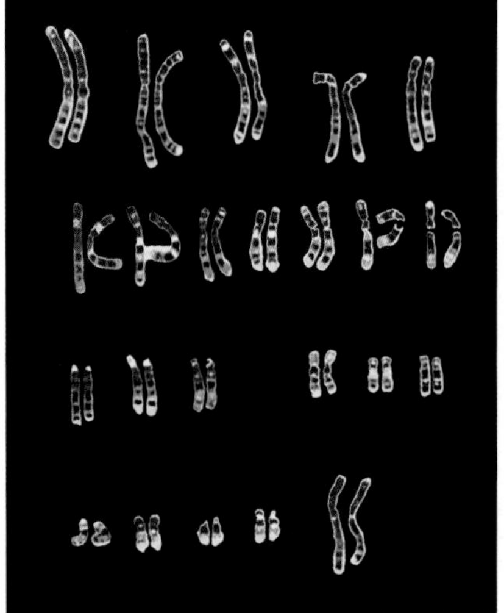

▲ **Figure 15** The chromosomes in a body cell from a human female.

Look at Figure 15. It shows the chromosomes from one cell from a human female. To make this, a photograph was taken of the cell using a camera and an optical microscope. The image of each chromosome was then cut out of the photograph and the images were arranged as you see them. Notice that they have been arranged in pairs. The members of each pair are the same size and shape. More importantly, they carry genes controlling the same characters in the same order. We call the members of each pair **homologous chromosomes**. You inherited one member of each homologous pair of chromosomes from your mother (**maternal chromosome**) and the other member of the homologous pair from your father (**paternal chromosome**).

A cell with pairs of homologous chromosomes is called **diploid**. A cell with only one chromosome from each homologous pair is called **haploid**. We often refer to diploid cells as **2*n*** and haploid cells as ***n***. If you look back to Figure 15, you will see that diploid human cells have 46 chromosomes ($2n = 46$). However, not all our cells are diploid. Our gametes – the egg and sperm cells that we produce – are haploid. Human gametes (the sex cells) have 23 chromosomes ($n = 23$).

Q4

We often use the symbol 2*n* to represent diploid cells. What does *n* represent?

The type of cell division that produces haploid cells from diploid cells is called **meiosis**. Most eukaryotic organisms have diploid and haploid cells during their life cycle. This means that meiosis occurs at some stage in the life cycle. Figure 16 shows two life cycles: our own and that of a fungus. Notice that, although humans produce gametes by meiosis, fungi do not.

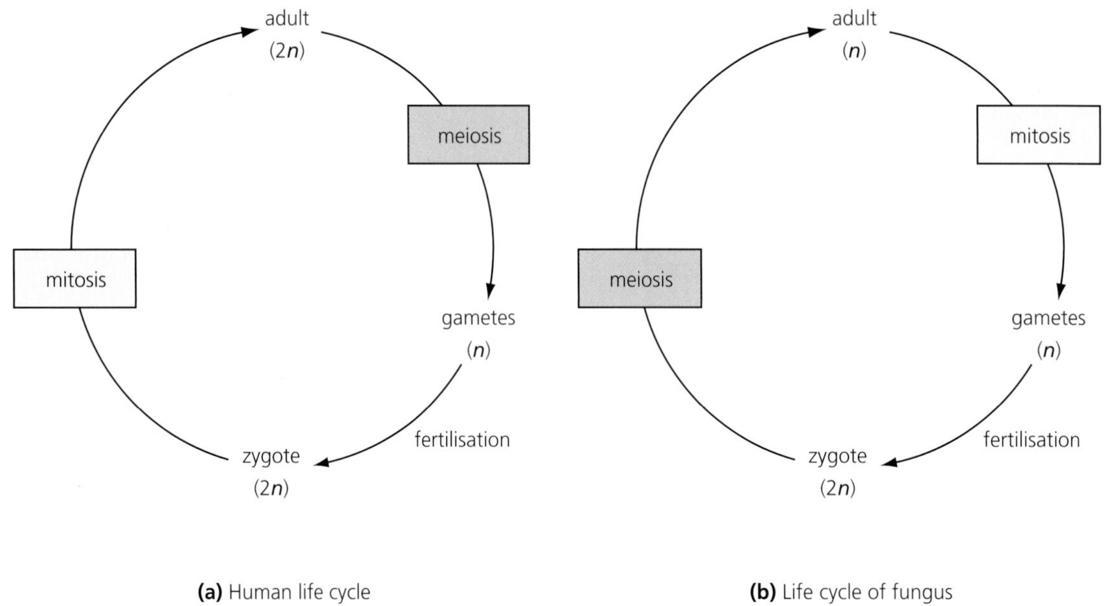

(a) Human life cycle

(b) Life cycle of fungus

▲ **Figure 16** Meiosis produces haploid cells (*n* chromosomes) from diploid cells (2*n* chromosomes). (a) In humans, meiosis occurs during gamete production. (b) In fungi, meiosis occurs after fertilisation, not before it.

Q5

Explain one advantage to humans of producing haploid gametes.

Meiosis has one other important effect: the haploid cells produced are genetically different from each other. There are two reasons for this: independent assortment of homologous chromosomes; and genetic recombination by crossing over.

Independent assortment of homologous chromosomes

The heading might sound a complicated description of the process, but the sequence is quite easy to follow. Figure 17 shows a cell with two pairs of homologous chromosomes. The members of each pair are colour-coded to distinguish the maternal and paternal chromosomes. Before meiosis starts, each chromosome makes a copy of itself.

Then two divisions occur:

- The **first meiotic division** separates the chromosomes in each homologous pair.
- The **second meiotic division** separates the two copies that each chromosome made of itself before meiosis started.

In the first meiotic division, the separation of one pair of homologous chromosomes is not affected by the separation of any other pair. In other words, if the maternal chromosome from one pair moves to one side of the cell, it does not cause the maternal chromosomes of other pairs to go in the same direction. This is **independent assortment of chromosomes**. The result is that gametes contain a mixture of maternal and paternal chromosomes.

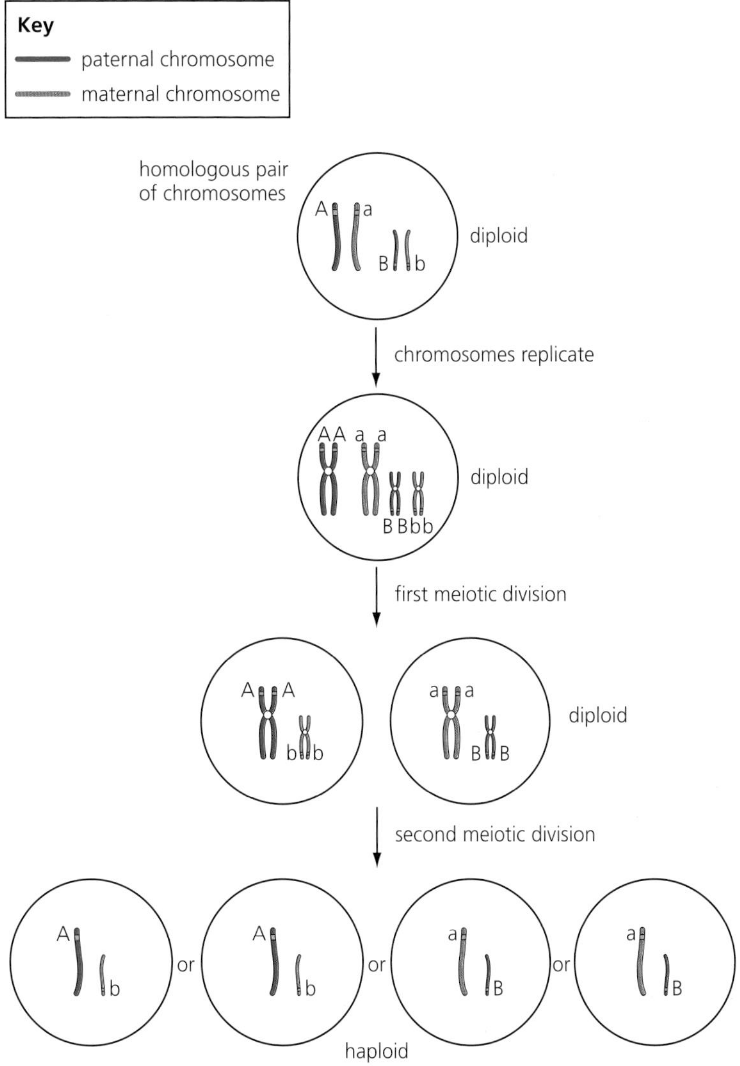

▲ **Figure 17** The result of meiosis in a cell with two pairs of homologous chromosomes. Before meiosis occurs, the chromosomes have copied themselves. As a result of meiosis, four cells (haploid gametes) can be formed, and there are two possible combinations. Another cell with the same two pairs of homologous chromosomes can produce another two different combinations (AB and ab), making four possible combinations in total.

Remember that homologous chromosomes carry genes controlling the same characters in the same order. However, each gene can have different forms, called **alleles**. To take a simple example, the human gene for haemoglobin has two forms; one leads to sickle cell anaemia and one does not. The maternal and paternal chromosomes in one homologous pair carry different alleles of many of their genes. Therefore, independent assortment produces different combinations of genes in the cells formed during meiosis. If you look back to Figure 17, you will see that a cell with just two pairs of homologous chromosomes could produce haploid cells with any one of four different combinations of maternal and paternal chromosomes. As you know, human cells have 23 pairs of homologous chromosomes. Independent assortment of 23 pairs of homologous chromosomes can result in 2^{23} different chromosome combinations in the haploid egg cells and sperm cells.

Q6

Use your knowledge of independent assortment of homologous chromosomes to determine how many genetically different children one human couple could have. Explain your answer.

Genetic recombination by crossing over

The chromosomes at the end of meiosis in Figure 17 are the same colour code as they were at the beginning. Figure 18 shows how homologous chromosomes can exchange pieces of their own DNA.

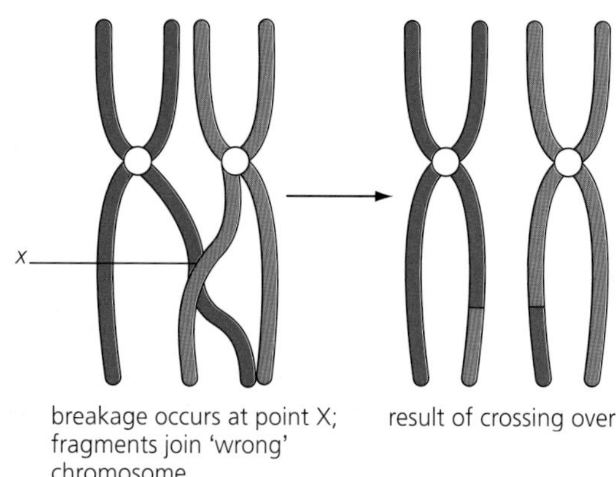

▲ **Figure 18** During meiosis, when the chromosomes of a homologous pair break at the same point, DNA is exchanged between the chromosomes. This is called crossing over.

During the first meiotic division, the members of each homologous pair lie side by side. If they break at the same point along their length, the broken segments can join the other member of the chromosome pair. This is called

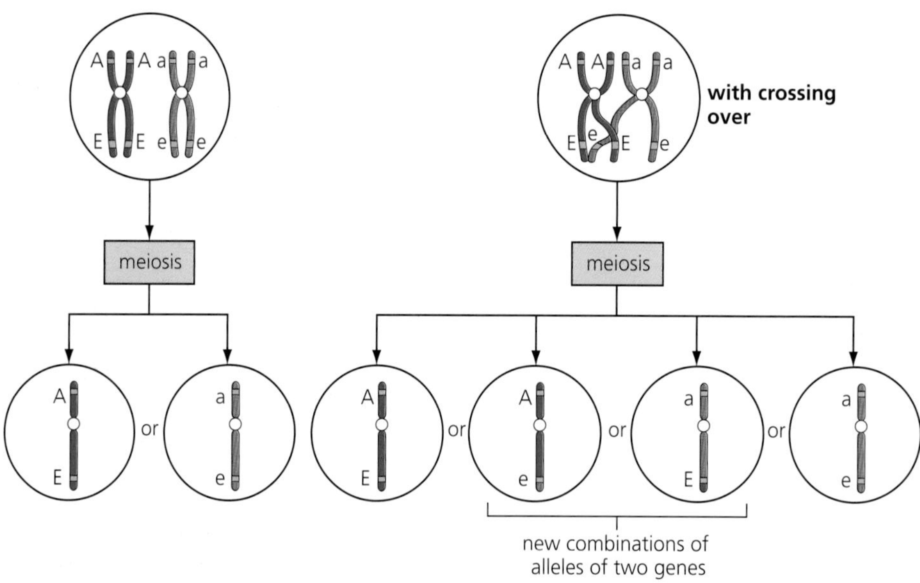

▲ **Figure 19** Crossing over results in cells with chromosomes that carry new combinations of alleles.

crossing over and results in **recombination** that gives rise to genetic variation.

The effect of crossing over is shown in Figure 19. You can see in this diagram that some of the haploid cells have chromosomes with part of the DNA from both the maternal and paternal chromosomes. They have a combination of alleles that was not present in either of the parental chromosomes.

Q7

What effect will crossing over have on your answer to Q6?

Chapter 7

DNA replication and the cell cycle

If you have visited the Royal Botanic Gardens at Kew, you probably enjoyed the variety of plants on display in the gardens and glasshouses. However, you are not likely to have seen laboratories full of plants in small containers like those shown in Figure 1. In addition to the staff who tend the gardens and glasshouses, there are teams of plant scientists working at the Royal Botanic Gardens.

▲ **Figure 1** A micropropagation unit. Inside each of the containers is a tiny plant that is growing on a sterile growth medium. Some of the plants are grown from seed. Others are grown from small pieces of growth tissue (an explant) taken from a mature plant.

One team works in the Micropropagation Unit. Members of this team are experts at propagating (reproducing) plants from seeds and from very small pieces of plant tissue, hence 'micro'. The containers in Figure 1 show plants that are not being grown in normal soil. Instead, they are in a special medium containing all the substances they require. They are kept in a sterile environment, which is why you will not have seen them if you visited the gardens.

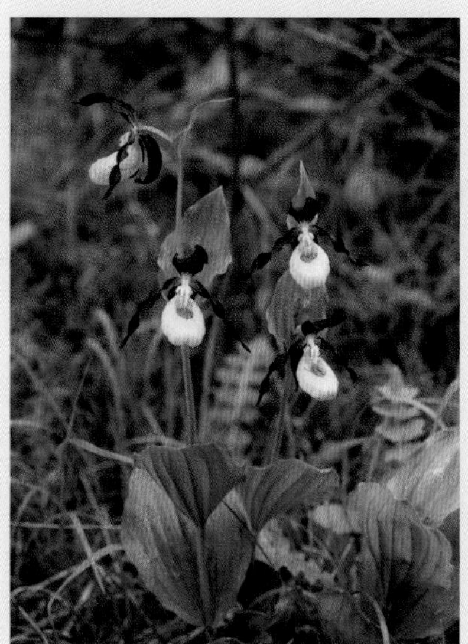

▲ **Figure 2** The lady's slipper orchid (*Cypripedium calceolus*). In the UK, the natural population of this species was reduced to only one flowering plant. Its location was a closely guarded secret.

You might wonder why plants are grown in sterile media. It is a way of making sure that the seedlings do not become infected by moulds, which could kill them. Some plants are grown in very large numbers. Often, they are plants of species from all over the world that are rare and possibly in danger of becoming extinct.

There are 50 species of orchid growing naturally in the UK. About one-third of these are thought to be endangered, mainly because their natural habitat has been damaged. For example, marshes that are the habitat of some orchids have been drained, and fertilisers added to the soil have favoured other plants which out-compete the orchids. Ten species of orchid are so rare that they are protected under an act of parliament. Figure 2 shows one of the rarest of these orchids – the lady's slipper orchid, *Cypripedium calceolus*. Over-keen Victorian collectors reduced its wild population in the UK to a single flowering plant. The team of plant scientists at Kew developed a recovery programme for this orchid that involved micropropagation techniques.

Plant scientists often use seeds in their micropropagation programmes. This was the case with the lady's slipper orchid. Where fertile seeds are not available, they develop new plants using samples of tissue from existing plants. This technique works best if the tissues taken are from a part of the plant that is actively growing. A small sample of tissue is cut from the plant and its outer layers of cells are removed. This leaves a tiny mass of cells, about 1 mm or less in diameter. This is called an explant. These cells are put into a flask containing a liquid growth medium. Eventually, a plant scientist can remove from this medium many small clumps of cells, and place each clump individually on sterile agar medium where it develops into a new plant. The plants are identical to the parent plant that was the source of the tissue, and therefore they form a clone.

Micropropagation is more successful with plants than with animals. This is because many plant cells retain their ability to divide even after they have matured and become specialised. Therefore, each clump of dividing cells, or **explant**, contains all the genetic information needed to form roots, stems and flowers in the developing new plant. In this chapter, we will examine how cells pass copies of their genetic information from cell to cell and about the type of cell division that produces new, genetically identical cells.

Replication of DNA

In Chapter 6, we saw that DNA contains two polynucleotide strands that are held together by hydrogen bonds between complementary base pairs. You will see that this base pairing is vital during **DNA replication**, that is, when DNA is copied in the nucleus of a cell. We can describe DNA replication using the three stages shown in Figure 3.

Stage 1: The polynucleotide strands of DNA separate

Replication of a DNA molecule begins when its double helix partially unwinds. As it does so, the hydrogen bonds between complementary base

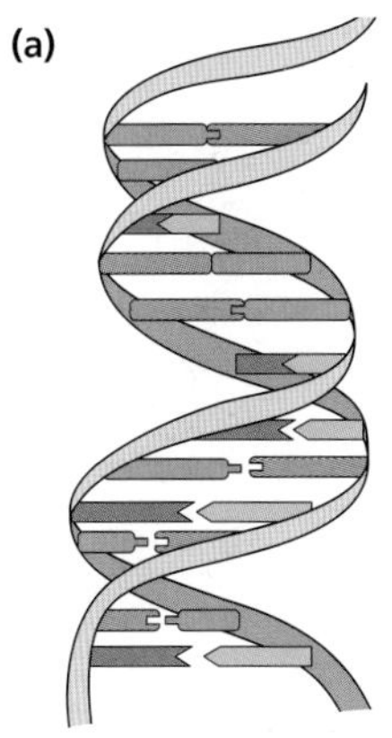

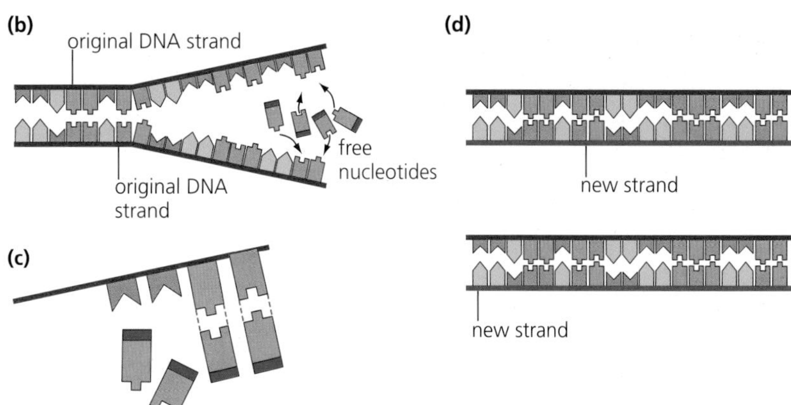

▲ **Figure 3** The process of DNA replication.
(a) The two strands of the DNA molecule begin to unwind when the weak hydrogen bonds between bases break. This happens at the point where the DNA is to be copied.
(b) Free DNA nucleotides pair with complementary bases that are exposed on the unwound DNA.
(c) Hydrogen bonds form between the new nucleotides and bases of each polynucleotide strand.
(d) At each DNA strand, the enzyme DNA polymerase joins the free nucleotides together. Each new strand is an exact copy of one of the old strands.

pairs break down. If you guessed that an enzyme is involved in breaking the hydrogen bonds, you are correct. The enzyme is called **DNA helicase**. The breakdown of hydrogen bonds allows the two polynucleotide strands to move apart. Figure 3(b) shows that we now have two separate strands of nucleotides with unpaired bases.

Stage 2: Free DNA nucleotides pair with exposed bases on each polynucleotide strand

The bases on the polynucleotide strands do not remain unpaired for long. Individual DNA nucleotides have already been made in the nucleus. They are attracted to the exposed bases on each polynucleotide strand, and hydrogen bonds form between complementary bases. For example, a free DNA nucleotide that includes the base adenine is attracted to an exposed thymine on one of the polynucleotide strands, and forms hydrogen bonds with it. This happens all along the unwound section of the DNA molecule. As a result, each of the polynucleotide strands of the DNA soon builds up a complementary sequence of nucleotides.

Stage 3: The new nucleotides bond together

You can see in Figure 3(c) that new nucleotides have formed hydrogen bonds with the bases of each polynucleotide strand. However, these new nucleotides are not joined together themselves. This happens in the final stage of DNA replication, shown in Figure 3(d). In this stage, deoxyribose–phosphate bonds are formed along the new chain of nucleotides (see Chapter 6, page 118). This linking of DNA nucleotides is controlled by the enzyme **DNA polymerase**.

We end up with two new DNA molecules, each formed from an original polynucleotide strand and a new, replicated, polynucleotide strand. We call this **semi-conservative replication** – one original strand remains intact (is conserved) and one new complementary strand is made using the old strand as a template for replication. The DNA molecules rewind as this process is completed.

Q1

During replication, a DNA molecule actually unwinds at many points along its length. Suggest one advantage of this.

Experimental evidence for semi-conservative replication of DNA

You might wonder how we know that DNA replication is a semi-conservative process. After all, we cannot see DNA actually replicating. The evidence is indirect. Let's look at one experiment that provides evidence about DNA replication.

Look back to Figure 3. The conserved polynucleotide strands and the new polynucleotide strands are coloured differently to help you to understand the replication process. We can do this in a diagram, but we cannot colour real DNA nucleotides to help identify them.

Scientists in one laboratory came up with a neat way of labelling nucleotides. It depends on the use of two isotopes of nitrogen. The more common isotope has 14 uncharged particles, called protons, in the nucleus of each nitrogen atom. The rarer isotope has 15 protons in the nucleus of each nitrogen atom. This makes the rarer isotope (^{15}N) heavier than the more common isotope (^{14}N). The difference in mass is tiny. However, there are so many atoms of nitrogen in a strand of DNA that a difference in mass can be detected.

1 Which component of a DNA nucleotide contains nitrogen atoms?

Under laboratory conditions, a bacterium rapidly replicates its DNA and divides into two new cells. Bacteria use nitrogen in their growth medium to make DNA nucleotides. In this experiment, the scientists used two types of growth medium containing nitrogen; in one medium, all the nitrogen atoms were the ^{14}N isotope, and in the other they were all the ^{15}N isotope.

At the start of the experiment, the scientists grew bacteria on a growth medium in which all the nitrogen was the ^{14}N isotope. After many generations of bacteria, they removed DNA from a sample of the bacterial cells, put it into a liquid and spun it in a centrifuge. The DNA formed a band in the liquid, shown in Figure 4(a).

2 What property of the DNA caused it to form a band when spun in a centrifuge?

The scientists then repeated this procedure exactly, but used a growth medium in which all the nitrogen was the ^{15}N isotope. The DNA extracted from bacteria in this experiment formed the band shown in Figure 4(b).

Figure 4 The results of an experiment to test the theory that replication of DNA is a semi-conservative process. Each tube shows the position of DNA taken from bacteria after it was centrifuged at the same speed for the same time in a liquid.

(a) DNA from bacteria grown for many generations in a medium containing only the ^{14}N isotope of nitrogen.

(b) DNA from bacteria grown for many generations in a medium containing only the ^{15}N isotope of nitrogen.

(c) DNA from bacteria grown for many generations in a medium containing only the ^{15}N isotope of nitrogen and then a single generation in a medium containing only the ^{14}N isotope of nitrogen.

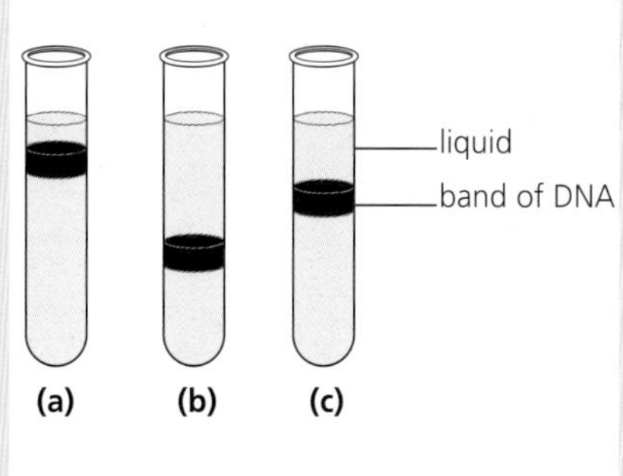

3 The bands of DNA in Figure 4(a) and (b) are in different positions in the centrifuge tubes. Explain why.

Finally, the scientists inoculated a sample of bacteria from the medium containing only the ^{15}N isotope into a medium containing only the ^{14}N isotope. After one generation, they removed DNA from a sample of these bacterial cells and spun it in a centrifuge. This DNA formed the band shown in Figure 4(c).

4 In the final part of the experiment, the scientists inoculated bacteria from a medium containing ^{15}N into a medium containing ^{14}N. Explain why.

5 The scientists removed the final sample of bacteria after only one generation in the medium containing ^{14}N. Explain why this timing was important.

6 The scientists went on to conclude that their experiment provided evidence for the theory of semi-conservative replication of DNA. Do you agree with this? In answering this question, consider whether there is another valid conclusion from these results?

Mitosis

Mitosis is a type of cell division that occurs in eukaryotic cells. During mitosis, a parent cell divides to produce two daughter cells. The two daughter cells contain some of the cytoplasm from the parent cell. They also contain a complete copy of the parent cell's DNA, making them genetically identical to the parent cell and to each other.

Q2

Mitosis produces clones. What is a clone?

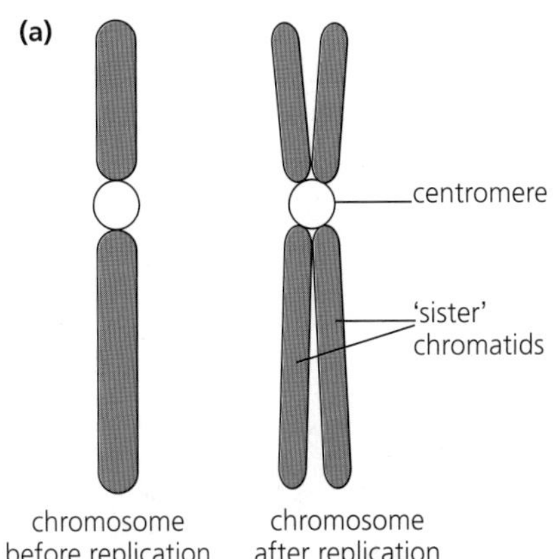

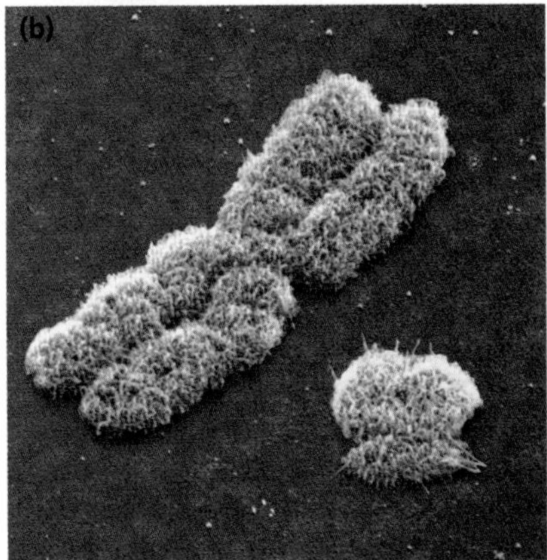

▲ **Figure 5** (a) Following the replication of DNA, a chromosome appears as a double structure composed of two chromatids. The chromatids are the products of replication of the DNA in the original chromosome. They are temporarily held together by a region called the centromere. (b) Human X (centre) and Y (lower right) sex chromosomes. Each chromosome has replicated and shows two identical strands (chromatids) joined at the centromere.

Table 1 A summary of the events occurring during each stage of mitosis.

Stage of mitosis	Main events that occur in each stage
Interphase	Cell makes a copy of its chromosomes by replication of DNA. Cell grows and undergoes its normal physiological functions.
Prophase fibre of spindle	Chromosomes coil, becoming shorter and fatter. We can now see them with an optical microscope. Nuclear envelope disappears. Protein fibres form a spindle in the cell.
Metaphase	One or more spindle fibres attaches to centromere of each chromosome. Chromosomes line up in the middle of the spindle.
Anaphase	Centromere holding each pair of sister chromatids together divides. Spindle fibres contract and pull sister chromatids to opposite poles of the spindle. We can now refer to the chromatids as chromosomes.
Telophase	The two sets of separated chromosomes collect at opposite ends of the cell. A new nuclear envelope forms around each set of chromosomes. Chromosomes become long and thin. We can no longer see them clearly with an optical microscope. Cytoplasm divides to form two new cells.

On pages 128–129, we looked at the replication of DNA. The DNA of eukaryotic cells is contained in linear chromosomes. Figure 5 shows you that the appearance of a chromosome changes after its DNA has been replicated. Before DNA replication, the chromosome is a single, rod-like structure containing one double helix of DNA. DNA replication gives rise to two rod-like structures, each containing one double helix of DNA. One region of the chromosome, the **centromere**, holds the two rod-like structures together. Whilst they are held together, they are called **chromatids**. We describe the chromatids in a pair as sister chromatids. During mitosis, sister chromatids are separated from each other. At anaphase (see Table 1), the chromatids become chromosomes.

Although mitosis is a continuous process, it is often described as a series of stages. The names of these stages, and the events that occur within them, are summarised in Table 1.

Examining cells undergoing mitosis

The diagrams in Table 1 are useful because they give you thumbnail sketches of what happens in a cell during each stage of mitosis. Figure 6 shows a photograph of cells in actively dividing tissue. The chromosomes have been stained so that we can see them. Cells in this tissue were at different stages of mitosis before they were killed and stained. The cells with indistinct nuclei were not dividing at the time the photograph was taken.

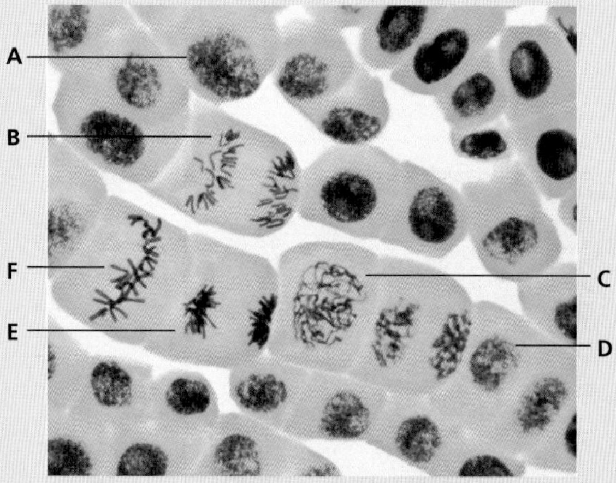

Look at cell **A** in Figure 6. Its nucleus is clear, but all we can see is a dark-stained nucleolus surrounded by granules that are the tightly coiled regions of DNA.

1 At which stage of mitosis was this cell?

▲ **Figure 6** Cells from the tip of a plant root. Many of these cells are dividing by mitosis.

Look at cell **B** in Figure 6. It has two groups of thread-like chromosomes. Look closely. Can you see that each chromosome looks v-shaped? This is because a spindle fibre, which you cannot see, is pulling its centromere to the left or right side of the cell. The arms of each chromosome lag behind its centromere, making the 'v'.

2 At which stage of mitosis is this cell?

Now look at cell **E**. It has chromosomes that are visible but are not such clear threads as in cell **B**. There are two clumps of chromosomes and a clear area is developing between them.

3 At which stage of mitosis was cell **E**? What is happening in the clear area between the clumps of chromosomes?

Cell **F** has a very distinctive appearance. The chromosomes are in a line across the centre of the cell. In which stage of mitosis was cell **F**?

Notice how some questions were easy to answer. Anaphase is always very easy to identify. In other cases, you needed to work through a logical pathway before you could answer the question. See how well you can identify more stages by answering the following questions.

4 Cells **B**, **C**, **D**, **E** and **F** were in different stages of mitosis. Put them into the correct sequence, starting with the earliest stage.

5 Was cell **D** in prophase or in telophase? Explain your answer.

The cell cycle

In actively dividing tissues, the new cells formed by mitosis grow before replicating their DNA and dividing by mitosis again. Thus a cycle is formed, called the **cell cycle**. Figure 7 shows this cell cycle. You can see that the two events we have described in this chapter, namely replication of DNA and mitosis, last only a short time during this cycle. Each part of the cycle involves specific cell activities. These are:

- G1 phase – the cell increases in size
- S phase – the cell replicates its DNA
- G2 phase – the cell increases further in size and replicates its cell organelles
- M phase – mitosis

Q3

Name two processes involving actively dividing tissue.

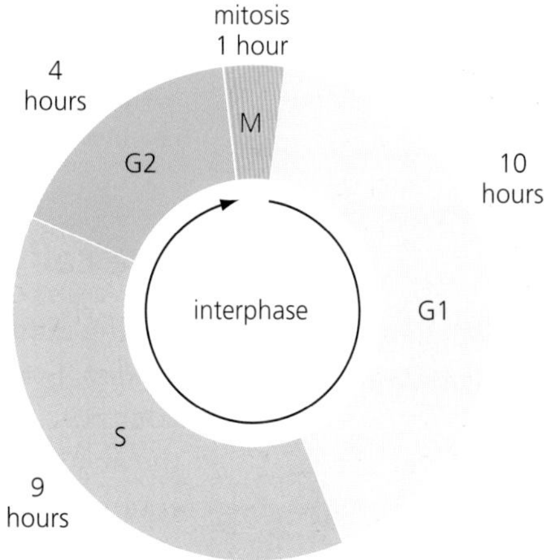

▲ **Figure 7** The cell cycle in a eukaryotic cell. The times shown represent a cell cycle of 24 hours, which might be found in actively dividing tissues. The actual length of the cycle varies from one type of cell to another.

Q4

How many double helices of DNA are present in each chromosome (a) at the start of the G1 phase, (b) at the start of the G2 phase?

Cell differentiation

Not all eukaryotic cells undergo the cell cycle shown in Figure 7. Some fungi grow as filaments that contain cells with more than one nucleus in them. As described above, during mitosis the DNA of these fungi replicates and then the new nuclei are formed. However, the cytoplasm does not then divide. Many cells in mature plants, and most cells in mature animals, lose the ability to divide. This is why, in plant micropropagation at the start of this chapter, it was important to use actively dividing cells to obtain the explants.

In most multicellular organisms, newly formed cells change their properties when they become specialised for specific functions. We call this process **differentiation**, and it does not occur at random. Cells in one part of a mature organism differentiate to form a grouping of similar cells performing the same function. This group of cells that performs one function is called a **tissue**. Different tissues are grouped together to form an organ. An **organ** performs a specific physiological function that combines the roles of its tissues. Finally, tissues and organs are organised into **systems**. You can see the relationship between cells, tissues and organs in Figure 8.

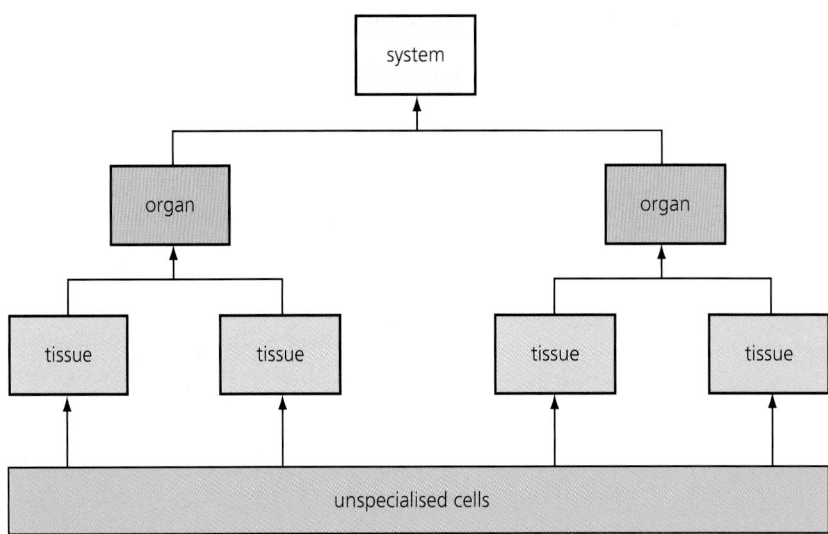

▲ **Figure 8** Tissues are groupings of similar cells, and organs are groupings of tissues performing specific physiological functions. Organs and tissues are organised into systems.

Q5

Name one tissue and one organ in your circulatory system.

The cell cycle and cancer

During differentiation, most human cells lose the ability to divide by mitosis. Even cells that continue to divide, such as those near the surface of your skin, normally divide only about 20 to 50 times before they die. Losing the ability to divide and programmed cell death are two ways in which cells control their own division. Sometimes these control mechanisms break down. The result is that, if kept supplied with the necessary nutrients, such cells undergo repeated, uncontrolled division. These are **cancer** cells, and they form a **tumour** – a large mass of cancer cells.

Benign tumour cells remain at the position where they were formed: they are localised. The main threat of a tumour is that, as it grows, it is liable to compress other, functional tissues. Being localised, benign tumours can usually be removed by surgery or destroyed by radiation. **Malignant tumour** cells do not remain where they were formed. They travel in the blood to other parts of the body, where they cause new tumours. This migration of cancer cells that form new tumours is called **metastasis**. Malignant tumours are more difficult to treat than benign tumours, simply because they spread.

In about 50 per cent of people with all types of cancer, a gene that helps to control cell growth (called *p*53) has mutated. However, there are many other reasons why the normal control of cell division breaks down. Consequently, there is no single treatment for cancer sufferers. Some cancer treatments work by interfering with the processes that we have just learned about in this chapter – stopping replication of DNA or stopping mitosis. For example:

- adriamycin and cytoxan stop DNA unwinding prior to replication
- methotrexate stops cells making DNA nucleotides
- taxol and vincristine inhibit formation of the mitotic spindle.

Q6

Which process is stopped by methotrexate? Explain your answer.

Chapter 8

Adaptation

In the Arctic, polar bears are able to survive in temperatures as low as −50 °C. A polar bear is so well insulated that snow on its fur does not melt. Below the skin is a thick layer of fatty tissue that provides insulation as well as being an energy store. The fur you can see consists of stiff, hollow hairs that stand up like a brush. Amongst this is dense woolly hair that traps air and prevents it from circulating by convection. The soles of its feet have thick pads of fat so that they lose little heat to the ice, as well as thick rough skin that prevents the polar bear slipping. The insulation is so efficient that the polar bear could easily overheat when it runs. The black skin round its nose where there is no fur reduces this problem because it radiates heat rapidly. The polar bear can also pant like a dog to speed up heat loss.

▲ **Figure 1** A polar bear has dense fur and a black nose and eyes. It has pads of fat on the soles of its feet.

These are some of the special features that make it possible for polar bears to survive and thrive in the Arctic environment. Biologists call such features **adaptations**. Adaptations are changes that have evolved as a result of natural selection.

Polar bears are closely related to brown bears, which also live in the Arctic, but further south in more forested areas. Polar bears are predators that feed on seals that live in the Arctic oceans. Seals are mammals that breathe air, so when the sea is frozen over they have to poke their heads through holes in the ice to breathe. They also must come out onto the ice to breed. Polar bears lay in wait near breathing holes and stalk seals that emerge to have their pups. Bears with white fur must be more likely to catch seals than bears with darker brown fur. Since most bears have dark-coloured fur, it seems very likely that in the white wastes of the Arctic, bears that happened to have pale fur were selected because they were more likely to survive. The genes that produced pale fur would be the ones that would be passed on through the generations.

The idea of adaptation to different environmental conditions explains the extraordinary variety that we see in living organisms. There may seem to be huge differences between polar bears, bacteria, whales, oak trees and humans, but they all share the characteristic features of life. You probably learned a list of characteristics at an early stage in your biological education, perhaps using the letters of 'Mr Niger' or 'Mrs Gren' to jog your memory. No doubt you soon realised that there were exceptions to some of the characteristics on the list. For example, many organisms do not move, at least not under their own steam. However, all carry out nutrition, respiration, growth and reproduction. Through evolution, organisms have developed a multitude of small differences in the ways that they carry out these and other processes.

For instance, most living things need oxygen for respiration. However, the availability of oxygen varies in different environments. Water has a much lower concentration than air, so a system for obtaining oxygen from air would be quite unsuitable in an aquatic organism. Gills work well in a fish, but in air they stick together and dry out. If a person's lungs become filled with water, that person drowns. In this chapter we will look at some of the ways in which the cells and gas exchange systems of organisms are adapted for different conditions.

Cells are adapted for their functions

▲ **Figure 2** An epithelial cell from the small intestine, taken with a transmission electron microscope and showing numerous microvilli projecting from a single epithelial cell.

In Chapter 2, pages 40–41, you studied the structure of a cell from the human intestine. This type of cell has many features that are common to most cells, such as the cell surface (plasma) membrane, nucleus, mitochondria and endoplasmic reticulum. But the intestinal cell is specially adapted for absorbing the products of digestion and transferring them through the intestine wall to the blood system. One adaptation is the presence of the microvilli that increase the surface area of the membrane exposed to the contents of the intestine.

Other cell types in the body have different adaptations. For example, alveolar cells are flattened (see page 63), and so the distance for gas diffusion is very short. Red blood cells are very unusual in that they have no nucleus, and very few of the other organelles normally present in cells. Instead, they are adapted for their function of transporting oxygen by being packed full of haemoglobin.

In general, animal cells have a similar basic structure, with variations in size, shape and organelles according to their function. Cells in flowering plants, however, have some fundamental differences. A key difference between plants and animals is that plants photosynthesise. This process requires light, and, to maximise the area exposed to sunlight, most plants have an upright, branching structure, usually with broad, thin leaves.

To make glucose by photosynthesis, plants need **chlorophyll**. Since chlorophyll is only useful in areas exposed to light, it is not present in all plant cells. For example, in underground roots chlorophyll would have no function. In most plants the leaves are where the majority of photosynthesis takes place. Even in the leaves, not all the cells contain chlorophyll. Some are adapted to keep the leaf extended and flat, some transport water to the leaf cells and some take the sugar produced to other parts of the plant.

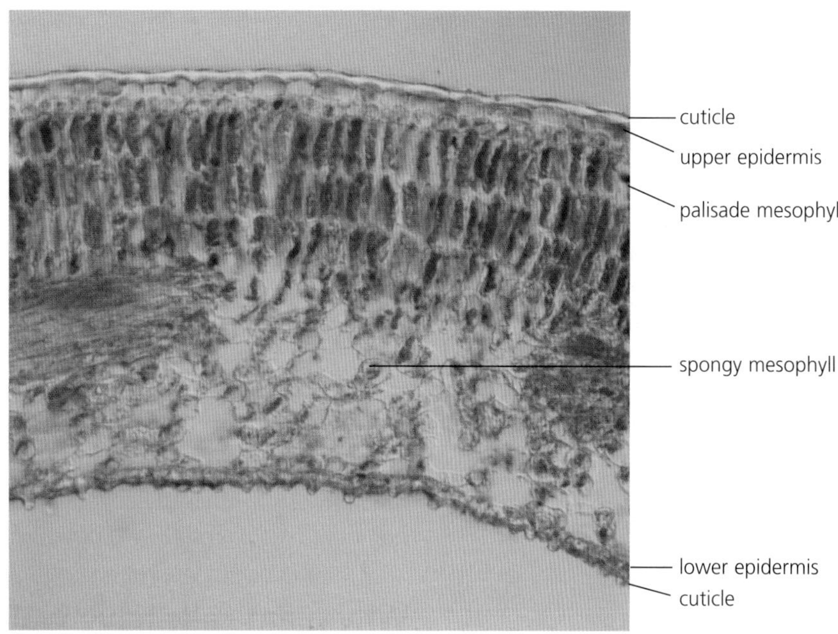

▲ **Figure 3** A photomicrograph of a vertical section across a leaf, as seen with an optical microscope (× 32).

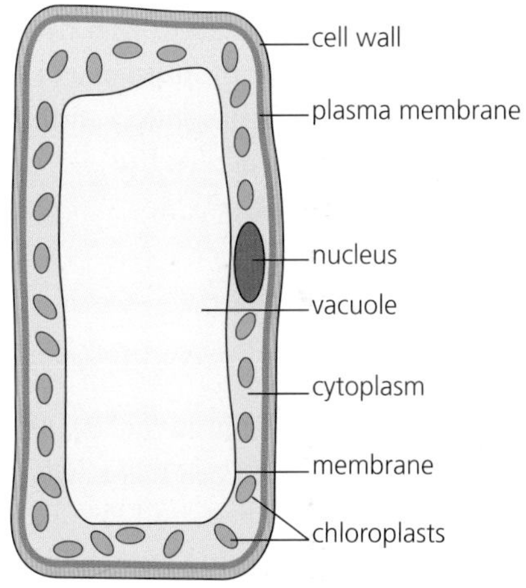

▲ **Figure 4** Diagram of a single cell from the palisade layer of a leaf.

Q1

Compare the diagram of the palisade cell with the photograph of the epithelial cell from the human small intestine on page 36. Describe three ways in which the structures of the cells are similar and three ways in which they differ.

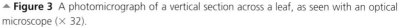

Figure 3 shows the cells in a section across part of a leaf seen through an optical microscope. You can see that most of the green chlorophyll is concentrated in the palisade mesophyll. Figure 4 is a diagram of one cell from the palisade mesophyll.

As you can see in the diagram of the palisade cell, the chlorophyll is not dispersed throughout the cells but is contained in separate organelles called **chloroplasts**. When viewed with an electron microscope, a chloroplast can be seen to have a complex structure that adapts it for photosynthesis.

The chlorophyll molecules are embedded in a system of double membranes. In some areas, the membranes are stacked up, rather like piles of coins. These stacks show up under low magnification in an electron microscope as dark, grainy patches. There are usually about 50 dark areas in a chloroplast, linked together by a network of the membranes. These structures hold the chlorophyll molecules in positions where the maximum

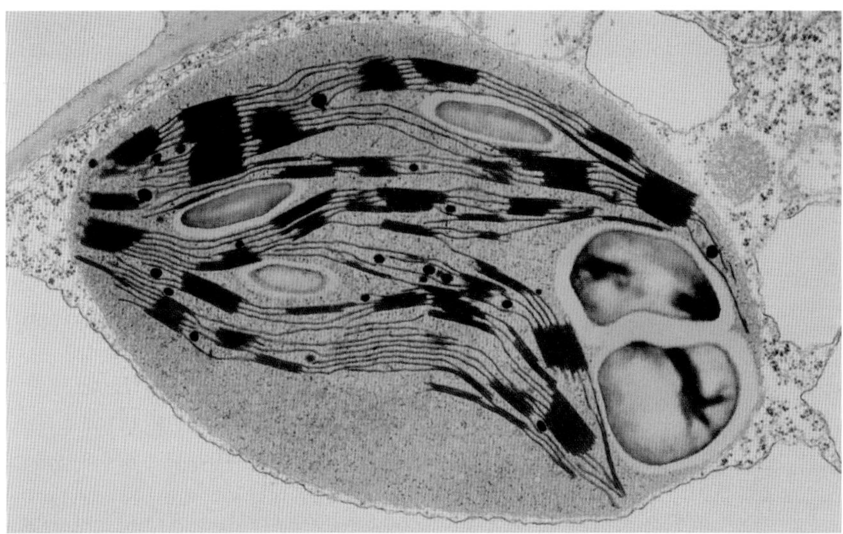

▶ **Figure 5** The electron micrograph of a chloroplast, × 16 000.

amount of the light that falls on the chloroplast reaches them. The chlorophyll molecules use the light energy to split water into hydrogen ions and oxygen.

The surrounding **stroma** contains enzymes. These enzymes catalyse a series of reactions that result in the hydrogen ions combining with carbon dioxide to make glucose. The chloroplast is surrounded by a double membrane which ensures that the enzymes are held inside the chloroplast close to the chlorophyll while allowing free movement of small molecules such as carbon dioxide and water. The structure of the chloroplast ensures that this complex process happens efficiently in a small space with optimum use of available light energy. Excess glucose is converted to insoluble starch and stored temporarily in starch grains in the chloroplast. This avoids the problem of the glucose concentration rising and affecting the water potential (see pages 48–49) of the chloroplast.

Q2

Calculate the actual length of the chloroplast in Figure 5 in micrometres. (Remember 1 μm = 10^{-3} mm.)

Q3

Explain how a rising glucose concentration might result in damage to a chloroplast.

Q4

Use your knowledge of osmosis and water potential gained in Chapter 2 to explain how water enters the palisade cells of a leaf.

Q5

Palisade cells have a large vacuole and only a thin layer of cytoplasm, whereas animal cells are filled with cytoplasm. Suggest how it is an advantage for the palisade cells to have a large vacuole rather than being full of cytoplasm.

Why plant cells have walls

You may have noticed that one major difference between animal and plant cells is that an animal cell has no wall, whereas the palisade cell has a wall outside the plasma membrane. This wall is quite thin. It is not rigid like a brick wall, but it does give the cell strength since it resists being stretched. It is the strength of the cell wall that stops a leaf cell from expanding and taking in so much water that it bursts.

The leaves of most flowering plants stick out from the stems. But, as you know if you have ever forgotten to water house plants, when a plant is short of water the leaves flop down – they wilt. For the leaves to stay flat, facing the light, they need water that is taken up through the roots. It enters a leaf cell by osmosis and fills the vacuole (see Figure 4). The water pushes against the wall and makes the cell firm, just as air pumped into a tyre makes the tyre hard. The cell wall is strong enough to prevent the cell from bursting. Animal cells, however, have no cell wall. If, for example, a red blood cell took in too much water, its cell surface membrane would burst. Animals have systems that control the water content of the blood and stop this happening.

The structure of cell walls

The main substance in a cell wall is the carbohydrate **cellulose**. Like starch, cellulose is a polysaccharide and is a polymer of glucose. All glucose molecules have the same formula, $C_6H_{12}O_6$. However, the molecules of glucose that go to make cellulose have a slightly different shape from the ones that make up starch. This is because the atoms in the glucose molecule can be arranged in different ways, called isomers. Figure 6 shows the arrangement of the atoms in the isomer of glucose that makes starch and the one that makes cellulose. The isomer in cellulose is called β-glucose.

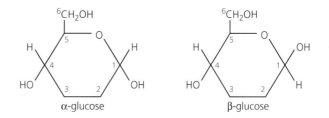

▲ **Figure 6** An α-glucose molecule and a β-glucose molecule to compare the arrangement of their atoms.

In β-glucose, look at the way that –H and –OH groups are bonded to the carbon atom on the right-hand side (C1). Now look at the –H and –OH groups bonded to the carbon atom on the left-hand side (C4). Notice that they are bonded the opposite way round. Compare this with the diagram of α-glucose that makes up starch. Here both –H groups are above the carbon atoms, and both –OH groups are below the carbon atoms.

Q6

Explain, using a diagram, how α-glucose molecules join together by condensation. If necessary, refer back to Chapter 1 to remind yourself.

In cellulose, the β-glucose molecules join together in chains by condensation. As when starch chains are made from α-glucose molecules,

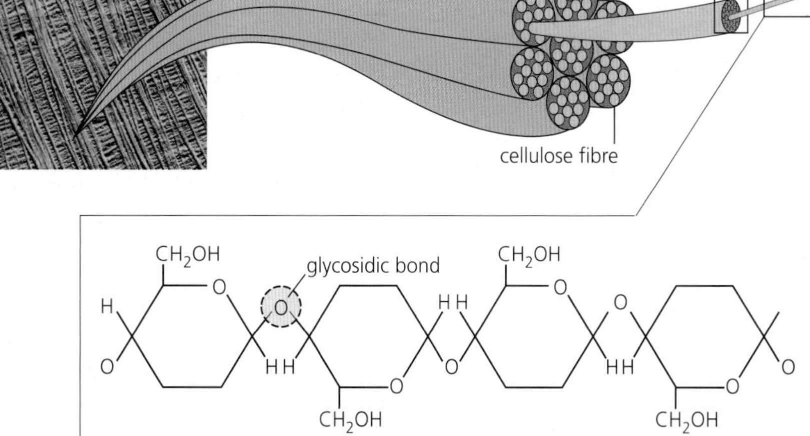

Long chain of 1,4 linked β-glucose residues. Hydrogen bonds link these chains together to form microfibrils

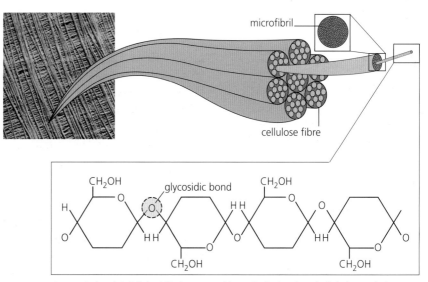

▸ **Figure 7** Cellulose is a polymer of β-glucose molecules joined by glycosidic bonds. Its molecules are long and straight and form fibres that are very strong. Cellulose gives cell walls their strength and resistance to being stretched.

glycosidic bonds are formed. But in the cellulose chains, every other β-glucose is 'upside-down', so the $-CH_2OH$ side-chains stick out alternately on opposite sides, as you can see in Figure 7. This 'alternate' bonding makes the cellulose molecules very straight. They are also very long. They line up parallel with each other and become linked together by hydrogen bonds.

Small bundles of cellulose molecules make very thin fibres, called **microfibrils**. These microfibrils are remarkably strong. They have much the same ability to withstand stretching as steel fibres of the same diameter. Groups of microfibrils are joined together to make thicker, stronger fibres, just as a piece of string is made from many thinner strands. In cell walls, these fibres are criss-crossed as shown in the photo in Figure 7, making the walls resistant to stretching in any direction.

Cellulose is structurally so well suited to its functions of supporting cells and limiting water intake that it is found throughout the plant kingdom. It is probably the most abundant carbohydrate. Surprisingly, neither humans nor any other mammal is able to make an enzyme that can digest cellulose. There are bacteria and fungi that do make such an enzyme, and these play an important role in recycling the constituents of cellulose. This is a good thing, since otherwise the world would have disappeared under cellulose long ago. Mammals such as cattle and rabbits, whose diet consists largely of plants, carry bacteria in their guts that break down cellulose, so they can make use of the energy in the large quantities of cellulose in their food. We, however, have no means of extracting the energy stored in cellulose.

Storage molecules

As you saw in Chapter 1, we use the starch from plants as our major source of energy. For many plants, **starch** is a storage compound, both for short-term storage overnight when photosynthesis cannot occur, and for long-term storage, for example in seeds and in the organs such as bulbs and tubers that survive through the winter. Like cellulose, starch molecules are polymers of glucose, but they are much more suitable for storage than

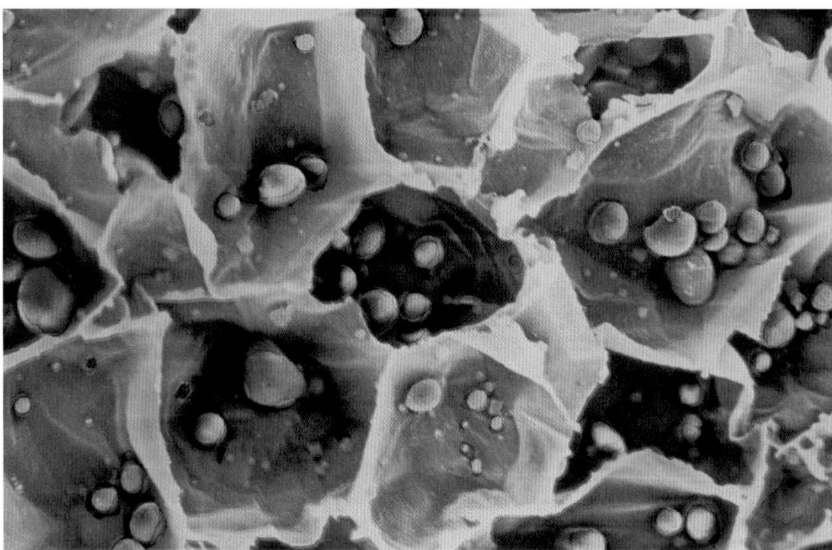

Figure 8 Starch molecules can fold up compactly and can therefore fit into small storage organelles, such as the starch grains in potato tuber cells, shown here. The grains are shown in green.

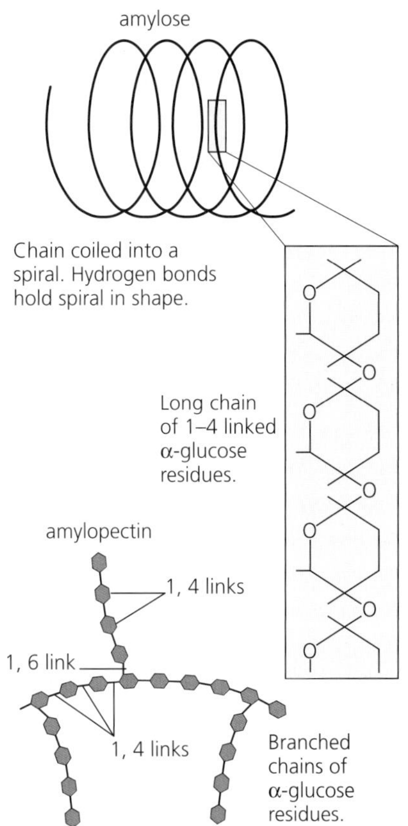

▲ **Figure 9** Because of the way that α-glucose molecules are linked to form starch, the chains form spirals that fold up in a compact way.

cellulose. As you can see in Figure 9, starch molecules have two sorts of chain, called amylose and amylopectin. In amylose, the α-glucose molecules are linked by 1,4 glycosidic bonds. Notice that the $-CH_2OH$ side-chains all stick out on the same side. This arrangement causes the chains of α-glucose molecules to coil into spirals as shown in Figure 9. Amylopectin molecules have branches because some of the α-glucose molecules form bonds between carbon atoms 1 and 6 instead of 1 and 4. This enables starch molecules to fold up compactly. As a storage compound it is important that starch can be easily synthesised and broken down. Plants have enzymes that can rapidly carry out these processes.

You have seen in Chapter 1 that we have a digestive enzyme called amylase which breaks down the starch in our diet to glucose. We need the glucose to provide a ready energy source in respiration. But we do not rebuild excess glucose into starch for storage. Instead, we make it into a polysaccharide similar to starch called **glycogen**.

Like amylopectin, glycogen also consists of α-glucose chains with both 1,4 and 1,6 glycosidic bonds, but the 1,6 bonds are much more frequent, so the molecules are much more branched. This makes glycogen molecules even more compact than starch molecules, and for animals this is an advantage because having a compact body makes it easier to move around to find food. In humans, some glycogen is stored in the muscles as a readily accessible store of glucose close to the site where the rate of respiration is regularly raised very rapidly. The liver stores larger reserves of glycogen and continually breaks it down to maintain a constant blood glucose concentration.

Q7

List the differences between the structures of cellulose and starch molecules.

Q8

Starch is insoluble and does not affect the water potential of cells in which it is stored. Explain how these properties make starch a good storage compound.

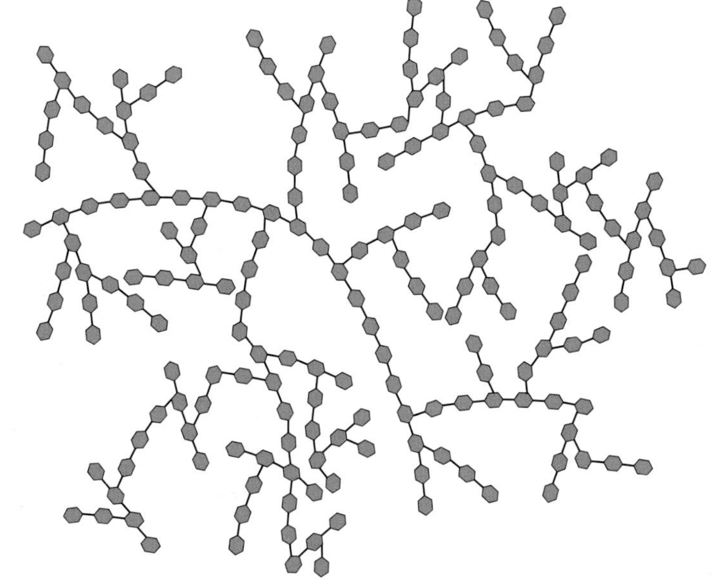

▲ **Figure 10** A glycogen molecule.

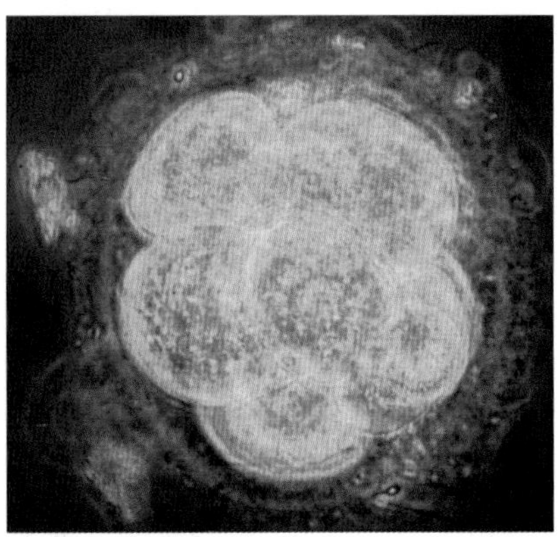

▲ **Figure 11** A human embryo consisting of eight cells. If cells are seperated at this stage, they can develop into any type of cell.

How do cells become specialised?

A fertilised human egg contains all the instructions necessary for it to grow into an adult human being with hundreds of different sorts of specialised cells. Moreover, somehow these cells normally all grow in the right order and in the right places so that we have functioning hearts, lungs, brain parts and so on. Scientists do not yet understand exactly how this extraordinary feat happens, but many scientists are doing research to find out.

In the first few days after fertilisation, an egg cell divides to form a ball of apparently identical cells. If one of these cells is separated off, it is still capable of growing into a complete person. Indeed, this sometimes happens naturally, when the first pair of cells, or even four (or more), split apart and develop into identical twins or quadruplets. Cells at this early stage are unspecialised. We call them stem cells, and they can develop into any type of cell. However, after the first few divisions, the cells lose this ability and most can then only divide to become a particular sort of cell, such as a nerve or muscle cell.

Researchers would like to find out how the unspecialised stem cells develop into specialised cells, because it might then be possible, for example, to grow hearts for use in place of transplants, or insulin-producing cells to treat diabetes. However, some groups of people oppose this stem-cell research because it uses embryo cells that have the potential to grow into an individual if they develop in the womb.

The process by which cells become specialised for particular functions is called **differentiation**. During the development of an embryo, some cells differentiate into large groups of similar specialised cells, for example muscle or skin cells. As you learned in Chapter 7 (Figure 8), such masses of similar cells are referred to as **tissues**. In complex plants and animals, most parts of the body consist of structures carrying out a particular function, but made up of several or many different types of specialised cell. These are called **organs**. The heart is an organ which is mostly muscle tissue but which also contains nerve cells, blood capillaries, elastic and connective tissue, valves and so on. A plant leaf is an organ, because, as Figure 3 shows, it contains several different sorts of cell. Another level of organisation consists of a **system** of organs and tissues that operate together to perform a major function, such as the blood system, which includes blood vessels and blood as well as the heart.

Does size matter? Is big better?

Tiny organisms are often considered simple and primitive compared with large ones. Yet it is precisely because they are simple and small that they have survived. The fact that there are now far more of them than there are large organisms shows how very successful tiny organisms have been. Each species is adapted to the particular set of conditions in which it exists, and there are many more sets of conditions suitable for small organisms than there are for large ones. Large organisms may seem to us to be dominant, more complex and more advanced, but increasing size brings a variety of problems.

For a large animal, a severe limitation is needing to find enough food to maintain its bulky body. This severely restricts the number of really large animals that can live in a particular habitat. Other problems include getting enough oxygen for respiration into the body and transporting it and food to all its parts. Larger organisms have a greater variety of specialised cells, tissues, organs and systems, but this does not make them better.

Life as a single cell

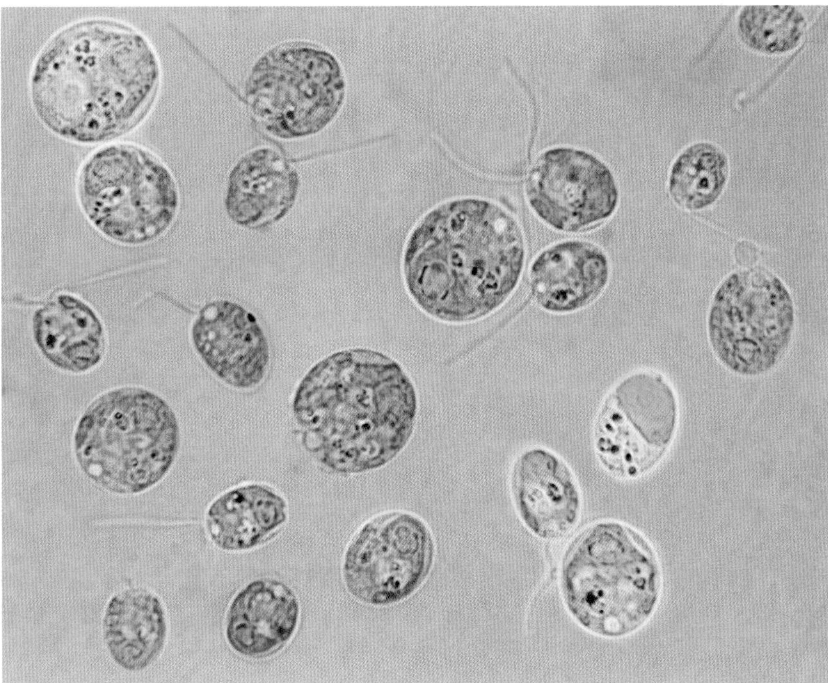

▲ **Figure 12** *Chlamydomonas* is a single-celled organism that lives in water (× 750).

Figure 13 shows a single-celled organism called *Chlamydomonas*. It lives in fresh-water ponds and ditches. It is roughly spherical and about 20 μm long. It has two flagella which enable it to swim around. It contains a chloroplast, so it can photosynthesise. Oxygen for respiration and carbon dioxide for photosynthesis are dissolved in the surrounding water and diffuse through the cell wall. Therefore *Chlamydomonas* has no need of a special area for gas exchange. The maximum distance that oxygen has to diffuse to reach the centre of the cell is about 10 μm, and this takes no more than about a tenth of a second (100 milliseconds).

However, if the distance is doubled, the diffusion time is squared, so to diffuse 20 μm would take about 400 ms, and to go just 1 mm would take 100 s. These figures are approximate because the actual rate depends on several factors, such as the concentration gradient and the material through which the oxygen is diffusing. However, it illustrates that, while diffusion is sufficiently fast to provide all parts of a small single-celled organism with oxygen, it is far too slow for a larger, multicelled animal.

As the size of an organism increases, the rate of gas diffusion becomes too slow. Also, the surface area available for diffusion becomes less and less in proportion to the volume. Imagine a cube-shaped animal in which the length of each side is 1 cm. Its volume is 1 cm^3, but since it has 6 faces each with an area of 1 cm^2, its surface area is 6 cm^2. The surface area to volume ratio is therefore 6 : 1. If you do the same calculation for 3 cm cube, the ratio is only 2 : 1. If you continue to do the calculations for larger and larger cubes, you will discover that the ratio gets smaller and smaller, so that if you were able to convert a human into a cube shape, the ratio would be less than 1 : 100. Animals aren't cubic, of course, but the general rule still applies: the larger the animal the lower the surface area to volume ratio.

Because it is essential to obtain oxygen and expel carbon dioxide, most animals have adaptations that increase the surface area available for gas exchange. We have already seen in Chapter 3 how the alveoli in our lungs do this for us. In the next sections we will see two completely different ways in which evolution has solved the problem of gas exchange.

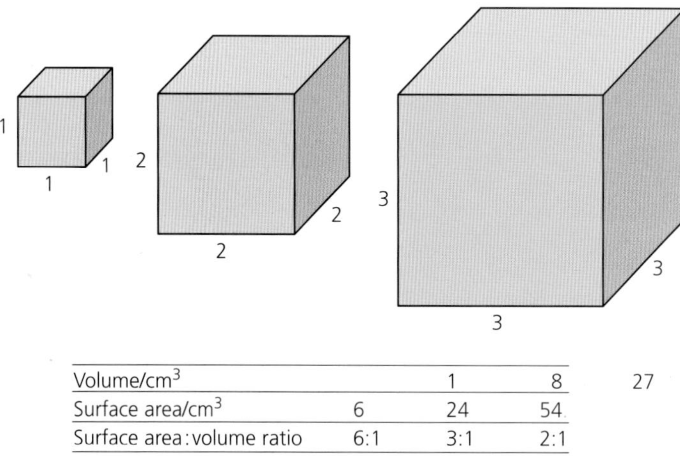

Volume/cm^3		1	8	27
Surface area/cm^3	6	24	54	
Surface area : volume ratio	6:1	3:1	2:1	

▲ **Figure 13** This diagram shows that, as the volume of a cube increases, its surface area to volume ratio decreases.

How do flies breathe?

Insects may seem to be small organisms that should have little difficulty in getting enough oxygen for their needs. Many, however, are very active fliers or jumpers and have a high rate of metabolism, as anyone who has chased a buzzing fly round the room will know. The problem for insects is that they have an outside skeleton, which is quite rigid and is coated with a waxy substance. This makes it waterproof, an adaptation a small creature living in air needs to prevent it from drying out. But a waterproof surface is also impossible for gases to diffuse through. Insects have been such an evolutionary success because they developed a breathing system of tubes that carry oxygen directly to all tissues and organs of their bodies.

Air can enter these tubes through a series of openings called **spiracles** arranged along the side of the body. These can be opened and closed. As you can see from Figure 14, air can pass through the spiracles into a system of **tracheae** and thinner **tracheoles**. The tracheae have rigid rings in their walls, similar to the rings of cartilage in the trachea and bronchi of humans. The tracheoles penetrate between cells and right into muscle fibres. It is here that gaseous exchange takes place.

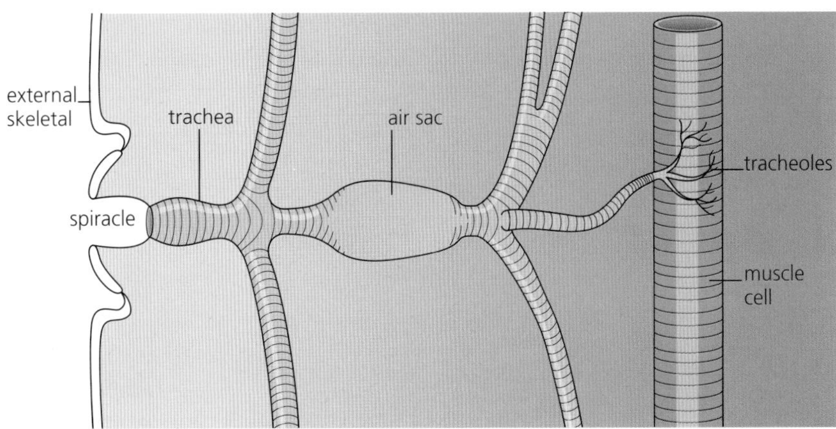

▲ **Figure 14** The tracheal system of an insect.

In some of the tiniest insects, this system can provide enough oxygen simply by diffusion. But larger insects, such as houseflies and grasshoppers, need oxygen more rapidly. To achieve this, the spiracles close and muscles pull the skeletal plates of the abdominal segments together. This squeezes the tracheal system and pumps the air in the sacs (see Figure 14) deeper into the tracheoles. If you watch a fly or wasp closely, you can often see these pumping movements that ventilate the tissues.

Q9

Suggest the function of the rigid rings in the walls of the tracheae.

Q10

Suggest how the breathing system of insects helps to minimise water loss.

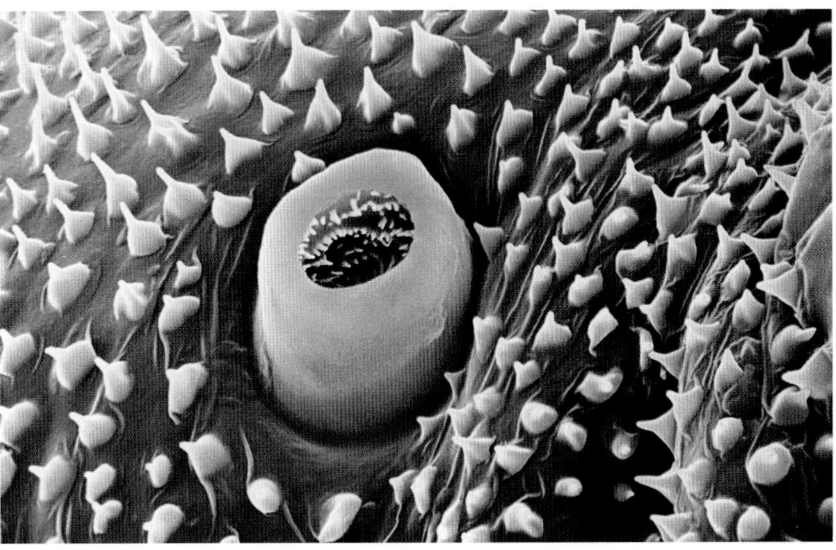

▲ **Figure 15** The scanning electron micrograph shows a single spiracle in the wall of the caterpillar of the tiger moth. Along the side of the caterpillar's body is a series of spiracles through which air enters the tracheae.

Q11

Explain how the increase in the lactate content of the muscle cells during flight causes the removal of water from the ends of the tracheoles.

One extra trick helps to get additional oxygen deep into the muscles during flight. When an insect is resting, a little water leaks across the cell membranes of muscle cells, just as it does in the alveoli of human lungs (see page 63). The very narrow ends of the tracheoles fill with water. When the wing muscles are working hard, they respire, partly anaerobically, and produce lactate, a soluble waste product of anaerobic respiration. This lowers the water potential of the muscle cells. As lactate builds up in the muscle cells, water passes from the tracheoles into the muscle cells. This draws air in the tracheoles closer to the muscle cells and therefore reduces the diffusion distance for oxygen when it is most needed.

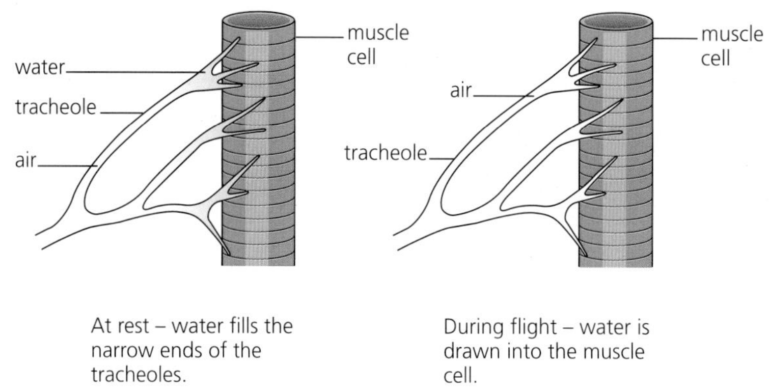

▲ **Figure 16** Gas exchange between the tracheoles and tissues.

How do fish get oxygen out of water?

A given volume of air contains about 30 times as much oxygen as the same volume of water. Oxygen does not dissolve readily in water, and as water warms up, even less can dissolve. This is bad news for fish living in lakes and rivers that are likely to get warmer as climates change. Fish are adapted to extract oxygen directly from water, unlike marine mammals such as whales and seals that have to come to the surface to take gulps of air. Not surprisingly, fish need a large surface area in contact with water through which to absorb oxygen, and this is provided by gills.

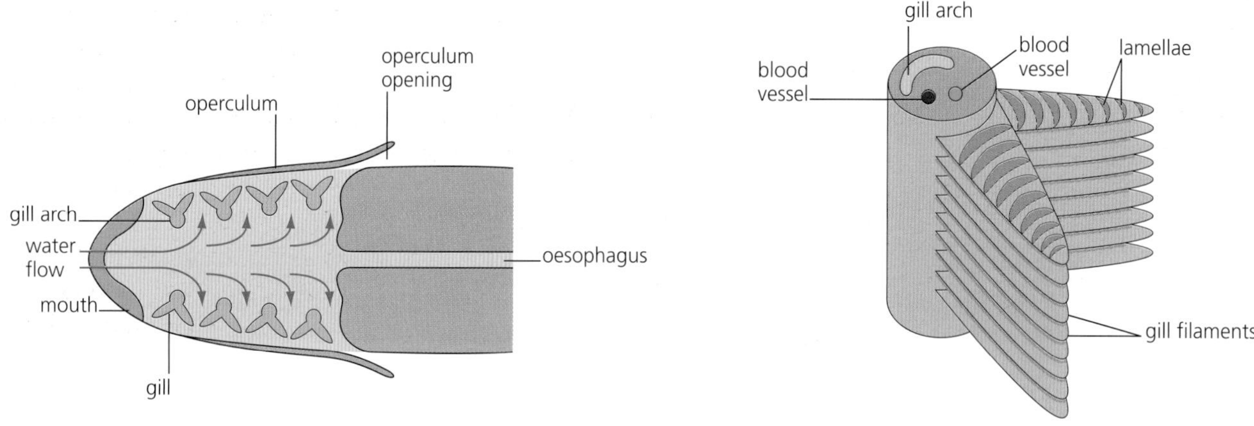

▲ **Figure 17** The arrangement of the gills of a fish.

▲ **Figure 18** Structure of a single gill.

Bony fish, such as trout, perch and cod, have a series of gills on each side of the head, as shown in Figure 17. Each bony gill arch has two stacks of thin plates called **filaments** that stick out like leaves. On the top of each filament is a row of very thin **lamellae** which stand up vertically, as you can see in Figure 18. The surface of each lamella is a single layer of flattened cells. This covers an extensive network of capillaries which is so close to the surface that oxygen has only a short distance to diffuse from the water into the blood. Since fish live in water, there is no problem with such thin

▲ **Figure 19** The head of a Blacktip grouper showing the operculum that covers and protects the gills.

surfaces drying out. But since they are so delicate they have to be protected under a bony flap on each side called an **operculum**.

The operculum on the side of a fish's head protects the gills from damage. Notice that the operculum opens at the rear edge. The fish takes in water through its mouth and forces it through the gills to maintain a current of water over them. The water then flows out from the back of the operculum, whether the fish is swimming slowly or rapidly.

The blood system in the lamellae is arranged so that the water flows in the opposite direction to the blood flow in the capillaries. This is called a **counter-current** system, as shown in Figure 20.

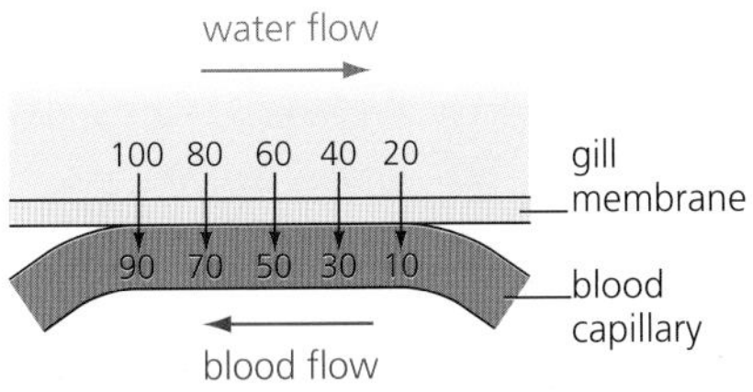

▲ **Figure 21** The diagram shows that, in the counter-current flow of water over a gill filament, the gradient of oxygen concentration is maintained between water and blood. The figures show the % saturation with oxygen.

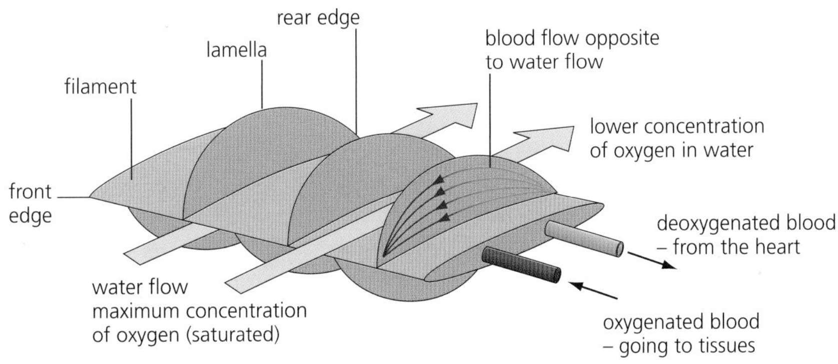

▲ **Figure 20** The counter-current flow of water over a gill filament.

Generally, the concentration of oxygen in the blood is lower than in the surrounding water, so oxygen diffuses into the blood. The advantage of the counter-current system is that it maintains an optimal diffusion gradient over the full length of the capillary. As Figure 20 shows, blood flows from the rear edge of the lamella to the front edge, and surrounding water flows in the opposite direction. So the blood at the front will have had the longest time for oxygen diffusion and therefore has the highest oxygen concentration. The front of the lamella is also where the surrounding water is most saturated with oxygen. At the rear edge, the blood has very little oxygen, and though there is now less oxygen in the flowing water, the diffusion gradient is about the same as at the front edge, as Figure 21 shows. This system therefore ensures that the concentration gradient is maintained.

▲ **Figure 22** Anglers use holding nets in the water to keep the fish they catch alive.

Q12

To keep the fish alive, competition anglers keep the fish they catch in a net in water. Their catch is weighed before being safely returned to the river after the competition. Suggest why fish cannot breathe in air, even though there is a much higher percentage of oxygen in air.

Gas exchange in leaves

The main function of a leaf is to carry out photosynthesis, and for this it needs a supply of carbon dioxide and water. Also, the chloroplasts require good access to sunlight. Sunlight will not penetrate far, so the leaves need to be thin, and to get enough carbon dioxide they need a large gas exchange surface. However, these requirements make them vulnerable to damage and dehydration. The leaves of different species are adapted to meet these requirements in a variety of different ways, depending on the conditions in which they live.

Figure 23 shows the cells and tissues in a section of the leaf of a plant that lives in the relatively moist and cool climate of Britain. The photograph, taken with a scanning electron microscope, shows in 3D what the cells inside the leaf really look like. Notice how much space there is between the cells in the mesophyll.

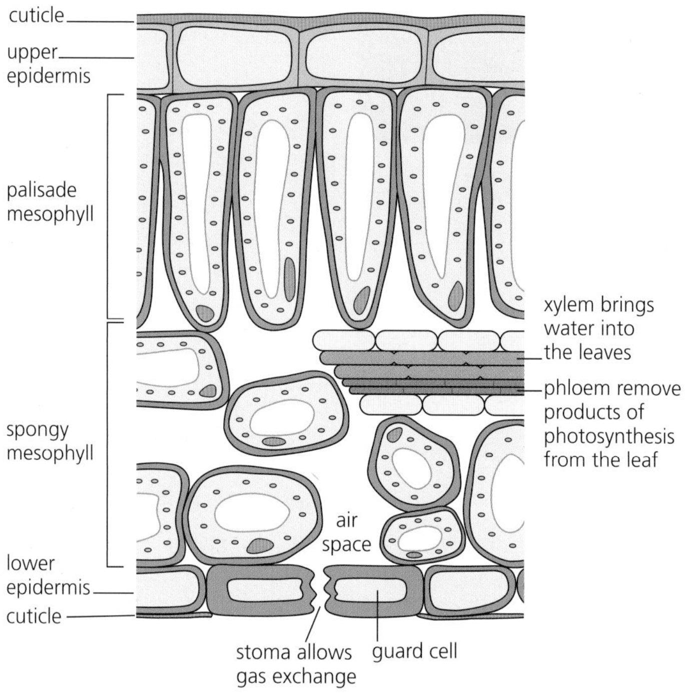

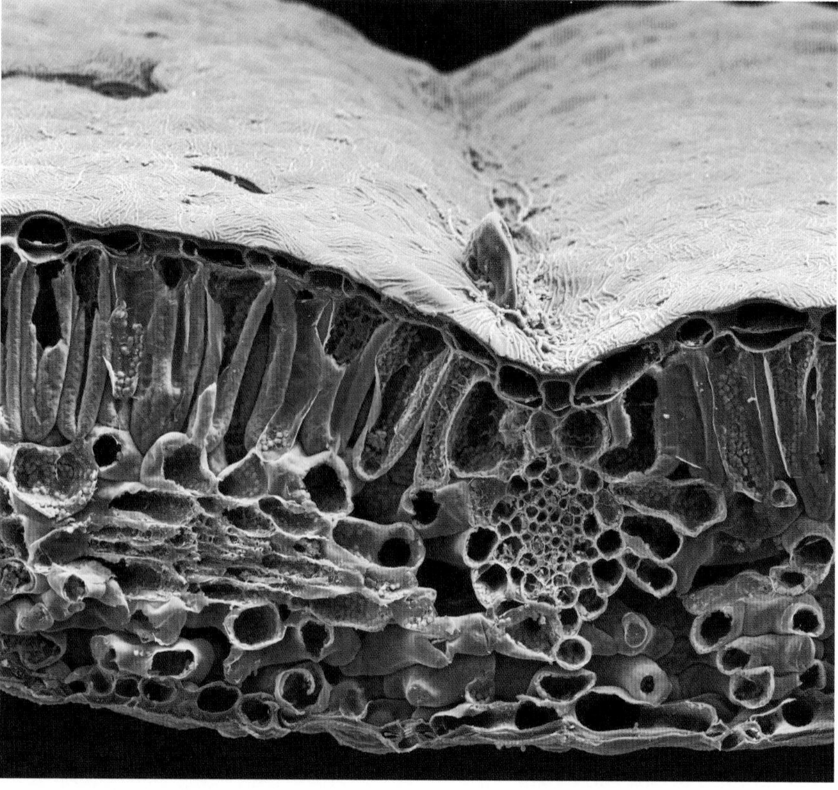

▲ **Figure 23** A cross-section of a leaf (× 210).

The outer cell layer on the upper and lower surface of a leaf is called the **epidermis**. It consists of cells that fit closely together. The outer walls of these cells contain a mixture of a lipid polymer and waxes that make a waterproof **cuticle**. Even in Britain, conditions can be dry enough for dehydration to be a problem. However, as well as stopping water from escaping, the cuticle prevents gas exchange. To allow carbon dioxide to get to the photosynthetic cells inside the leaf, there are pores called **stomata** (singular: stoma) in the epidermis. In most leaves, the stomata are mainly on the under-surface of the leaf.

Each stoma is surrounded by a pair of **guard cells**. These are banana shaped. If the guard cells lose water they collapse and close the stoma, which helps to prevent further water loss. They can also be closed at other times, for example during darkness when, without light, carbon dioxide cannot be used in photosynthesis.

Q13

Suggest an advantage of the stomata being on the under-surface.

The central tissue of the leaf, called the **mesophyll**, has an extensive network of air spaces, as you can see in Figure 23. These spaces allow gases to circulate to and from the cells by diffusion. There is no active system of ventilation, so this tissue has to be thin to keep the diffusion pathway short. The upper layer, or sometimes two or three layers, is the **palisade mesophyll**. It has elongated cells that contain large numbers of chloroplasts, as we saw earlier in this chapter. The spongy mesophyll, below it has more air spaces and the cells have fewer chloroplasts. Water reaches the leaves through the xylem, and we will look in more detail at this process in the next chapter.

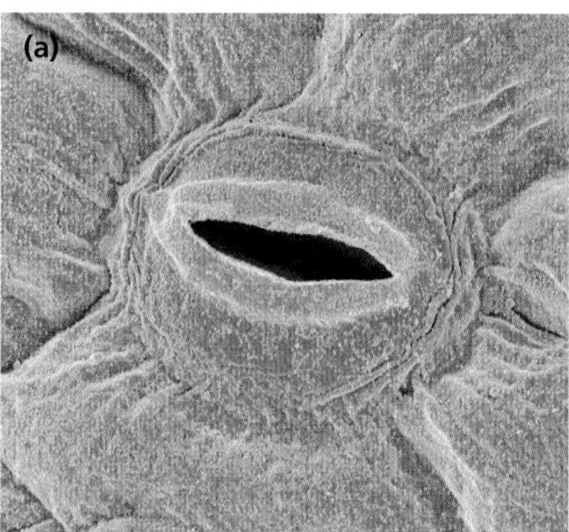

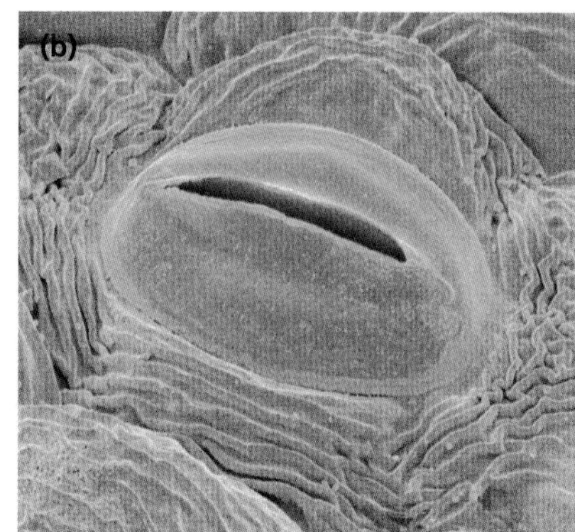

Figure 24 The surface view of guard cells of a stoma, (a) shown open; (b) shown closed.

Despite the amount of fossil fuels that we have burned, the proportion of carbon dioxide in the atmosphere is still low, only about 0.036%. In other words, out of every hundred thousand molecules in the air, fewer than 40 are molecules of carbon dioxide. This means that efficient gas exchange is vital for leaves to get enough carbon dioxide for rapid photosynthesis.

Large numbers of stomata dot the lower surface of leaves. The air spaces in the mesophyll allow fast carbon dioxide diffusion to the cells. The palisade cells are elongated, so they have a large surface area exposed to the atmosphere inside the leaf. The large number of chloroplasts in the thin layer of cytoplasm next to the cell wall means that carbon dioxide rapidly takes part in photosynthesis and is therefore removed. This maintains the diffusion gradient.

The downside is that the adaptations that boost the entry of carbon dioxide also allow water to be lost rapidly. Water evaporates from the mesophyll cells to become water vapour in the air spaces and, although the cuticle prevents water loss, water vapour easily passes out through the stomata. In a damp climate, such as Britain's, plants can overcome this problem simply by taking in large amounts of water from the soil. On a hot day, an oak tree may absorb over half a tonne of water, and most of this will evaporate from its leaves. During water shortage, the stomata close to reduce evaporation. Although this tends to stop photosynthesis, it avoids the more catastrophic results of dehydration. Most plants also economise on water by closing the stomata during darkness, when photosynthesis is impossible anyway. The leaves must have a constant supply of oxygen for respiration, because energy is required to keep the cells alive. However, enough oxygen remains in the air spaces for the hours of darkness. The excess carbon dioxide produced by respiration overnight is then available for photosynthesis as soon as it becomes light.

How do plants survive in dry environments, such as deserts?

Plants that live in very dry conditions have additional adaptations that enable them to conserve water very effectively. Such plants are called **xerophytes**. Some of the best known xerophytes are the cacti, which typically populate the deserts of the American Wild West.

The cactus in Figure 25 is adapted to desert life by having leaves that are reduced to spines. They have also lost the ability to photosynthesise. Instead, the stem has chloroplasts, as you can see from its green colour. The stem is very wide, enabling it to store water in its tissues, and it has a thick cuticle. The number of stomata is much reduced. Overall, the cactus has a low surface area to volume ratio, which reduces water loss. The spines may be just as important as deterrents to grazing animals as in reducing the surface area for evaporation. Many desert plants have two sets of roots. One

▲ **Figure 25** Cactus growing in the desert.

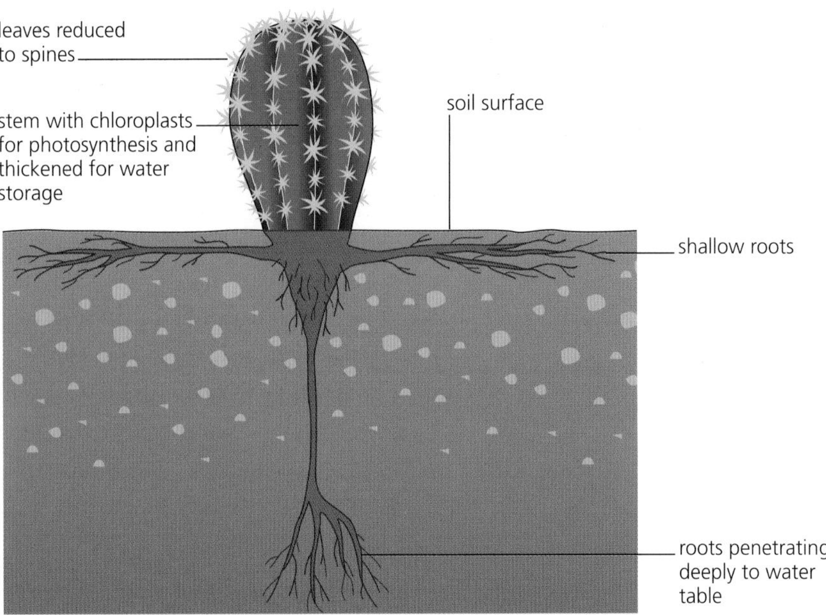

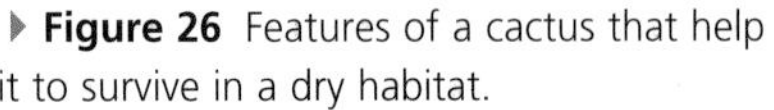

▶ **Figure 26** Features of a cactus that help it to survive in a dry habitat.

set grows out sideways near the surface of the soil, and is able to take advantage of occasional heavy showers. The water from such showers never penetrates far into the soil and very quickly evaporates. The second set of roots is a small number that grow straight down and may be very long. These roots are able to obtain water from a low water table.

Deserts are not the only habitats that require plants to be adapted to dry conditions in order to survive. The water supply in sand dunes is also limited. Marram grass is an example of a plant that is particularly well adapted to life in dry conditions, and as a result it is one of the first species to colonise new sand dunes on a beach.

Leaves of marram grass have several adaptations that help to reduce water loss. In Figure 27, you can see that:

- the leaf can roll up so that only one surface is exposed to the wind
- the exposed surface has a thick cuticle and no stomata
- when the leaf is rolled up the stomata are protected in deep grooves
- the inner surface has many hairs.

The advantage of the leaf rolling up is that water vapour becomes trapped and kept near the stomata because there is no wind or air current to move the vapour away. The hairs also help to reduce air movement. The air just

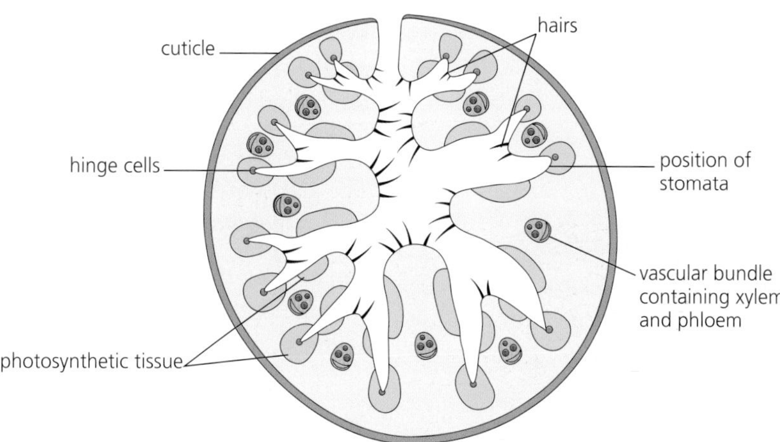

▲ **Figure 27** Marram grass is very well adapted to restrict water loss, and is an early coloniser of newly formed sand dunes in the UK.

outside the stomata becomes much more humid, so the diffusion gradient across the stomata is much reduced. The rate of evaporation is therefore much slower. How does the leaf roll up? In dry conditions, the special hinge cells at the base of the grooves lose water rapidly by evaporation. These cells shrink and pull the sides of the grooves together, making the leaf curl up.

Describing and analysing xerophytic adaptations

Features that are common in plants exposed to dry conditions include:

- thick cuticle
- small or needle-shaped leaves
- few stomata
- stomata sunk into pits in the epidermis
- hairs around the stomata and over the leaf surfaces.

General principles

When analysing and interpreting adaptations, it is important for you to present information that supports your ideas. For example, when suggesting how water loss is reduced in a xerophytic plant:

- Identify clearly the particular feature, such as sunken stomata or epidermal hairs.
- Describe the structure or appearance of the feature, for example, the guard cells at the base of a pit in the epidermis with a narrow opening at the entrance to the pit. You can also draw a diagram to illustrate this (see Figure 28).
- Suggest an explanation of how the rate of water loss is reduced, for example, that the hairs reduce air currents and trap a layer of humid air next to the leaf surface, thus lowering the diffusion gradient.

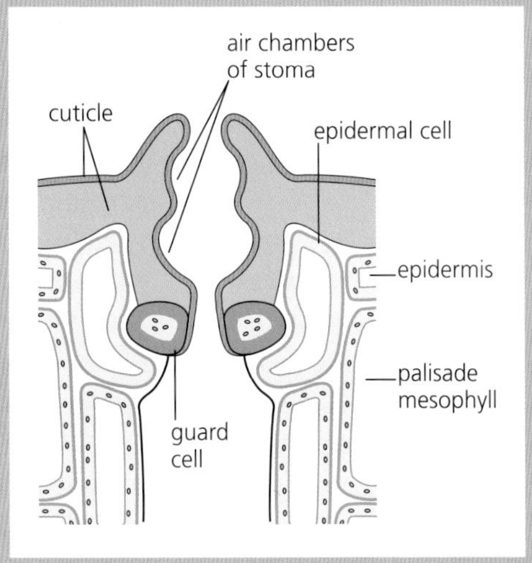

Figure 28 Sunken stoma.

We can make suggestions but we cannot be certain that a particular feature really does affect water loss without further experimental evidence. Look at the following evidence relating to the effect of hairiness on the rate of water loss.

The graph of Figure 29 shows the difference between the rate of water loss from a leaf without hairs in still and in moving air.

You can see that in moving air the rate of water loss rises steeply as the stomata open, but in still air there is a much lower rate and little difference as the stomata open wider.

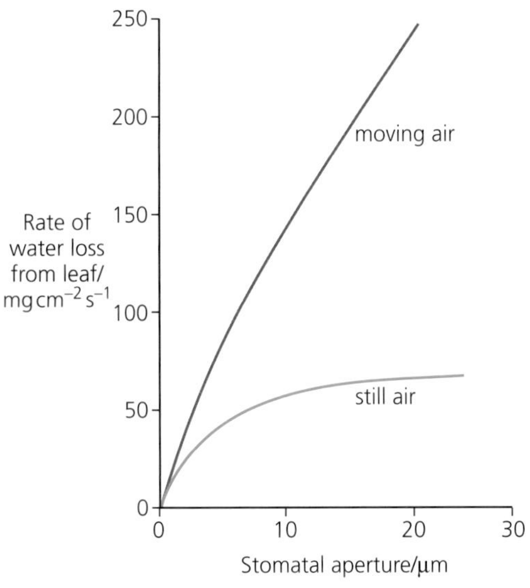

Figure 29 Rate of water loss for a leaf in still air and in moving air.

Table 1 gives the results of measuring the rate of water loss in leaves from three species of flowering plant with differing amounts of hairiness on the leaves.

Table 1 Rate of water loss for flowering plants with leaves of different hairiness.

Name of flowering plant	Hairiness of leaves	Rate of water loss from leaf surface/g $cm^{-2} h^{-1}$
Sweet violet	Slightly hairy	0.04
Storksbill	Quite hairy	0.09
Woundwort	Densely hairy	0.13

■ What do these results tell you about the effect of hairs on the rate of water loss in these particular plants?

You would expect from the data in the graph of Figure 29 that in Table 1 the rate of water loss from the hairiest leaves would be lowest because they would trap a layer of still air best. However, the results in the table do not fit with this hypothesis. They clearly do not suggest that the hairs on the woundwort leaves are adaptations to reduce water loss. They may have some other function, such as deterring animals from eating them. Alternatively, any reduction in water loss may be offset by different numbers of stomata, or by some other factor.

Moral: Look carefully at data before assuming that the answer you are expecting is correct!

Chapter 9

Adaptations for mass transport

If you have ever squashed a fly, you will have noticed that the contents that ooze out are yellowish, with no sign of red blood. This is because, although the fly does have a blood system, it does not have the bright red haemoglobin that gives our blood its colour. The absence of haemoglobin in flies is not because they are simple or primitive. As you saw in the last chapter, flies don't use their blood system to carry oxygen to their muscles. Haemoglobin, however, occurs widely in the animal kingdom, even, for example, in such apparently lowly organisms as earthworms. It must have first arisen at quite an early stage in evolution.

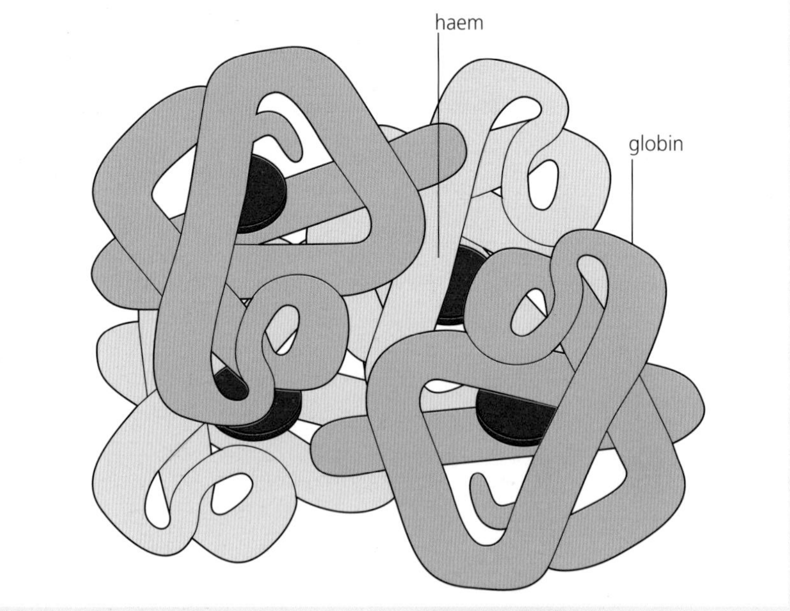

Figure 1 Diagram of the structure of a haemoglobin molecule.

Haemoglobin is a complex molecule that consists of four chains of a polypeptide called globin, with a haem group tucked in the centre of each, as you can see in Figure 1. It is the haem that is the key to the oxygen-carrying function of haemoglobin.

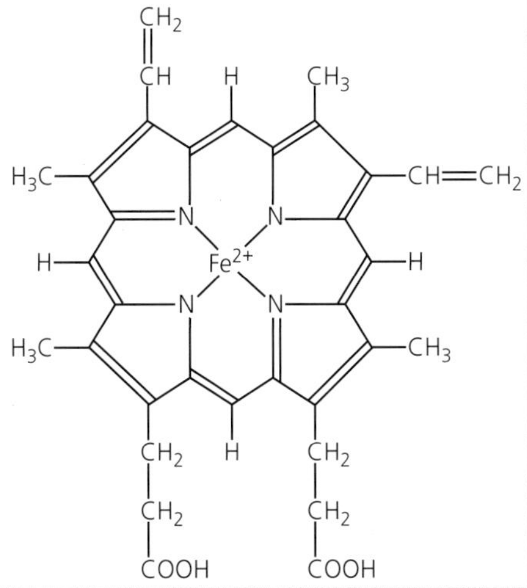

Figure 2 The chemical structure of haem.

You will notice from Figure 2 that haem contains iron (symbol: Fe) at its centre. The iron exists as an Fe^{2+} ion, which has the remarkable ability to combine reversibly with one oxygen molecule, making it ideal as a means of picking up and delivering oxygen, as we shall see later.

Haemoglobin may seem a complex molecule, and indeed it is. Even the haem part is quite complex, and it may be hard to imagine how it arose by evolution. However, it may have evolved through minor changes to a relatively small number of basic molecular structures.

Haem belongs to a group of substances called porphyrins, which all have a common chemical structure and include a metal ion at the centre. Porphyrins occur in several substances with surprisingly different functions. One is cytochrome, which is found in mitochondria and plays a vital part in respiration. Like haemoglobin, it consists of haem attached to polypeptides, but haem's role in cytochrome is as a temporary carrier of electrons rather than oxygen.

Chlorophyll molecules, too, contain a porphyrin similar to haem, but here it has a magnesium ion at the centre. There are also animals that have blood pigments for transporting oxygen in which the key component is a slightly different porphyrin. Lobsters, for example, have bluish blood because they use a porphyrin containing cobalt instead of iron.

The structure of haem is the same in all haemoglobin, but the globin chains vary considerably between species. It is actually the globin component of haemoglobin that determines its precise function, and many varieties exist. Different forms of haemoglobin vary both in their ability to combine with oxygen and in the conditions in which they take up and release oxygen. The haemoglobin of a developing baby in the womb differs from the haemoglobin the baby makes after its birth. Fetal haemoglobin is better at absorbing oxygen at low concentrations. This is necessary because it has to obtain its oxygen from the mother's blood, which has a much lower concentration than the air in the lungs. After birth, the baby starts to make haemoglobin which is better suited for the uptake of oxygen in the lungs.

One of the remarkable features of living things is that, despite the extraordinary variety, all species have an essentially similar basic chemistry and physiology. As we have seen in earlier chapters, all have a structure based on proteins, lipids and carbohydrates. All depend on DNA or RNA for their coded instructions and replication. The story of porphyrins shows how adaptations of one particular form of chemical structure have served many different functions through the course of evolution.

In this chapter we shall see how haemoglobin performs its role in transporting oxygen, but first we will look at the structure of the transport system itself.

The blood circulation

The main function of the blood system is to transport substances round the body. As a process for moving substances, diffusion of molecules is much too slow for an animal any larger than a pinhead. Larger animals have a system of **mass transport** that enables them to move substances around in bulk, just as a country depends on a transport system carrying large quantities rather than on people carrying individual items on foot.

In Chapter 4 we saw that the human heart is the pump that forces blood round the body. In effect, it is a double pump, because the left half pumps blood to the majority of the body tissues, while the right half pumps blood through the lungs. In this section we consider how the vessels that carry the blood around the body are adapted for their function.

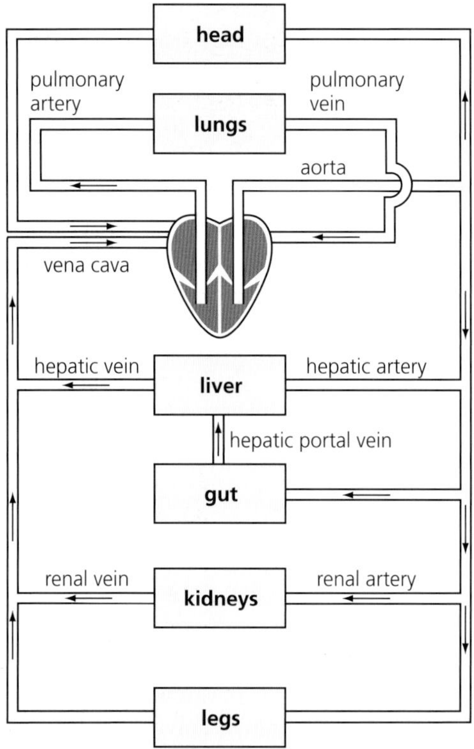

Figure 3 Diagram showing the main blood vessels in the human circulatory system.

Figure 3 is a diagram showing the basic plan of the human blood system. Blood is pumped out of the heart into **arteries**. These branch into thinner **arterioles** within the organs, and the arterioles branch to form the mass of very narrow **capillaries** which penetrate the tissues. From the capillaries the blood flows into **venules** and **veins** that transport it back to the heart.

Arteries

The arteries have to withstand the full force of the pumping action of the heart's ventricles. They are adapted for this by having thick but flexible walls. You can see from Figure 4 that an artery wall has three layers. The thick middle layer consists of a mixture of muscle cells and elastic fibres. Outside this is a layer of tough protein fibres. The innermost layer, the

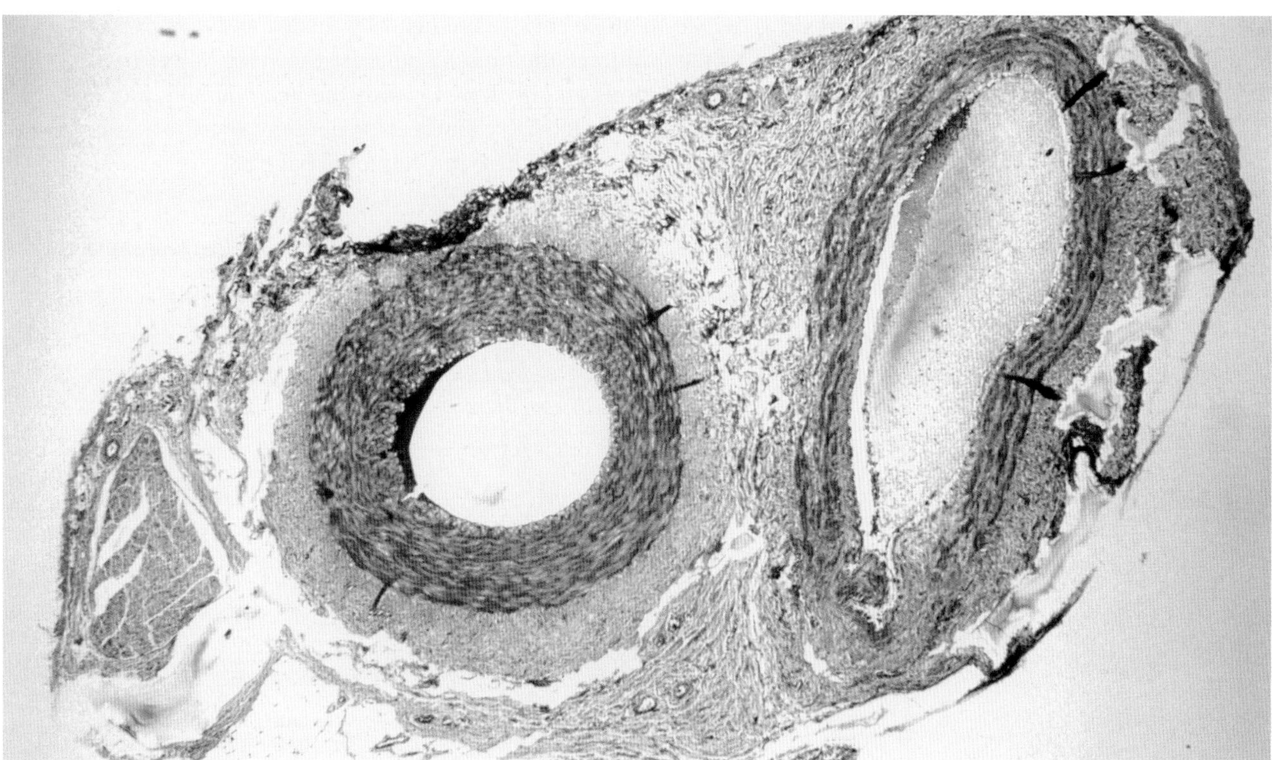

Figure 4 Photomicrograph of the cross section of an artery (left) and a vein (right).

endothelium, consists of flattened cells which have an extremely smooth surface. This ensures that blood flows freely and does not stick to the walls. As we saw in Chapter 4, if this surface does get damaged, blood clots are liable to form and may block the artery.

The elastic fibres in the middle layer allow the artery to expand each time the heart beats. This is better than having a rigid tube because the stretching of the fibres absorbs the shock waves caused by the heart's forceful pumping action. The other advantage of the elasticity is that the fibres recoil to their original length between heartbeats. This smoothes out the changes in pressure and maintains a more constant blood flow. Close to the heart, arteries have a high proportion of elastic fibres and few muscle cells. In the smaller arterioles the balance is the opposite way round. Here, muscle cells can contract and partially shut off blood flow to particular organs. For example, during exercise, blood flow to the stomach and intestines is reduced, allowing greater blood flow to the muscles.

Veins

Veins have much thinner walls than arteries. The blood pressure is much lower and the blood moves more slowly. This is because they have a considerably wider central lumen – the same volume of blood returns to the heart as leaves it, but the returning flow is slower. It is like a wide river moving slowly compared with a narrow mountain torrent that joins the river. Like the arteries, the veins have walls of three layers, but the middle layer is much less muscular and has only a few elastic fibres. The walls have only a limited ability to contract and push blood along. During exercise, the blood is helped to move back to the heart by the leg and arm muscles because, as they contract, the muscles squeeze the veins. Valves in the veins ensure that the blood can only flow towards the heart. Finally, blood is drawn into the heart when the chambers expand and there is a brief period of negative pressure (see Figure 6 in Chapter 5, page 88).

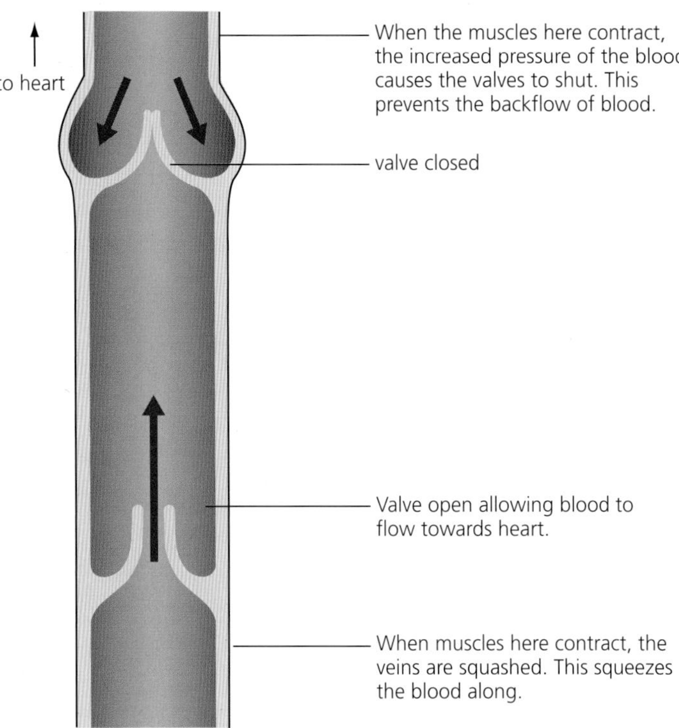
to heart
When the muscles here contract, the increased pressure of the blood causes the valves to shut. This prevents the backflow of blood.
valve closed
Valve open allowing blood to flow towards heart.
When muscles here contract, the veins are squashed. This squeezes the blood along.

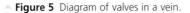

Figure 5 Diagram of valves in a vein.

The smallest arterioles and venules are connected by capillaries. A capillary is only about 8 μm in diameter, and it is estimated that an adult human has nearly 100 000 km of capillaries. That is more than twice the distance round the equator! As you might expect, this provides an enormous surface area for the exchange of gases, glucose and other substances, and no cell in the body is more than a very short distance from a capillary. The walls of many capillaries, especially those in muscles and the lungs, consist of a single thin endothelial cell wrapped into a tubular shape, as shown in Figure 6. Others have two or three cells linked together, but all have very thin walls only one cell thick which allows for rapid diffusion.

Leaky vessels

Capillaries are so thin-walled that most substances can easily pass through. Only substances with particularly large molecules, such as most proteins, cannot escape from the blood. This has the advantage that oxygen, carbon dioxide, glucose, amino acids, hormones and many other substances are easily exchanged between the blood and the tissues. It also means that water freely leaks out.

The blood vessels are so leaky that there is more water outside the blood system than in it. The leaking water produces a solution that fills the spaces

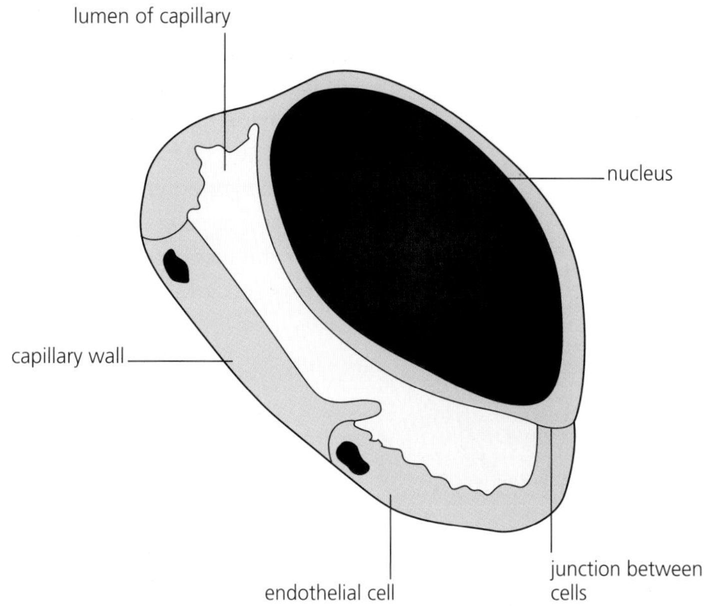

Figure 6 A section across a capillary.

between cells. This is called **tissue fluid**. Obviously, water cannot simply drain out of the blood vessels without being replaced. In fact, in the tissues there is constant movement of water into and out of the capillaries. By the time blood enters the capillaries from the arterioles it is at a much lower pressure than when it left the heart in the arteries. Nevertheless, this **hydrostatic pressure** is still large enough to force water out of capillaries into the tissue fluid. Therefore, as the blood passes along the capillaries, the water content decreases. Small solutes including glucose and ions also pass out, but the soluble proteins in the blood plasma cannot go through the walls of the capillaries. As water is lost, the concentration of proteins in the blood plasma increases. This lowers the water potential inside the capillary. The result is that at the venule end of the capillary the water potential of the plasma is lower than the water potential of the tissue fluid. Therefore, water goes back into the capillary by osmosis.

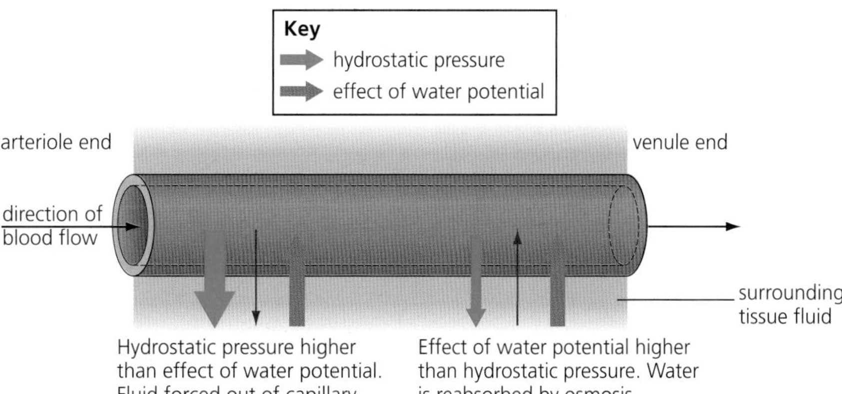

Figure 7 The effects of hydrostatic forces and water potential at the arteriole end and the venule end of a capillary.

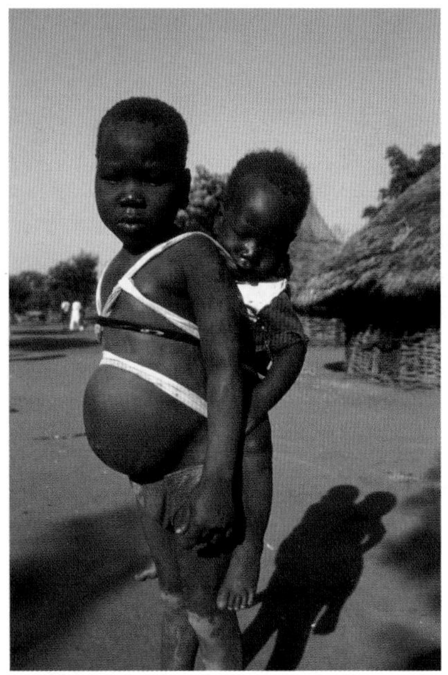
Figure 9 A child with kwashiorkor, a condition caused by malnutrition.

Q1

Explain why shortage of plasma proteins causes fluid to collect in the tissues.

Not all of the excess water in the tissues is reabsorbed into the blood capillaries by osmosis. The tissues also have a drainage system that consists of tubes slightly wider than capillaries. These tubes are called **lymph capillaries**. They are not part of a circulatory system like the blood. They have closed ends which are sufficiently porous for tissue fluid and large molecules to enter. This is important because some proteins do escape from the blood capillaries. If they accumulated in the tissue fluid, they would lower the water potential of the tissue fluid until water would no longer be reabsorbed into the blood.

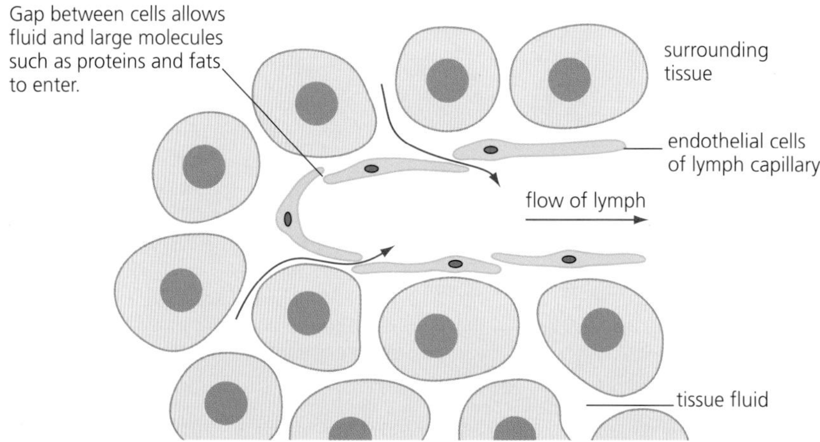

Figure 8 Section through the end of a lymph capillary.

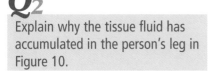

Figure 10 A person with elephantiasis, caused by parasitic worms that block lymph vessels.

Q2

Explain why the tissue fluid has accumulated in the person's leg in Figure 10.

The lymph capillaries drain the excess fluid through a system of larger vessels that connect with large veins in the neck where the fluid returns to the blood system. The lymph vessels have very thin walls and also have valves similar to those in veins. There are some muscle cells in the walls of the lymph vessels to move the fluid along and, as in veins, this movement is assisted by the squeezing action of leg and arm muscles.

Figure 9 shows a child suffering from severe malnutrition. The child's diet contains very little protein. Consequently his blood is very short of plasma proteins. One result is that fluid collects in the tissues. This causes the child's belly and limbs to swell, as you can see in the photo.

Figure 10 shows a woman suffering from a condition called elephantiasis. The woman has been infected with parasitic worms that have blocked the lymph vessels in one leg. Tissue fluid has accumulated in this leg, making it swell massively so that it looks like an elephant's leg.

How blood is adapted to transport oxygen

Blood has two main constituents, the liquid plasma and the cells.

When blood is centrifuged, the red blood cells are forced to the bottom of the tube because they are heaviest. The pale yellow plasma is a fluid that makes up just over half the volume. Its role is to transport dissolved glucose, amino acids, urea, mineral ions and hormones. The great majority of cells

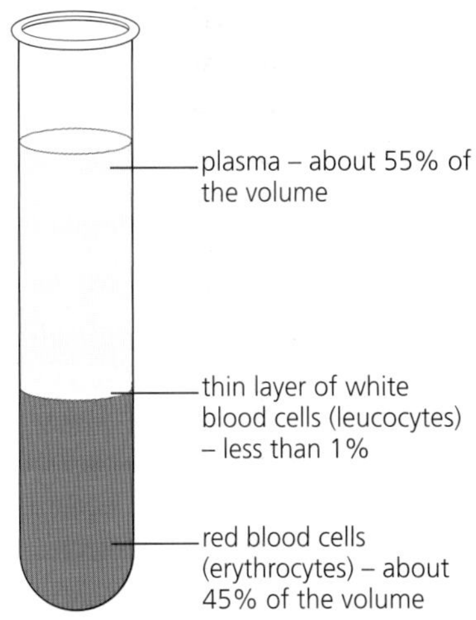

Figure 11 A tube of centrifuged blood.

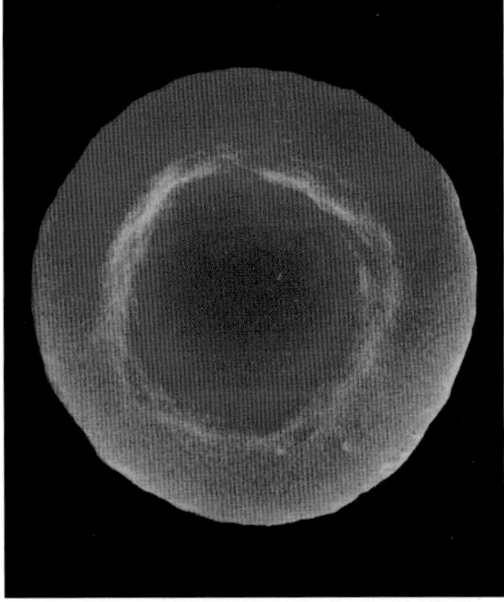

Figure 12 The shape of a red blood cell (× 15 000).

are the red blood cells (technically called erythrocytes), which transport oxygen and some carbon dioxide. There are many fewer white cells (leucocytes) and these form a barely visible layer on top of the red cells.

The proportions of plasma and cells are important. There has to be enough plasma for the blood to flow easily. On the other hand, an efficient oxygen supply requires a large proportion of red blood cells. A quite small decrease in the proportion of plasma makes the blood more viscous (sticky), and the heart has to pump harder to push it round. This increases blood pressure and places additional strain on the heart. Increased blood viscosity is one way in which dehydration can affect the performance of an athlete.

Red blood cells have several adaptations for the transport of oxygen. Consider how each of the following features assists in efficient oxygen transport, before reading the explanations. A red blood cell:

- is small in size – each cell is just over 7 μm in diameter. A blood capillary has an outer diameter of about 8 μm; the diameter of its lumen is rather less
- is flattened; shaped like a disc
- has a thin central part of the disc
- has no organelles such as a nucleus or mitochondria
- is filled with haemoglobin.

How is its small size an adaptation for efficient oxygen transport?

The small size allows the red cells to pass through the narrow capillaries. By being about the same diameter as the lumen of the capillary, they touch the sides, which reduces the distance that oxygen has to diffuse once it enters the capillary. The narrowness of the capillaries is an associated adaptation in that they can penetrate the spaces between cells.

How is its flattened disc shape an adaptation?

The flat shape increases the surface area to volume ratio and greatly increases the area through which oxygen can diffuse. It also results in all the haemoglobin being close to the surface. If the cells were spherical, much of the haemoglobin in the centre would be of little use because it would be too far for oxygen to reach it in the time available.

How is its thin central part an adaptation?

The thin centre allows the cell to be flexible so that it can bend and squeeze through the narrow capillaries. As blood flows through a capillary, the cell tends to form a dome shape with its edges scraping along the wall of the capillary.

How is the absence of organelles an adaptation?

The absence of organelles provides maximum space for haemoglobin.

Q3

Red blood cells do contain some enzymes. These are important for carbon dioxide transport. But red cells cannot replace the enzymes. Explain why the enzymes cannot be synthesised in the red cells.

■ How is the cell being filled with haemoglobin an adaptation?

The haemoglobin greatly increases the oxygen-carrying capacity of the blood. Oxygen is not very soluble in water, so only small amounts would be transported by plasma alone.

Haemoglobin

In the introduction to this chapter, we learned that the haemoglobins are a group of chemically similar substances that occur in a very wide range of different animals. Haemoglobins are so widespread because of an exceptionally useful property. Their molecules combine with oxygen when it is present in high concentrations, but – and this is the important feature – the process is reversed when the concentration is low. This means that adult human haemoglobin takes up oxygen in the lungs, but when it reaches a tissue where there is little oxygen, the haemoglobin releases it again.

The dissociation curve for haemoglobin

The graph shows the oxygen dissociation curve for adult human haemoglobin. This shows how much oxygen is combined with haemoglobin at different oxygen concentrations. However, if you look at the *x* axis of the graph, you will see that the scale shows not a concentration but the 'partial pressure' of oxygen. Scientists use **partial pressure** as a measure rather than concentration because it is a more useful indicator of how much oxygen is available to haemoglobin.

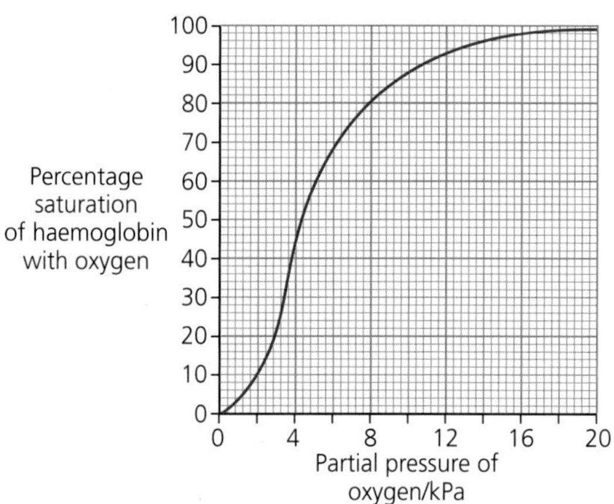

Figure 13 The oxygen dissociation curve for adult human haemoglobin.

■ When discussing how much oxygen is available to haemoglobin, why is it more useful to measure partial pressure of oxygen in air than its oxygen concentration?

The air is a mixture of gases. Each gas exerts a pressure proportional to its concentration. Atmospheric pressure at sea level is about 100 kPa. (It varies a bit according to weather conditions, so forecasters refer to low pressure areas and high pressure areas.) The atmosphere contains about 21% oxygen. So at sea level, oxygen exerts a partial pressure of about 21% of the total atmospheric pressure, that is, about 21 kPa. Up a high mountain, the atmospheric pressure is much lower because the air is much thinner. But the *proportion* of oxygen is still about 21%. However, there is far less oxygen in each cubic metre of air, so the *pressure* exerted by the oxygen is much lower. On the summit of Mount Everest it is only about 7 kPa.

■ Explain what we mean if we say that haemoglobin is 100% saturated.

In Figure 13, the *y* axis shows the saturation of haemoglobin with oxygen. Each haemoglobin molecule can combine with a maximum of four molecules of oxygen, making **oxyhaemoglobin**. If all the haemoglobin molecules in a red blood cell combine with four oxygen molecules, the haemoglobin will be 100% saturated, and obviously it cannot possibly take on any more oxygen. (If 80% of the oxygen is released, the haemoglobin will then be only 20% saturated.)

Let us look at the shape of the curve on the graph. It is like a partly flattened letter S.

■ The graph shows that haemoglobin reaches nearly 100% oxygen saturation when the partial pressure is much lower than atmospheric partial pressure of 21 kPa. Explain the advantage of this.

In the alveoli of the lungs, the partial pressure of oxygen is less than the 21 kPa in the air outside the body. This is because the alveolar air contains a lot of water vapour and a relatively high concentration of carbon dioxide. The partial pressure of oxygen is usually about 15 kPa. From the graph you can see that even at this lower partial pressure the haemoglobin becomes almost 100% saturated.

Therefore, as the blood passes through the lung capillaries, the haemoglobin in the red cells becomes loaded with oxygen. This happens extremely quickly – the haemoglobin will become almost fully saturated within a fraction of a second.

■ The blood system carries the red cells through a pulmonary vein into the heart from where they are pumped out through arteries and arterioles to the tissues of the body. Explain why the haemoglobin does not unload its oxygen before it reaches the capillaries in the tissues.

The walls of the veins, arteries and arterioles are too thick to allow oxygen to escape. The partial pressure around the red cells remains constant, so the haemoglobin stays saturated.

■ **Use the data in Figure 13 to explain why oxygen is unloaded from the haemoglobin when the red cells reach the capillaries in the tissues.**

When the red cells reach a capillary in, for example, a muscle or the brain, the surrounding tissue will have a low partial pressure of oxygen because these tissues will have been using oxygen for respiration.

Suppose that the partial pressure of oxygen in a muscle is 4 kPa. From the graph, at 4 kPa the haemoglobin can be no more than 55% saturated. Therefore, the oxyhaemoglobin rapidly unloads oxygen until the haemoglobin is 55% saturated. This unloading is called **dissociation**. Assuming that the haemoglobin became 100% saturated in the alveoli (in practice it is usually slightly less), it will unload 45% of its oxygen. This will rapidly diffuse into the muscle. Bear in mind that this all happens very fast as the blood circulates. (It is not like a truck that has to stop to load or unload.) So, although it may seem inefficient for haemoglobin to release only some of its oxygen, the muscle gets a continuous supply.

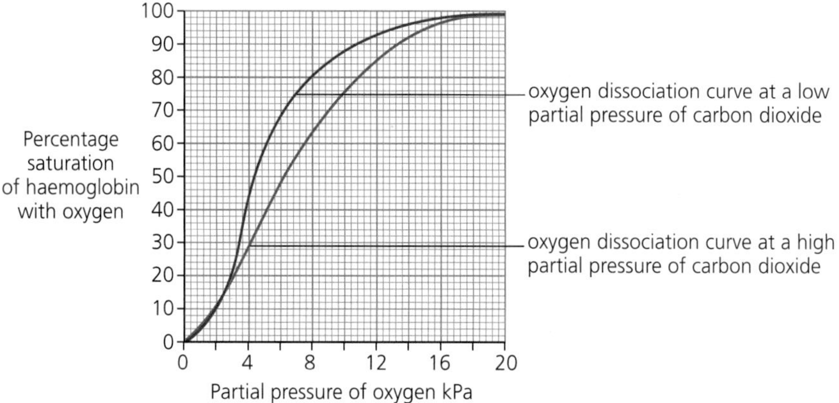

Figure 14 The oxygen dissociation curve in low and high partial pressures of carbon dioxide.

■ **In practice, more than 45% of the oxygen is unloaded in active muscles. An active muscle is respiring and rapidly producing carbon dioxide. Use the data in the graph in Figure 14 to explain why more oxygen is unloaded.**

Look at the curve for oxygen dissociation at a high partial pressure of carbon dioxide. You will see that it forms a more forward-sloping S. It is to the right of the curve for oxygen dissociation at a low carbon dioxide partial pressure. This is also the curve in Figure 13. You will recall that muscle contains a 4% partial pressure of oxygen, when oxygen in haemoglobin above 55% saturation is unloaded into the muscle. Now read off the percentage saturation of haemoglobin when the partial pressure of carbon dioxide is high, as it will be in active muscle. It is only 30%. The oxyhaemoglobin will dissociate more completely and release 70% of its oxygen. The advantage of this is that when a muscle is respiring actively it receives an increased oxygen supply.

Oxygen dissociation in a fetus and its mother

The introduction explained that there are different forms of haemoglobin, adapted for different conditions. Figure 15 shows the dissociation curve for the type of haemoglobin that babies have before birth as well as for the mother's adult haemoglobin. While in the womb, a fetus receives its oxygen from the mother's blood by diffusion across the placenta.

1 The partial pressure of oxygen in the placenta may be 3 kPa. At that value, what percentage of the oxygen in the mother's haemoglobin will dissociate?

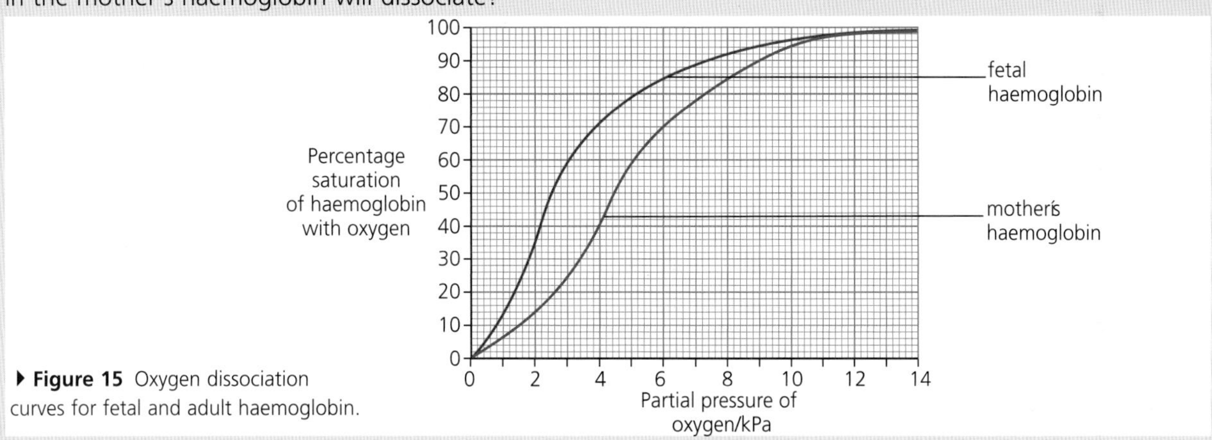

▸ **Figure 15** Oxygen dissociation curves for fetal and adult haemoglobin.

2 At the same partial pressure of 3 kPa, what percentage of the fetal haemoglobin will become saturated?

3 Explain the advantage of the fetal haemoglobin having a different dissociation curve from the mother's haemoglobin.

A fetus starts to manufacture more and more adult haemoglobin as it gets closer to the time of birth. After birth, the proportion of fetal haemoglobin in the blood normally declines quite rapidly.

4 Explain why it is important for the baby to have adult haemoglobin after birth.

Muscles contain a substance called **myoglobin** that is similar to haemoglobin and which also combines reversibly with oxygen. It provides muscles with a store of oxygen which is quickly available when the muscles become active. Like haemoglobin, myoglobin contains haem, but each molecule has only one polypeptide chain and therefore just one haem group.

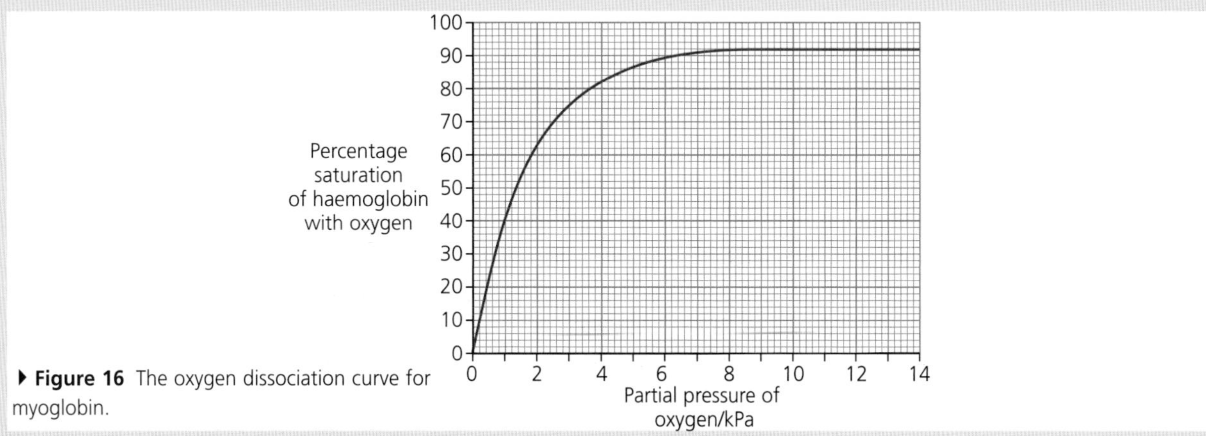

▸ **Figure 16** The oxygen dissociation curve for myoglobin.

5 With how many molecules of oxygen can a molecule of myoglobin combine? Explain your answer.

6 Use the graph to explain how the myoglobin in a muscle acts as an oxygen store that is only used when the muscle is particularly active.

7 How can the oxygen store in the myoglobin be replaced after use?

(a)

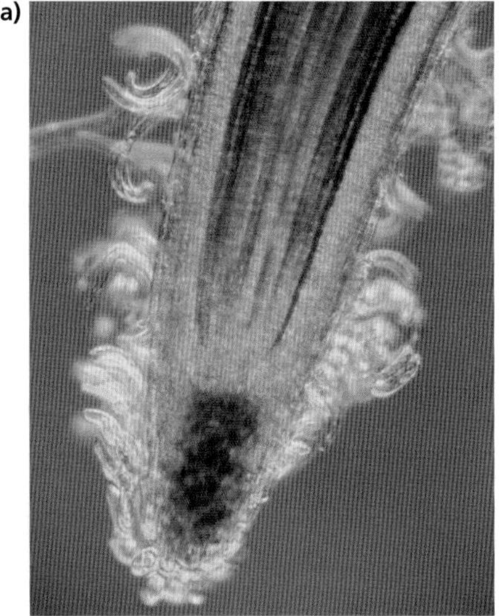

(b)

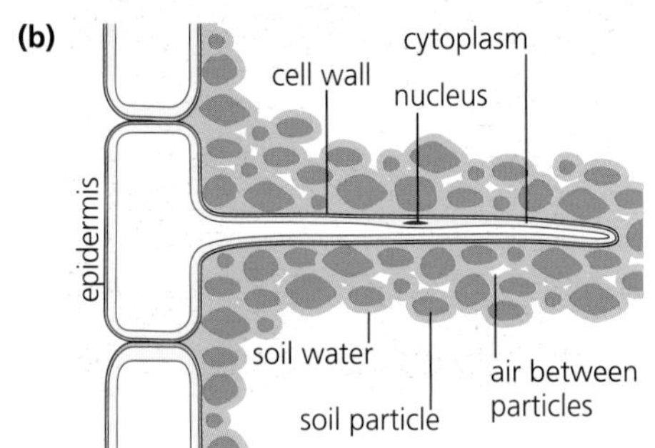

Figure 17 (a) Photograph of a root tip showing root hairs. (b) Diagram showing a root hair extending into soil water between soil particles.

How does water get to the top of a tree?

An oak tree can be at least 30 m high and have a huge array of leaves and branches. You may have seen a physics experiment using a pump in which water is 'sucked' up a long tube, perhaps up the side of a school building. No matter how good the pump, the water never goes up more than about 10 m. So, how can a tree get water to the leaves at the top?

First, the water has to get into the tree. The tree has a massive branching network of roots that penetrate deep into the soil and absorb water from the soil. The job of the larger roots is to anchor the tree into the soil. They have a waterproof coating and do not absorb water. They branch many times, ending in young, very fine roots. At the end of each one is a section near the tip which has no waterproof coating, and its role is to absorb water. Many of the cells in its outer layer, the **epidermis**, have extensions that penetrate between the soil particles, as seen in Figure 17. These extensions are the **root hairs** and they greatly increase the surface area through which water can enter.

Water enters the root hairs by osmosis. The water in the soil usually contains only a low concentration of mineral ions, so this solution has a water potential just below zero. The root hair cells accumulate mineral ions by absorbing them from the soil by active transport (see pages 49–50). This makes the water potential of the solution inside the cell lower (more negative) than the soil water, so water enters through the partially permeable plasma membrane inside the cell wall.

Once inside the root, the water crosses to the xylem tissue in the centre. The **xylem** is the mass transport system made up of continuous tubes that distributes the water to other parts of the plant. Water crosses the **cortex** by two different pathways. Some passes through the cells of the cortex, moving from cell to cell through the membranes that separate them, as you can see in Figure 19. This is called the **symplastic pathway**. Water moves by this route down a water potential gradient, since the cells near the centre have a more negative potential than those near the outside of the root. However, this is a slow route because the cytoplasm and membranes restrict the rate at which water can move. There is much less resistance in the cellulose walls where water can move quite freely between the fibres. Much of the water passes by this route, called the **apoplastic pathway**.

Q4

When land is flooded by seawater, the land plants may wilt because they lose water from the roots into the soil. Explain why.

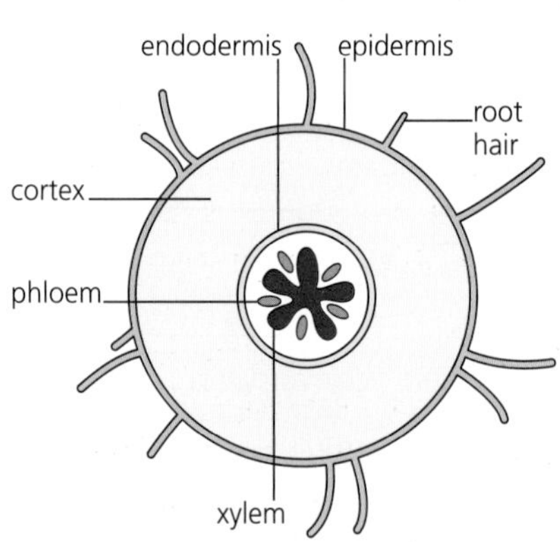

Figure 18 A cross-section of a root.

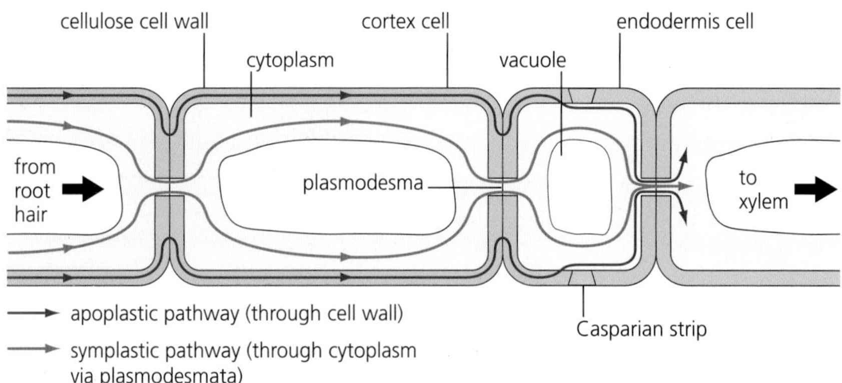

Figure 19 The symplastic and the apoplastic pathways by which water moves through the cells of the cortex and the endodermis.

However, before the water can get into the xylem it has to pass through a single layer of cells called the **endodermis**. Here, the water cannot continue its fast route through the cell walls because of a waterproof barrier, the Casparian strip. Instead, it is forced to pass through the membranes and cytoplasm of an endodermis cell before it can reach the xylem. This may seem an unnecessary obstacle, but this barrier means that ions have to go *through* the endodermis cells, and the ions are pumped through by active transport. A high ion concentration is therefore built up in the cells inside the endodermis. This ion concentration establishes a water potential gradient from the root hairs to the centre of the root, which enables water to reach the centre of the root by osmosis.

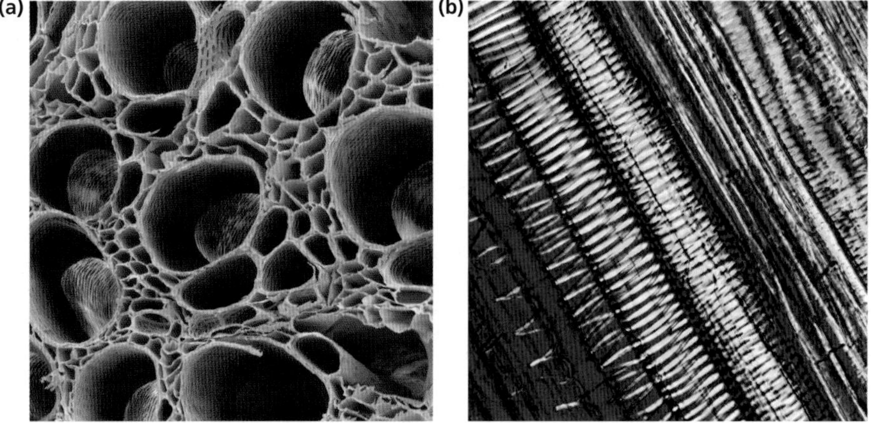

Figure 20 (a) Cross-section of xylem in old root. (b) Vertical section of xylem in young root.

In the centre of the root is the specialised transport system through which water moves rapidly upwards to the stem and leaves. Look at Figure 20(a). The brown cells are **xylem vessels**. Notice that they appear to be empty. This is because the vessels are long tubes consisting of dead cells linked end to end and containing no cytoplasm. Near the tip of a young root they develop as elongated cells. The cellulose walls of these cells become thickened with a waterproof substance called **lignin**. At first, the lignin is in rings, as you can see in Figure 20(b). The rings allow the cells to stretch and grow longer. The spaces between rings also allow water to enter the cells easily. In older cells, the lignin fills in the spaces between the rings so that the walls are almost completely lignified, apart from small gaps, called **pits**, that allow water to move sideways into surrounding tissues or between vessels if any get blocked. The end walls of the original cells break down, so the vessels are continuous pipes going all the way up the trunk of a tree to the uppermost leaves.

Q5

List four features of xylem that make it well adapted to the transport of water.

To understand how water reaches the top of the tree, we need to go to the leaves. In Chapter 8 we looked at the structure of leaves. You will remember that leaves have stomata which must open to let in carbon dioxide for photosynthesis. An unavoidable result of this is that water can get out. Normally there is relatively little water in the air around a leaf, so water diffuses to the lower water potential of the air through the stomata whenever they are open. This process is called **transpiration**, and vast amounts of water can be lost from a large tree. As water vapour diffuses from the air spaces in the mesophyll and through the stomata, it is replaced by water from the mesophyll cells. This in turn is replaced by water from the xylem in the veins of the leaf.

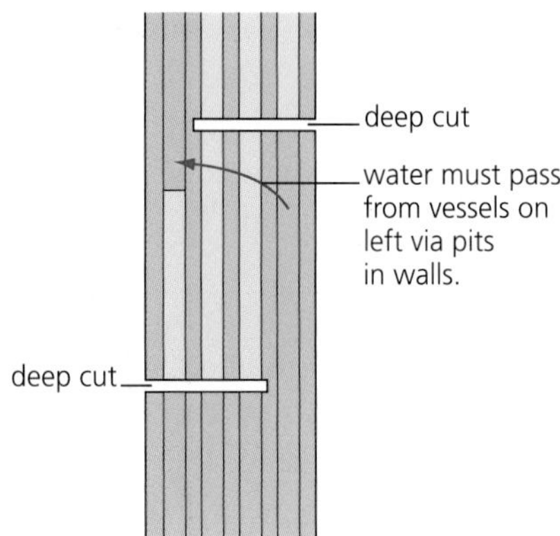

Figure 21 Diagram to illustrate the cut stem experiment.

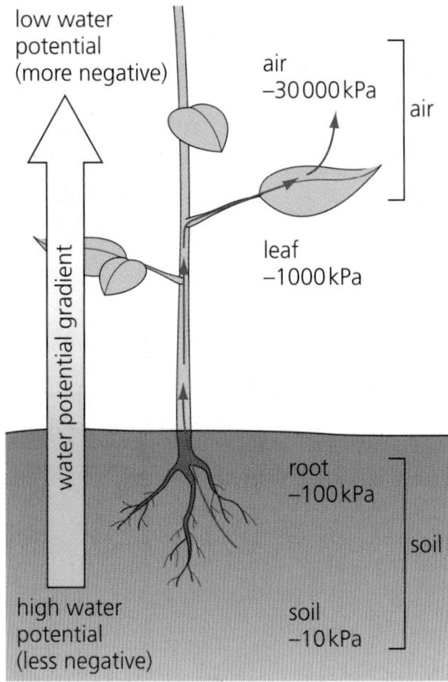

Figure 22 The passage of water through a plant.

Since the xylem is a continuous system of tubes, water is drawn through to replace the water lost from the uppermost ends of the xylem, in the same way as a drink can be sucked through a straw into your mouth. However, since water cannot be pulled up more than ten metres, even the most fantastic 'sucker' cannot drink through a straw longer than 10 metres. Trees are often much taller than this, so how do they overcome this problem?

The answer is that xylem vessels are very narrow, and water molecules tend to stick together. This is why water drops form at the end of a tap – the water does not fall off until the weight is greater than the force holding the molecules together. This property of water is called **cohesion**. As water moves out of the xylem in a leaf, it drags other molecules of water behind it. Because the vessels are so narrow, the column of water behind does not break, and water is pulled up all the way from the roots. The pulling force is so great that the column of water is actually being stretched. It is under **tension**, just as an elastic cord being pulled up would be. The tension in the column of water tends to make the xylem vessels slightly narrower. However, the lignin in the walls is strong enough to stop the vessels collapsing, just as the cartilages in the trachea and bronchi prevent them from collapsing as we expand the chest to breathe in.

Surprisingly, the diameter of a tree trunk is reduced very slightly, but measurably, when the tree is transpiring rapidly on a hot day, because the tension in the xylem is sufficient to pull in the walls of the many vessels just a little. If the column of water in a vessel is broken, for example by an air bubble or a cut, the water will ping apart like elastic, leaving an empty section above and below the bubble or cut. This is why the pits are important. They permit water to move from one vessel to a neighbour if a vessel is damaged. A simple experiment showed this. The stem of a young tree was cut over half way across at two positions, one above the other, as seen in Figure 21. This ensured that all vessels were cut. Even so, water continued to rise up the stem by moving sideways between the cuts.

The two ideas, of cohesion and tension, used to explain how water is pulled up in a plant, are brought together in the **cohesion–tension** theory. The theory largely explains how water reaches the leaves of a plant from its roots. However, there is some evidence that water can also be *pushed* up from the roots. If a young tree is cut down near the base, water continues to spill out onto the cut stump for some time. This cannot be due to the pulling force of transpiration. It has been shown experimentally that water can be forced a few metres up a cut stem, although certainly nowhere near to the top of tree. This **root pressure** is generated by the endodermis. As we saw earlier, ions are carried by active transport through the cells of the endodermis into the cells surrounding the xylem. Water therefore enters these cells by osmosis. Both water and ions enter the xylem, and the force of the incoming water is sufficient to push it some way up the xylem. Evidence for this theory comes from observations that root pressure is stopped by low temperatures and by respiratory inhibitors.

Q6

Explain why (a) a respiratory inhibitor and (b) a low temperature stop active transport and hence root pressure.

Transpiration

Water enters the roots by osmosis and passes up the stem to the leaves where it evaporates into the air spaces inside the leaf and then passes out to the atmosphere. The air has a low water potential because it normally has a low percentage of water vapour.

Most of the water taken in through the roots of plants living in damp climates simply passes through the xylem and then out from the leaves. Only a small proportion is used in photosynthesis to manufacture glucose. The loss of so much water by transpiration may seem very wasteful, but it is the unavoidable effect of the need for leaves to take in carbon dioxide. It does, however, have some advantages. The stream of water also transports mineral ions around the plant. The evaporation of water from the leaves has a cooling effect, just as the evaporation of sweat from our skin does. When leaves are exposed to bright sunlight, transpiration can reduce the possibility of the leaves overheating and the enzymes being denatured.

The rate of transpiration is affected by four main factors.

Temperature

As the temperature rises, the rate of diffusion of water vapour increases. The water molecules gain kinetic energy and move more rapidly, so they are more likely to pass through the stomata by random movement. (We use the term transpiration rather than just evaporation for this loss of water, because the water both evaporates from the cells into the air spaces and also passes out of the plant by diffusion.)

Humidity

The air spaces of the leaf mesophyll are normally saturated with water vapour, whereas the air outside is usually much less humid. The greater the difference in humidity, the faster the water vapour will diffuse out of the leaf. This is because of the greater difference in water potential.

You will remember that xerophytes often have adaptations that increase the humidity around the leaf surface, for example by having stomata that are sunk into the epidermis or having a coating of hairs that trap water vapour. The diffusion gradient is therefore less steep and the rate of water loss is lower.

Air movements

The movement of air over the surface of the leaf clears the water vapour away as it passes out of the stomata. This maintains the steep water potential gradient between the inside and outside of the leaf. The more rapidly that water vapour is moved away from the leaf surface, the more rapid will be the rate of transpiration.

Light

Light does not affect the rate of evaporation directly. The rate of diffusion is not changed by the brightness of the light. But indirectly, light does alter the rate of transpiration because of its effect on the opening and closing of the stomata. Since stomata are usually closed during darkness and are stimulated to open by daylight, the rate of transpiration increases markedly in the light. In many plants, however, the stomata close well before darkness falls, so bright sunlight does not necessarily mean a high rate of transpiration.

Chapter 10

Classification

Figure 1 shows four different birds. Three of them are common in Britain – the European robin, the blackbird and the song thrush. You have probably seen them at some time. It is less likely that you will have seen the New Zealand robin.

▲ **Figure 1** Four species of birds; (a) blackbird; (b) song thrush; (c) European robin; (d) New Zealand robin. The first three are common in Britain and the fourth is from New Zealand.

Let us consider the three British species. Look at the photographs carefully. The blackbird and the song thrush are very similar in general appearance. The blackbird is a female and, like the song thrush, has a spotted breast. Both birds also have similarly shaped beaks. We might guess from this that they were closely related. The European robin, however, is different from these two. It is dumpier in shape and has a smaller, thinner beak. Apart from its red breast there seems to be a close similarity between the European robin and the New Zealand robin. We might conclude, then, that blackbirds and song thrushes are closely related and that the same is probably true of the European and New Zealand robins.

The common names of the first three don't help us to decide. But from the names of the two robins, we might imagine that there is a relationship between them. This is where scientific names are much more helpful.

Each species of organism has a unique scientific name made up of two words. The scientific name of the blackbird is *Turdus merula*. The blackbird's **species** name is *merula*, and only the blackbird has this name. The blackbird is one of a larger grouping of species, the thrushes, which are all related to each other. The thrush group, or **genus** (plural **genera**), is called *Turdus* and all the different types of thrush found in Britain are named *Turdus* something. The song thrush is *Turdus philomelos* and another, the mistle thrush, is *Turdus viscivorus*.

The scientific names of the four birds in the photographs therefore tell us a lot more about relationships. *Turdus merula* (the blackbird) and *Turdus philomelos* (the song thrush) are clearly related. As we have seen, they both belong to the *Turdus* genus. From the names, we can now tell that the European robin *Erithacus rubecula* and the New Zealand robin *Petroica australis* are in fact not related at all. The New Zealand robin was only called a robin because it reminded early settlers in New Zealand of the familiar bird that they had known in Britain. When scientists came to look more carefully at the two species, they decided that these two birds were in different genera.

What is a species?

We like to organise and classify things. For example, a cookery book can have recipes grouped into starters and main courses, meat and vegetarian dishes, and the weekly television guide divides programmes according to the day of the week and the channel. If knowledge wasn't classified in this way, we would never know where to look for information. Imagine, for example, a library full of books that were placed randomly on the shelves. If you wanted information on a particular topic such as growing roses or the French Revolution, you would waste a lot of time trying to find it.

We really don't know how many different species of organisms there are, but it certainly runs into millions. Just as with a library, we need a system that classifies all the organisms we know about, and to be of real use, the system must be universal – it has to be usable by biologists anywhere in the world. The system we use is based on dividing living organisms into **species**. To use this system we need to have a clear idea of exactly what we mean by a species. There are three things that we consider in defining a species:

- Organisms belong to the same species if they are similar to each other and different from members of all other species.

So we need to look for similarities and differences. They might involve physical features. For example, in the blackbird and song thrush, we see differences in the colour of their feathers and their size. Similarly, flowering plants may differ in features such as the colour of their petals and the shape of their leaves. However, it is not just physical features that we should be looking at. The features that distinguish different species are controlled by genes, so we should expect to find differences in the DNA of different species. Genes code for proteins (page 119), and there will be differences in proteins such as the haemoglobins that transport oxygen in different species. We could also expect members of different species to show different behaviour patterns.

Q1

Suppose you wanted to investigate the difference between the distribution of silk button galls and common spangle galls on oak leaves.
Explain why you would:
(a) take a large sample of leaves;
(b) select the leaves at random.

- Organisms belong to the same species if they are able to breed together in their natural environment and produce fertile young.
- Different species of organism have different ecological niches.

Galls are abnormal growths produced by a plant. They are often caused by insects. The spangle galls shown in Figure 2 are found on the underside of oak leaves.

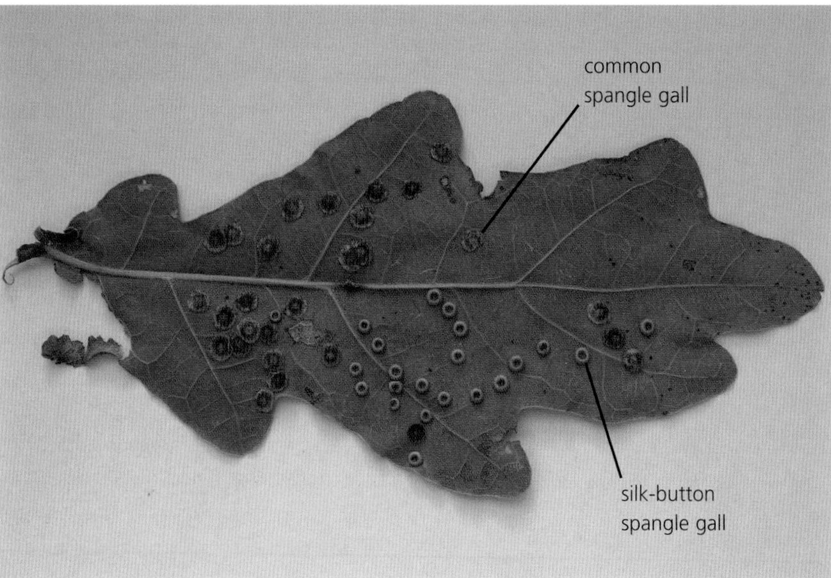

▲ **Figure 2** The lower surface of an oak leaf showing silk-button and common spangle galls. The silk button spangle galls are found more towards the tip of the leaf.

These galls are caused by the larvae of small wasps. Two types of gall are shown in this photograph. The single button spangle gall is a golden brown colour and has a dense covering of fine hairs, making it look rather like a tiny velvet-covered button. The common spangle gall is larger and has a raised central mound. It is green with tufts of red or brown hairs.

Q2

A horse and donkey can interbreed. The offspring is called a mule. Cells in a mule can undergo mitosis but not meiosis. Are a horse and a donkey different species? Give an explanation for your answer.

Although the gall wasps that produce these galls are very similar to look at, they have different ecological niches. They lay their eggs on different parts of an oak leaf, so the larvae which hatch from the eggs give rise to galls on different parts of the leaf.

When is a species not a species?

We can define a species, then, as a group of organisms that share certain observable characteristics, are able to produce fertile young and occupy the same ecological niche. If we use this definition, it ought to be easy to decide whether or not two organisms are separate species. Unfortunately, though, it is not always easy to decide whether or not two organisms are the *same* species.

A thorny problem

Hawthorn is a common woody plant. There are two species of hawthorn – *Crataegus monogyna* (common hawthorn) and *Crataegus oxyacanthoides* (Midland hawthorn). There are some obvious differences between these two species. Table 1 shows some of these.

Table 1 Some differences between the two British species of hawthorn.

Feature	*Crataegus monogyna* (common hawthorn)	*Crataegus oxyacanthoides* (Midland hawthorn)
General appearance		
Number of seeds in berry	One	Two
Shape of leaf	Many indentations	Few indentations
Hairs on leaf veins	Tufts of hairs present	No tufts of hairs present
Habitat	Along edges of woods and in open areas	In mature woods

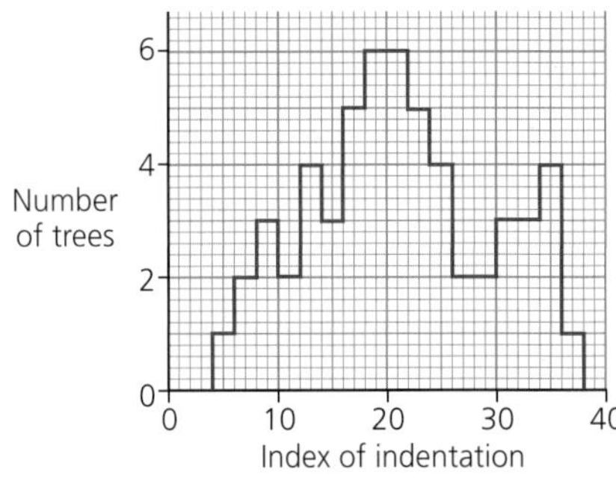

▲ **Figure 3** Graph to show variation in leaf shape in the hawthorn trees growing in a hedge planted over 900 years ago.

The evidence in the table suggests that *C. monogyna* and *C. oxyacanthoides* are different species. But are they? Hawthorns have always been planted as hedges. To grow the earliest hedges, farmers would have taken young hawthorn plants from nearby woodland and planted these. It is likely that they would have collected plants of both types.

Now look at the graph in Figure 3. It shows data about the leaves of hawthorn trees growing in a very old hedge, thought to have been planted over 900 years ago. The x axis is an index of indentation of the leaves. This index was calculated by comparing the total depth of indentations with the length of the leaves. The more indentations there are on a leaf, the greater the value of the index of indentation. The *y* axis shows the number of trees with each value.

We need to make sure that we understand the underlying biology before we look at the graph in detail.

- **This hedge was planted over 900 years ago. How old are the hawthorn trees in the hedge now?**

  The answer to this is that we don't really know. It is very likely that all of the original hawthorn trees have died. Those present now are their descendants and they will have a range of ages. Some will be very old trees; some may be young.

The scientists who collected and analysed the data in the graph calculated the index of indentation by comparing the total depth of indentations with the length of the leaves.

- **What was the advantage of presenting the data in this way?**

  The leaves on a particular tree vary in size. Size is bound to affect the total depth of leaf indentation, the bigger the leaf, the greater the depth of the indentations. Calculating an index like this enabled the scientists to compare leaves of different size.

The scientists calculated the index of indentation for a sample of *C. oxyacanthoides* trees growing in their natural environment. The mean value was 10.

- **Explain why some of the trees growing in the hedge had values less than 10.**

  There will be variation in leaf indentation. When we say that the mean value for *C. oxyacanthoides* was 10, some trees will have a value less than 10 and some will have a value more than 10.

The scientists also calculated the index of indentation for a sample of *C. monogyna* trees growing in their natural environment. The mean value was 34.

- **Explain why there are a large number of hawthorn trees in the hedge with an index between 10 and 34.**

  We can explain some of these intermediate values as being due to variation. A lot of these plants, however, are hybrids between *C. oxyacanthoides* and *C. monogyna*.

When we look at these hybrid plants in more detail, we find that they are intermediate in a wider range of characteristics. What is more, they are fertile and in turn produce fertile offspring.

■ Are *C. oxyacanthoides* and *C. monogyna* different species?

This is a difficult question to answer. Table 1 shows us that there are some very obvious differences between the two types of hawthorn. But, when they are planted together, they breed and produce fertile offspring. This makes these offspring **hybrids**. Since hybrids between the two are very rare in the natural environment, it seems reasonable to suggest that there are two different species of hawthorn. Examples such as the two types of hawthorn, and the two types of duck shown in Figure 4, illustrate the problems that biologists have in defining species. Biologists also find that new evidence constantly leads them reconsider how closely organisms are related. Sometimes this means that they have to change the scientific names of organisms. You will read about an example of this on page 178 (bug orchid).

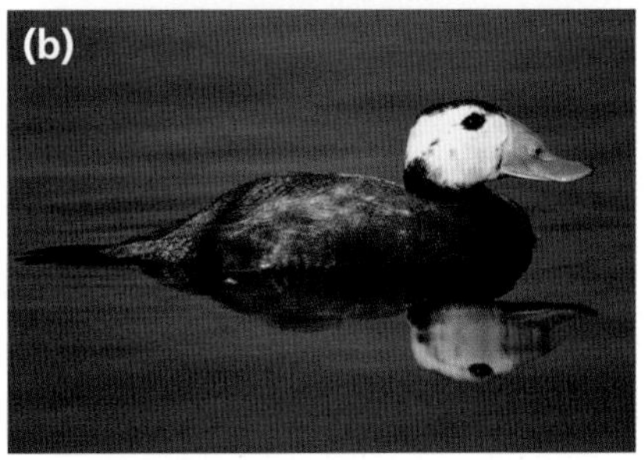

▲ **Figure 4** (a) The ruddy duck. (b) The white-headed duck.

Figure 4(a) is a ruddy duck, *Oxyura jamaicensis*. Ruddy ducks were brought to the UK from North America. Then, in 1953, some of them escaped from captivity. Now they are widespread in Western Europe. The white-headed duck, *Oxyura leucocephala*, seen in Figure 4(b), is a native of Europe. It is also now a globally threatened species. Its numbers worldwide have fallen in the last hundred years from perhaps 100 000 birds to just over 5000.

White-headed ducks face extinction because they produce hybrids with ruddy ducks. Before this was known, the two ducks were thought to belong to different species. There are now about 550 white-headed ducks in the whole of Spain, the largest population in western Europe. To protect them, Spain decided to exterminate all their ruddy ducks. There are no white-headed ducks in the UK, and the policy is to kill all the ruddy ducks here to protect the Spanish white-headed ducks. But should we be doing this? This is the type of question that we have to ask ourselves as biologists.

Sorting out species

In the system we use to classify different organisms, we put them into groups. These groups are based on things that organisms have in common and how they evolved. If two organisms have common features and if there is evidence that they also have the same ancestor, we assume that they are related, and put them into the same group. Often, but not always, the features they have in common reflect their evolutionary history.

Look at the organisms in Figure 5. We could divide them into those organisms that can fly and those that are unable to fly. This classification gives us no information about their evolutionary history. However, if we look carefully at the structure of their wings, we can see that, though an albatross wing and a penguin flipper are used for different purposes, they are really very similar. We can recognise the pattern of bones in an albatross wing as being the same as the pattern of bones found in a penguin flipper. This similarity points to the albatross and the penguin having a common ancestor at some stage in the distant past, and so being quite closely related.

▲ **Figure 5** (a) A dragonfly. (b) An albatross. It has very long wings and can fly huge distances. (c) A penguin. It cannot fly, but swims using its flippers as paddles.

A dragonfly's wing has a very different structure. Clearly, a dragonfly is not closely related to either an albatross or a penguin. A natural classification makes use of features like wing bones that show a common evolutionary history.

We divide living organisms into a number of groups called kingdoms. They are the largest groups. Kingdoms are divided into smaller and smaller groups until finally we end up with individual species. This classification system is summarised in Figure 6.

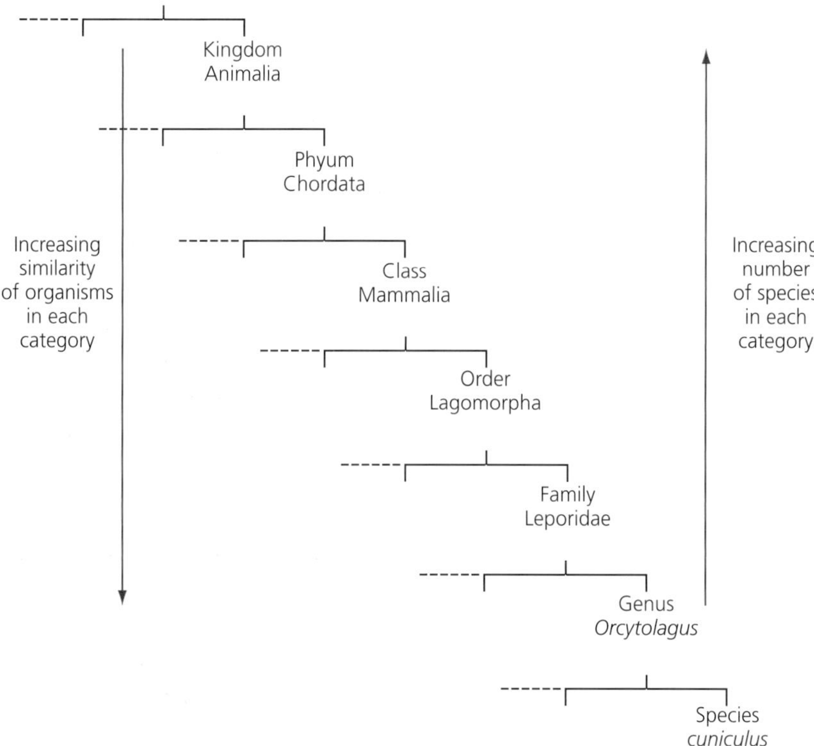

▲ **Figure 6** How the rabbit, *Oryctolagus cuniculus*, is classified.

▲ **Figure 7** The bug orchid, first named *Orchis coriophora* but now called *Anacamptis coriophora*.

DNA, proteins and classification

The examples you read about earlier in this chapter show that biologists are not always certain whether organisms belong to the same or different species. Relying on physical features to sort organisms into different species can be misleading.

Biologists also have difficulties deciding how closely different species are related. Look at Figure 7. This wild orchid is called a bug orchid because it smells rather like crushed bed bugs! Its scientific name was *Orchis coriophora* and that is the name you will find in many books. In natural conditions it forms hybrids, not just with closely related species, but with orchids of a different genus. Because of this, biologists now think they might have classified it wrongly. They have suggested that it ought to be placed in the same genus as the orchids with which it forms hybrids, so they have changed its scientific name to *Anacamptis coriophora*.

Do two species belong to the same genus? Are two families of organisms closely related? Biological research that finds the answers to questions such as these helps us to understand evolutionary relationships.

The physical features that help us to classify an organism are determined by its genes. A gene is a piece of DNA that codes for a protein, and proteins are the molecules that control the physical features of an organism.

Looking at DNA base sequences

In Chapter 6 you learned about DNA and its structure. Molecular biologists use machines to analyse DNA. They have worked out the complete DNA base sequences of a number of different organisms including humans. They have also found the DNA base sequences of particular genes in many different organisms.

In Chapter 7 you learned how DNA is copied in the process of replication. Errors sometimes arise when base sequences are being copied. When a base sequence in a gene has a copying error, we say there has been a **mutation**. A base may be added to the sequence, replaced by another base, or may be deleted altogether. If this happens in a body cell, it occurs only in that individual. If it happens to sex cells, the next generation inherits the change. Such mutations may either make no difference to the characteristics we see in a species, or they can cause the species to change very slowly over a period of many thousands of years. Either way, the DNA that codes for a particular protein in an organism alive today is slightly different from the DNA that coded for the same protein in its distant ancestor.

We can use computers to compare DNA base sequences in different organisms. If the sequences are very similar, it suggests that the organisms concerned are closely related and that they originated from a common ancestor relatively recently. If there are more differences between the sequences, it suggests that the organisms are not so closely related and probably originated from a common ancestor a longer time ago.

Classifying whales

There are two groups of whales. Large whales such as fin whales and humpback whales do not have teeth. Instead, they have large plates like huge combs which they use to filter small organisms from the water. They are put into one group. Dolphins and porpoises have teeth and are put into a second group. The sperm whale is a large whale, but it does not have the baleen plates. Instead, it has teeth, so, in the past, biologists classified sperm whales with the dolphins and porpoises.

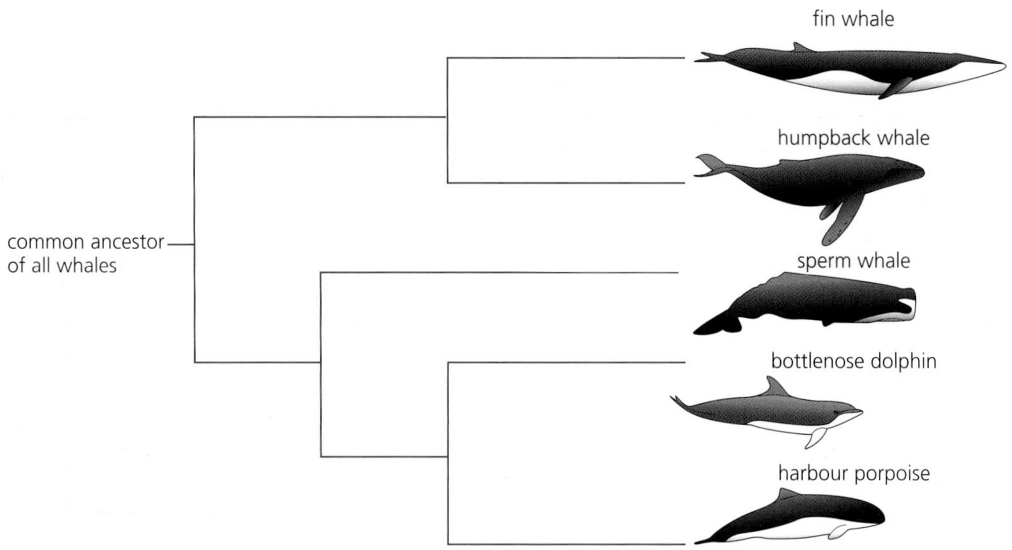

▲ **Figure 8** This diagram shows how five species of whale could be related to each other.

Figure 8 shows this information in a diagram. The fin whale and humpback whale are closely related to each other and they split off from a common ancestor relatively recently. The bottlenose dolphin and the harbour porpoise are related in a similar way. The relationships shown in this diagram have been built up by looking at physical characteristics such as teeth. What do we find when we look at their DNA?

fin whale	TAAACCCCAATAGTCA–CAAAACAAGACTATTCGCCAGAGTACTACTAGCAAC
humpback whale	TAAACCCTAATAGTCA–CAAAACAAGACTATTCGCCAGAGTACTACTAGCAAC
sperm whale	TAAACCCAGGTAGTCA–TAAAACAAGACTATTCGCCAGAGTACTACTAGCAAC
bottlenose dolphin	TAAACTTAAATAATCC–CAAAACAAGATTATTCGCCAGAGTACTATCGGCAAC
harbour porpoise	TAAACCTAAATAGTCC–TAAAACAAGACTATTCGCCAGAGTACTATCGGCAAC

▲ **Figure 9** Matching DNA base sequences in different whales and dolphins.

Now look at Figure 9. It shows DNA base sequences in part of a gene that these different species of whales and dolphins have in common. In this diagram, the bases are lined up with each other so that they match as closely as possible. Biologists use a computer to give the best possible match.

We can analyse the differences between these pieces of DNA by using a simple scoring system. We will start by comparing the humpback whale DNA with the DNA from the sperm whale. Some bases match. These have been highlighted in orange. We will score 1 for each match; these two sequences score 48. In other words, there are 48 matches between them. This tells us very little. To get a more detailed picture, we need to count up the matches between all the other pairs of species as well. These scores are shown in Table 2.

Table 2 Similarities between DNA sequences in some whales and dolphins.

	Fin whale	Humpback whale	Sperm whale	Bottlenose dolphin	Harbour porpoise
Fin whale					
Humpback whale	51				
Sperm whale	48	48			
Bottlenose dolphin	43	43	41		
Harbour porpoise	40	45	45	48	

Let us work through this table and see what it tells us.

■ **Using only the evidence from the table, which two species appear to be most closely related?**

The fin whale and the humpback whale are most closely related. The score of 51 tells us that they have 51 matching bases. The greater the numbers of matching bases the more closely are two species related.

Here are the scientific names of some whales:

Fin whale	*Balaenoptera physalus*
Sperm whale	*Physeter catodon*
Southern right whale	*Eubalaena australis*
Northern right whale	*Eubalaena glacialis*

■ **Suppose you analysed the same piece of DNA in these four species. Between which two would you expect the highest score, and why?**

The two right whales belong to the same genus, so they should be the most closely related to each other, and should have the highest score.

The sperm whale is a large whale that has teeth. Figure 8 shows the sperm whale classified with the bottlenose dolphin and the harbour porpoise.

■ Does the evidence in the table suggest that this is the best way of classifying the sperm whale?

If you look at the table carefully, you will see that the sperm whale has 48 matches with the fin whale and 48 matches with the humpback whale. It has fewer matches with the dolphin (41) and the porpoise (45). This seems to suggest that Figure 8 does not show the best way of classifying the sperm whale. It would be better to classify it in the way shown in Figure 10. This diagram suggests that the sperm whale is more closely related to the other large whales than it is to the bottlenose dolphin and the harbour porpoise.

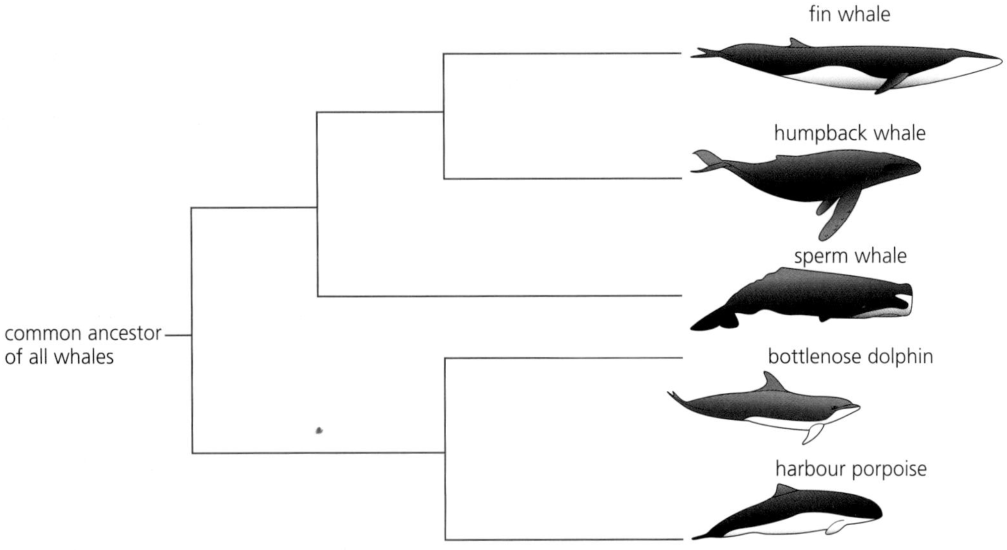

▲ **Figure 10** An alternative way of showing how the whales and dolphins shown in Figure 8 may be classified.

■ We have two different ways of ways of classifying the sperm whale. Which is the correct one?

We have to be very careful about how we interpret evidence about DNA base sequences. Here we have looked only at the similarities and differences in one piece of DNA. Sometimes the evidence we get from another piece of DNA may suggest something else. In coming to their conclusions, biologists have to weigh up data from different sources. In this case, all the available evidence now suggests that Figure 10 is a better interpretation than Figure 8 of how the five whales should be classified.

Another way of looking at differences in DNA – DNA hybridisation

In the previous section, we looked at a method of comparing DNA that relies on the similarities and differences in short sequences of DNA bases. Biologists also use a method called **DNA hybridisation** to compare DNA from different species. This lets them compare whole DNA molecules rather than just short sequences.

To understand how DNA hybridisation works, you may need to remind yourself about the structure of a DNA molecule. On page 118, you learned that DNA is a double helix. Each DNA molecule consists of two strands held together by the hydrogen bonds that form between complementary base pairs. Figure 11 shows how we use this pairing to compare DNA from different species.

In the process, biologists make a hybrid DNA molecule. This consists of a strand of DNA from one species joined to the complementary strand from another species. Where a base on the first strand lines up with a complementary base on the second strand, hydrogen bonds form.

Look at Figure 11. As you can see, all base pairs in (a) are complementary. This is because both strands are from the same species. In (b), most of the base pairs in the length of DNA are complementary, showing that the strands are from closely related species. Far fewer of the base pairs in (c) are complementary because the strands are from two species which are not closely related. The general rule is that the more closely two species are related, the greater the number of hydrogen bonds formed, and so the more strongly the two strands are held together.

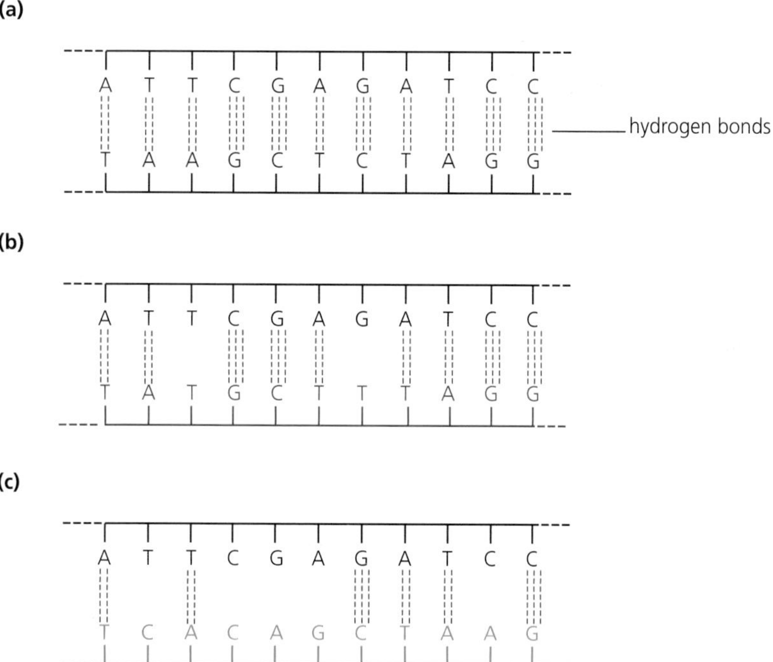

▲ **Figure 11** (a) Part of a DNA molecule from a single species. All base pairs are hydrogen bonded because the strands are completely complementary.
(b) Part of a hybrid DNA molecule formed from two closely related species. There are many hydrogen bonds holding the two strands together.
(c) Part of a hybrid DNA molecule formed between two species that are not closely related. There are only a few hydrogen bonds holding these strands together.

When we take a sample of DNA and heat it, the hydrogen bonds break and the DNA separates into its two strands. If we are using DNA from a single organism, we have to heat it almost to boiling before its strands separate. This is because there are many hydrogen bonds between the bases in the two strands and it takes a lot of energy to break them all. Less heat is required to separate the strands of a molecule of hybrid DNA because there are fewer hydrogen bonds holding the strands together. As a general rule, a difference in the temperature of 1 °C is equivalent to a 1% difference in the DNA base sequences of the two species from which the hybrid was formed.

Who are our nearest relatives?

We can use DNA hybridisation to investigate the relationships between humans and three species of ape, the chimpanzee, the gorilla and the orang utan. Table 3 shows some data that scientists obtained from a study of the DNA of these four species. In each sample, the DNA has one human strand and a strand from one of the apes.

Table 3 Data from a study investigating the relationships between humans and three species of ape.

Species from which hybrid DNA was produced		Difference between the temperature at which half of a sample of human DNA split into its two strands and that at which half of the sample of hybrid DNA split/°C
Human	Chimpanzee	1.6
Human	Gorilla	2.3
Human	Orang utan	3.6

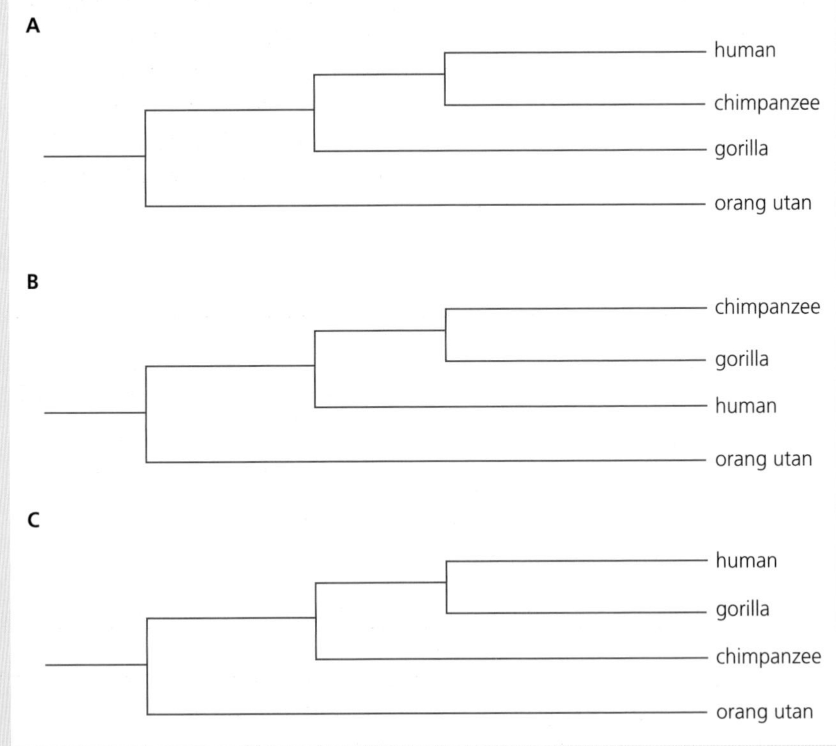

Figure 12 Possible relationships between humans and three species of ape: chimpanzee, gorilla and orang utan.

The temperature at which half of a sample of human DNA split into its two strands was 94.0 °C.

1 At what temperature would you expect half of a hybrid strand between human DNA and gorilla DNA to split into its two strands?

The scientists measured the temperature at which *half* the DNA split into its two strands.

2 Why did they measure the temperature at which half of the DNA had split?

3 Which species in the table has DNA that is most similar to human DNA?

The diagrams in Figure 12 show three possible relationships between the four species.

4 Using only the evidence in the table, explain why you think:
(a) B is incorrect
(b) C is incorrect.

Proteins and classification

Q3

Proteins are polymers of amino acids. Give two ways in which the primary structure of proteins may be different.

The human body contains many different proteins. You will already have come across some of them, such as enzymes, carrier molecules and antibodies. Each protein is made up from a particular sequence of amino acids. If we look at a protein present in several species, we may see that the sequence of amino acids in this protein differs slightly from one species to another. We can find out more about how closely humans are related to different species of apes by comparing the amino acids in their proteins.

We will start by looking at human haemoglobin. Every haemoglobin molecule in an adult human contains four polypeptides – two identical α chains and two identical β chains. Each α chain consists of 141 amino acids joined to each other by peptide bonds. The β chains are slightly longer. They each contain 146 amino acids. Together then, we have 141 + 146, that is 287, amino acid positions that we can compare. Surprisingly, if we take the four species that we looked at in the previous section, 282 of these amino acids are exactly the same in all four. There are differences in only five amino acids, and these are shown in Table 4.

Table 4 Differences in amino acids in the haemoglobin of humans and three species of ape.

Species	α chain		β chain		
	Position 11	Position 23	Position 87	Position 104	Position 115
Human	alanine	glutamic acid	threonine	arginine	proline
Chimpanzee	alanine	glutamic acid	threonine	arginine	proline
Gorilla	alanine	asparagine	threonine	lysine	proline
Orang utan	threonine	asparagine	lysine	arginine	glutamine

In the table, the blue tint shows the places where amino acids are the same as on the human α and β chains. You can see that both chains in chimpanzee haemoglobin have exactly the same sequences of amino acids as both chains in human haemoglobin. We need to be careful how we interpret this. It doesn't mean that humans and chimpanzees are the same species! Remember, the data are for only one molecule, haemoglobin. A much more likely explanation is that it takes a very long time for differences in the amino acid sequence of haemoglobin to evolve. It is possible that only a few million years have passed since humans and chimpanzees split apart from a common ancestor. Perhaps this is too short a time for differences in their haemoglobin to have evolved.

Look back at Figure 12. You will remember that DNA hybridisation was used to investigate how closely humans and apes were related, and that the findings supported the relationships of diagram **A**. The amino acid sequences in haemoglobin give further support. Human and chimpanzee haemoglobin is identical. It differs by only two amino acids from gorilla haemoglobin, but by four from orang utan haemoglobin. Therefore, by combining the evidence from DNA hybridisation and from analysing the amino acid sequences of haemoglobin molecules, we have some very convincing support for the relationship between humans and apes shown in diagram **A**.

Immunology and classification

Blood plasma is a complex fluid. It contains many of the substances transported round the body: nutrients such as glucose and amino acids, mineral ions, hormones and proteins. One of these proteins is **albumin**. As proteins go, it is a fairly small molecule, made up of 584 amino acids. By the 1960s, scientists were already aware that there were differences in the amino acid sequence of the albumin from different species of animals. But

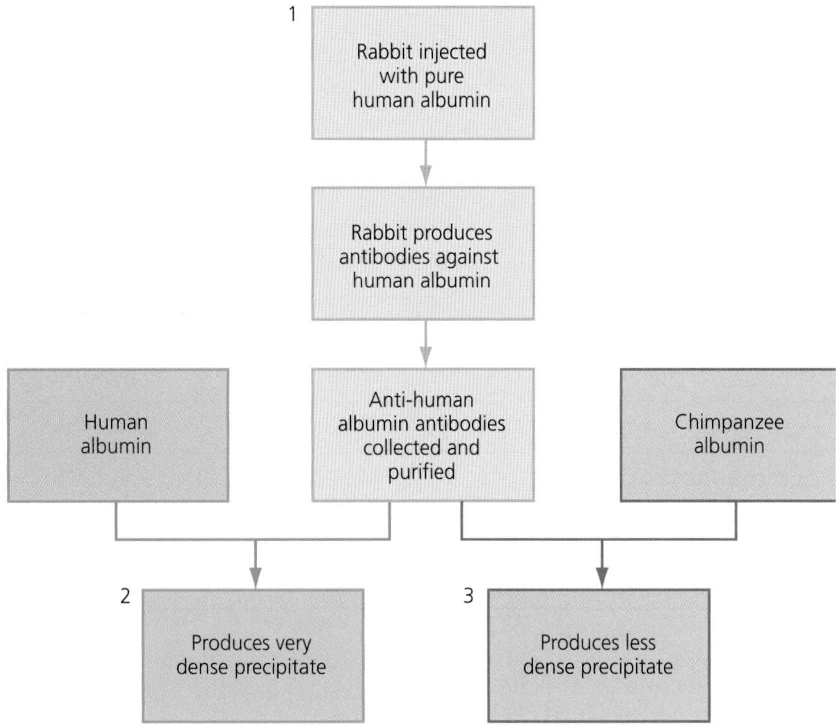

▲ **Figure 13** This flow chart shows how antibodies can be used to investigate the differences between human albumin and chimpanzee albumin.

working out the entire amino acid sequence for a particular protein took a lot of time. Scientists wanted a quick and reliable way of measuring the differences between albumin from different species. They developed a method based on their understanding of the principles of immunology.

In Chapter 5 we saw that the white cells in the blood are involved in defending the body against invasion by pathogenic bacteria and viruses. Molecules on the surface of these microorganisms act as antigens. When a pathogen causes an infection, some of the white cells divide rapidly and produce antibodies against the pathogen's particular antigens. The antibodies bind to the antigens and form a complex network of molecules that is eventually destroyed by other cells in the body. Scientists used this antibody–antigen reaction to measure how similar human albumin is, for example, to chimpanzee albumin. The flow chart in Figure 13 summarises the steps in the procedure they used.

We will look at the information in this flow chart, a step at a time.

1 The rabbit is injected with a sample of pure human albumin.

■ Why is it necessary to make sure that the sample is pure?

Blood plasma contains many different proteins. If the sample of albumin isn't pure, it might be contaminated with some of these other proteins. Then, the rabbit's white cells will make antibodies against these other proteins as well.

2 When a solution of anti-human albumin antibodies is mixed with human albumin, a precipitate is formed.

■ What causes this precipitate to be formed?

The antibody molecules have a specific shape which is complementary to the shape of human albumin. Therefore the antibodies bind to the albumin and form a precipitate.

3 Chimpanzee albumin binds in fewer places than human albumin to anti-human albumin antibodies.

■ Why is this?

The sequence of amino acids in a molecule of chimpanzee albumin is slightly different from the sequence in human albumin. Therefore there will be fewer places where chimpanzee albumin will bind to the antibodies, so less precipitate will be formed.

We look now at Table 5 which shows some of the results obtained by using this technique to compare albumin from humans and apes.

Table 5 The results of testing albumin from different species with anti-human albumin antibodies.

Species tested against anti-human albumin antibodies	Amount of precipitation measured as a percentage of the amount of precipitation with human albumin
Human	100
Chimpanzee	95
Gorilla	95
Orang utan	85

We have to think carefully about interpreting this information. There are clearly more differences between human albumin and orang utan albumin than there are between human albumin and that from chimpanzees and gorillas. This suggests that orang utans were the first apes to split off from the line that eventually led to humans. This is confirmed by the evidence that we obtained from looking at the amino acids in haemoglobin (page 185) and from DNA hybridisation (page 183). The evidence in the table, however, doesn't help us to decide whether we are more closely related to chimpanzees or to gorillas. It was only after we developed the techniques to analyse proteins and DNA that we were able to establish the relationship between humans, gorillas and chimpanzees.

Courtship behaviour

We saw earlier in this chapter that if different species of animals mate, they are very unlikely to produce offspring. If offspring are produced, they will almost certainly be infertile. It is therefore very important for the survival of

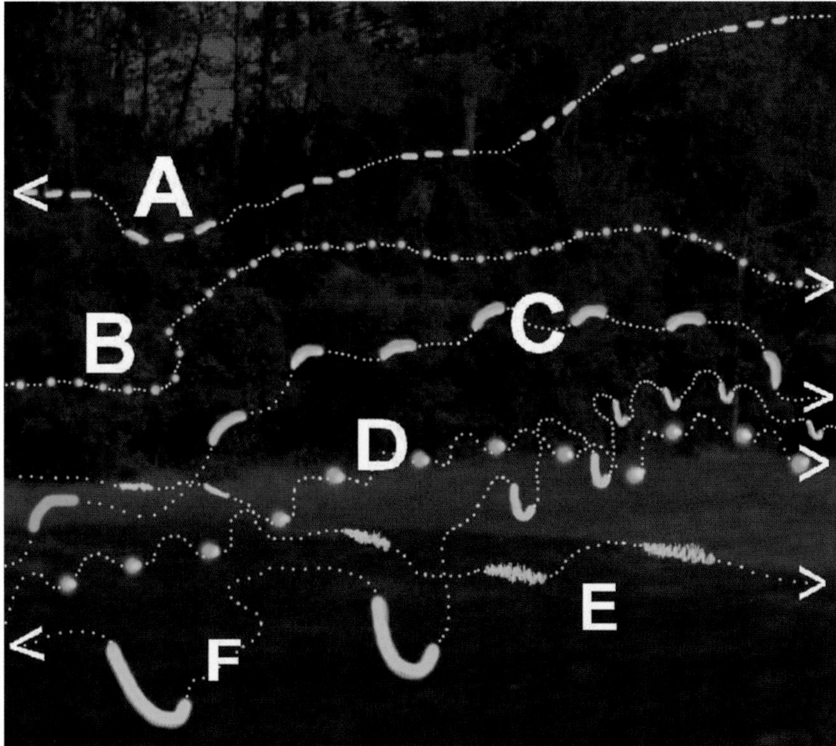

▲ **Figure 14** Male fireflies of the genus *Photinus* produce different patterns of flashes.

a species that mating takes place only between members of the same species.

Fireflies are small beetles. About 2000 species have been identified worldwide, but they are very difficult to tell apart, even if you are a firefly expert. So, how does a firefly recognise a member of its own species? This is where courtship behaviour is important. It helps to ensure that mating occurs only between fireflies of the same species.

Several species of firefly of the genus *Photinus* live in the eastern United States. The adults have light-producing organs on their abdomens. These organs produce flashes of light which come from a chemical reaction controlled by an enzyme called luciferase. Courtship takes place at night. The males of each species of firefly produce a unique pattern of flashes as they fly. Some species only flash once. Others flash several times. Some of these flashing patterns are shown in Figure 14.

The female firefly stays on the vegetation. She responds to the flashes of a male by flashing in turn, but she only responds to the specific flash pattern produced by males of her species.

Courtship behaviour in fence lizards

Fence lizards are small American lizards. The courtship display of the males involves bobbing their heads up and down. Figure 15 shows the head bobbing movements of two species of fence lizard.

1 Use Figure 15 to describe the head-bobbing movements of *S. cyanogenys*.

2 In a particular area, both of these species of fence lizards are found. Use Figure 15 to explain why it is not likely that mating will occur between males of *S. cyanogenys* and females of *S. ornatus*.

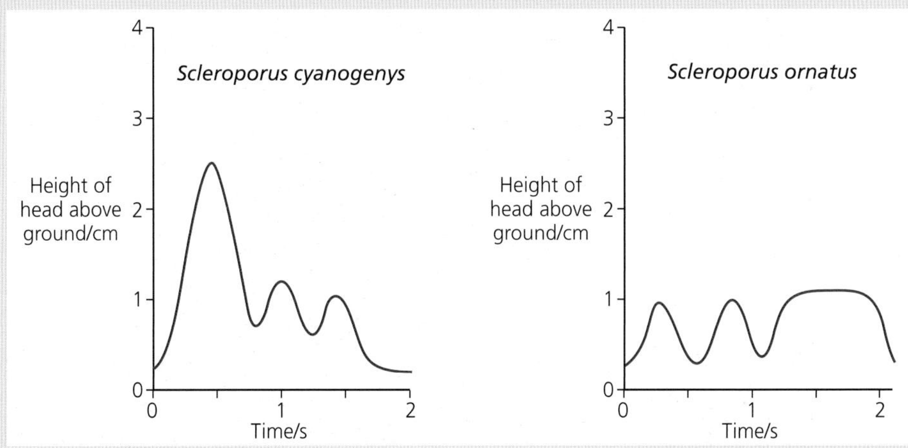

▲ **Figure 15** The head-bobbing movements of two species of fence lizard, *Sceloporus cyanogenys* and *S. ornatus*.

Chapter 11

Genes, alleles and natural selection

Bacteria are single-celled organisms. Figure 1 shows cells of the bacterium called *Mycobacterium tuberculosis*. As its name suggests, this bacterium causes tuberculosis, commonly called TB. The bacterium is transmitted from person to person in droplets of water in the breath, coughs and sneezes of people who have TB. The World Health Organization (WHO) estimates that, each year, there are about 9 million new cases of tuberculosis and about one and a half million people die from the disease.

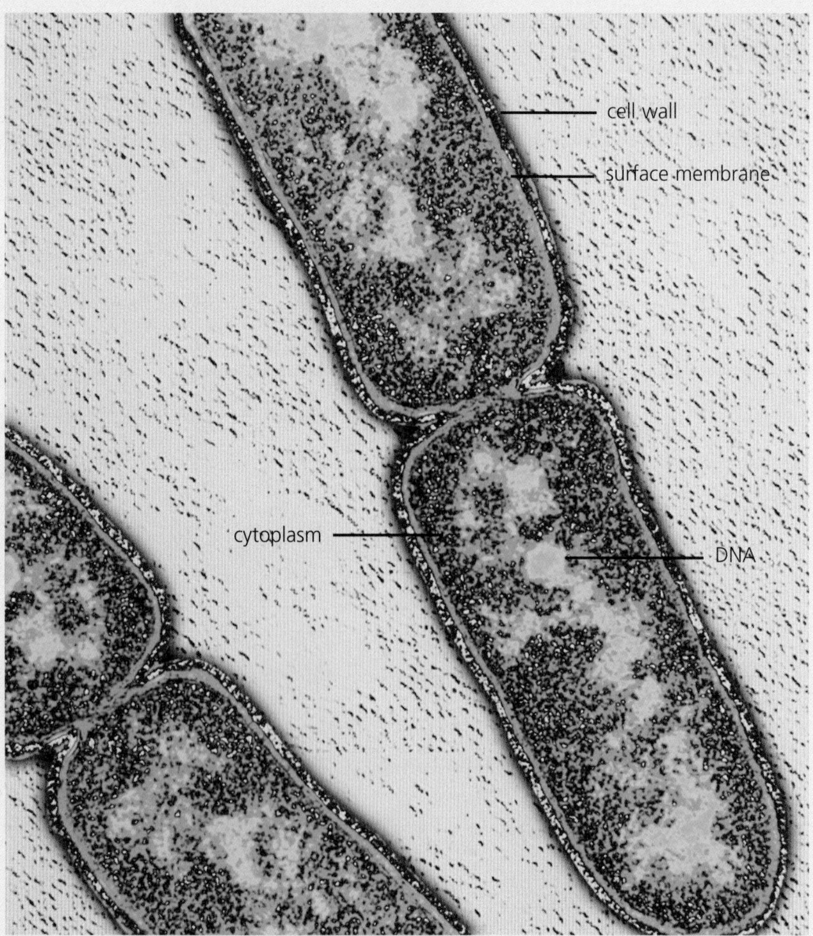

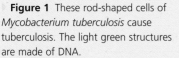

Figure 1 These rod-shaped cells of *Mycobacterium tuberculosis* cause tuberculosis. The light green structures are made of DNA.

About 50 years ago, TB was also a major cause of death in the UK. However, during your lifetime, there have been antibiotics to treat TB sufferers and a national vaccination programme. Both these measures have ensured that TB has not been a major threat in the UK. However, in the early years of the 21st century, medical workers became concerned by a sudden increase in the number of people suffering from TB in London. The medical workers already knew that, between 1984 and 1991, there had been a major epidemic of TB in New York City. Then, the number with TB reached 50 cases per 100 000 of the city's entire population. At the start of investigations into the London outbreak, scientists in the UK looked at the research reports from New York to see if there were similarities in the TB outbreaks. They found many aspects in common, and this helped them to understand the London outbreak and to control it so that it did not become an epidemic.

Table 1 contains information about *M. tuberculosis* found in samples taken from TB patients during the New York outbreak. Different strains were resistant to different antibiotics. What can we conclude from this information? Start with the first row of data, for 'Any antibiotic'. This shows that, in 1991, almost one-quarter of New York's TB patients were infected with *M. tuberculosis* that was resistant to at least one of the antibiotics commonly used to control the disease. The rest of this row shows that the percentage of patients with antibiotic-resistant bacteria fell and then remained roughly steady. From the first column of data, you can see that some strains were resistant to more than one antibiotic: we call this **multiple resistance**. Notice that the trends in resistance were different for different antibiotics. Clearly, resistance to antibiotics is complex.

Table 1 Percentage of TB patients in New York City with strains of *M. tuberculosis* bacteria that were resistant to different antibiotics.

Name of antibiotic	Percentage of patients each year infected with *M. tuberculosis* that was resistant to the named antibiotic			
	1991 (312 patients)	**1994** (225 patients)	**1997** (212 patients)	**2003** (217 patients)
Any antibiotic	24.4	16.0	18.9	18.9
Kanamycin	1.9	2.2	13.5	0.5
Isoniazid alone	17.0	10.7	11.3	9.7
Both isoniazid and rifamprin	9.0	5.8	4.2	2.8
Rifamprin alone	10.9	6.2	8.0	3.2
Streptomycin	8.3	8.9	10.4	10.1

Now look at Figure 2, which shows information about infection rates in different parts of New York City.

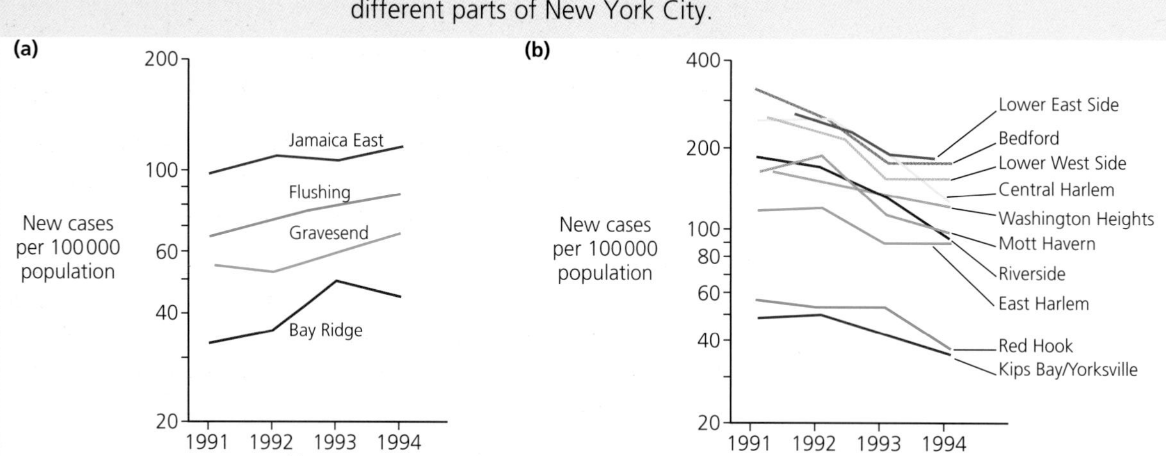

Figure 2 Annual TB cases in New York: (a) health districts with low levels of poverty; (b) health districts with high level of poverty.

The data show that the resistant strains of *M. tuberculosis* were restricted to the poorer districts of the city. UK scientists found a similar pattern in London, where the boroughs of Brent, Newham and Tower Hamlets had the highest infection rates, of between 77 and 79 cases per 100 000 of the local population.

Among the research findings of the New York reports were the following patterns.

1 In the 1970s, the amount of money available to control tuberculosis in New York City had been drastically reduced. At the same time, there was a poor flow of information on the treatment of TB patients in hospital and in the community. Both these problems meant that the medical authorities failed to react effectively when TB broke out in the city.

2 There were cases in New York of TB patients with bacteria that showed multiple resistance (were resistant to more than one antibiotic). These cases were found to cluster, meaning that they were not distributed evenly across the city, but were found among small groups of people living in particular streets or even parts of streets. This clustering of multiple resistance cases also appeared in those London boroughs that were worst affected.

3 In 1990, there were an estimated 86 000 homeless people in New York City. Up to 25% of the city's cases of TB occurred among these homeless people. In 1992, there were an estimated 50 000 homeless people in London. In both cities, these homeless people with TB tended to cluster.

4 In different parts of New York City, between 40% and 89% of patients failed to complete a full course of antibiotic treatment. This seemed to be linked to levels of poverty, since TB patients in the city

had to buy the antibiotics themselves and often bought them on a daily basis. Sometimes, TB patients felt better after a day or so of treatment and so stopped buying more antibiotics. In other cases, the TB patients could not afford to buy another daily dose of antibiotic.

Failure to complete a course of antibiotic treatment allowed infectious TB patients to remain a threat to others. It also contributed to the development and spread of antibiotic-resistant strains of *M. tuberculosis*.

5 In the period 1993–94, 28% of new TB cases were people who had recently arrived in New York from a country where TB was **endemic**, that is, where there was a constant, low level of infection. At that time, data on where patients had come from were not routinely collected in the UK.

6 Early in the New York epidemic, 38% of TB patients were also infected with the human immunodeficiency virus (HIV). At that time, data on HIV infection among TB patients were not routinely collected in the UK.

The reports of the TB epidemic in New York City showed that social and political problems were just as important as medical problems in allowing TB to spread. This information assisted the authorities in London when TB broke out there some years later. By comparing the two cities, London's medical authorities could react to the increase in TB cases faster than would otherwise have been possible. For example, they could test arrivals from countries where TB was endemic, target treatment at homeless people, take special care of TB patients who were also infected with HIV and take steps to ensure that patients completed a course of antibiotics that were free of charge. As a result, the risk of a TB epidemic in London was greatly reduced.

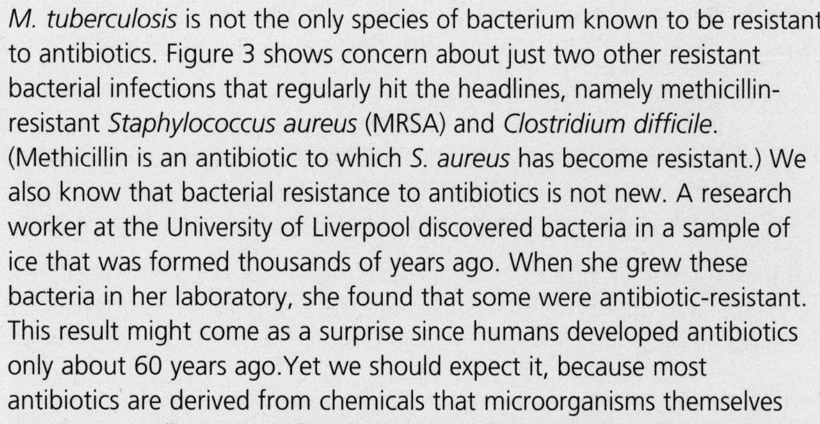

MRSA DEATHS UP

Rampant superbug and lethal C.Diff kill 5,500

Figure 3 This headline reflects public concern about antibiotic-resistant bacteria. Most of the people affected were infected by the antibiotic-resistant bacteria whilst in hospital.

M. tuberculosis is not the only species of bacterium known to be resistant to antibiotics. Figure 3 shows concern about just two other resistant bacterial infections that regularly hit the headlines, namely methicillin-resistant *Staphylococcus aureus* (MRSA) and *Clostridium difficile*. (Methicillin is an antibiotic to which *S. aureus* has become resistant.) We also know that bacterial resistance to antibiotics is not new. A research worker at the University of Liverpool discovered bacteria in a sample of ice that was formed thousands of years ago. When she grew these bacteria in her laboratory, she found that some were antibiotic-resistant. This result might come as a surprise since humans developed antibiotics only about 60 years ago. Yet we should expect it, because most antibiotics are derived from chemicals that microorganisms themselves secrete naturally, to stop their competitors from growing. This is exactly what we hope antibiotics will do for us, to restore us to health.

To understand how bacteria become resistant to antibiotics, we need to look more closely at how genes work, how genes can change from one form to another, and how new forms of genes can spread through a population. We shall do this in the rest of this chapter.

Genes and antibiotic resistance

Look back to the cell structure of *M. tuberculosis* in Figure 1. Each cell is rod-shaped, and much of its interior is taken up by a large, folded loop of bacterial DNA. The cell also has one or more small circular pieces of DNA called **plasmids**. Genes for antibiotic resistance are usually located on these plasmids. Together, the loop and plasmids contain the **genome** – the *entire* genetic code of the bacterium. Enclosing it is a cell wall that prevents the cell from bursting when it takes in water by osmosis.

1 Infection with HIV has led to a rise in deaths from tuberculosis. Suggest *one* reason why.

Pathogenic bacteria affect us by invading specific cells in our bodies. *M. tuberculosis* invades macrophages – scavenger cells that normally engulf and destroy bacteria that enter our bodies (see Chapter 5). You can see this happening in Figure 3. One of the antibiotics used in the treatment of tuberculosis is called isoniazid (see Table 1). This antibiotic is effective because it interferes with the activity of enzymes that control the production of the cell wall that surrounds the *M. tuberculosis* bacterium. Chapter 8 describes how cell walls in plants prevent cells from bursting. In a similar way, so do the cell walls of bacteria. Without a surrounding cell wall to limit the volume it can reach, a bacterial cell is liable to burst when it takes in water by osmosis; bursting in this way is called **osmotic lysis**.

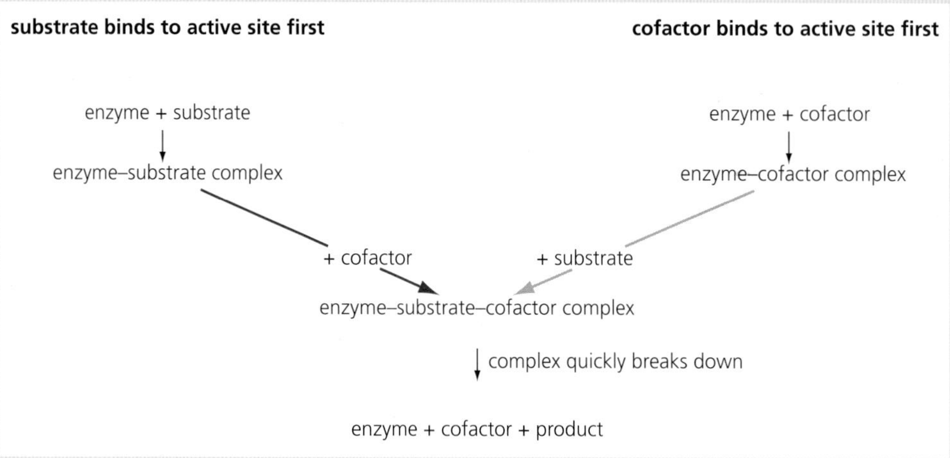

▲ **Figure 4** The enzyme InhA catalyses a reaction that produces a substance used to make the cell wall of *M. tuberculosis*. A molecule of substrate and a molecule of cofactor both bind to the active site of the enzyme.

2 *M. tuberculosis* infects only specific types of cells in the human body. Use your knowledge of the structure of cell surface membranes to suggest why.

3 (a) A bacterial cell present in human blood tends to take up water by osmosis. Using your knowledge of water movement across membranes, suggest why this is so.
(b) The cell wall prevents osmotic lysis of the bacterial cell. Explain how.

The reasons why *M. tuberculosis* is resistant to antibiotics are complicated. To understand its resistance, we must first learn about two of its enzymes. The first enzyme is called InhA. It controls the production of one of the substances of the bacterial cell wall. In the *M. tuberculosis* cell, the active site of this enzyme binds to:

- a substrate
- a cofactor (called reduced NAD).

You learned on page 19 in Chapter 1 how an enzyme binds to a substrate to form an enzyme–substrate complex. The action of enzyme InhA is a bit more complicated. The active site of a molecule of InhA binds both to a substrate molecule and to a cofactor molecule, forming an enzyme–substrate–cofactor complex. Once formed, this complex quickly breaks down, giving a product that is the substance used in making the cell wall. Figure 4 shows two ways in which binding at the active site of the enzyme can normally occur. It does not seem to matter whether the substrate binds first or the cofactor binds first. In either case, an enzyme–substrate–cofactor complex forms, then breaks down to release the enzyme, the cofactor and the product.

4 Use your knowledge of enzyme action to explain the advantage to cells of *M. tuberculosis* in using the pathways shown in Figure 5 rather than the simpler pathway of substrate → product.

Isoniazid is an antibiotic. It acts as a competitive inhibitor of the InhA enzyme; it competes with the substrate. (You learned about competitive inhibitors in Chapter 1, page 24.) The antibiotic isoniazid binds with the cofactor at the active site of InhA in place of the substrate. As a result, an enzyme–antibiotic–cofactor complex is formed, which cannot break down to release the product. This explains how the antibiotic stops the normal activity of InhA. Look again at Figure 4, and you will realise that the antibiotic can only bind in this way when the active site of the enzyme binds first with the cofactor (as shown on the right-hand side), because this leaves the substrate position available for the antibiotic. When InhA binds first with the substrate, the antibiotic cannot bind. Remember this – it becomes important later.

5 Isoniazid can combine with the enzyme–cofactor complex but not with the enzyme–substrate complex. Explain why.

A second complication is that, before isoniazid can bind to the active site of the InhA enzyme, it must first be activated. Fortunately, this can be done by an enzyme that *M. tuberculosis* itself normally uses to help invade macrophages. This enzyme is called KatG:

$$\text{Inactive isoniazid} \xrightarrow{\textit{KatG enzyme}} \text{Active isoniazid}$$

6 The KatG enzyme normally acts on substances produced by human macrophages, helping the bacterium to invade the macrophage cell. You have seen above that it also activates isoniazid, a manufactured antibiotic. Suggest why the KatG enzyme can act on two different substrates like this.

Scientists have analysed the DNA of *M. tuberculosis* and found two ways in which the bacterium has become resistant to isoniazid. Both ways involve changes in the base sequences in the genes encoding KatG and InhA.

- A change in the base sequence of the gene encoding KatG reduces this enzyme's ability to activate isoniazid. If it is not activated, the antibiotic cannot bind to the InhA enzyme and so cannot inhibit the activity of the InhA enzyme. Thus, bacteria with the mutant KatG gene are resistant to isoniazid.
- A change in the base sequence of the gene encoding InhA reduces this enzyme's ability to combine with the cofactor. Look back to Figure 4. If the enzyme cannot bind easily to the cofactor (right-hand side of the diagram), the enzyme will combine with the substrate first (left-hand side of the diagram). This reduces the chance of an enzyme–antibiotic–cofactor complex forming. Thus, bacteria with the mutant InhA gene are resistant to isoniazid.

These are only two ways that *M. tuberculosis* has evolved resistance to isoniazid. Others have been found. Some of them involve the bacterium developing different pathways to produce the substances for its cell walls.

7 Using the information above, suggest why it is difficult for scientists to overcome bacterial resistance to antibiotics.

Genes and enzymes

You learned in Chapter 1 that enzymes control reactions in cells and that enzymes are protein molecules. You learned in Chapter 6 that a gene is a section of DNA encoding the sequence of amino acids in a particular polypeptide or protein. Figure 5 summarises the relationship between DNA and proteins. Although their cell structures are different, prokaryotic cells and eukaryotic cells use their genes to make polypeptides in a similar way.

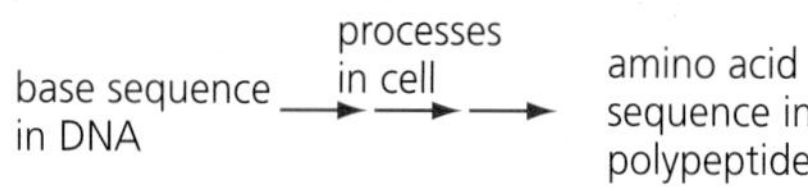

Figure 5 A polypeptide is made from the genetic code held in the DNA base sequence of a gene

The Activity on page 192 shows how we can use our knowledge of DNA and proteins to understand bacterial resistance to antibiotics.

Gene mutations

We have seen in the Activity above that resistance to antibiotics results from changes in the base sequence of more than one gene.

A change in the base sequence of a gene is called a **gene mutation**. A gene mutation generally happens when DNA is replicated. In the case of bacteria, this occurs only during simple cell division. You learned about DNA replication in Chapter 7. A gene mutation is a rare event, occurring about once every 1 million times that a gene is copied, and is a completely random event. Sometimes a gene mutation causes the encoded protein to lose its function as an enzyme. In the Activity above, this type of mutation must have occurred in the gene encoding KatG, since this enzyme lost its ability to activate isoniazid. Sometimes a gene mutation causes only a slight change in the properties of the encoded protein. In the Activity, this type of mutation must have occurred in the gene encoding InhA, since the ability of this enzyme to bind with its cofactor (as in Figure 4) was reduced but not destroyed.

A gene mutation causes a change in the sequence of amino acids in the encoded protein. Often this has no effect on the function of that protein. These mutations are called **neutral mutations** and are, probably, the most common type of gene mutation. However, some gene mutations cause a change in the amino acid sequence of the encoded protein such that its function is lost. As a result, these mutations are harmful. It is extremely rare for a gene mutation to produce a beneficial change in the activity of the encoded protein. But, when we look at beneficial mutations in *M. tuberculosis*, remember that populations of bacteria contain vast numbers of individual cells and that these cells copy their DNA and divide very quickly. To give you an idea of just how large bacterial populations are, about 90% of the cells in your body are bacterial cells, most of them in the gut; only the remaining 10% are your own. The rate at which bacterial cells reproduce is extremely rapid. Again using an example from our own bodies, the bacterial population in the gut of an individual human has the potential to double its number every 20 minutes or so. For comparison, at its present rate of increase it would take about 50 years for the human population of the UK to double its number. Thus, in a bacterial population, even a rare event such as a beneficial gene mutation, is quite likely to happen in a relatively short time.

Q1

A gene mutation involves a change in a DNA base sequence. Where in the DNA would a mutation *not* cause a change in the encoded protein?

Passing on genes to other cells

Figure 6 shows two ways in which a bacterial cell can pass its DNA to another cell. In the first method, the cell copies its DNA and then divides into two daughter cells. Each of the daughter cells gains some of the cytoplasm from the original cell and one of the copies of its DNA. This is called **vertical transmission** – DNA passing from parent cell to daughter cells during cell division. In the second method, DNA is transferred from one bacterium to another. Often a plasmid is transferred. This is **horizontal transmission** – DNA passing from one cell to a different cell.

Q2

Suggest one reason why scientists are concerned about the use of genetically modified bacteria in agriculture.

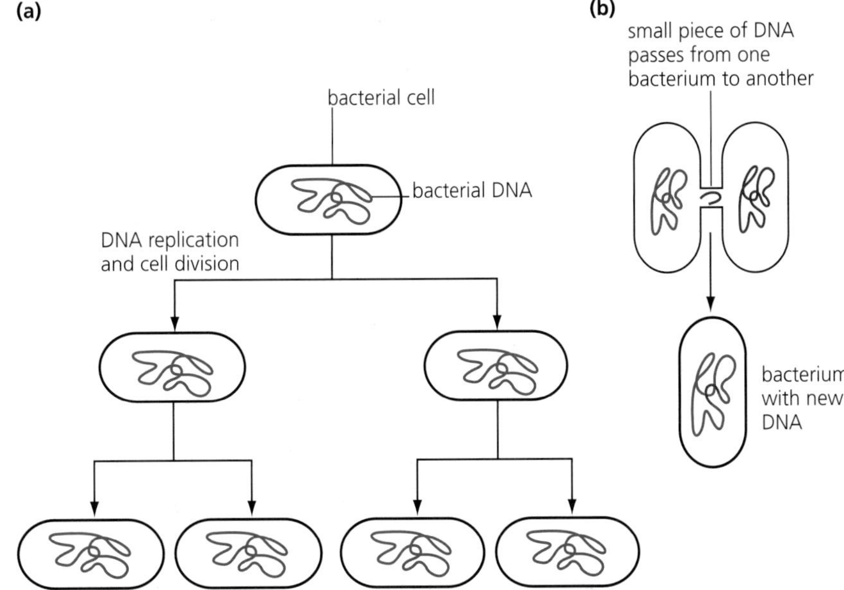

Figure 6 (a) Vertical transmission of DNA. Like multicellular organisms, a bacterium passes a copy of its DNA to two new cells during cell division. (b) Horizontal transmission of DNA. Bacteria can also pass DNA from one mature cell to another.

Spread of a gene for antibiotic resistance through a bacterial population

Imagine a population of *M. tuberculosis* in the body of a TB patient. Figure 7 represents a small sample of these bacteria. Initially, none of the bacterial cells is resistant to the antibiotic isoniazid. By chance, a mutation happens in one bacterium. As a result, it becomes resistant to isoniazid. The patient is being treated with isoniazid, and so cells without the mutation – the susceptible cells – are killed by the antibiotic. Only the one cell carrying the gene mutation – the resistant cell – survives. The patient now has just one bacterial cell. However, as bacteria can double in number in a matter of minutes, the patient soon becomes infected by a population of millions of isoniazid-resistant bacteria. There has been a fundamental change in the bacterial population; all the TB bacteria now carry a gene that gives a new characteristic beneficial to the bacterium.

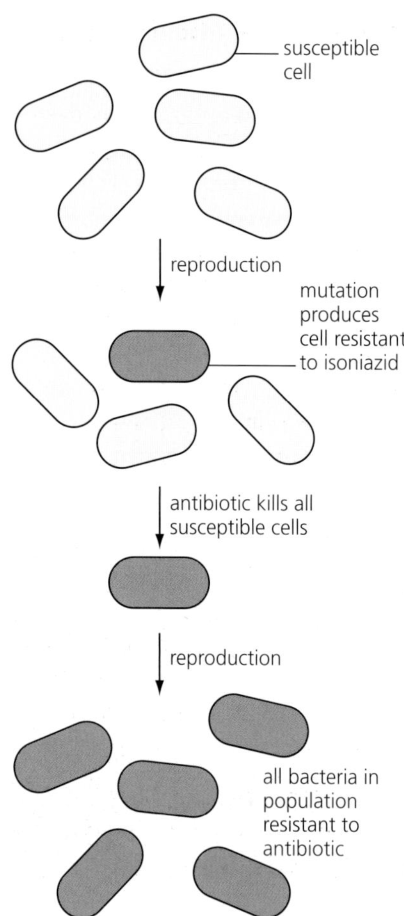

Figure 7 Evolution of antibiotic-resistant populations of *M. tuberculosis* bacteria in the body of a TB patient. As a result of a gene mutation, a single bacterial cell becomes resistant to the antibiotic isoniazid, and this one cell survives the patient's treatment with the antibiotic. All the offspring of the cell inherit the gene for resistance, and so the patient's whole population of *M. tuberculosis* is resistant to isoniazid.

Q3

Bacteria have been found in samples of ice that was formed in the Antarctic thousands of years ago. Some of these bacteria were found to be resistant to antibiotics. Suggest why.

Natural selection – a change in the frequency of alleles in a population

We can work from the particular example of the TB bacterium to learn how any population can evolve. When a gene mutates, it has two forms – the original form and the mutated form. We call the different forms of the same gene **alleles**. The genes encoding the enzymes KatG and InhA in *M. tuberculosis* each have alleles – the original form and the mutated form. If one of the alleles of a gene confers an advantage over the alternative allele of the same gene, it will become more common (its frequency will rise) in the population. We call this process **natural selection**, and the development of a population of bacteria that are resistant to an antibiotic is just one example of natural selection.

Figure 8 shows on the left a general example of how natural selection can change the frequency of alleles in a population of bacteria, and shows how this can be applied to antibiotic resistance in *M. tuberculosis*.

General feature of natural selection in bacteria	Evolution of antibiotic resistance in M. *tuberculosis*
For any characteristic, there is genetic variation in a population, i.e. there are two (or more) alleles of a gene. ⇓	Gene mutation produces a new allele of the gene encoding InhA. ⇓
One mutation produces an allele that confers a favourable advantage on organisms that possess it, so that organisms with the original allele are at a relative disadvantage. ⇓	Cells with the mutated InhA gene are more resistant to the isoniazid than cells with the normal allele. ⇓
Organisms with the favourable allele are able to grow and reproduce more successfully than those with the original allele. ⇓	When the patient is treated with isoniazid, bacteria with the mutated InhA gene are able to grow and reproduce more successfully than bacteria with the original allele ⇓
Organisms with the favourable allele have more offspring than those with the original allele. ⇓	Bacteria with mutated InhA gene have more offspring than those with original allele ⇓
As the favourable allele is passed on to more offspring, the frequency of the favourable allele will be greater in the next generation than it was in the parental generation.	The frequency of the mutated InhA gene increases in the bacterial population as the frequency of the original allele decreases.

Figure 8 Populations of bacteria become resistant to antibiotics through natural selection.

Does natural selection work only on populations of bacteria?

The answer to the question posed in the heading above is no. Natural selection can also change the frequency of alleles in populations of all other organisms, including human populations.

Figure 9 shows two adults of a species of snail called *Cepaea nemoralis,* the banded snail. One of the snails has a yellow shell and the other has a pink shell. The difference in shell colour is controlled by two alleles of the gene for shell colour. The frequency of the alleles for yellow and pink shells is different in populations in different habitats. Table 2 summarises how natural selection affects the frequency of these alleles in two different populations. Notice that natural selection changes the population as a whole, not the individuals within it.

Figure 9 The banded snail, *Cepaea nemoralis*, is common throughout Europe. The difference in shell colour is controlled by two alleles of a single gene.

Table 2 Natural selection causes differences in the frequency of two alleles controlling shell colour in populations of the banded snail, *Cepaea nemoralis*.

Habitat in which snail population lives	More frequent allele in population	How natural selection affects frequency of alleles
Beech woodland in England	Pink allele	Snails are eaten by song thrushes, which can distinguish colour. Pink shells are camouflaged amongst the leaf litter but the yellow shells are conspicuous. The song thrushes eat more yellow-shelled snails than pink-shelled snails.
Grassland of Pyrenees (a mountain range dividing France and Spain)	Yellow allele	No song thrushes live in these mountains. The yellow shells reflect heat from strong sunlight. The pink shells absorb more heat and the snails die.

Q4

Song thrushes in a beech woodland eat more yellow-shelled snails than pink-shelled snails. Explain why this changes the frequency of these alleles in a population of snails.

Some populations lose their genetic diversity

All members of the same species have similar DNA. However, in most populations, their DNA is not identical. There are differences in the DNA of individuals of one species. We call this **genetic diversity**. As we have seen above, natural selection depends on genetic diversity within a population. If anything happens to reduce the genetic diversity of a population, natural selection becomes less effective. A population with low genetic diversity loses its ability to adapt to new conditions. Table 3 summarises three ways in which populations are known to lose their genetic diversity.

Table 3 Reasons why populations might lose their genetic diversity.

Cause of reduction in genetic diversity	Explanation
Artificial selection	Humans have domesticated many animals and plants. In doing so, we breed these animals and plants using only those which best show the characteristics we desire. Individuals not showing these characteristics are not allowed to breed. As a result, we reduce the genetic diversity of the domesticated organisms. When we domesticate animals or plants for food, we select those that provide the highest yield. For example, we breed from cows that produce the most milk, from bulls that produce the most muscle and from wheat plants that produce the largest ears.
Founder effect	Sometimes, a new environment is colonised by one individual, or a few, from a population elsewhere. These founders of the colony carry only a small sample of the genetic diversity of the population from which they came. This is most common when islands are colonised from a mainland nearby and accounts for the differences in the populations of offshore islands.
Genetic bottleneck	Occasionally, the majority of a population is wiped out. Only a few survivors remain. This small group of survivors carries only a small sample of the genetic diversity of the population from which it came. We believe this is the explanation for the low genetic diversity of cheetahs. All the cheetahs in the world are derived from a small group that survived a worldwide disaster.

Q5

Seed banks contain seeds of the ancestors of modern crop plants. Suggest why these seeds are kept.

Variation can be caused by environmental factors as well as by genetic factors

Tall people tend to have tall children. This suggests that height is inherited. However, children born after the introduction of the National Health Service in 1948 grew to be taller, on average, than those born before 1948. It is unlikely that there had been a genetic change in the population. It is more likely that children grew taller because they had a better diet and were free from disease. These are environmental, not genetic, factors.

How easy is it to tell whether variation is caused by genetic or environmental factors? A student measured the height of the students in her AS Biology year. Figure 10 summarises her results. What can we conclude from these bar charts? You can see that there is no clear-cut 'tall' or 'short' person. The range of heights shows continuous variation. You can see that the distribution of heights is different for males and females. This suggests that these differences result from genetic differences between females and males. You can also see that there is a range of values around the peak values. Is this caused by genetic factors or by environmental factors? Without further information, we cannot easily draw conclusions about which of these two types of factors is the more important.

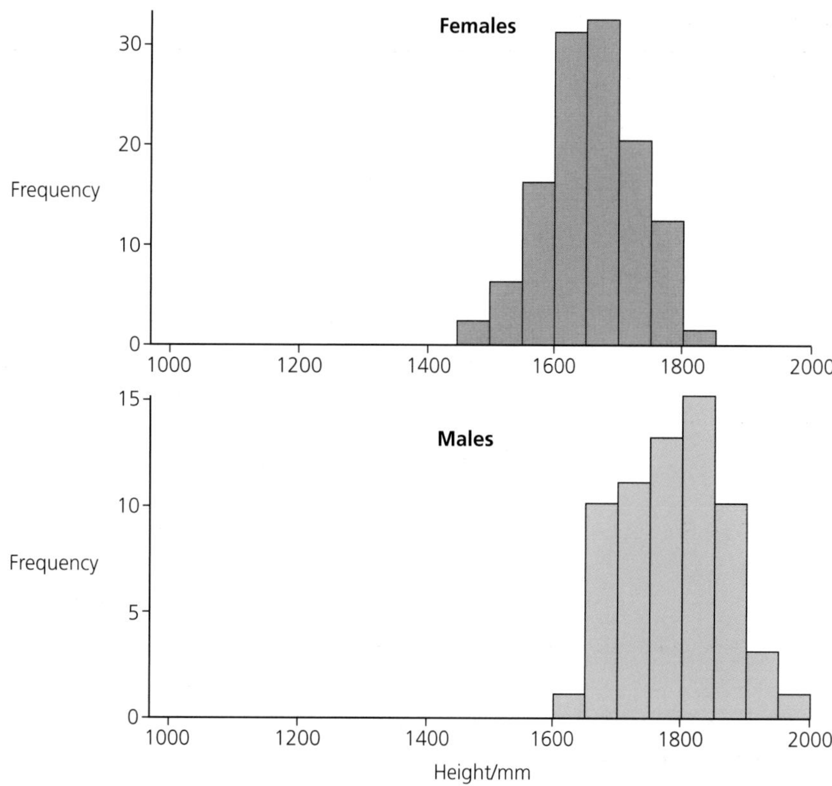

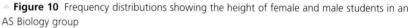

Figure 10 Frequency distributions showing the height of female and male students in an AS Biology group

Q6

Suggest one environmental factor that might account for the variation in the height of females in Figure 10.

Investigating variation

Figure 10 may suggest to you the problems that we might have in finding the average height of humans in the UK. We could not measure every human in the country. Instead we would have to measure a small group of the population, called a **sample**. But would this sample be representative of the country as a whole? For example, if we had more females than males in our sample, this would give us a lower average height.

Any sample might not be representative of the population from which it is taken. This might happen for two reasons.

- Chance – what we commonly call 'luck'. We can reduce the effect of chance by taking several samples, instead of just one, and finding their average value.
- Sampling bias – this happens when the investigator, knowingly or unknowingly, chooses which measurements to include in the sample. We can reduce the effect of sampling bias using a **random sampling** technique. Random sampling is a technique of selecting the individuals in a sample that removes the investigator's choice, and ensures that the measurements are representative of the whole population.

Look back to Figure 10. Each bar in the chart shows the number of individuals falling into a particular category. This bar chart is called a **frequency distribution**.

Figure 11 shows another frequency distribution. The sample used to make Figure 11 was much bigger than that for Figure 10, so the distribution is shown as a smooth curve rather than as a bar chart. The frequency distribution in Figure 11 is of a special type, called a **normal distribution**. It has several important features:

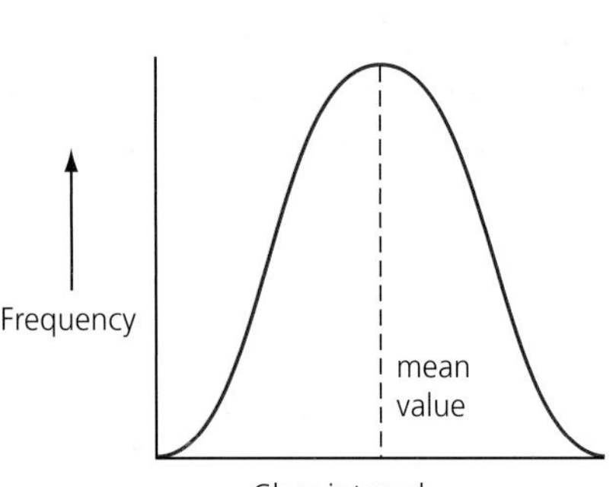

Figure 11 A normal distribution curve.

- The value at the peak of the curve is the sample's most frequent value. In a normal distribution, the peak is also the middle value in the range and the average value (**mean**).
- The curve of a normal distribution is symmetrical with 50% of the values below the peak (to its left) and 50% above the peak (to its right).
- 95% of the values are within two standard deviations of the mean.

We have introduced two new terms here – mean and standard deviation. Let's examine them further.

Mean

The **mean** value is what we commonly call the average value. We find it by adding up all the measurements we made and then dividing this total by the number of measurements we made. We can represent this in words as

$$\text{Mean} = \frac{\text{sum of all measurements}}{\text{number of measurements}}$$

In mathematical notation, this is written as: $\bar{x} = \frac{\Sigma x}{n}$

where $\bar{x}$ (pronounced x'bar') is the mean value, Σ stands for 'sum of', x represents each measurement made and n is the number of measurements made.

Standard deviation

The standard deviation is a measure of the variation within a sample. Think back to your practical work in class. You will have carried out an investigation to determine the effect of a variable, say temperature, on the activity of an enzyme-controlled reaction. When you did this, you probably used at least three replicate tubes at each temperature and calculated from them the mean time for the reaction to finish (the end time). Suppose you had found the end times in your three replicate tubes were 44 s, 45 s and 46 s. You would probably have felt pleased with these results because they show little variation. You would have been confident in the reliability of your result. Now suppose your end times were 25 s, 45 s and 65 s. Although they give the same mean time as the first example, i.e., 45 s, you would probably not have been pleased with these results. The second set of results shows too much variation; you would have doubted that the mean value represented the true value you had tried to measure.

From these two examples, you will realise that the mean itself does not give us enough information about our sample. We want to know how spread out the results were that gave us our mean. If they are not spread out, we are more confident about their reliability than if they are very spread out. This is where the standard deviation is helpful, since it is a measure of the variation within a sample. Figure 12 shows two normal distribution curves;

they represent the measurements made on two different samples. You can see that the two curves have the same mean but they have different shapes. Curve (a) has a narrow spread of measurements, i.e., the measurements in this sample were very similar. Curve (b) has a much broader spread of measurements, i.e., there was much more variation in the measurements in this sample. Because there is greater variation within the sample in curve (b), it will have a larger standard deviation than curve (a).

Q7

A student measured the heights of two different groups of people. Group A had a mean height of 185 cm and a standard deviation of 3.7. Group B had a mean of 185 cm and a standard deviation of 7.5. What does this information tell us about the two samples?

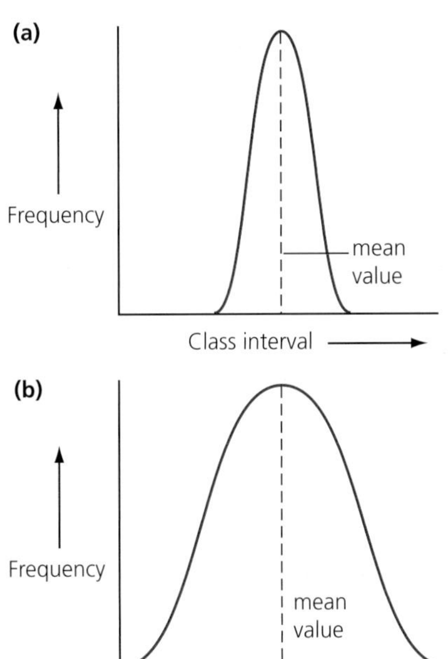

Figure 12 These two normal distribution curves have the same mean value. Curve (a), with the smaller spread of values, has a smaller standard deviation than curve (b).

Scientists and government

We began this chapter looking at how bacteria evolved a resistance to antibiotics, so let's end with this topic as well. In 1997, a study by a team of scientists estimated that about 100 000 inpatients in National Health hospitals in the UK picked up an infection while in hospital. Many of the pathogens causing these hospital-acquired infections, such as methicillin-resistant *Staphylococcus aureus* (MRSA), were immune to antibiotics. Hospital-acquired infections pose a serious threat to the health of the UK population.

In England, final responsibility for hospitals rests with the UK Government. In 1998, the Government published an action plan to cope with antibiotic resistance. It included the following action.

- Outbreaks of antibiotic resistant infections to be monitored and recorded.
- Advice to be given to general practitioners (GPs) and to the public on the use of antibiotics.
- Measures to be put in place to control infection.
- Funding for further scientific research into antibiotic resistance.
- Procedures introduced in hospitals which ensure that infections are immediately diagnosed and treated.

In the same year, the Government also:

- set up a Specialist Committee on Antimicrobial Resistance (SACAR). One of its major tasks is to persuade GPs to reduce the number of prescriptions they issue for antibiotics. Many are unnecessarily prescribed to treat minor infections in children, in theory prescriptions for antibiotics could be reduced by between 60% and 70%.
- launched a health education programme, known as CATNAP – the Campaign for Antibiotic Treatment and National Advice to the Public. One of the aims of this campaign is to encourage members of the public not to request antibiotics unnecessarily from their GP.

Q8

One of the aims of the CATNAP campaign was to encourage people not to request antibiotics from their doctors. Explain why this would be helpful in reducing the evolution of resistant bacteria.

Despite these initiatives, the UK is no closer to being able to control hospital-acquired infections, such as MRSA. The UK continues to have the highest rate of MRSA infections amongst the 15 countries monitored by the European Antimicrobial Resistance Surveillance System (EARSS).

Chapter 12

Biodiversity within a habitat

Figure 1 shows a wood at the edge of Hauxley Nature Reserve in Northumberland. The area the wood occupies was once part of an open cast coal mine. When the mine closed, the whole coalmining area was landscaped to include a lake with islands. Then in 1983 the Northumberland Wildlife Trust bought the land to develop into a wildlife reserve. The Trust decided to plant trees and create the small wood that you see in the photograph.

▾ **Figure 1** Woodland at the edge of Hauxley Nature Reserve in Northumberland.

Questions the Trust asked were: What trees should we plant? and Where should we plant them? These decisions would influence the number and kinds of other organisms that came to live in the wood, including birds, insects and mammals, and the Trust wanted to make the mix of species in their wood – its **biodiversity** – as wide as possible.

Scientists carry out investigations that can help to answer questions such as these. We will look at the results of some of the research that has been done on woodland birds. These results are shown in Figure 2. We have a much better picture of the factors determining the different species of birds that live in a wood than we have for most other groups of animals and plants. This is because so many scientists have studied bird populations. Also, it is generally true that a wood that supports many different species of birds will also support many different species of other organisms. This makes studies on birds very useful when selecting types of trees and deciding where to plant them to form a new wood.

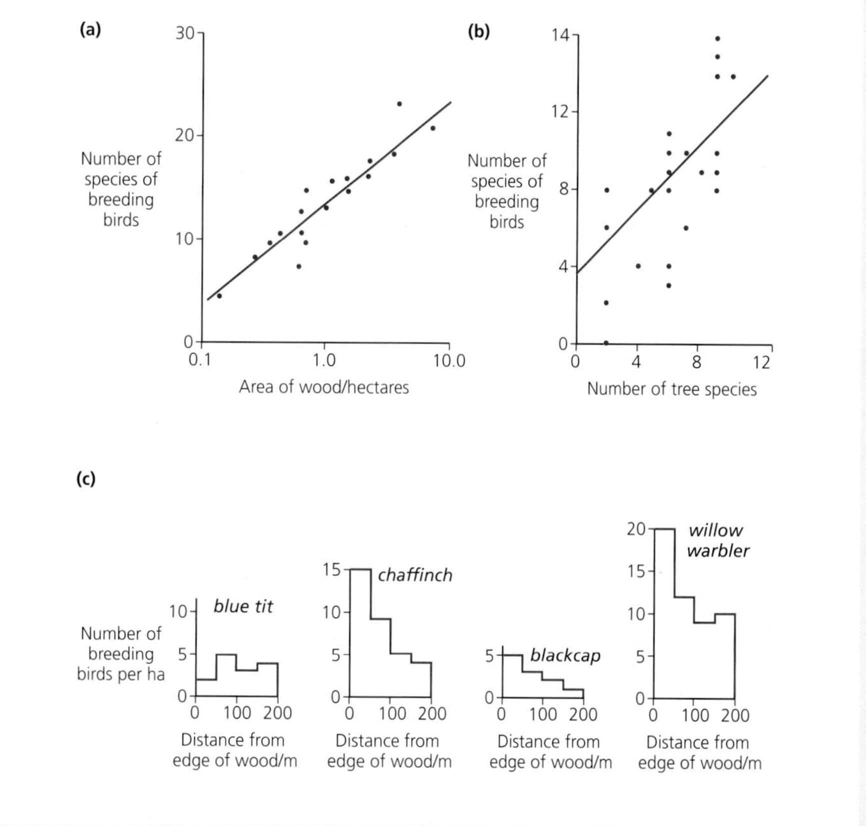

▲ **Figure 2** Graphs showing the results of some research on woodland birds. (a) Number of species found in woods of different sizes. (b) The relationship between the number of species of birds and the number of species of tree growing in a wood. (c) The effect of distance from the edge of the wood on the breeding populations of blue tit, chaffinch, blackcap and willow warbler.

We will start by looking at the data in Figure 2(a). The graph shows the number of species of birds found in woods of different sizes. On the *x* axis in this graph, the numbers for the size of the wood have been plotted on a log scale. This means that the values on the *x* axis increase by a factor of ten each time. Instead of going up in equal increments – 0, 0.2, 0.4, 0.6 hectares etc., the scale goes from 0.1 to 1.0 to 10.0 hectares. The advantage in plotting data this way is that we can show a far greater range of sizes.

A lot of studies have been carried out on the effect that wood size has on the number of bird species. They have all produced similar results to those in Figure 2(a). The line drawn through the points is called the line of best fit. It shows the overall trend of the data. Since the slope is upwards, the trend is upwards, so there is a 'positive correlation' between number of species and wood area. This means that we can conclude that as the size of the wood increases, so does the number of bird species.

Figure 2(b) shows data collected from a second investigation. In this graph, the number of breeding species of birds has been plotted against the number of different species of tree present. Again, there is a clear correlation between the two. The more species of trees that are present, the more species of birds that breed.

Finally, we look at Figure 2(c). The scientists who collected the data for these graphs investigated the effect of distance from the edge of the wood on the number of times that particular species of birds were recorded. The graphs show the results for four different species. Notice that records for blue tits are spread roughly evenly. For the other three species, however, more birds are found near the edge of the wood, and there are fewer in the interior.

The results from scientific investigations such as those shown in the graphs help us to make decisions about biodiversity, such as those made by the Northumberland Wildlife Trust at Hauxley Nature Reserve. The results suggest three things:

- As large an area as possible should be planted with trees because there is a clear correlation between the area of a wood and the number of species of birds.
- Different species should be planted. Again, there is a clear correlation between the number of species of tree and the number of breeding bird species.
- The wood should have an irregular shape or should have open areas within it. This will allow for more woodland edge, and this is the habitat favoured by most species of bird.

Wherever habitats such as at Hauxley Nature Reserve's wood are developed, compromises need to be made. One compromise is that making a wood will inevitably destroy open ground which is the habitat of species that do not live in woods. Also, particular species of tree have specific ecological needs and this limits the choice of suitable trees. Alder and willow grow in moist soil; birch will not grow in heavy shade and beech requires alkaline soils. Clearly, not all species of trees will grow in a particular area. In the Trust's project and others like it, the second compromise is to plant different tree species to encourage a wide range of birds, yet to plant only species that will grow well in the area.

▲ **Figure 3** There are a number of different species of tree in this wood. An index of diversity is a single number that takes into account both the number of species and the number of individuals of each species.

Measuring diversity

Look up the word 'diversity' in a dictionary, and you will see that it simply means 'being different'. So **species diversity** means 'different species'. The simplest way of measuring species diversity in a particular area is to count the number of species present. The data in both Figures 2(a) and 2(b) are for species diversity measured in this way. Producing a list of species can, however, be misleading.

The photograph in Figure 3 is taken inside a wood. If you were to look carefully at the trees there you would find quite a lot of species present. Some will be commoner than others. A really useful measurement of species diversity for the trees in this wood should take into account both the number of species present and the number of individuals of each species. We call such a measurement an **index of diversity**. It describes the relationship between the number of species present in a community and the number of individuals in that community. This index would be high for the wood shown in the photograph. Let us look at how a biologist who gathered information about the diversity of trees in this wood used the formula for an index of diversity.

Table 1 The numbers of trees of different species along a path through a wood.

Species	Number of trees
Beech	2
Cherry	1
Hawthorn	1
Hazel	4
Holly	7
Lime	14
Oak	6
Rowan	1
Total	36

The biologist walked along the path through the wood shown in Figure 3. He recorded all trees within 5 m of the path along a 50 m length. His results are shown in Table 1.

Here is the formula for calculating the index of diversity, d:

$$d = \frac{N\,(N - 1)}{\Sigma n\,(n - 1)}$$

In this formula:

N = the total number of organisms of all species
n = the total number of organisms of each species.

The symbol Σ means 'the sum of', so in this formula it means the sum of all the values of $n \times (n - 1)$.

We can substitute the figures for N and n from the data in the table:

$$d = \frac{36\,(36 - 1)}{2(2 - 1) + 1(1 - 1) + 1(1 - 1) + 4(4 - 1) + 7(7 - 1) + 14(14 - 1) + 6(6 - 1) + 1(1 - 1)}$$

$$d = \frac{36 \times 35}{(2 \times 1) + (1 \times 0) + (1 \times 0) + (4 \times 3) + (7 \times 6) + (14 \times 13) + (6 \times 5) + (1 \times 0)}$$

$$d = \frac{1260}{268} = 4.7$$

Q1

Willow trees are planted in some areas to provide fuel. These trees are planted close together. Would you expect the index of diversity for trees in such a willow plantation to be higher or lower than that for the wood shown in Figure 3? Explain how you arrived at your answer.

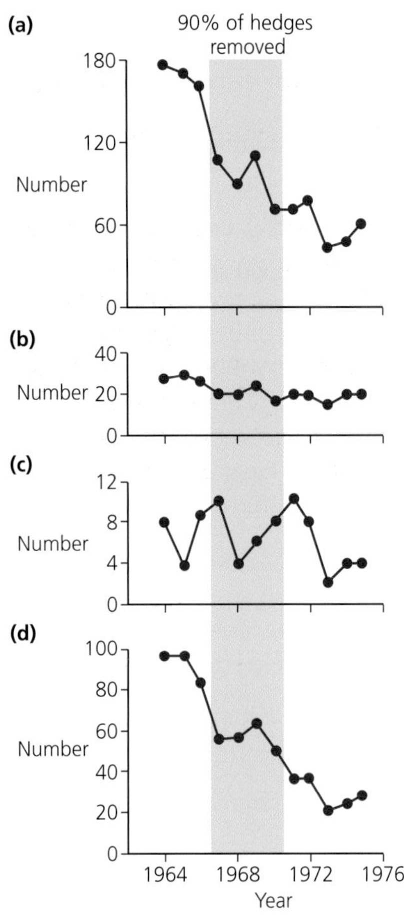

▲ **Figure 4** Graphs to show the effect of hedge removal on the bird population on a Cambridgeshire farm. (a) The total number of birds holding territories on the farm. (b) The total number of bird species holding territories on the farm. (c) The number of skylark territories (skylarks breed in open fields). (d) The total number of territories of eight bird species that are resident all year round and live mainly in hedges.

On its own, this figure for the diversity index of the wood does not mean a lot. Its value is that it allows us to compare the diversity of the trees in this wood with tree diversity in different woods and other habitats. Biologists concerned with species diversity find it very valuable to make comparisons like this.

Farming and diversity

Since the Second World War there have been huge changes in the way that land has been farmed. Agricultural machines have become larger and more powerful, and to work efficiently they need very big fields. Farmers rear more productive varieties of livestock, and grow more productive varieties of plants. They control insect pests and weeds with chemical pesticides. As a result of these changes, farming has become more intensive, with more food produced per hectare. Also, farms have become more specialised, concentrating for example on just crops or just livestock. All this adds up to larger quantities of food being produced more cheaply.

Farmers are under pressure to use all available land for food production. In the drier east of England, for example, most farmers now concentrate on growing crops such as cereals. They have removed hedges to create larger fields, and have filled in most farm ponds because they no longer have farm animals that need water. Changes in farming practices like these have reduced the diversity of wild plants and animals found on farmland. We will look at some specific examples of changes in the way that land is farmed which have affected diversity.

Removing hedges

Look at the graphs in Figure 4. They show the effects that hedge removal has on populations of birds. The data used to draw these graphs were collected from a farm in Cambridgeshire for the period 1964 to 1976. From 1966 to 1971, 90% of the hedges on the farm were gradually removed.

During the breeding season, each pair of birds holds a territory. A territory is an area in which a pair of birds breeds and collects food for their young. They defend it against other birds of the same species and do not allow these other birds into their territory. The scientists who carried out the investigation on the Cambridgeshire farm counted these territories.

■ The scientists wanted to collect reliable data on the numbers of birds on the farm. To do this they counted the territories of breeding birds. What were the advantages and disadvantages of counting territories in this investigation?

In answering this, let us start by considering the advantages. If the birds moved round all over the farm, the scientists couldn't be sure that a chaffinch they saw at one side of the farm was a different bird from one they saw at the other side. However, at the time when the birds were breeding, they stayed in their territories, and this made it easier to count them.

There are some disadvantages with counting territories, though. This method will only tell you the number of breeding pairs of birds. It won't include any that are not breeding; it won't include young birds and it won't give you any idea of the winter bird population.

■ What trends are shown in the graphs?

Graph (a) shows that there is a fall in the total number of birds holding territories and, according to graph (d), there is a fall in those species that live mainly in hedges. Graph (b) shows that the total number of species of birds holding territories remains more or less constant. Similarly, graph (c) shows that the number of skylarks remains more or less constant.

■ Can we conclude from the results of this investigation that the fall in the number of birds holding territories is caused by removing hedges?

It is very likely, but we must remember that just because two things are correlated, it does not mean that one causes the other. In this case, although the fall in numbers of birds holding territories occurs at the same time as the hedges were removed, other changes might have happened on the farm at the same time that also influenced the number of bird territories. Perhaps the farm was changing from a mixed to an arable farm, or new pesticides were being used. Either of these could have produced a fall in the numbers of birds holding territories.

Changing the way we farm

In this second example of the way in which changes in farming have affected organisms living on farmland, we will again look at birds, but this time at the species that live on arable fields (fields in which crops are grown). For these birds, the two most important events in the farming year are ploughing and harvesting. When a field is ploughed, the soil is turned over and many invertebrates are brought to the surface. Large numbers of birds are often attracted to newly ploughed fields and feed on these invertebrates. This supply of food, however, only lasts for a day or two after ploughing. Harvesting is also a time when food is plentiful. Seed-eating species of birds can feed on spilt grain and seeds from weeds growing in the crop. Insect-feeding species also benefit because soil-living invertebrates become more accessible once the cover provided by the crop plants has been removed.

One of the main changes in arable farming is a switch from spring planting to autumn planting of cereal crops. Look at Table 2. You will see that spring sowing involves ploughing the soil in early March. The grain is sown in March or early April. It germinates in April and is ready for harvest in September. Fields are left with stubble over winter before being ploughed again the following March. Autumn sowing involves ploughing immediately after a harvest in July. The grain is then sown in September and starts to germinate. The young plants grow rapidly once spring comes, and the grain is ready for harvesting in late June or early July.

Table 2 This table summarises the differences in the timing of the spring and autumn sowing of cereal. The shaded columns show when rooks rely heavily on arable fields for their food.

Spring sowing		Month		Autumn sowing
Stubble	shaded	January		
	shaded	February		
Ploughing	shaded	March		
Sowing and germination	shaded	April		
	shaded	May		
		June		
		July	shaded	Harvesting
		August	shaded	Ploughing
Harvesting	shaded	September	shaded	Sowing and germination
Stubble	shaded	October	shaded	
	shaded	November		
	shaded	December		

Rooks (see Figure 5) are omnivorous birds. Their food includes plant and animal material. Surveys of rook numbers were carried out by biologists and showed a decrease, particularly in eastern England. The biologists thought that this decrease was due to the change from spring to autumn sowing of grain crops.

1 Look at the first column in the table. This shows information about spring sowing. In which months would you be unlikely to find rooks feeding in arable fields?

2 When they were feeding in spring-sown fields, on what do you think the rooks would be feeding in: (a) October; (b) March?

3 With autumn-sown crops, for what proportion of the year is food available in arable fields?

4 Between 1975 and 1980, rook numbers decreased in southeast England but remained more or less the same elsewhere. Use the data in the table to suggest an explanation for this.

▲ **Figure 5** The rook often feeds in fields, eating soil invertebrates. It also eats seeds including newly planted and spilt grain.

Forests and diversity

In the whole of Europe, west of Russia and north of the Alps, there are only about fifty native species of tree. That is not very many when compared to the number of species growing in the tropical rain forests of South America and South-east Asia (see Figure 6).

▲ **Figure 6** Tropical rain forest growing along the banks of the Kinabatangan River in Borneo. Forests like this have a high diversity of trees and other woody plants.

Biologists obtain data on the diversity of trees in tropical rain forests by counting the number of different species in sample plots. They start with a small plot and count the number of species there. Then they look at bigger and bigger plots, each time counting the number of different species present. They use the data they collect to plot species–area curves like the two shown in Figure 7. The first of these is for Yanamomo in Peru. The second is for the Kinabatangan forest on the island of Borneo (see Figure 6).

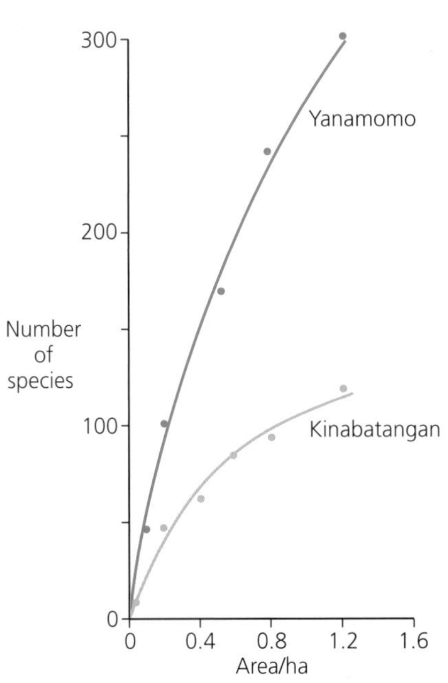

▲ **Figure 7** The curves on this graph are called species-area curves. They show the number of species of tree in plots of different sizes in areas of two tropical rain forests.

Q2

You could use the species-area curve for Kinabatangan to estimate the total number of species of tree present in the Kinabatangan forest. Explain how.

Why is there such a high diversity of trees in tropical rain forests? There are many factors that contribute to this high diversity. Here are some of them:

- Temperatures are high and it rains frequently. There are no frosts and drought is rare. Many trees are able to grow in these hot, wet tropical conditions.
- Physical conditions are different at different places in a forest. The ground may be swampy or it may be drier; the soil may be acid or alkaline; altitude varies from just above sea level to high in the mountains. Each area has its own characteristic species.
- Breaks occur in the forest canopy. Trees are occasionally blown down and produce clearings. Species that live in these clearings are different from those found in mature forest.

Sharing the resources

Rain forests are very rich in different species of animals as well as plants. These animals share the resources of the forest in different ways. Some are found in a particular layer in the forest canopy. Some are active during the day and others are active at night.

Look at Figure 8. It is a profile of part of a rain forest. You can see that the trees form layers. The uppermost layer consists of scattered giant trees called **emergents** – they emerge through the main canopy, towering above it, and are often over 40 m in height. Underneath them is a second layer in which the canopy is almost continuous. The trees in this second layer are between 25 and 35 m tall. Finally, there is a third layer of species that are adapted to live in the shady conditions beneath the main canopy.

Different species of animals are able to exploit different layers in the forest. We will look at one group of mammals found in rain forest in West Africa – squirrels. In the UK we have two species of squirrel, the native red squirrel and the introduced grey squirrel. There are many more species, however, in West African rain forests. They differ from each other in size and in the height in the trees at which they feed. Figure 9 shows the results of an investigation into the distribution of different species of squirrels in one area of forest. All the squirrels in this investigation were active during the daytime and fed on plant material.

1 Which is the largest species of squirrel?

2 Which of the species in the diagram feeds over the greatest range of heights above ground?

3 (a) Species B, D and F feed at the same height above the ground. What does the diagram show about how these three species are different from each other?
(b) How do you think this difference allows these three species to live together in the same area of forest?

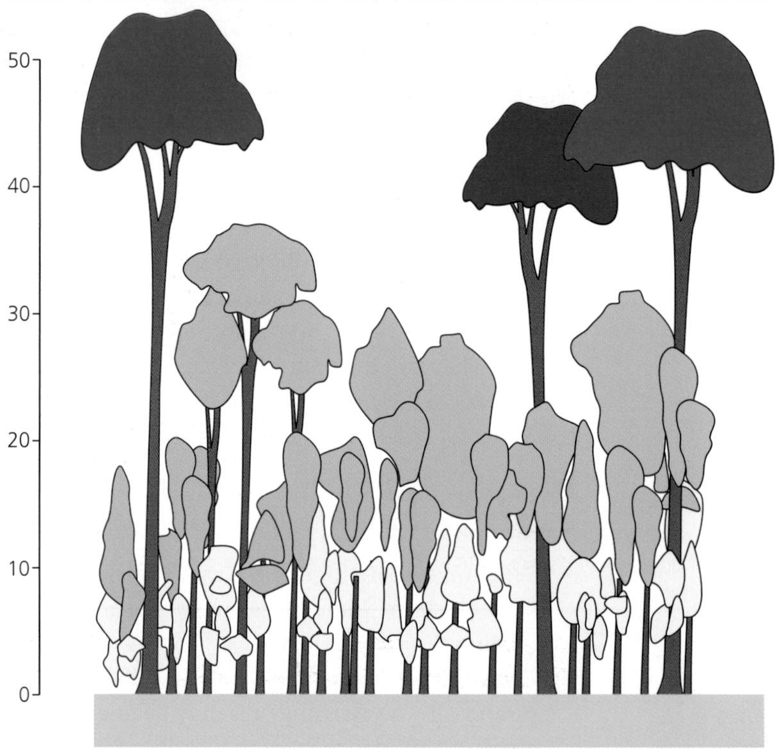

▲ **Figure 8** A typical tropical rain forest profile. It shows three main layers of trees. The upper layer, shown dark green in the diagram, consists of scattered giant trees called emergents. The second layer is the main canopy. The species that form the third layer can live in the shade.

When rain forest is cut down, many species of trees are lost, and so are many of the flowering plants that grow on and climb up them. This clearly results in a huge loss of biodiversity. Not only do the plants disappear, but also the animals that are dependent on them. Forest is often replaced with agricultural crops and pasture for grazing. This has another important consequence. Instead of a forest with its different layers of trees such as that shown in Figure 8, we usually end up with a single layer of vegetation. We can say that the structure of the plant community is much simpler.

4 In areas of Gabon where the forest has been cleared for agriculture, there are fewer species of squirrel. Use the information in the previous paragraph to explain why.

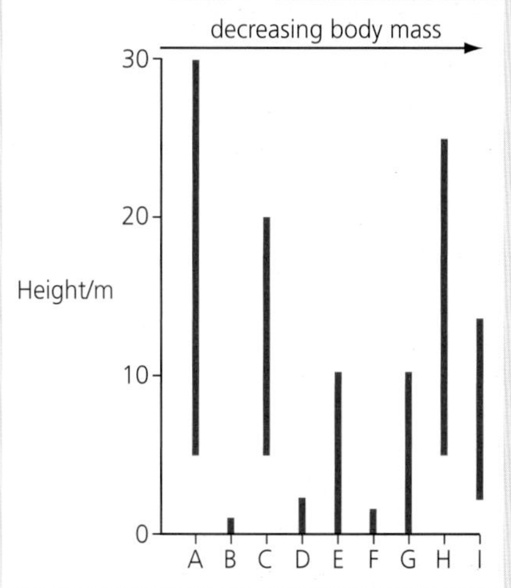

▲ **Figure 9** The heights at which nine different species of squirrel feed in an area of rain forest in Gabon, West Africa. The arrow at the top of the diagram shows the direction in which body mass decreases.

Deforestation and the diversity of animal life

Figure 10 shows a view of an area of forest. It measures 40 km by 40 km. A road was built across this area in 1970. The brown areas show where land was cleared for agriculture. Look at the first square. This shows that in 1973 forest covered 94% of the area. The second square shows the situation in 1980 with forest covering only 56% of the area.

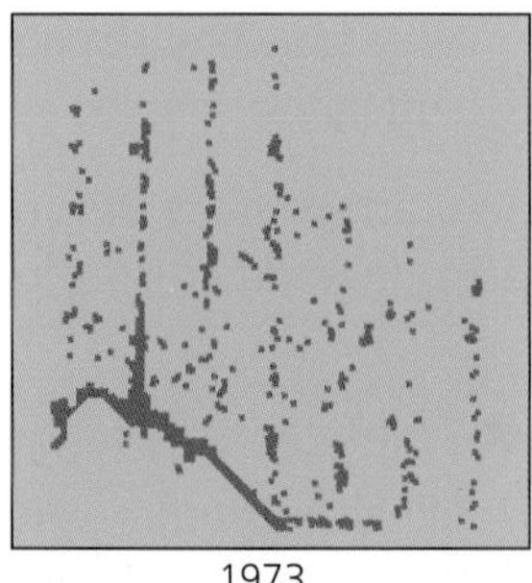

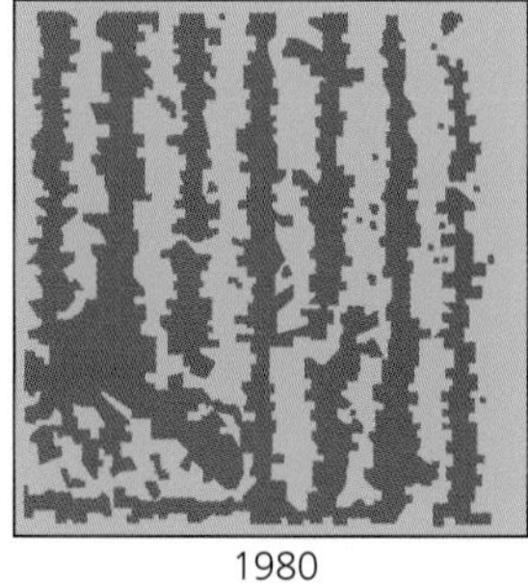

▲ **Figure 10** Maps showing the clearing of an area of forest for agricultural land between 1973 and 1980. The brown areas show farmland and the green areas show forest.

As forest is destroyed, the number of species of animals falls. Table 3 shows the change in numbers of some of the apes and monkeys in the forests of Malaysia between 1958 and 1975. During this time the forest area was reduced from about 84% to 51%.

The last column of the table shows the percentage loss in population for each species.

Table 3 Estimated change in number of some of the apes and monkeys in Malaysia between 1958 and 1975.

Species	Population in 1958	Population in 1975	Loss in population	Percentage loss in population
Gibbon	144 000	71 000	73 000	50
Dusky leaf monkey	305 000	155 000	150 000	49
Banded leaf monkey	962 000	554 000	408 000	42
Silver leaf monkey	6 000	4 000	2 000	33

■ Suggest why it useful to give the percentage loss for each species.

There were different numbers of each species to start with, so using percentage losses allows us to compare the loss for different species. If you just looked at the loss in population numbers, you might think that only 2000 silver leaf monkeys had been lost and that this was a very small number. There were only 6000 to start with, however, so a loss of 2000 is quite a large proportion of the original number.

Scientists have estimated that the area of forest necessary to support a breeding population of 500 adult gibbons is 171 km^2. The area necessary to support a breeding population of 500 dusky leaf monkeys is 34 km^2. Five hundred is the minimum number of animals they think is necessary to ensure long-term survival.

■ Explain why the deforestation shown in Figure 10 affected the gibbons more than the dusky leaf monkeys.

The forest has been split up into patches separated from each other by agricultural land. None of these patches is large enough to support a large breeding population of gibbons. But the patches are still large enough to support a large breeding population of dusky leaf monkeys.

You can see from the previous question that some mammals need larger areas than others to support a large breeding population.

■ What can you suggest about the size of the mammals that are most likely to require very large areas of forest in order to support a large breeding population?

They are likely to be large. The most difficult animals to conserve are mammals such as tigers and elephants that either live at very low population densities or have very large territories.

Turning to a group of much smaller animals, carpenter bees are big fat tropical bees, a bit like dark blue-black bumble bees to look at. They feed their young on pollen and nectar that they collect from rain forest flowers. They collect from different flowers at different times in the year. Figure 11 shows the flowering times of some plants visited by one species of carpenter bee.

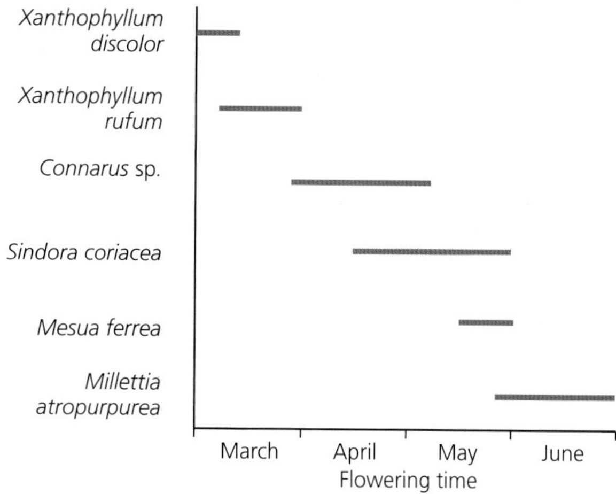

▲ **Figure 11** Flowering times of some rain forest plants visited by one species of carpenter bee over part of a year.

■ Use the information in this chapter to suggest why this species of carpenter bee is found in the rain forest but not on the agricultural land.

Each of the rain forest plants shown in Figure 11 flowers for only a short period of time. There are many species of plants in the forest, so there will always be some in flower and there will always be some food for the carpenter bee. The diversity of plants is much lower on the agricultural land, so when farmers clear the rain forest, it is likely that food will not always be available.

■ Would it matter to the farmers if this particular species of carpenter bee became extinct?

Without a great deal more research, the answer to this is that we cannot tell. It is possible, though, that this particular bee could be an important pollinator of one or more of the crop plants grown by the farmers. It might also pollinate plants growing in the forest that could be harvested for food, medicines or other useful products.

Reports on environmental issues

If you read articles about environmental issues in newspapers or on the internet, you will find that comments are often very dramatic. Writers sometimes deliberately exaggerate so as to scare us into paying attention. They seem to be more concerned with making an impact than with reporting accurately.

You can see this for yourself quite easily. Try, for example, a simple web search for the rate at which rain forest is being lost based on 'rain forest + acre + minute'. You will come up with a lot of references, but very little agreement between the figures quoted. They vary from as low as 8 hectares a minute to as high as 60 hectares a minute. That is a huge disagreement and ought to make you think about the accuracy of data such as these.

You will also come across some very dramatic statements. The rain forests are, for example, described as 'the lungs of the earth, turning carbon dioxide into oxygen'. If you have read Chapter 3, you will realise that there is some pretty dreadful biology here!

General principles

Writing about environmental issues

When you write about environmental issues such as those described in this chapter, remember that you are a scientist and you should write as a scientist. Here are some hints for you to follow:

- Avoid dramatic statements that contain very little accurate biology. It might seem a good idea to finish your account by saying that, 'The last remaining rain forest will be felled in less than 40 years,' but we cannot possibly support statements like this with evidence.
- Avoid general comments about 'animals' and 'plants' unless what you are going to say applies to all of them.
- Back up what you say with evidence. Use real examples wherever you can.
- Use proper scientific terms and use them accurately. It is not a good idea to write, for example, about animals 'losing their homes' and 'having nowhere to live' because the forest has been cleared.

Index